The Foreign Connection
Writings on Poetry, Art and Translation

LEGENDA

LEGENDA is the Modern Humanities Research Association's book imprint for new research in the Humanities. Founded in 1995 by Malcolm Bowie and others within the University of Oxford, Legenda has always been a collaborative publishing enterprise, directly governed by scholars. The Modern Humanities Research Association (MHRA) joined this collaboration in 1998, became half-owner in 2004, in partnership with Maney Publishing and then Routledge, and has since 2016 been sole owner. Titles range from medieval texts to contemporary cinema and form a widely comparative view of the modern humanities, including works on Arabic, Catalan, English, French, German, Greek, Italian, Portuguese, Russian, Spanish, and Yiddish literature. Editorial boards and committees of more than 60 leading academic specialists work in collaboration with bodies such as the Society for French Studies, the British Comparative Literature Association and the Association of Hispanists of Great Britain & Ireland.

The MHRA encourages and promotes advanced study and research in the field of the modern humanities, especially modern European languages and literature, including English, and also cinema. It aims to break down the barriers between scholars working in different disciplines and to maintain the unity of humanistic scholarship. The Association fulfils this purpose through the publication of journals, bibliographies, monographs, critical editions, and the MHRA Style Guide, and by making grants in support of research. Membership is open to all who work in the Humanities, whether independent or in a University post, and the participation of younger colleagues entering the field is especially welcomed.

ALSO PUBLISHED BY THE ASSOCIATION

Critical Texts
Tudor and Stuart Translations • *New Translations* • *European Translations*
MHRA Library of Medieval Welsh Literature

MHRA Bibliographies
Publications of the Modern Humanities Research Association

The Annual Bibliography of English Language & Literature
Austrian Studies
Modern Language Review
Portuguese Studies
The Slavonic and East European Review
Working Papers in the Humanities
The Yearbook of English Studies

www.mhra.org.uk
www.legendabooks.com

TRANSCRIPT

Transcript publishes books about all kinds of imagining across languages, media and cultures: translations and versions, inter-cultural and multi-lingual writing, illustrations and musical settings, adaptation for theatre, film, TV and new media, creative and critical responses. We are open to studies of any combination of languages and media, in any historical moments, and are keen to reach beyond Legenda's traditional focus on modern European languages to embrace anglophone and world cultures and the classics. We are interested in innovative critical approaches: we welcome not only the most rigorous scholarship and sharpest theory, but also modes of writing that stretch or cross the boundaries of those discourses.

www.legendabooks.com/series/transcript

TRANSCRIPT

1. *Adapting the Canon: Mediation, Visualisation, Interpretation*, edited by Ann Lewis and Silke Arnold-de Simine
2. *Adapted Voices: Transpositions of Céline's Voyage au bout de la nuit and Queneau's Zazie dans le métro*, by Armelle Blin-Rolland
3. *Zola and the Art of Television: Adaptation, Recreation, Translation*, by Kate Griffiths
4. *Comparative Encounters between Artaud, Michaux and the Zhuangzi: Rationality, Cosmology and Ethics*, by Xiaofan Amy Li
5. *Minding Borders: Resilient Divisions in Literature, the Body and the Academy*, edited by Nicola Gardini, Adriana Jacobs, Ben Morgan, Mohamed-Salah Omri and Matthew Reynolds
6. *Memory Across Borders: Nabokov, Perec, Chamoiseau*, by Sara-Louise Cooper
7. *Erotic Literature in Adaptation and Translation*, edited by Johannes D. Kaminski
8. *Translating Petrarch's Poetry: L'Aura del Petrarca from the Quattrocento to the 21st Century*, edited by Carole Birkan-Berz, Guillaume Coatalen and Thomas Vuong
9. *Making Masud Khan: Psychoanalysis, Empire and Modernist Culture*, by Benjamin Poore
10. *Prismatic Translation*, edited by Matthew Reynolds
11. *The Patient, the Impostor and the Seducer: Medieval European Literature in Hebrew*, by Tovi Bibring
12. *Reading Dante and Proust by Analogy*, by Julia Caterina Hartley
13. *The First English Translations of Molière: Drama in Flux 1663-1732*, by Suzanne Jones
14. *After Clarice: Reading Lispector's Legacy in the Twenty-First Century*, edited by Adriana X. Jacobs and Claire Williams
15. *Uruguayan Theatre in Translation: Theory and Practice*, by Sophie Stevens
16. *Hamlet Translations: Prisms of Cultural Encounters across the Globe*, edited by Márta Minier and Lily Kahn
17. *The Foreign Connection: Writings on Poetry, Art and Translation*, by Jamie McKendrick
18. *Poetics, Performance and Politics in French and Italian Renaissance Comedy*, by Lucy Rayfield

The Foreign Connection

Writings on Poetry, Art and Translation

❖

JAMIE MCKENDRICK

LEGENDA
Transcript 17
Modern Humanities Research Association
2020

Published by Legenda
an imprint of the Modern Humanities Research Association
Salisbury House, Station Road, Cambridge CB1 2LA

ISBN 978-1-78188-500-0 (HB)
ISBN 978-1-78188-504-8 (PB)

First published 2020

Copy-Editor: Richard Correll

CONTENTS

In memory of Michael O'Neill

ACKNOWLEDGEMENTS

All translations are my own unless indicated explicitly or by context.

I have a debt of gratitude to all the editors who have commissioned these pieces, especially to the late Mick Imlah and Anna Vaux at the *Times Literary Supplement*, to Mary-Kay Wilmers and Daniel Soar at the *London Review of Books*, to Anthony Lane, Natasha Walter and Suzi Feay at the *Independent*, and to Karen Wright at *Modern Painters*. I would like to thank my sister Posy O'Neill for her expertise in locating several articles long lost in the limbo of the internet. And I'm immensely grateful to the Legenda Transcript series editor Matthew Reynolds and to the reader Patrick McGuinness for all their helpful suggestions, and to Graham Nelson for all his expert assistance. Another great debt is to the many with whom I've been lucky to discuss art, poetry, translation, and all kinds of other things. I'd have been considerably more ignorant and unprepared, and far less entertained, without them, so I'd like to record my gratitude also to the late Michael O'Neill, to whom this book is dedicated (and without whom it wouldn't exist), to Romesh Gunesekera, Tom Paulin, William Boyd, Stella Tillyard, Michael Hofmann, the late Tom Lubbock, Peter Hainsworth, the late Rachel Owen, Simon Carnell, Erica Segre, Antonella Anedda, Valerio Magrelli, Bernard O'Donoghue, Christopher Reid, Pawel Pawlikowski, Mina Gorji, Amit Chaudhuri, Jo Shapcott, Stephen Romer, Gunnar D. Hansson, Paul Keegan, Kathryn Maris, Emma Smith, Andrew Laird, Sarah Hopkins, Laetitia Zecchini and Tatiana Faia, in more or less the order in which I met them. The list should go on — and probably should also include the critics of this and other ages who have broadened my understanding of poetry and art (on Dante alone, Giorgio Agamben, Erich Auerbach, Teodolinda Barolini and Benedetto Croce... and that's just the first three letters of the alphabet) but my particular thanks go to Xon de Ros who has been the tolerant and incisive first reader of most of these writings for something like thirty years and whose own critical work is far better researched, to say the least.

J. McK., Oxford, February 2020

INTRODUCTION

The prospect of gathering together these writings on poetry, translation and the visual arts in a single volume began to seem less presumptuous when I saw that a number of the subjects from the visual arts — not just the more literary-leaning ones such as Jack Yeats or Odilon Redon, or the illustrative ones such as Blake's and Botticelli's Dante — were also connected to poetry, and that translation often formed a bridge of sorts. The ambidextrous Michelangelo is here represented as a poet in translation; Blake as a painter. Kurt Schwitters, being painter, master collagist, sculptor, architect of weird interior space, poet, sound poet, graphic artist, and just about everything else, might serve as a tutelary spirit. The paintings of my fellow Liverpudlian (and Neapolitan) Arturo Di Stefano are haunted by the ghosts of poets. In Elizabeth Bishop's poems, the visual imagination is remarkably heightened and subtle, and for her the visual arts, especially the 'primitive' as in her fine essay on Gregorio Valdes, are a topic of both her poetry and her prose. I was drawn to write on the use she makes of the visual in her poetry as well as to review, as chance would have it, her paintings — a chance, now I think of it, which I contrived myself with a pleading phonecall to the *Times Literary Supplement*. Her imagination often locates itself at the crossroads of the verbal and the visual, and her descriptions are like translations — carryings-across — from one medium to another. The longer piece on her poems also considers her intricate connections with Charles Baudelaire.

Translation is a subject which elicits a pious but slightly glazed respect from many readers. The presence of the translator is an embarrassment to the illusion of reading an untampered-with original — and better for all concerned if that obtrusive go-between would discreetly disappear. If the translator is even noticed by the critic, it is usually only to deliver a rebuke. When I began writing poems, translation appeared to me as a decent but secondary resource. Yet it soon began to seem both more fascinating in itself and more integral, not only to the whole activity of composition but also to the whole history of poetry.

Those who make use of Pierre Bourdieu's still influential terminology refer to translation (the translations they disapprove of) as one of the strategies for amassing 'cultural capital', as if such tokens could be slotted into a kind of ceramic piggy bank. The employment of this term always presupposes on the part of the critic (or practitioner) a status morally superior to those busily trying to bolster their literary careers. And yet that perspective is just as vulnerable to the same critique. While some translations might have the air of poets gratuitously in search of canonical fodder, it's fairer to judge them by their results rather than by a cynically presumed motive. Even though the theoretical manner in which poetry translation is often scrutinized within the academy can be disheartening (slow down — haven't I been teaching an academic course on translation myself?) it may also be a welcome sign that the activity is considered worth some attention and argument.

I start the book with three pieces on translation that touch on some of these arguments. For the rest, instead of separating the writings into three categories, I've chosen chronology as the best way of arranging things, not the chronology of when the pieces were written but that of the births of the writers and artists themselves, in the hope that the visual arts, poetry and translation will have the chance of connection, wherever appropriate. As for when the essays were written, noted after each, the first I've included is on Hart Crane from 1984 — a disturbingly distant date as witnessed by its reference to Reagan's 'star wars' — and the last on Catullus was finished just a few weeks ago. A span of thirty-five years might suggest a ragbag, but I've excluded a great deal that didn't bear on the book's central concerns, and I've almost successfully resisted the temptation to rewrite some of the reviews, on the principle that these were my responses at the time, and to change them now would be to falsify the record. Besides, there's little here, at least in terms of judgement, that I'd want to reverse or revise. Call it consistency or stasis, the poets and painters I admired when I started out I admire as strongly now, only for sometimes better and more tested reasons.

The pieces themselves are of very varying lengths, often dictated by commission or occasion, and a fair number are reviews for papers or magazines. A review is the ghost of the essay — at best, it carries traces of what it might have been if unconstrained by deadline and word limit. The essay is amateur, in the finer sense: unrequired, disinterested, self-impelled. The review is (usually) paid-for, occasional, perhaps ephemeral. And yet the brevity of the form, the incitement to think decisively about a given topic, the immediacy of its remit are all factors that potentially work in its favour. Even the ghostly contours of the buried essay may be discerned in the review. With this in mind, I've collected together, alongside the more extended pieces, a fair number of reviews which show at least the traces of deeper engagement with the writer or artist, and which suggest something of where that engagement might lead. The only inclusions which stray from these parameters, apart from an introduction to Tom Lubbock's writings on graphic art, are some writings on poets' prose, and an introduction to my translation of Giorgio Bassani's *The Novel of Ferrara*, but as he began and continued as a poet, and saw his prose as poetry by other means, he is arguably relevant.

Because the great majority of the reviews I've included have been assigned by editors rather than sued for by me, I'm keenly aware that there are many poets, artists and topics I'd have liked to have dealt with here but have not. More women artists for a start — Hannah Höch, Eileen Agar, Nasreen Mohamedi and Grace Ringgold in particular, but also painters from beyond Europe and the U.S. such as Bhupen Khakhar and Xu Bing. Of relevance to this book, Ringgold's *Dancing at the Louvre* story quilt, which depicts the *Mona Lisa* and two other Da Vincis in sombre contrast to the dancing black girls, on one level irreverently upstages the old masterpieces but on another, with the two maternal canvases behind, makes a claim of continuity, and confidently repossesses the Renaissance for the present. Even if I'm ill-equipped to properly comprehend Xu Bing's use of calligraphic motifs, his sinuous shifts between ideogram and representational image, between the miniscule and the macro-scale, and his agile referencing of the classical Chinese tradition, would have shed a challenging cross-light on many of the other pieces. Another time, perhaps, or another world.

A further word on that drab phrase 'the book's central concerns'. In assembling these writings I began to see a recurrent motif that connected many of them, and this had to do with what I'd loosely call the transmission, or even transfusion, of images from one poet or artist to another, or from one culture and language to another, or from one art form to another. Strange meetings, deliberate or fortuitous; overlappings; convergences. Obvious examples here would be Catullus adopting a poem by Sappho or Shakespeare's and Cavafy's re-imagining of a passage of Plutarch or Chaim Soutine's re-working of Rembrandt's carcass of beef; and more generally the relations between Modigliani and both Verlaine and Akhmatova, Giacometti and Beckett, Soutine and Kafka, Tuymans and Conrad. A more covert example is Elizabeth Bishop's refiguring of several images of Baudelaire. Perhaps the most explicit instance can be found in the commentary on Dante's *Purgatorio* Canto XXX, with all its images of 're-clothing', in which a line of Virgil is given a new emotionally charged context in Tuscan, then a passage from the same canto is reworked, a generation later, by a Petrarch sonnet, which in turn is translated and utterly reshaped by Thomas Wyatt. This constitutes four steps of a long recursive journey through three different languages, over a millennium and a half, and represents for me not merely an exercise in allusion-spotting, nor even a study in influence (anxious or otherwise) but rather an attempt to show how the arts flourish in, even depend upon, a spiritual context of open borders, and how they are replenished by sometimes hidden sources. Poetry, which of all the arts one would think of as the most rooted in and confined by its language, is as vagrant and disrespectful of frontiers as art or music. In an essay exploring the relations between art and poetry, Wallace Stevens suggestively describes their traffic as 'migratory passings to and fro, quickenings, Promethean liberations and discoveries',[1] and my hope is that such migrations and kindlings will become perceptible in these pages.

One objection to this approach might be that it valorizes the 'traditional' and the received over what might be called the free and spontaneous aspects of poetry and art, and it's an objection that troubles me to a certain extent. A second which is an extension of the first, is that this approach overstresses the artistic milieu rather than the life — the historic moment, the personal circumstances — out of which any art grows. My tentative defence to the first objection is that it is especially where poems and art seem most original that they are most indebted, and their originality can be best seen in relation to their departures from, as well as to the depth of their receptivity to, their forebears; to the second is that this attention in no way excludes

1 Wallace Stevens: *The Necessary Angel* (London: Faber and Faber, 1960), p. 169.

what is personal and contingent, or what is social and political, and may even bring those elements into sharper focus.

A third objection might be summed up in Philip Larkin's witty dismissal of the 'myth-kitty'.[2] Quite reasonably this scorns the idea that in writing a poem you can hitch a ride on the back of some classical myth like Persephone or Ariadne and with that your job's done. It's consistent with his self-parodic and insular reply in an interview with Ian Hamilton: 'Foreign poetry? No!'[3] (a question this book would answer very much in the affirmative). The irony, of which he was probably well aware, is that there is no escaping myth or foreign poetry. The title to his final and conclusive poem 'Aubade' betrays a Provençal source while its prospect of 'Extinction's Alp' boldly reimagines Claudio's 'regions of thick-ribbed ice' in *Measure for Measure*. And even the ending of that most glumly English poem 'Toads Revisited': 'Give me your arm, old toad; | Help me down Cemetery Road' is indebted to Baudelaire's 'Recueillement': 'Ma Douleur, donne-moi la main; viens par ici...'. Similarly 'This Be the Verse' — 'They fuck you up, your mum and dad' — apart from borrowing its home-grown title from R. L. Stevenson's 'Requiem' is a spirited re-working of Horace's Ode 3.6:

> Damnosa quid non imminuit dies?
> aetas parentum, peior avis, tulit
> nos nequiores, mox daturos
> progeniem vitiosiorem.

> [What hasn't been worsened by harmful time? Worse than our grandparents, our parents then made us, still worse than them, and soon enough we'll bear progeny even more riddled with vice.]

Larkin, of course, has a point. The reliance on previous literature or art is as likely to be deadening as enlivening. Though I'm largely concerned with the latter effect, the question in each case remains open. In 'Music of Hautboys', an essay on Shakespeare's use of Plutarch, and Cavafy's use of both, a third example of T. S. Eliot's allusions to *Antony and Cleopatra* in 'Burbank with a Baedekker, Bleistein with a Cigar', however sonorous, seem to me to close off the poem. Intentionally or not, its echoes are trammelling and oppressive.

In the present circumstances when the UK is in the prolonged and painful process of withdrawing from the European Union, and has been engineering a 'hostile environment' for both long-settled and recent immigrants, and shows ever less interest in other languages and cultures, I would like these writings to stand very much in opposition. The overall title, with its nod towards the two films that treated the Marseilles drug trade, would hope to give the word 'foreign' a distinctly positive value. After all, its Latin root *foris* means 'door' and is suggestive of the openings and interconnections which these writings examine. For a related reason I've taken 'Silent Parishes' as the title of the first essay from a phrase that George

2 'Statement on Poetry', in Philip Larkin: *Required Writing: Miscellaneous Pieces, 1955–1982* (London: Faber and Faber), p. 79.

3 Philip Larkin: *Further Requirements: Interviews, Broadcasts, Statements and Book Reviews* (London: Faber and Faber, 2001), p. 25.

Steiner long ago coined to warn of the linguistic and cultural impoverishment of isolationism. Fortunately the chosen topics of this book are far from silent or parochial, and offer the alternative of openness, receptivity and a decidedly welcoming environment.

29 August 2019

PART I

Translations/Transfusions

— 1 —

Silent Parishes

The Portuguese cafe, fronting the busy road in south Oxford, has some outside tables where a few smokers sit out in any weather, but this morning being fine the tables were all full. I was reading a frontpage article about Theresa May's stand against the EU's demand that Britain up its quota of boat people. Easy to see how this could further fuel the anti-European controversy in the run-up to the proposed yes/no referendum: Syrian and Libyan refugees to add to the Eastern European economic migrants. (Even though of the 200,000 Syrian refugees who have arrived in Europe, Britain has so far granted asylum to only 187.) At the table behind me, a conversation between a Madeiran builder and an English biker about the customized BMW bike parked on the pavement was being translated by a second Portuguese man. In response to an apparently derisory offer from the Madeiran, the biker's reply was 'Ask him if he'd like a kick in the balls. That might just buy him the back wheel.' Duly interpreted, this won a grim chuckle from the big builder. Judging by his response, I'd say the translator got the tone exactly right.

Before leaving the house I'd been reading George Steiner's introduction to the *Penguin Book of Modern Verse Translation*, published in 1966 and now out of print. Steiner quotes Goethe writing to Carlyle on the topic: 'Say what you will of its inadequacy, translation remains one of the most important, worthwhile concerns in the totality of world affairs', and then Steiner comments: 'Without it we would live in arrogant parishes bordered by silence'.

Parishes: clever of Steiner to use that churchy term, but it's also ironic that its derivation is far from parochial, arriving in English via Anglo-Norman French and Old French *paroche*, from late Latin *parochia*, and from Greek *paroikia* 'sojourning' (*para-* 'beside, subsidiary' + *oikos* 'dwelling' as Wiki explains). The ancient root could, I suppose, span various modern senses: from living abroad in a second home on the Mediterranean to economic migration, or other more threatening necessities that drive people from their homes. *Paroikia* might then describe the state of a good number of the cafe's clientele, even of those from within England — the biker's accent is clearly North London, and my own home town is 170 miles away. Not so far perhaps, but I don't see I therefore have any greater claim on this parish than the Madeiran builder does. (Though it would help him to learn the language.)

Three years before Steiner's book was published, the French had vetoed the UK's entry into the EEC, as it then was, and it would be another seven years before Britain joined. His remark remains as eloquent and monitory as ever, and yet I feel a certain pride in my own suburban parish, this small cafe where mainly Portuguese and English are spoken, but where in the last few weeks I've heard Spanish, Italian, Urdu, Polish, Neapolitan and, a week ago, Tagalog. It's certainly not bordered by silence — and is a kind of mostly convivial Babel. Other parishes may differ. Despite gaining only one seat in the general election, UKIP garnered near enough four million votes, presumably from those who approved of its anti-EU, anti-immigrant agenda. As to the run-up to the referendum, much may depend on what concessions the Prime Minister can wrangle out of Europe, though how far that will appease the divided Conservative Party remains to be seen.

There is a prospect in the nearish future of an independent Scotland (56 seats for SNP) *and* a withdrawal from the EU. Will this entail a growing silence on a new northern border, as well as from our European neighbours?

Since I've spent a good part of my days, the last few years, translating literature from one of the EU's 24 'official' languages into English (with one excursion into unofficial 'dialect'), the silence that Steiner speaks of is a matter of particular interest to me. Admission to university language courses, the same newspaper records, has markedly slumped in the last few years. Perhaps the privilege of being a dominant world language has made us whose first language is English complaisant and incurious. Another passage from Steiner's introduction remains relevant today: 'There are, at every moment and on every horizon worlds beyond our words, hence our urge to cross the barriers of national speech, the effort to make other insights, other tools of awareness, available.' Not just for the clarity and passion of its introduction but also for its fine choice of poems the book is worth reprinting.

Royal Society of Literature Magazine, 24 June 2016

— 2 —

Sinister Experiments

In one famous episode of Alan Bleasdale's TV series *Boys from the Blackstuff*, the head-the-ball case Yosser Hughes paces alongside a groundsman who is marking the lines of a football pitch. After some grim reflection, he announces 'I can do that. Gi'us a job'. The starting point for translating a poem is often a Yosser-like confidence: the lines are already marked out — even in the faintness of another language — and it can't be that hard to follow them with lines of, and in, your own.

The first unhappy lesson of translation is that a 'literal' translation is a dead duck. It's not just that idioms and wordplay often resist translation, that rhythm and rhyme may be unavailable, but that the entire pace and economy of a poem, its subtlest interconnections and internal shaping risk being lost in the process.

* * * * *

Osip Mandelstam speaks somewhere of writing a poem as being 'work in the dark'. The same goes for translating a poem, except that this dark is faintly lit by the glow of the original — there's at least a shape and a direction to follow. But for a translated poem to work the same fortuitous discoveries of sound and of alignments of image need to occur. Nothing much is *guaranteed* to the new poem by the force of the original; and whilst it's irresponsible to jettison the original, it's lazy to mimic it.

* * * * *

I usually begin trying to be as faithful to the original as possible, and then find myself looking for excuses for my infidelities. But when I see the infidelities of other translators, my inclination is to be morally outraged. Who gives them permission?

Questions of fidelity may be beside the point — all that *tradurre* = *tradire* stuff we've heard so often. Anyone would choose fidelity if it was the happiest condition; if it worked. It's when it doesn't and it isn't that the translator starts looking elsewhere.

* * * * *

There's a kind of brutal empiricism about the process — does this work or not?

There's also something fatuous about the process. If a poem already exists why bring it into re-existence? To help those who can't read the original or to help the new language by including something from beyond — a kind of philanthropy? Or to help oneself (in both senses)? Maybe the impulse is other than either: rather a question of seeing if the poem can resonate in circumstances — cultural and linguistic — different from those into which it was born; of seeing what survives even such a radical transition. A sinister experiment in language: to find out if some shivering essence can be uprooted and then transplanted, evicted and then relocated.

⋆ ⋆ ⋆ ⋆ ⋆

Does it help to know the original language well? — At least it (usually) saves the translator from unnecessary gaffes and misprisions. If you can't hear the sound of the original (however impossible it is to reproduce in the target language) how on earth, short of some unearthly promptings, are you going to know by how far you've missed it or what you need to do to move your own version closer?

Though compared to many translators my experience is small, I've translated poems from languages I know and those I don't know well, from poets living and dead as well as from languages living and dead. In the end, no one set of conditions has made the process much easier for me, although the chance to confer with the poet over any ambiguity is welcome — so as to avoid unforced errors, as they're called in tennis. The translator's knowledge of *language* is more important than their knowledge of *languages*.

⋆ ⋆ ⋆ ⋆ ⋆

In translation, often as not, there's a vandalizing imbalance in the equation — the sad likelihood is that the original poet will have a markedly superior gift to that of his or her translator. But this gradient of talent isn't always disastrous; something good may be salvaged from the wreckage of an inferior talent. And it doesn't always work to have an attitude of humble reverence (however appropriate that would be) towards the original. A temporary blindness to the glaring inequalities might even help.

⋆ ⋆ ⋆ ⋆ ⋆

Following from this, we all acknowledge the inevitable losses. Where for example the nuance or secondary meaning of a word in one language has to be sacrificed in the other. We tend to be more sensitive to these losses in our own language. I remember reading an Italian translation of Hardy's 'An Afterwards':

> When the Present has latched its postern behind my tremulous stay,
> And the May month flaps its glad green leaves like wings,
> Delicate-filmed as new-spun silk...

in which the first line became : 'Quando il Presente avrà chiuso la sua porta dietro il mio tremulo soggiorno' which gives the gist of the idea (the present will have shut its door) but loses at a stroke all the intimacy and particularity of 'latched' and the slightly antiquated, provincial quality of 'postern' — all this damage done before the second line's monosyllables and the third's compound adjectives were irrecoverably lost to sight.

This doesn't discount the possibility of certain gains. Even excellent poems may have weak moments or connections (Homer nodding) which the translator could profit from, and it seems to me legitimate for the translator to turn the poem in the direction of his or her own strengths. Again, the legitimacy of this will depend not on any aprioristic theoretical position adopted but on the efficacy of the result. Most readers would prefer a good poem in the new language than a static and slavish translation. That said, certain kinds of merely careless or would-be virtuoso inaccuracies are unnecessary and dispiriting. Perhaps blind hubris and excitement at the outset and more humbled reflection in the reworking are the best conditions for translating.

★ ★ ★ ★ ★

Rhyme and rhythm are areas in which the losses are most often encountered, and the skills, or lack of them, in the translator are most apparent. There's so much luck involved in finding a rhyme that works in your own language that finding a rhyme for a rhyme in another language would seem to make the odds even more dizzyingly against. There are also structural differences in rhyme from language to language. In Italian and Spanish, for example, the rhyme of the *finale* or final vowel alone doesn't count as a rhyme.[1]

I've twice put an unrhymed Montale poem into rhyme. This might appear labour-intensive and at best redundant, and yet recognizing how much of the internal rhyming and acoustic play of the original was being lost in my own version I felt that rhyme might somewhat repair the loss, even if by substituting a more obvious sound device for a subtler one.

As regards rhythm, even if were possible to follow a rhythmic pattern in certain languages, there may be nothing more than a technical equivalence: a dactylic rhythm in English would not necessarily have the same effect say as a *sdrucciolo* in Italian.

I was once given a helpful crib as well as a rhythmic breakdown for a Brecht poem by a German scholar. The original sonnet was in *terza rima* and a trochaic metre, quite possible to reproduce in English, and the rhyme scheme had the additional significance of a nod towards Dante's form and his Paolo and Francesca. So no excuse really, but still I felt that I had a better chance of making something worthwhile of the poem if I gave myself a freer hand. I used a more random rhyme scheme and abandoned the metre for looser iambics. The question is whether something worthwhile has been salvaged. Likewise in translating Dante's Ulysses Canto, I've kept the ghost of a rhyme scheme going, but let it disappear wherever I felt I was stretching too far or abandoning something I thought more important. In

1 From T. S. Eliot to Don Paterson, the claim has been made again and again that Italian is a rhyme-rich language compared to English, and it's probably based on the misconception that the final vowel represents a rhyme. It doesn't (except in rare circumstances). On the one hand there are far fewer vowel sounds in Italian, seven, and only five in Spanish, which would make full rhyme easier than in English; on the other hand the requirement for more than one syllable to rhyme makes it considerably harder.

that sense there is an audible acknowledgement of failure, a kind of 'modesty topos' in the effect. A more rigorous view might state that it should go one way or the other — either full *terza rima* or no rhyme at all. My own view is that flexibility of strategy is of more use than rigour.

* * * * *

After considering translation as 'like viewing Flemish tapestries from the wrong side, when, although one can make out the figures, they are covered by threads that obscure them, and one cannot appreciate the smooth finish of the right side', Don Quixote cheers up the translator he meets by saying that 'there are worse and less profitable things that a man can do' — or at least he says this in John Rutherford's distinguished translation.

Poetry News, Winter 2003–04

— 3 —

Forms of Fidelity: Poetry Translation as Literary Activism

It may seem odd to consider the activity of poetry translation within the context of literary activism. That phrase suggests polemical criticism, manifestos, public protests and other interventions such as anthology-making that seek to effect change in the literary realm, whereas poetry in translation, by contrast, conjures images of ill-paid labour, commercial losses, the reticence of publishers and a dearth of reviews.

And yet, not only is translation a central place where a form of passionate advocacy can be found, where the linguistic contours as well as the perspectives of a culture may be challenged and even expanded, but it can also be a kind of cultural catalyst. Ezra Pound is the embodiment of more than one kind of literary activism: a *caposcuola* for the Imagists, a central figure for the Vorticists and for Modernism itself, an untiring polemicist writing on poetry, sculpture and music (leaving aside his baleful economic and political propagandizing), but it's arguable that his collection *Cathay* (1915), a translation of classical Chinese poems, changed the literary map just as profoundly.[1] They represented a challenge of a radical nature to prevailing ideas about poetry. By importing perspectives from far afield but also by rethinking the ways in which such perspectives might become apprehensible and audible within his own environment, Pound challenged the literary culture of his day.

Though I have plenty of reservations about Robert Lowell's *Imitations* (of which more later) that book too has been profoundly influential, not only on subsequent translating practice but also, and relatedly, in sweeping aside linguistic and cultural barriers.[2] Of course there's an argument for respecting those barriers rather than sweeping them aside, but for the moment I'm considering the impact of the work within English-speaking culture.

Within almost every generation of poets a claim could be made for the transformative and challenging effects of translation. After all, in terms of the genesis of 'modern' English poetry, two of Thomas Wyatt's versions of Petrarch's 'Whoso list to hount' and 'My galley, charged with forgetfulness' stand as superb and paradoxically originary creations, formative for the whole development of the sonnet as well as for a native lyric tradition.

1 No longer in print as an individual volume, but included in Ezra Pound, *Personae: Collected Shorter Poems* (London: Faber and Faber, 2001), pp. 13–146.
2 Robert Lowell, *Imitations* (London: Faber and Faber, 1962).

Although for the most part reviews ignore the translator as a creature best neither seen nor heard, and translators themselves are content — or resigned — to remain as invisible as glass through which another world may appear, it's not surprising that every now and then quarrels rage within the vocation's confines that make it far from a peaceable kingdom populated by ghosts or ghost-writers.

A 2011 article in the *New York Review of Books* blog by Tim Parks, the English novelist and translator of Italian, picks a quarrel with a culture of poetry translation thriving in the absence of any knowledge of original languages, which he accuses of being irresponsible, and goes on to highlight some of the more casuistical claims that support these endeavours.[3] I'm flattered — well, both flattered and irked — that he also takes issue by proxy with one of my own declarations from long ago, which had been quoted by the Scottish poet Robin Robertson in the introduction to his translations of Tomas Tranströmer — these being the main target for Parks's attack.[4] As the argument interests me, in both senses, I'd like to quote at length:

> Robertson also calls on the British poet Jamie McKendrick who, he feels, is 'surely right' when he says 'The translator's knowledge of language is more important than their knowledge of languages.' How vague this remark is! Does it mean that the translator has one kind of knowledge of how language in general achieves its effects, and another of the nuts and bolts of the different languages he knows, the first kind being 'more important' than the second? If that is the case, then to what degree more important? Wouldn't the two, rather, be interdependent and mutually sustaining? These perplexities apart, the thrust of McKendrick's argument is clear enough: we are sweeping aside the objection that a profound knowledge of a foreign language might be required to translate its poetry, or prose for that matter, thus clearing the path for a translation by someone who is an expert in the area that counts: our own language.

In my defence I should say that had Parks bothered to look up my remark's original context he would have seen that it was very much in a dialectic with contrary statements, and part of an argument not that different from his own. Immediately preceding the sentence he quotes, I had written: 'If you can't hear the sound of the original (however impossible that is to reproduce in the target language) how on earth, short of some unearthly promptings, are you going to know by how far you've missed it or what you need to do to move your own version closer?'[5]

I still feel somewhat torn in this dispute: I think Parks is right about the cavalier manner in which numerous poets brush aside the question of their competence in another language by claiming that the poet somehow trumps the humble translator — 'It does seem', he observes, 'that a serious issue is being dispatched with indecent haste here.' It is assumed that the poet–translator is able mysteriously to intuit the dynamics of a poem without knowing the language, and that such knowledge

3 Tim Parks, 'Translating in the Dark', from NYR Daily 30th November 2011, <http://www.nybooks.com/daily/2011/11/30/translating-dark/>.

4 Tomas Tranströmer, *The Deleted World*, trans. by Robin Robertson (London: Enitharmon, 2006).

5 Jamie McKendrick, 'Sinister Experiments?' in *Poetry News* (Winter 2002/–3) <www.poetrysoc.com/content/publications/poetrynews/pn2003/translation/>. See p. 12 above.

might even be an encumbrance to the swiftness and depth of a presumably telepathic rapport. And yet I'm impressed by the translations of some of the poets his arguments would seek to expose, and feel that their practice should be defended. Their practice, that is — not their theory.

To give a quick résumé of these theories, if they could be called that, I'd say their founding father was Robert Lowell's *Imitations* which is an assemblage of free translations from several European languages, from poets that include Rimbaud, Pasternak and Montale. Probably no book of poetry translations in the English-speaking world has been as influential since Ezra Pound's *Cathay*. Both poets share an ignorance of the original languages, though Pound based his work on Ernest Fenollosa's notes. In Lowell's introduction he speaks about 'tone' as though this were the exclusive preserve of the poet–translator: 'Boris Pasternak has said that the usual reliable translator gets the literal meaning but misses the tone, and that in poetry tone is of course everything.'[6]

Parks also cites this argument and comments wryly:

> Here the 'of course' skates over the fact that tone is always in relation to content: if the content were altered while diction and register remained the same, the tone would inevitably shift. One notes in passing the disparagement of the 'usual reliable translator' — the fellow knows his foreign language, but doesn't understand poetry.

What seems to me even more questionable about Lowell's use of Pasternak's statement is that only adept speakers of a language are likely to infer tone, by which we understand the emotional coloration of words, and yet Lowell is boldly asserting that only poets, regardless of their linguistic competence, have access to this elusive quality of another language. One example where this regal confidence has led Lowell astray is his translation of Montale's 'L'Anguilla' — 'The Eel'. Not only does Lowell mistakenly splice another thirty-line Montale poem with a completely different topic on to what is perhaps the most celebrated example of twentieth-century Italian poetry, but he completely misunderstands the final lines of the original poem and ends up saying almost the opposite to Montale.[7] Despite these serious flaws, Lowell achieves effects of sinewy brilliance 'threading | delicate capillaries of slime', and you could set some of his lines very much to his advantage against most other English translations of the poem, including those of translators with a good knowledge of Italian. But it's a high price to pay, and the theoretical justification that precedes it makes one even less willing to pay.

Many of Lowell's followers reproduce both the hubristic and the aggressive-defensive quality of his introduction. Perhaps the most influential in Britain at the time of writing is Don Paterson, who has published *The Eyes*, a translation of Antonio Machado, and then *Orpheus*, a translation of Rilke's *Die Sonette an Orpheus*. I should say at the outset that these are two outstanding works, inventive, supple and, in both cases, lifted by Paterson's deft handling of the sonnet and his skill with rhyme, a formal intelligence that arguably makes him one of the best translators

6 Lowell, *Imitations*, p. xi.

7 Ibid., pp. 125–27.

of the Spanish as well as of the German poet. My dissent is confined to the accompanying essays to both collections — the theory not the practice. And I really believe the two can be divorced, especially as the latter may well have been devised defensively (against all those pedants Eliot warned Lowell about) and perhaps a shade naively. To adapt Lawrence's remark, we should trust the translations not the accompanying paraphernalia, and yet these arguments become influential when a practitioner of Paterson's gifts makes them.

On the front cover of *The Eyes*, there's no mention at all of Machado (just as Rilke is absent from the cover of Orpheus).[8] Whether this signals his publisher's preference to steer the book's reception away from the dowdy straits of translation or Paterson's own feeling that these are really his not Machado's poems, it's alarming that the cover should erase the name of arguably twentieth-century Spain's foremost poet and sport only that of his translator. I can think of no other country where this kind of usurpation could happen.

In his 'Afterword', Paterson declares:

> These poems are versions, and not translations. A reader looking for an accurate translation of Antonio Machado's words, then, should stop here and go out and buy another book — again, probably Trueblood's, which although it isn't poetry, at least gives a more reliable reflection of the surface life of Machado's verse.[9]

In this and the following passage, Paterson makes far too neat a distinction between 'surface' and 'depth', 'lexis' and 'vision', 'literal meaning' and 'spirit', and I would disagree that Alan Trueblood's translations are not poetry, or that he was essentially trying to do something significantly different from Paterson. Translators of poems, whether or not they are accomplished poets, don't just plonk down the literal word and think their job is over. No more than Paterson would Trueblood consider the 'surface life of the verse', or mere verbal accuracy, to be an adequate response to the original. It is true that Paterson has allowed himself more liberties, though further on he confesses that Trueblood's 'solid literal translations have more poetry in them than most poems, because of the integrity and self-delighted purity of his enterprise', and apologizes for having on two or three occasions 'stolen lines of his because they seemed pretty much unimprovable'. With this mixture of swaggering critique and honest generosity, it's clear that Paterson is tying himself in knots in order to maintain what is in essence a specious distinction between a translation and a version. Having compared the two, poem by poem, in most cases I prefer Paterson's translations to Trueblood's, from which they have evidently profited, so I'm far from having any objection to Paterson's practice.[10]

The same argument, only in a slightly more exaggerated form, resurfaces when Paterson in his *Orpheus* introduction employs the ugly gerund 'versioning' to distinguish his practice from that of jobbing translators (and it's a term that is now

8 Don Paterson, *The Eyes* (London: Faber and Faber, 1999).

9 Ibid., pp. ix–x.

10 For a fuller exploration of Paterson's translations, see Xon de Ros, *The Poetry of Antonio Machado: Changing the Landscape* (Oxford: Oxford University Press, 2015), pp. 178–238.

brandished about by a younger and older generation of his admirers). The argument in both the Machado and Rilke books is often acute and observant about language, but it's his assumption that only poets are really qualified to translate that is suspect and, perhaps unwittingly, fosters a kind of linguistic insularity that Britain can ill afford, given the dwindling of language teaching in schools, the imperilled position of language departments in universities, and the general disregard for other languages that has long been a feature of British cultural life. I rather think the same could be said of America. The excuse of having a language that enjoys global sway and the resulting prestige is no excuse. And besides, such incuriosity about other languages is, I'd argue, a severe handicap for poets and writers in general. There are many examples of non-poets' translations of poetry that are of the highest standard and from which most poets could learn a great deal — you only have to think of Constantine Cavafy translated by Edmund Keeley and Philip Sherrard or Zbigniew Herbert translated by John and Bogdana Carpenter.

Political questions lie very close to the surface of translation. The perpetual tussle between domesticating and estranging strategies in translation, which has been highlighted by various contemporary theorists, often starts from the assumption that it is a battle between the prestige of two cultures and languages, that what is going on is somewhat similar to colonial appropriation if English is the target language in question. Whereas for the translator of poetry (of poetry especially but not exclusively) it's very often the deviation from normal usage that can characterize a particular style, and that sets a whole other kind of procedural difficulty in motion. The theory in this case operates at some distance from the real interests of the job, and so offers a facile politicization of the métier. The hegemonic status of English, the argument would go, flattens out the local elements and particularities of other languages and cultures for a kind of insular readership — insular here referring just as much to the continental US.

And yet, especially between Romance and Germanic languages, the cultural differences are not that insurmountable, and only in rare instances require footnotes. Translations from remoter languages and cultures may well stand in greater need of explanatory apparatus. More often the problems facing a translator of poetry have to do with slight shifts in conventional usage — say, an unexpected preposition or an eccentric word-choice that signals a calculated departure from the norm, but which might risk sounding like inept translation if literally rendered. Such subtle alterations can be the lifeblood of a poem and yet are the kind of things about which a poet–translator with no knowledge of the language would be blithely unaware. With these kinds of micro-problems the whole political discourse that argues on the macro-scale about the unwieldy blocks of different languages becomes inappropriate. Such is the complexity of the task, most of the time, that having some kind of aprioristic ideological or theoretical position about translation is likely to be irrelevant or distracting. Decisions have to be taken on the hoof, on a one-by-one basis, with a kind of pragmatism which I'd like to hope could also include aesthetic discrimination. There is, however, a kind of politics in this refusal of ideology: not simply a fidelity to the original text, because we understand that fidelity to one aspect or element can be a betrayal of another, to sound let's say at the cost of lexical accuracy, or vice versa, but a fidelity to an aesthetic whole. No sooner have I risked a phrase like this than I realize how open it is to attack, how close I'm getting to the arguments of those poet–translators who work without knowledge of the other language. But still I can think of no other way of putting it. This aspiration to a deeper kind of fidelity is an attempt to respect not just the alterity of another language and culture but also that of another individual sensibility. The translator's task is to listen out for what is happening on as many levels as possible and tentatively to move the target language in the right direction. If it puts strains on the receiving language well and good, but those strains have to be such that the reader can still intuit something of what made the original poem of value.

To return to Parks's argument, he begins with Robertson describing 'a process wherein his Swedish girlfriend gives him a literal line-by-line translation into English, then reads the Swedish to him to give him 'the cadences', after which he created 'relatively free' versions in English'. And yet Parks ends with what he obviously believes to be a telling contrast with the husband-and-wife team of Robert and Jean Hollander, who have adapted, he claims with I'm not sure how much accuracy, Sinclair's earlier version of Dante's *Commedia*. He invites us to try an experiment: to look into a book which he says is 'misnamed' — *Dante's Inferno*, a gathering of poets who have attempted a canto each:

> Sometimes it is Heaney's Inferno, sometimes it is Forché's, sometimes it is W. S. Merwin's, but it is never Dante's. Then dip into the 1939 prose translation by the scholar John Sinclair. There is immediately a homogeneity and fluency here, a lack of showiness and a semantic cohesion over scores of pages that give quite a different experience. To wind up, look at Robert and Jean Hollander's 2002 reworking of Sinclair. Robert Hollander is a Dante scholar and has cleared up Sinclair's few errors. His wife Jean is a poet who, while respecting to a very large degree Sinclair's phrasing, has made some adjustments, under her husband's meticulous eye, allowing the translation to fit into unrhymed verse. It is still a long way from reading Dante in the original, but now we do feel that we have a very serious approximation and a fine read.[11]

It's strange that Parks seems unaware that he has come full circle and proposed a model of scrupulous collaboration that almost exactly replicates the one he began by gently mocking. The fact that this second team are married doesn't make the translation, per se, more respectable, and nor does the presence of two 'scholars' on this second squad guarantee anything about the translation. In the case of Dante, there's an argument, and one that Benedetto Croce makes forcefully, to free up the *Commedia* from the encrustations of centuries of scholarship. When he says of the Hollanders' translation 'now we do feel that we have a very serious approximation and a fine read' we realize that, in his hands too, 'a serious issue is being dispatched with indecent haste', and his clinching finale is an anti-climax that leaves the whole question of quality unresolved. Having more people at work by no means ensures the superiority of that venture over the individual poets' cantos, or for that matter

11 Parks, 'Translating in the Dark'.

over Robertson's Tranströmer. As it happens, I think highly of the Hollanders' translation but I would suggest a counter-experiment: to read the Hollanders' translation of the *Inferno* Cantos XXXII and XXXIII and compare it with Seamus Heaney's Ugolino in *Field Work*.[12] If we allow Heaney a few vivid departures from the original, such as 'carnal melon' — like a gory anagram of 'Menalippo' — his image of Ugolino sinking his teeth into Archbishop Ruggiero's skull:

> Gnawing at him where the neck and head
> Are grafted to the sweet fruit of the brain,
> Like a famine victim at a loaf of bread.
> So the berserk Tydeus gnashed and fed
> Upon the severed head of Menalippus
> As if it were some spattered carnal melon

is both far more Dantesque and far more compelling than the Hollanders':

> We had left him behind when I took note
> of two souls so frozen in a single hole
> the head of one served as the other's hat.
> As a famished man will bite into his bread,
> the one above had set his teeth into the other
> just where the brain's stem leaves the spinal cord.
> Tydeus gnawed the temples of Melanippus
> with bitter hatred just as he was doing
> to the skull and to the other parts.[13]

Not only does Heaney have a finer feel for the line, but his rhymes (head/fed/bread) give the reader an echo of Dante's *terza rima*, which is the miraculous engine of the original. Parks's idea that the Hollanders have adapted Sinclair's prose 'to fit into unrhymed verse' betrays scant respect for anything we should want from, or associate with, a poem. While Heaney's botanical 'grafted' as well as his 'sweet fruit of the brain' are his own inventions, which foreshadow the 'spattered carnal melon', the whole texture of the verse is far closer to Dante's. The Hollanders' line, 'where the brain's stem leaves the spinal cord', rather too coolly anatomical, is no less of an invention for the Italian 'la 've 'l cervel s'aggiunge con la nuca' — literally 'there where the brain joins itself to the nape'. The first quoted line by the Hollanders is dull pentametric filler and the last two are especially flat. Though you could claim that the phrases 'he was doing' and 'the other parts' are more literal than Heaney's, they fail to give the sinister feel of the grey and bloody matter in Dante's 'e l'altre cose' — 'cose' meaning 'things' rather than body parts, things he would prefer not to specify.

The Russian poet Osip Mandelstam describes this canto as 'enveloped in the dense and heavy timbre of a cello like rancid, poisoned honey' and Heaney's version, however he deviates from the literal, gives us access to these acoustics.[14]

12 Seamus Heaney, *Field Work* (London: Faber and Faber, 1979), pp. 61–64.

13 Dante, *The Inferno*, trans. by Robert and Jean Hollander (New York: Doubleday, 2001), p. 547.

14 Osip Mandelstam, *The Collected Critical Prose and Letters*, ed. by Jane Gary Harris (London: Collins Harvill, 1991), p. 427.

He knows about the visceral hatred of internecine warfare and his lines carry that sinister freight unerringly. If Parks can hear nothing of this, he should step a great deal more warily into the zone of poetry translation.

Dwelling at such length on a blog entry may seem excessive but it has been republished in a book of essays and even if Parks pays scant attention to elements that are among the most crucial in poetry translation — such as form, sound and linguistic texture — his arguments regarding the unexamined premises of poet–translators deserve serious attention.[15]

I began with the claim that translation could be a form of literary activism but I should also stress that I don't consider the translation of well-established figures such as Montale, Machado, Rilke or Tranströmer, however valuable, to qualify, though I wouldn't altogether exclude that possibility. Perhaps among those works that have inherited the mantle of Lowell, Tom Paulin's *The Road to Inver* is the most original, the most like literary activism — a gathering of translations from Pessoa to Mayakovsky, all shamelessly and entertainingly wrestled into his own quirky vernacular.[16] Another equally free venture, more like reply poems than translations, can be found in Jo Shapcott's *Tender Taxes* where Rilke's original poems in French, the sequences *Les Fenêtres* and *Les Roses*, evoke subtly intimate and culturally entangled, often eroticized responses:

> speaking aphids and bees to you in silence,
> speaking English through a French mouth.[17]

Among translations published in Britain over the past two decades, however, none seem to me to earn this title as surely as do those of the poet Michael Hofmann, whose exemplary volumes of Durs Grünbein, Gunter Eich and Gottfried Benn have carried these three very distinct and divergent voices into English and made them audible for the first time, combining passionate advocacy with an equal depth of knowledge both of German and English.[18]

To return to the instance of Pound's translations with which I began, one conspicuous aspect that I have left without comment is the temporal distance that his Chinese translations have had to traverse. Inevitably, this entails dealing not only with linguistic and cultural difference but also with the even more formidable distance between eras. (Elsewhere, Pound's translations from Cavalcanti, which make that distance evident even when addressing moments that are relatively straightforward in the original, seem to me often wilfully obscure and archaic.) How does one simultaneously preserve that distance and discover proximity and connection? Among the most engaging work of this kind, a literary activism that

15 Tim Parks, *Where I'm Reading From: The Changing World of Books* (London: Harvill Secker, 2014). Nowhere in Parks's essay does he venture to say whether he thinks Robertson's translations are any good — surely this would be the crucial test, or an inconvenient complication, for his argument.

16 Tom Paulin, *The Road to Inver* (London: Faber and Faber, 2008).

17 Jo Shapcott: *Tender Taxes,* Faber, 2001, p. 59.

18 Durs Grünbein, *Ashes for Breakfast*, trans. Michael Hofmann (London: Faber & Faber, 2006); Gunter Eich, *Angina Days: Selected Poems*, trans. Michael Hofmann (New Jersey: Princeton University Press, 2010); Gottfried Benn, Impromptus: *Selected Poems and Some Prose*, trans. Michael Hofmann (New York: Farrar Straus Giroux, 2013).

approaches alchemy, are A. K. Ramanujan's translations from Classical Tamil, (*c.*100 BC–250 CE) and Arun Kolatkar's translations from various Marathi poets.[19]

Kolatkar's version of the thirteenth-/fourteenth-century poet Namdeo:

> in the beginning
> is the ant
> mouth of the triple river
> is the mouth of the ant[20]

manages to sound at once chthonic and contemporary. Arvind Khrishna Mehrotra's translation of the first- and second-century CE Mahārāshtrī Prākrit anthology Gāthāsaptaśatī is another exemplary work. Since we've been considering the costs of fidelity in translation, I'll end with one of his sinuous and vivid versions:

> Let faithful wives
> Say what they like,
> I don't sleep with my husband
> Even when I do.[21]

Literary Activism: A Symposium, ed. by Amit Chaudhuri
(Norwich: Boiler House Press, 2017)

19 A. K. Ramanujan, *Poems of Love and War* (New Delhi: Oxford University Press, 1996).

20 Arun Kolatkar, *Collected Poems in English* (Tarset, Northumberland: Bloodaxe, 2010), p. 298.

21 Arvind Krishna Mehrotra, *Collected Poems 1969–2014* (New Delhi: Penguin Books India, 2014), p. 206.

PART II

Afterworlds and Otherworlds

— 4 —

Naming Names: Ideas of Address in Catullus and Others

We are poor passing facts
warned by that to give
each figure in the photograph
his living name.
— Robert Lowell, *Day by Day*

Catullus's 116 mainly short poems abound in names. Often enough there's a name in the first line, or the first sentence, or as the first word. At school we were taught about a part of speech called Proper Nouns: names of persons, names of places, names of seas, names of winds. Although Catullus's poems may be cooled by the odd Zephyr and chilled by Boreas and travel to far flung places, it's the names of persons that stand out. Many of his poems are addressed to a particular named person, usually, we assume, a friend, and often referring to one or more named (or unnamed) person known to both. It's a good ruse to generate both a casual speaking voice and a shared experience, and seems effortlessly to establish a tone that can be jokey, bitchy, mocking, acerbic, mock-acerbic, affectionate, tender, even loving. Hard as it is in another language, especially a dead language, to hear a speaking voice — and Robert Frost asserts the impossibility of doing so — Catullus seems instantly identifiable by his tone, or rather by his mercurial range of tones.

It's not only Catullus's voice, though, that we hear in his poems. Other voices interrupt, arraign or arrest him — a phenomenon we might associate more with drama or epic than with the lyric, especially the short lyric. A typical example is 10, where Varus's mistress, presumes to take him at his word and asks to borrow the sedan-chair bearers he lyingly boasted were his. Curiously, it was having to parse this poem in a Latin class at thirteen that I had my first inkling of what a poem is, till then a topic which had never prompted in me the remotest interest. However removed the situation and the language, I had heard a voice I recognized, I saw the whole scene in my head. The poet — I had no idea then that he could have just been making the whole thing up — was reliving an acute social embarrassment, and was getting his belated revenge.

The first poem in Catullus's book, written, it's likely, in the last year of his brief life, is a witty ten-line dedicatory poem addressed to his friend, the historian Cornelius Nepos, presenting him with this 'new elegant little book', his 'lepidum novum libellum'; it is a poem which in passing also swears by Jupiter and invokes an unnamed 'virgin' who may be either Minerva or one of the Muses. The vocative mode of this opening poem is maintained in the next, which is addressed not to a person but to Lesbia's sparrow, although in this case the person is only referred to as 'my girl', 'meae puellae'. The small scale — from the little book to the sparrow — is already asserted in neoteric fashion, perhaps in deference to the saying attributed to Callimachus, '*mega biblion, mega kakon*' — big book, big evil. Cornelius Nepos, however, is acknowledged in the poem as the author of an ambitious three-volume historical work, so the *libellum*, buffed with dry pumice, is offered in arch contrast.

How do names function within a poem? On one level they're words like any other. They can be metrically scanned or subsumed in the rhythm of the line, and in Latin, obviously, they decline like every other noun. (Jupiter has a particularly irregular and eccentric set of cases.) Although they can be avoided by pronoun, epithet or periphrasis, names stand unambiguously for one thing, one person, unsubstitutable by another. But a name is already a substitution for the presence of an actual (or imagined) person. A friend who has a stutter explained to me that he had the most difficulty with names and numbers, for which there was no evasive manoeuvre possible. In other cases, his large vocabulary and speed of mind could often seize on another word, but names remained obdurately non-interchangeable. More on numbers later, but names cast a solid, unambiguous shadow: 'L'ombra di un nome', the poet Giovanni Pascoli wrote, turning a name into a gravestone. They say everything and nothing, being arbitrary, fated and immutable. Even a nickname shares with poetry an element of invention and characterization. Could names then be thought of as antithetical to a poem's freedom to play with sound and image, to use suggestion rather than statement? A stumbling block, an obstacle, an obstruction to a poem's flow?

For Catullus it seems not. His use of names is excessive by any standard. Not name-dropping so much as name-sowing and name-planting, a field and a forest of names. Instead of weighing down the verse, as it easily might, his use of names is sociable and frivolous, and helps, just as the everyday situations he describes do, to make these terse poems conversational, so the tight metres he employs constantly play against the idiomatic, gossipy, often obscene language. Surely there's no better example of what Frost calls 'sentence sounds'.

The *fons et origo* of poetic name-calling, at least for the Western tradition, is the catalogue of ships and men in Homer's *The Iliad* (ll. 584–989), a portion of which, in Robert Fagles's translation reads:

> Then Schedius and Epistrophus led the men of Phocis —
> two sons of Iphitus, that great heart, Naubolus' son —
> the men who held Cyparissus and Pytho's high crags.
> the hallowed earth of Crisa, Daulis and Panopeus,
> men who dwelled round Anemoria, round Hyampolis,
> men who lived along the Cephisus' glinting waters,
> men who held Lilaea close to the river's wellsprings.
> Laden with all their ranks came forty long black ships
> and Phocian captains ranged them column by column,
> manning stations along the Boeotians' left flank.[1]

1 Homer, *The Iliad*, trans. by Robert Fagles (London: Penguin, 1990), p. 116.

Sixteen place-names and men's names in ten lines; five hundred and five lines which maintain this resounding, heroic roll-call. Each strophe packed, and organized by the anaphora 'men who...' and ending with the number (and type) of ships they brought. Beside this martial catalogue, Catullus's naming is decidedly informal and unheroic.

Many of Milton's sonnets, to take one, more local, example, begin with the name of the addressee as the subject of the poem — Vane, Fairfax, Cromwell, Cyriak Skinner, H. Lawes etc. It's a habit he may have picked up from the Roman poets, most likely Horace, another great namer of names, and gives further weight to the cumbersome mighty movement of the verse. But in his case, the names for the most part are already in the public zone, already presences occupying the historical stage on which Milton was at home:

> Vane, young in yeares, but in sage counsell old,
> Then whome a better Senatour nere held
> The helme of Rome, when gownes not armes repelld
> The feirce Epeirot & the African bold

and the poems are squarely centred on the figure addressed. By contrast Catullus's names proliferate and are only sometimes those of known public figures — one resounding exception being 93, his curt dismissal of Caesar — and tend to find street encounters with, say, the ill-mannered mistress of the bankrupt Formian merchant more engaging than public affairs. In fact, a fair number of public figures do crop up in his poems — Pompey, Cicero and so on — and many others would have been known to his contemporaries. It's rather that Catullus, despite being very much of the senatorial class, is insistently informal and irreverent, and any hierarchy has to do with personal affection rather than social status.

But it is surely George Gordon Byron who is our closest poet to Catullus, in his speed of reflex, swift passage of mood, and his delight in naming. The 'dedication' to Southey of *Don Juan* begins, as many a Catullus poem, with the name about to be flayed:

> Bob Southey! You're a poet — Poet-laureate,
> And representative of all the race.
> Although 'tis true that you turned a Tory at
> Last — yours has lately been a common case...

before turning his tender attentions to Coleridge and Wordsworth. No doubt the multitude of poets' names in Pope's *Dunciad* — 'Dennis and dissonance, brangling and Brewall...' — gave Byron licence, but the cornucopia of names that follow in stanzas 2 and 3 of the poem proper, as he pretends to flounder about in search of an appropriate hero for his poem, are very much in the spirit of Catullus:

> Vernon, the butcher Cumberland, Wolfe , Hawke,
> Prince Ferdinand, Granby, Burgoyne, Keppel, Howe...

followed in the next stanza, as if this wasn't enough, by:

> Barnave, Brissot, Condorcet, Mirabeau,
> Petion, Clootz, Danton, Marat, La Fayette

were French, and famous people as we know;
And there were others, not forgotten yet,
Joubert Hoche, Marceau, Lannes, Desaix, Moreu,
With many of the military set,
Exceedingly remarkable at times,
But not at all adapted to my rhymes.

Here it's as though he's determined to out-Catullus Catullus, and his knowing, worldly tone owes much to the Latin forebear, whose sexual candour and obscenity he would also likely have found appealing.

As for numbers, that other stumbling block, which like names are unique and unsubstitutable, Catullus is also prolifically numerate.[2] Not only do we know his poems by their number, but like our 'numbers', in Latin 'numerus' refers to metre, so 50 has the poet amusing himself with Licinius : 'ludebat numero modo hoc modo illuc' — (each of us) played at writing in this or that metre. At times, metre and number combine as in the threat to expose Asinius Marrucinius, who has stolen his napkin, with 'hendecasyllabos trecentos'. Numbers occur often enough with relation to sums of money, and can be very specific, as in 26 where the debt incurred by his farm, worse than anything the climate can throw at him, is fifteen thousand two hundred ('milia quindecem et ducentos'). But mostly they occur as extravangance and exaggeration, as in 5 where he asks of Lesbia : 'da mi basia mille, deinde centum | dein mille altera, dein secunda centum' — and so on up to three thousand three hundred kisses, and then more to confuse the initially precise reckoning. Also 48 counts kisses to his friend Juventius (300,000) and ends with the inadequacy of the number, even if it were fuller than a harvest of ripe ears of corn. These multiplications are at once worldly and lyrical.

★ ★ ★ ★ ★

It's a singular and poignant feature of the three poems Catullus wrote about his brother's death (65, 68, and 101) that nowhere in them is his brother named. He is addressed only as 'frater'. We know — and learn — nothing of his life. All we can suppose, because he tells us so, is that Catullus visited his grave in the Troad in Bythinia, modern day Anatolia, by land and sea, almost exactly a thousand miles from Rome — no mean journey. The poems supply no details about him other than his death. This name avoidance is reminiscent of the taboo still practised by indigenous Australians, but sufficiently widespread also in Africa, South America and Southern India to suggest some instinctive and universal dread of naming the dead, of calling them by name, and so calling them up. Here at the very least, in the context of such a plethora of names, the omission of his brother's creates a dark

2 In relation to my earlier claim that numbers are resistant to poetic inclusion, Clarence Brown in his discussion of Osip Mandelstam's great early poem 'Hagia Sophia', writes that the poet 'insists upon the precision of the numerals — 107, 40, 4 [respectively, the marble columns, the windows and the archangels] — of all grammatical categories the most "unpoetic"...' Although the context of his argument is far removed from that of Catullus, the essential idea is similar, and the fact that the word 'unpoetic' is in inverted commas suggests his own contrary intuition. Clarence Brown, *Mandelstam* (Cambridge: Cambridge University Press, 1973), p. 187.

invisible border exiling him from the vivid social world of so much of Catullus's work.

Poem 65 is addressed to Hortalus, 68 to Manius, but 101, the last and most renowned of these elegiac poems, speaks directly to his brother:

> multas per gentes et multa per aequora vectus
> advenio has miseras frater ad inferias
> ut te postremo donarem munere mortis
> et mutam nequiquam alloquerer cinerem
> quandoquidem fortuna mihi tete abstulit ipsum
> heu miser indigne frater adempte mihi
> nunc tamen interea haec prisco quae more parentum
> tradita sunt tristi munere ad inferias
> accipe fraterno multum manantia fletu
> atque in perpetuum frater ave atque vale

For which a rough (and unready) translation of mine might serve:

> Crossing many lands and many seas,
> I have come, brother, for these wretched funeral rites
> to present you with the last tribute of death
> and to speak in vain to voiceless ash,
> since Fortune has cut you off from me,
> alas, poor brother, and cruelly bereft me of your very self,
> so now meanwhile, according to age-old ancestral custom,
> in sad observance of the funeral rites, receive
> these things, drenched with fraternal tears:
> now and forever, brother, hail and farewell.

Words echo each other throughout this brief ten-line poem, from the first line's pairing of 'multas' and 'multa' and the penultimate line's 'multum' (with 'mutam' between); with 'miseras' and 'miser'; with the doubling of 'inferias', 'munere' and of 'atque' and the final almost anagrammatic 'ave' and 'vale'. But the echo that we hear most resoundingly in the hollowed acoustics of the poem is 'frater, 'frater', 'fraterno'. Even the emphatic personal pronoun 'tete' is a repetition built on an absence. Dead centre of the poem is the single mournful exclamation 'heu'. That's a great many repetitions for a short poem, and the vocabulary is predictable and conventional — funeral rites, ashes, sadness, tears. It reprises almost verbatim the phrasing of 68B:

> sed totum hoc studium luctu fraterna mihi mors
> abstulit. o misero frater adempte mihi.
>
> [But all this interest [in poetry] has been wrested from me by
> my brother's death. O woe is me, with you, brother, taken from me.]

However predictable the language of 101 sounds, the wonder is that it somehow embodies the numbness of grief and the depth of love. Arguably, its very namelessness gives it such force, as does the flat tone and conventional vocabulary, set against the sociable multitude of names and the dazzling play and tonal variety in so many of his other poems.

* * * * *

Anne Carson's *Nox*[3] makes an uncanny use of this famous poem, and appropriately turns it into a lament for her own brother's death. In this case, however, we do encounter the name of her brother, Michael, and in the slow and meandering course of *Nox* we receive fragmentary information about his life. The work is arranged in a concertina of attached pages, not as a book but rather as a gathering of scattered leaves, which, when opened like a book, mainly uses the verso for a word-by-word parsing of Catullus's poem and the recto for a miscellany of texts and images. The verso columns mimic a Latin–English dictionary entry for every one of the poem's 63 words with repetitions referred back to the first instance. Most of the entries — even those of adverbs and pronouns — ingeniously contrive some reference to 'nox' so that the hidden theme is a perpetuum of night — 'nox est perpetua' (the phrase occurs first in Catullus 5, a poem on the death of Lesbia's sparrow). This is both a grim scholastic joke and a searing confrontation with the ineluctable fact of her brother's death and the incomplete knowledge she has gathered to piece together his life. (For readers whose Latin is as wretched as mine, it also provides a helpful gloss to the poem and a crash course in vocabulary and grammar.)

Roughly midway through the work, the poet gives her own 'translation' of Catullus 101, which does little to accord with the ramifying meanings listed in the word-by-word verso entries, or rather it marks a minus sign, a shortfall, in deference to the complex unity of the original poem. By being more or less 'word-for-word', the translation deliberately does violence to the usual English word order, but still includes the odd striking condensation such as the interrogative 'Why?' to register the adverb 'nequiquam' (in vain, to no purpose).

Every sheet, verso and recto, is a collage, whether text, drawing, letter or photograph, so the work is like a memorial album but, though reproduced in this grey box, the edges of each glued-in section still retain a jagged and puckered appearance, as well as faint signs of staplings, and so match the serrated edges of the Fifties photographs included, but also suggest the torn-off, fragmentary nature of the life and the poet's meditation on loss. For even the information about his life, sparse as it is, is interrupted by reflections on history, Herodotus 'the father of history', Plutarch and others. Most heart-breaking are details of their mother's thwarted love for her son and his widow's account which alludes to episodes from his life and funeral. It's a work of extraordinary restraint and, as so often in Carson's writings, her narrative skill is witnessed by what she leaves out as much as by what she includes, though here what is omitted is poignantly due to a lack of knowledge and a lack of contact with the brother, whose vagrant and disturbed life and loves are fragments that can only ever be incompletely fitted together.

* * * * *

Of all the names that occur in his poems Catullus shows an inordinate fondness for his own — as anyone might if they were called Catullus; if they *were* Catullus.

3 Anne Carson, *Nox* (New York: New Directions, 2010).

'Catullus' occurs in every singular case of the first declension noun that he is (so in English translation it's as though his name is shorn of all the variant endings): in self-communing (46), as a reminder to friends (38 begins in ironically mournful style 'Your Catullus, Cornificius, is unwell...'), as a person spoken to within his own poem: in 10, 'mi Catulle', he is addressed, as we've seen, by Varus's mistress.

We see 'Catullus' surrounded by an extended, convivial and promiscuous social circle in Rome, his poems addressing his lover Lesbia, his friends Cornelius, Flavius, Veranius:

> Verani, omnibus e meis amicis
> antistans mihi milibus trecentis...
>
> [Veranius, my favourite among the three
> hundred thousand of my friends...]

Here name and number combine. Then we have Fabullus, inseparably paired with Veranius, Varus, Furius, Aurelius and Calvus, and that only covers the first fifteen poems, without listing the various named enemies. The so frequent presence of his own name amid this circle gives us the delightful illusion of knowing the 'actual' living Catullus, though of course this is an illusion that is artfully constructed by the poems. It reminds me of the poet Antonio Machado, who created among his various apocryphals a figure called Antonio Machado who seems to have shared a great many biographical features with his namesake, only he died in Teruel several years earlier than his author.

The Manchester Review of Books, July 2020

— 5 —

The Seeing Ocean and the Heartless Theseus: Catullus, Dante, Titian

As a student, having been chucked off the twentieth-century art course I was hoping to study, for reasons I can only guess at, by the brilliant but irascible Ronald Pickavance, I settled for a consolatory course in Renaissance art and architecture with the eminent art historian Professor Alastair Smart. I have a clear memory of one late afternoon, sitting in a small dark room on the first floor of Nottingham University's vast, slightly pompous, neo-classical Portland Building — its elder neighbour, also in Portland stone, was the Trent Building which D. H. Lawrence described as resembling 'an iced cake'. Accompanied by the low hum of the stack-loaded projector's fan, the darkness was comforting and soporific, but I was jolted awake by the sudden vivid colours of Titian's *Bacchus and Ariadne* as it clattered onto the screen.

I had little idea at first of what was going on in the picture — a bright welter. A woman was turning her seaward gaze back at the very moment the god was leaping from his cheetah-drawn chariot, so that their gazes met across the upper left-hand third of the canvas at a slight gradient, human up to god. A dramatic crossing of eyes, an intersection. Everything seemed both out of kilter and oddly balanced. His leap, suspended in mid-air; her twisting, suspended in mid-turn. It looks like a kind of predatory leap, with the attendant big cats as models, but even that is equivocal. It could just be a protective act, given her proximity both to the cheetahs to her right and the cliff edge to her left. The folds of his pink mantle billow behind him, her blue gown is bunched in pleats. At her left, shoulder-height, the wind-filled sails of Theseus's ship are perched on the horizon as the faithless Greek deserts her — a small shape about to fall off the edge of the picture. The right-hand two thirds are occupied by a seething rout of bacchanals clashing cymbals, tambourines, with a snake-girdled Silenus beside another celebrant flailing the torn-off leg of an ox or a deer.

The picture was commissioned by Alfonso I d'Este for his Ferrara palazzo and I read somewhere that he was the proud owner of a pair of cheetahs. I can't recall much else of what was told us except that the literary source was Ovid's *Metamorphosis*, a set text for the literature course I was also studying, but one I'd culpably avoided till then. Out of curiosity I checked Ovid's account. Looking again at a reproduction of Titian's picture there seemed to be a disconnect. Some details tallied, others very evidently didn't. Though I hadn't read the Ovid, by chance

I was leafing through Peter Whigham's brilliant and inventive translations of Catullus published in 1974, a couple of years earlier, and alighted on no. 64. There, indeed, were all of the relevant details missing from Ovid. Doubtless this is now common knowledge, as the recent Oxford Classics edition sports Titian's painting on the cover, but then, at least, my professor seemed startled and interested by this information. Anyway, it was mere chance and not scholarship that led me to resolve a question I was asking about Titian's sources. What I learnt from the experience was the way these extraordinary images in Catullus's poem had sparked a vision in the painter. Their two gazes had crossed a sea of time, more than fifteen hundred years and two art forms, and intersected. Something the Latin poet had imagined had been re-created, had been sumptuously re-imagined in oil paint, and that recreation, in turn, had become a source of many Renaissance paintings. Just as one example, Velázquez, who had seen several of Titian's mythological paintings in the Palacio de Buen Retiro, went on to create his own mythological versions such as that of Arachne, this time more securely sourced in Ovid.

Perhaps because I had to figure it out myself, the nature of this dynamic transmission struck me even more forcefully. Till then, despite everything I was meant to be studying telling me the opposite, I suppose I had considered art and poetry to be the unmediated original creation of a solitary mind. Now I was faced with the puzzle of 'translation' — of time, place, language, culture, medium.

There is a further irony or recursive twist in that the mythological events that Catullus narrates are presented by him as ekphrastic accounts of what is depicted on a cover on the goddess of love's bed, so the imagined visual art is translated into poetry by Catullus, and Titian then retranslates it back into the visual.

Even though these may well be rather obvious insights about the nature of the imagination, I'd like to pause a little longer on this same epyllion — little epic — by Catullus. Rereading it again recently in Whigham's translation, with an opened Latin text that I was stumblingly trying to parse, I noticed a further arresting fact. The opening describes the very first sea voyage, undertaken to plunder the golden fleece, and the wonder with which it is beheld by 'the Nereids of the deep':

> Quae simul ac rostro ventosum proscidit aequor,
> tortaque remigio spumis incanduit unda,
> emersere freti candenti e gurgite vultus
> acquorcae monstrum Nereides admirantes. (ll. 12–15)

The 1913 prose version by F. W. Cornish — 'ex-Provost of Eton College' — in my (bowdlerized) edition gives this:

> So when she [the boat] ploughed with her beak the windy expanse, and the wave churned by the oars grew white with foam-flakes, forth looked from the foaming surge of the sea the Nereids of the deep wondering at the strange thing.

I'm not competent to give an accurate account of how these lines work, but I can glimpse their precipitant, echoic quality: *aequor* (a flat level, of desert or sea) and *acquorcae*, *incanduit* and *candenti*, and how *rostro* (beak of a bird, hence ship's prow, hence face) meets that other face *vultus*. An encounter of two faces that have never before met: the pine-clad boat and the sea. The human world enters the realm of Neptune, who is named in the second line of the poem. My Latin dictionary defines *monstrum* as 'a significant supernatural event, a wonder, portent'. Which makes Nietzsche's put-down for Socrates, '*monstrum in fronte, monstrum in animo*', considerably less insulting.

Yet, trying to figure out these lines, I had a sense of *déjà-vu*. This same scene is used as a spectacular simile in the final canto of Dante's *Paradiso*:

> Un punto solo m'e' maggior letargo
> che venticinque secoli alla 'mpresa
> che fe' Nettuno ammirar l'ombra d'Argo.
> (Canto xxxiii, ll. 94–96)[1]

It's a crucial passage, at once unforgettable and obscure, in which Dante is trying to 'measure' how much of a single moment of the divine vision he has forgotten — far more than Neptune has forgotten in the 2500 years since he first stared in amazement at the shadow of the Argo passing overhead. The obscurity yields to careful attention but even then the image remains difficult to grasp, so much of human history and so much emotion is condensed into a single line, a second subclause which hinges on 'Un punto solo', a single point, a single moment. It's significant that at the same time these lines are a further condensation of another poet's lines.

Here I have to proceed warily as none of the Italian glosses for these lines makes any reference to Catullus, and they are written by scholars steeped in the Classics. However, in the late thirteenth century, Catullus's *Carmina* appeared in Verona, and Dante was to spend six years (1312–16) in the city. If I'm right to think that Dante is recollecting the image from Catullus's epyllion this is a further condensation of human history and culture. Still, whether it's been noted before or not, the similarity of the scene, Catullus's 'admirantes' and Dante's 'ammirar', and the epic sweep of both descriptions suggest that Dante had this passage in mind or at least reverberating in his inner ear.

This succession of images doesn't end with Dante, for his 'Un punto solo' finds a new home in the seventh octave of Torquato Tasso's *La Gerusalemme Liberata*. God is looking down on the Crusades from his throne, as high above the stars as the starry sphere is above hell, imagined to be, as in Dante's cosmos, at the centre of the earth:

> Gli occhi in giù volse, e in un sol punto, e in una
> vista mirò ciò ch'in sé il mondo aduna.

> [He cast his eyes down, and in a single point, and in one | glance saw that which the world contains in itself.]

The upward gaze of Catullus's nereids becomes Neptune's gaze in Dante before turning into God's downward gaze in Tasso, effecting a counter-Reformation

1 This and all subsequent quotations from Dante Alighieri: *La Commedia secondo l'antica vulgata*, ed. by Giorgio Petrocchi (Milan: Società Dantesca Italiana, Mondadori, 1966–67). William Anderson in *Dante the Maker* (London: Hutchinson, 1985), p.10, gives a helpfully expanded translation of these three lines: 'A single point [of that vision of eternity] is a greater weariness to me [to describe or recall] than the twenty-five centuries that have elapsed since the enterprise of the Golden Fleece made Neptune wonder at the shadow of the *Argo*.'

'conversion' of the pagan imagery that nevertheless nourishes his poem. Implicit in all three is a vast compression of time and space, as well as a compression of poetic imagining into 'un punto solo'.

Maybe this is a sign of a 'classic': that it continues to reverberate in the mind. The idea takes us onto T. S. Eliot terrain, where I'm loathe to trespass, as does the notion of borrowing: 'Immature poets imitate; mature poets steal; bad poets deface what they take, and good poets make it into something better, or at least something different.' Whatever truth this famous remark has, it posits a progressive and hierarchical order to poetry whereas I'm trying to think about a different set of relations. If Eliot's idea has a Darwinian slant, or at least a social-Darwinian slant, what I'm proposing is more like the anarchist Kropotkin's idea of mutual aid among the species, a model he set up in opposition to inter-species competition. Or, to abandon these analogies, a situation in which one imaginative leap fosters another. Dante's dizzyingly compressed use of this image comes as a culmination to a whole series of boat and voyaging images throughout the *Commedia* which represent not only his pilgrim's journey but that of the reader alongside his own — see for instance his warning to the 'lettor' in his 'piccioletta barca' (the reader in his little boat) as he sets forth into the deeper waters of the *Purgatorio.* If his own image figures as a kind of *summa* that includes this developing series of representations, it seems even more resonant that it should include also the sweep of classical learning that informs his poem.

This one poem by Catullus, then, has provided two subsequent artists not merely with matter, or with arresting imagery, but with an inclusive vision. I suspect the lineage could be traced back via Apollonius of Rhodes's *Argonautica*, ad infinitum (and forward as we've seen with Tasso) and so is something like the 'song lines' Bruce Chatwin considers in indigenous Australian culture. In this case, whatever spurred Catullus, it was his poem that was carried forward long after by two artists at the very height of their powers.

July 2019

— 6 —

Dante: *Inferno*, translated by Robin Kirkpatrick

Dante, *Inferno*, trans. by Robin Kirkpatrick (London: Penguin, 2006)

The past ten years have brought a spate of *Inferno* translations. We have had Steve Ellis's Yorkshire-inflected *Hell*, Ciaron Carson's tour de force in terza rima, still to come is Sean O'Brien's version; and that's just this side of the Atlantic. Now Robin Kirkpatrick, a distinguished Dante scholar, has published his first instalment of the entire *Commedia*. What is behind all this industry — apart, that is, from Dante's work being the pre-eminent long poem of the last millennium? Its entirety, compassing *Hell*, *Purgatory* and *Heaven* in a hundred cantos, records the poet's journey through the three realms of the afterlife. Osip Mandelstam refers to the poem as a vast crystal made of 30,000 facets — a tall order, then, for any translator. What makes it harder still is that the translator must find a way not only to embody Dante's own narrative voice, but also the hundreds of utterly distinct and unforgettable voices that he records — most famously, from Hell, Francesca, Pier della Vigna, Brunetto Latini, Cavalcanti (père), Farinata, Ulysses and Ugolino. Some of the characters are mythical, others historic, others still Dante's contemporaries. In fact the afterworld, especially Hell, has much in common with the faction-ridden world of Dante's Tuscany and, as this uninterrupted flow of translations may strongly suggest, with our own world too.

The difficulties do not stop there. Stylistically, Dante is one of the most omnivorous of poets. Here Mandelstam's beautiful image does scant justice to the fluvial, all-inclusive, perpetually self-transforming nature of the poem. Linguistically it ranges from the most colloquial to the most courtly, from the sepulchral to the burlesque. It is unfair to expect this span from any single contemporary poet: but, doomed to failure, the translator must at least offer one strand that holds.

Despite its history furnishing so many examples, the last century gave us few poems that attempt to understand evil. Hell in Pound's *Cantos* merely draws on the obscene, ordure-laden elements of Dante without a convincing moral context. *The Waste Land*, deeply indebted to Dante, emphasizes the sterile and mechanical life of the living, damned without Dante's sense of their towering potential and magnetism — no Francesca, no Brunetto, no Ulysses. This lack of a modern equivalent may account for the continuing challenge that Dante throws out to translators and readers.

In T. S. Eliot's critical prose, Dante was fashioned into a forbidding, infallible classic. The figure we meet in the poem is far more engaging. We may find some of Hell's punishments vindictive and repellent — those for homosexuals or heretics or even adulterers, for example — but the journey that Dante takes us on allows us to hear, though not necessarily to believe, the sinners' own versions, brought to a point of absolute self-definition.

Kirkpatrick's introduction and canto-by-canto notes are remarkably level and lucid, as attentive to structure as to syntax, language and motif, and deftly cross-reference the whole poem. On their own, they would justify the price. He also brings a more nuanced sense of the Italian and a more meditated appreciation of the poem's construction than nearly all of his competitors.

At times, however, this advantage can work against him, especially when he is tempted to gloss the original. In the opening, for example, Dante's one word *smarrita* becomes 'blurred and lost', the three adjectives describing the wood become the Hobbesian combo of 'savage, brute, harsh and wild', where the last adds little to the first. For my taste, the iambic beat is too insistent, and can lead him to fillers such as 'firmly' in these otherwise powerful lines describing the prodigals and misers:

> Their frenzied sprees or febrile hoardings-up
> have wrung from them the beauty of the world
> and brought them firmly to this ugly brawl.

Earlier in the same canto, he has Virgil address Pluto as 'you execrable wolf' and continues: 'May fury gnaw you inwardly away'. Dante's 700-year-old Italian sounds decidedly more contemporary.

In the long run, any translation of this poem will fall short, but there is much to recommend here — certainly the intelligence, the energy, the linguistic range — and Kirkpatrick's ability to enliven even doctrinal discourse bodes well for his final two instalments.

The Times, 29 April 2006

— 7 —

More Hell

Sean O'Brien: *Dante's Inferno* (London: Picador, 2006)
Dante, *Inferno*, trans. by Robin Kirkpatrick (London: Penguin, 2006)

Sean O'Brien is surely right to claim that the *Inferno* 'is the most frequently translated poem in the Western tradition' and his own version, arriving just a few months after that of Robin Kirkpatrick, is further confirmation. Both employ blank verse. Otherwise the translations could not be more dissimilar. As far as I can see the only thing that reads identically in both versions is the beautiful line, with its ripple of 'o's, describing the foul Harpies: 'who drove the Trojans from the Strophades'.

Although the Italian hendecasyllable is often much longer than eleven syllables (as adjacent vowels don't count), the pentameter would seem the natural English choice, and has been employed again and again in translations since Henry Cary's 1814 version. Dante's metre, though, secures very different effects: its unstressed final syllable, combined with its interlocking rhyme scheme, the *terza rima*, and often radical enjambment, gives it the capacity for greater forward propulsion and pace than the pentameter has, in anyone but Shelley's hands. A useful attribute in a poem so shaped by continuous walking, climbing, wading, sailing and flying.

Kirkpatrick's translation, which comes accompanied by a dual text and an excellent introduction and notes, is the odder, the riskier of these two. A renowned *dantista*, his treatment is surprisingly free and improvisatory though always prompted by a strong sense of the original. Lines such as 'Our tread now fell | on voided nothings only seeming men' make something inventive and strange out of the regular iambic beat.

With years of practice behind him, O'Brien has formidable skill with the pentameter, and gives it a stately, marmoreal quality — here emphasized by the way Dante's *terzine* are laid out as three-line stanzas, and each canto given a title. Some of the finest moments occur when this disciplined and chiselled line sparks against obdurate matter with grim energy:

> The demon Charon, with his eyes like coals,
> Then summons each to take his place aboard
> And clubs the laggards with his dripping oar.

The language is deliberately plain, without being plodding and tuneless like C. H. Sisson's version. O'Brien often deploys runs of monosyllabic words — one advantage English does have over Italian — to impressive effect:

> I saw a broad ditch bent into an arc,
> And seeming to encompass all the plain,
> Just as my guide had told me that it would.

This landscape from Canto XII perfectly prepares the reader for the arrival of the centaur archers, and their leader Chiron, who takes 'An arrow out and with the notch of it | Brushed back his heavy beard upon his jaws' and in both instances, the English does justice to the original.

One of the most testing problems for a translator is the way Dante's poem keeps developing — it abhors stasis — and each canto extends the voice and voices of the poem. The Wood of the Suicides, for example, introduces the courtier Pier della Vigna whose spidery, intricate wordplay is a translator's nightmare. The whole canto is knotted with such ingrown resonances as can be heard in the line: 'Cred'io ch'ei credette ch'io credesse' which Kirkpatrick quirkily renders as 'Truly I think he truly thought that, truly,' and O'Brien more straightforwardly as 'It seems my master thought that I believed'. Pier della Vigna's own twisted repetitions, which Kirkpatrick energetically registers, are pruned back to the bare wood by O'Brien. A legitimate claim could be made for both approaches, though one *terzina* goes missing in O'Brien's taut canto.

What O'Brien has achieved is a compellingly readable version of the whole poem, with little slack, and a steady incandescence to the language. Any reader with no Italian could do a lot worse than turn to both of these new translations, and readers who know the original could still learn much from them.

The Independent, 15 December 2006

— 8 —

A Commentary on Dante, *Purgatorio* XXX

It's strange that a canto so concerned with beauty, so rich in colours, so involved with the end of a long upward journey should be darkened by so many negatives at the level both of syntax and of the psyche. Instead of triumphalism, there's shame; instead of relief there's discomfort; instead of congratulations there are reproaches.

In *Purg.* IV, l. 88, Virgil had encouraged Dante with the promise that

> Questa montagna è tale,
> che sempre al cominciar di sotto è grave;
> e quant'om più va su, e men fa male.
> Però, quand'ella ti parrà soave
> tanto, che sù andar ti fia leggero
> com'a seconda giù andar per nave,
> allor sarai al fin d'esto sentiero:
> quivi di riposar l'affanno aspetta.

[This mountain is such, | that beginning below is always hard; | and the more a man climbs up, the less pain he suffers. | When the slope seems to you to level out | so much that ascending will be easy | as if you were voyaging on a boat, | then you will be at the end of this road | where you can expect to recover from the weariness.]

Having arrived at the end of this road, it would only seem right that Dante should recover his breath and well-being. But instead he must face an even harder trial, and weep for another sword 'per altra spada'. His imagination is carried away towards other peaks and harsher climates:

> si come neve tra le vive travi
> per lo dosso d'Italia si congela
> soffiata e stretta dalle venti schiavi...

[just as snow among the living rafters | along the backbone of Italy freezes | blown and compacted by Slavic winds (north-easterlies)...]

In *Purg.* XXIII, readers are offered a concise résumé of the whole *cantica*:

> salendo e rigirando la montagna
> che drizza voi che il mondo fece torti

[climbing up and circling round the mountain | which straightens you that the world has twisted] as if the ascent was a spiralling movement that unwinds something within, straightening what has been twisted, unscrewing the self that the world has deformed, so the spirit may ascend towards the light. In Canto XXX, clearly Dante has as yet not attained a sufficiently untwisted condition, and for all the felt emotion, there's something of an anti-climax in the long-awaited meeting with Beatrice.

The canto is concerned with transformations, albeit hindered ones: the transformation of the flesh to spirit, which Beatrice has experienced, the future transformation — back — into 'la revistita carne' [the re-clothed flesh] at the Final Judgement, the transformation of solid to liquid in the central image of the snow on the Alps (along the spine of Italy), which will melt like candle wax in the 'perdita', the loss, of shadow (implying negatively the presence of the sun). And even more significant for the canto's plot is the baton change from Virgil, who has been the guide for two thirds of the whole poem, to Beatrice.

It has often been noted that here is the only occasion in the *Commedia* — chockful of names — in which the poet gives, or rather is given, his name, for which he immediately offers an excuse: 'Dante, perchè Virgilio se ne vada...' (55) [Dante, as Virgil is about to leave...]. Beside the five repetitions of Virgil's name (in the 9 lines 46–55), his own name sounds out in solitary prominence:

> quando mi volsi al suon del nome mio,
> che di necessità qui si regista, (62–63)

[when I turned at the sound of my name | which here I am forced to record]

This hesitancy is in heightened contrast with Beatrice's assured self-assertion: 'Guardami ben: ben son, ben son Beatrice' [Observe me well — I am, I am indeed Beatrice]. She is prone to repetition, as can be seen earlier in l. 56: 'non pianger anco, non pianger ancora' [don't weep yet, don't weep yet], a bit as though speaking in a singsong emphatic voice to a child.

Dante himself says not a word, but only turns to an absent Virgil as if 'to speak' (per dicere). Among many songs, some Latin and the stern rebukes of Beatrice, Dante stays mute. His words are transformed into trembling, tears and sighs.

At the beginning of the canto, interposed between the Latin hymns, there's a quote from Virgil: 'Manibus... date lili plenus' [Give lilies from full hands] *Aen.* VI. 883, which is already a sign that the angels are cultured and have read the classics dear to the poet. Yet, given that this canto is both a valediction to Virgil and a welcome to Beatrice it's especially fitting that the last line that Dante addresses to his already disappeared guide is 'conosco i segni de l'antica fiamma' [I recognize the signs of the ancient flame] which, as has often been noted, reprises in his own dialect Virgil's line: 'agnosco veteris vestigia flammae'. It is as if Dante has had to undertake his own laborious personal journey to earn and inhabit these words. On the poetic plane it's 'la rivestita carne' [the reclothed flesh] which the poet earlier anticipated for human bodies in the future Judgement.

Concerning the future and the body once more clothed in flesh, this canto provides a startling image of 'redressing' and reincarnation which, as far as I'm aware, has not been noted. It is the reworking of Dante's lines:

> sopra candido vel cinta d'oliva
> donna m'apparve, sotto verde manto,
> vestita di color di fiamma viva.

[in an olive-girdled white veil | a woman appeared to me, in a green cloak | dressed in the colour of living flame]

in Petrarch's famous sonnet 190 which begins:

> Una candida cerva sopra l'erba
> verde m'apparve, con duo corna d'oro,
> fra due riviere, all'ombra d'un alloro,
> levando 'l sole a la stagione acerba...

[A white deer upon the green | grass appeared before me | with two golden horns, | between two rivers, in the shadow of a laurel tree, | as the sun was rising in the early spring...]

where the lexical sequence 'sopra candido...m'apparve verde' is transformed into the sequence 'candida...sopra...verde m'apparve', and the woman into a deer, the olive plant into a laurel. Whether deliberate citation or unconscious prompt, the proximity in the two passages is unmistakeable. Although Dante's vivid colours are changed, in both passages there is an abundance of springtime colouration. Dante's earlier lines

> Così la madre al figlio par superba,
> com' ella parve a me, perchè d'amaro
> sente il sapor della pietate acerba (79–81)

[Thus the mother to the son seems severe | as she seemed to me, though he senses the pity behind the bitterness [of the rebuke].]

are again taken up in Petrarch second quatrain:

> Era sua vista sí dolce superba,
> ch'i' lasciai per seguirla ogni lavoro:
> come l'avaro che 'n cercar Tesoro
> con diletto l'affanno disacerba.

[The sight of her was so sweetly severe | that I abandoned all other pursuits | like the miser who in search of treasure | with delight makes the weariness less bitter.]

Here the rhyme of 'superba/disacerba' echoes Dante's 'superba/acerba', and Petrarch's final line 'quand'io caddi ne l'acqua, et ella sparve' [when I fell in the water, and she disappeared] seems already prefigured by Dante's l. 76: 'Gli occhi mi cadder giù nel chiaro fonte' [My eyes 'fell down' into the clear fountain], as well as reprising the earlier mentioned 'affanno'.

It's an important moment where a profound memory of Dante has risen in Petrarch's mind (and ear), and this in its turn, has given light and life to English Petrarchism and, one could almost say, to the modern English lyric, in the free, inventive and incomparable translation of Thomas Wyatt, 'Whoso list to hount, I know where is an hind'.

This account, I now see, is a brief parable of transmission, of translation in its widest sense: a winding road that takes us from Dante's citation of Virgil, to Petrarch reworking Dante, to Wyatt re-imagining Petrarch. A transmission from Latin to Tuscan vernacular, a refiguring of an image within the same culture and language, then a further shift from Tuscan to English, the first a leap over some thirteen hundred years, the second a mere fifty years, the third of almost two hundred years. Interestingly, Wyatt lapses into Latin in his translation — 'Noli me tangere, for Caesars I am' — where Petrarch has none, a worldly, almost blasphemous, twist to Christ's words to Mary Magdalene '...for I am not yet ascended', but also translating a Latin maxim written on the collars of white stags: 'Nole me tangere, caesaris sum'. It reveals one way in which the sometimes occult, sometimes overt transfer, or transfusion, of material in poetry crosses the barriers of time and language, and how that process may constitute the life blood and living fibre of the art, and of language itself.

This essay was originally written in Italian, and published in Melodia meridiana: il paradiso terrestre letto dai poeti, La bella scola *(Rovigo: Il ponte del sale, 2014). I have translated it and added a final paragraph.*

— 9 —

Beyond the Human: Dante's *Paradiso*

What do humans do in heaven? Not too much, though not too little, according to St Augustine who foresees 'leisure for the praise of God' with 'no inactivity of idleness, and yet no toil constrained by want'. But eternity is a fair stretch: over millennia any activity, even such leisure, might begin to pall. The Roman dialect poet, Giuseppe Giacchino Belli in his sonnet 'Er paradiso' claims:

> in paradiso
> Nun perdi tempo co ggnisun lavoro:
> Nun ce trovi antro che vviolini, riso
> E ppandescelo...'

> [in heaven | you don't waste time with any work: | there's nothing but violins, laughter and heaven's bread...]

For Belli's Roman worker, heaven mainly means not having to graft and there's the bonus of free food — a cross between communion wafers and *panettone*, his 'ppandescelo' probably a nod to the 'pan de li angeli' in Dante's *Paradiso*. With Dante, though, it's a different story. In the first canto of this third part of his *Commedia*, he links the words 'valore' and 'lavoro', worth and work, as near anagrams and almost synonyms. But Belli's knowingly satirical rhyme (*paradiso / riso*), common at least since the thirteenth-century Sicilian sonneteer Giacomo da Lentini, is one which Dante employs with frequency, and the almost interchangeable 'riso' and 'sorriso' (laughter and smile, though both are usually translated into English as smile), in nominal, verbal or adjectival forms, figure prominently in every canto of *Paradiso*. Beatrice is constantly wreathed in smiles, as the sinister saying goes. Her 'santo riso', which we first meet at the end of *Purgatorio*, comes with such emotional force because it slakes what Dante calls his 'decade long thirst' following her death. Christina Rossetti, in a note to one of her poems, complains that both Dante's Beatrice and Petrarch's Laura 'have come down to us resplendent with charms, but [...] scant of attractiveness'. These smiles at least partly offset that impression: they're the encouraging accompaniment of what for Dante, ascending through the Ptolemaic heavens, from the moon and the planets to the Empyrean, is, to say the least, a steep learning curve.

Paradiso, I suspect, is the least read of the *Commedia*'s three *cantiche*, and surely the hardest work. If for no other reasons, and there are many, these two new English translations, one by Robin Kirkpatrick, the other by the husband-and-wife team of Robert and Jean Hollander, are to be welcomed. Each edition is the completing third volume of a long labour, and each helps the reader see this last *cantica* in the context of the previous two. With Virgil as his guide, Dante has already spiralled down through hell, seen what goes wrong, and progressively wronger, with the human spirit, and has then been taken up in an opposite spiral through the rocky terraces of Mount Purgatory, where souls are gradually mended. Dante describes this movement with beautiful economy in *Purgatory* 13 as 'salendo e rigirando la montagna | che drizza voi che 'l mondo fece torti...' [Climbing up and turning round the mountain | which straightens you whom the world twisted awry]. Heaven, we're told in *Paradiso* 19, is where we're no longer twisted by our appetites ('là dove appetito non si torce'). So no wine and *panettone*. Beatrice, who takes over as guide when the Latin poet reaches his permitted limit at the summit of Purgatory, in the Earthly Paradise, has been assigned this job for the rest of the journey or rather until she, in her turn, is replaced by St Bernard for the last cantos, so whatever else she eternally does has been temporarily set aside. On route, she instructs Dante in the significance of what he beholds and of much else besides, including astronomy, the properties of light, theology, free will, degree, human diversity, the history of language and the nature of God. If this makes the poem seem like a combined honours course, or several at once, the impression isn't mistaken, for Dante himself undergoes an intense viva on the Christian virtues by Saints Peter, James and John. Beatrice begins one typical lesson by saying 'secondo il mio infallibile avviso' ['in my infallible opinion'] but her teaching is administered not only with smiles but with a whole firework display of inner glowing. The words for light indefatigably multiply through the poem — *luce, lume, raggio, sfavilla, bagliore, splendore, fulgore*, and so on. In the notes accompanying his translation, Kirkpatrick makes helpful distinctions between Dante's use of the first three, though this is far from exhausting the language of light in which the *Paradiso* excels. A representative line, from Canto XIX, is 'raggio di sole ardesse sì acceso' where, apart from the two slender monosyllables, there's no lightless word to cast a shadow.

The journey proper begins with an instantaneous ascent through the sphere of fire and a moon landing. There, after a dull lesson on moon spots, Dante meets the not quite immaculate spirits who have failed to keep their vows. From the moon they ascend to Mercury, zone of the law-makers and politicos, and thence to Venus, where they meet the amorous and attractive Cunizza da Romano (and the repellent Folco). Their next stop is the Sun on which the wise, such as Thomas Aquinas and Solomon, are congregated. Thence they travel to Mars and meet heaven's warriors, the Church Militant, including Dante's great-grandfather, Cacciaguida. Jupiter, which follows, is the heaven of justice; and moving on to Saturn, Dante finds the contemplatives ascending and descending a Jacob's ladder. In Canto XXII, two-thirds of the way through the poem, Dante and Beatrice are assumed into the Heaven of Fixed Stars where Dante is catechized on faith, hope and charity. There he also meets Adam. Then they rise to the ninth heaven, the Crystalline Sphere and the Empyrean, which occupy the poem's final five cantos.

As we might expect, Paradise resounds with hymns and circle dances. Different spheres of the heavens are adorned with different shaped arrangements of souls, so in the heaven of the just they take the form of an eagle, among the contemplatives that of a cross. For all its symbolism, this aspect of the poem comes across as part pageantry, part Olympic opening ceremony. And yet there is the complication that these figures reside both there and in the Empyrean, where at the end of the poem Dante will see them arrayed in the shape of a rose, in the presence of God. They are almost like the 'measurement problem' in physics in which atoms are where they are observed and yet simultaneously elsewhere. St. Augustine had wondered about hierarchy in heaven: 'But what will be the grades of honour and glory here, appropriate to degrees of merit? Who is capable of imagining them? But there will be such distinctions, of that there can be no doubt.' Dante proves capable of imagining them, of arranging them geometrically and, better still, has found a way to graduate these distinctions so as not to cause envy and resentment among the blessed.

God, 'il sommo fattore', the Great Maker, is forever about His own business. Even before the creation, Dante is at pains to point out that He was occupied : 'Nè prima quasi torpente si giacque...', translated by the Hollanders as 'Nor, before then, did He rest in torpor, | for until God moved upon these waters | there existed no "before" , there was no "after" '. God had no time to waste since there was no such thing as time, but even in denial the line agreeably conjures up a loafing God — like Bellaqua among the indolent spirits of *Purgatory*. Those jobs that need doing are done by angels who govern the movement of the heavenly spheres. Dante's argument for their being co-nascent with the Creation is that had they been made earlier they'd have been redundant, a thing nature abhors (and he has Beatrice rebuke St. Jerome for that hypothesis). His Paradise's occupants have various time-saving devices, such as telepathy and accelerated travel, although, again, there is no time to save. Angels, according to Dante, have no language of their own, and the spirits of the blessed no need for words, but Dante is coaxed to express his thoughts anyway. This is a didactic device to help him formulate his ideas, and one that, besides, his readers profit by.

In Canto I Dante confronts the difficulties ahead with the tricky neologism 'transumanar': 'Transumanar significar *per verba* | non si poria...' The line with its two opening four-syllable words, capped with Latin, has a thundering grandeur which seems to achieve what it denies to be possible. The Hollanders translate this flatly as 'To soar beyond the human cannot be described | in words.' Kirkpatrick highlights the linguistic in his version: 'To give (even in Latin phrase) a meaning | to "transhuman" can't be done...' and argues incisively in his introduction that this verb 'implies not the transcendence of humanity but its transference from one dimension to another', in effect, its translation. It sounds like hedging, but I'd prefer the word to carry both these meanings at once. That way, it registers the tug between the transcendental and an obdurately held-on-to human state which the reader keeps sensing in the poem. The inadequacy of language to describe what occurs in heaven is a recurrent trope in Dante as it is in much Christian writing from Acts onwards. When St. Paul uses the image of a darkened mirror (variants of which Dante plays on in the poem) he says that 'now we know in part, but then we shall know, even as we are known'. Dante has set himself the tougher task actually to describe this knowing and being known. Where at the beginning of the *Inferno* he had protested 'Io non Enëa, io non Paolo sono' [I am not Aeneas, nor am I Paul], he finally leaves the author of the *Aeneid* behind and outreaches Paul. He even contrives his own Damascene moment of blinding, at the brightness of Beatrice's gaze in Canto IV.

The poem's impulse to go beyond the human makes my opening question out of place. Doing belongs to the earthly realm, being to heaven. The drama and narrative of the first two *cantiche*, dependent on the past doings of the souls Dante meets, are for the most part left behind. The individual's biography, so often asserted in the *Inferno*, recedes where souls have moved beyond themselves to form a united community. In Canto XIX, the Eagle hovers between first person singular and plural pronouns as it does between sight and sound:

> I saw and heard that Eagle's beak form words
> that rang, in what they voiced, as 'I' and 'mine'
> although in meaning they were 'we' and 'us'. (Kirkpatrick)

This kind of syntactical fusion or synaesthesia is one of Dante's devices to takes us outside of our usual modes of perception. Another is a whole series of neologisms with the prefix 'in-'. Just one example of how translator-confounding this can be occurs in *Paradiso* XIII:

> ché quella viva luce che sì mea
> dal suo lucente, che non si disuna
> da lui né da l'amor ch'a lor s'intrea...

Kirkpatrick, to his credit, doesn't shy away from the problems:

> For Living Light, which, from the Fount of Light,
> cascades in ways that do not disunite it,
> from Him or from the Love en-three-ing them...

The Hollanders offer something that sits more happily in English, but sacrifices some of the oddness of the original:

> For that living Light, which so streams forth
> from its shining Source that it neither parts from it
> nor from the Love that is intrined with them....

(Let him who has tried a canto of *Paradiso* cast the first stone.) Apart from any numerological significance, these invented words erode and then recreate the whole notion of a singular identity, which is invaded with plurality. Such being is beyond earthly powers to fully describe, but Dante dedicates his supreme verbal skills to giving the reader a glimpse, or rather a progression of ever-widening glimpses of what this beyond might be like.

Canto II opens with a warning, or a challenge, to the reader. Kirkpatrick renders this with style:

> You in that little boat, who listening hard,
> have followed, from desire to hear me through,
> behind my bowsprit singing on its way,
> now turn, look back and mark your native shores.
> Do not set out upon these open seas
> lest losing me you end confused and lost.

The substitution of 'bowsprit' here for the metonymic 'legno' [wood] is spirited. The whole line in Dante is 'dietro al mio legno che cantando varca' and the word 'varca' with its sense of going beyond permitted limits is integral to the poem and intends an echo of and contrast to Ulysses's 'folle volo' [mad flight] recounted in the *Inferno*, which also employs the word 'legno'. (Kirkpatrick on that occasion translated the word as 'prow'.)

This passage may well be a warning to himself that he is about to embark on a poem for which there's no real precedent: a Classical–Christian amalgam that presumes to describe Heaven as if he had visited it. Effectively it's also a warning to his future translators setting out to translate a poem which makes such dizzying demands. Both these translations know the dangers of the enterprise and the threats of these 'open seas'. When I read Kirkpatrick's *Inferno* I thought he'd been hampered by the regularity of his iambic pentameters, but reading his *Paradiso* I'm not so sure. Given that the original's *terza rima* is jettisoned, having some sustained rhythmic structure to stand in for Dante's hendecasyllables now seems to me a good working method. The translation by Jean Hollander is far looser metrically and can vary from eight to thirteen syllables per line, though based on a pentametric scheme. This gives her translation a certain flexibility which often has the advantage of clarity, a gain at the loss of structure. The accompanying introductions and notes are the product of a life's work on the part of Kirkpatrick and Robert Hollander, and both are 'transhumanly' knowledgeable about the text. Hollander's vast notes succeed in summarizing the many knots and disputes of almost seven hundred years of commentary. He can be quirky (as when he introduces, in the context of a Chaucerian remake, a fond note on *Some Like It Hot*, 'one of Billy Wilder's greatest films') but there's a moving sense of fairness in his accounts of other scholars' positions, with only the odd asperity. The sheer quantity of these notes — the book is almost a thousand pages long — may be more than some readers would want but their existence is still a reason for celebration. One small example will have to stand for a multitude: the problematic word 'aiuola' which Dante uses to describe the earth when, in Canto XXII in one of the great moments of the poem, he is invited by Beatrice to look down on it from the Heaven of Saturn, and sees 'L'aiuola che ci fa tanto feroci'. In Kirkpatrick this is given as 'That little threshing floor that makes men fierce'; in Hollander as 'The little patch of earth that makes us here so fierce.' Hollander's notes explain why 'threshing floor', first introduced by Longfellow, is dubious, tracing the word's roots back to the Latin diminutive 'areola', a small area. Still, the image of the threshing floor has a Biblical resonance which is not out of keeping. Just once in a while, Kirkpatrick's succinct and passionately argued notes are the fuller, as when he deals sorrowfully and at length, with the jarring, anti-Judaic sneer in Dante's otherwise humane and subtle argument for the necessity of Christ's sacrifice. Hollander is silent here, but elsewhere, as if to defend Dante from the taint of medieval prejudice, he observes drily that 'It will come as a shock to some readers to learn that fully half of those in Paradise are, in fact, ancient Hebrews'.

Milton begins his *Paradise Lost* by pronouncing that his epic 'with no middle flight intends to soar | High above th'*Aonian* Mount' and is careful throughout to establish a pious hierarchy between Christian and Classical imagery: 'For thou art heavenly, she an empty dream' (vii, l. 39). This element can be found in Dante too, but the mix is more volatile. Again and again, Dante grafts a Classical to a Christian or Biblical image, and the Classical image often seems richer in resonance for him (and his readers). It is not necessarily a case of divided loyalties but a desire to have both, to sacrifice nothing from an accumulated poetic tradition which he is heir to. This lies behind his question about the salvation of pagans, which both questions exclusionary Christian doctrine and betrays a deep regret for the fate of his former guide. The reply he receives is unsatisfactory, but it seems that in special circumstances God can find ways round some of the rules He created (at least the rules according to St. Paul).

Samuel Johnson's complaint that in *Paradise Lost* 'a want of human interest is always felt' is one that could also be aimed at Dante's *Paradiso*, if the reader feels that the upper reaches of human emotion are lacking in interest. And yet one of Johnson's resounding tributes to Milton could at least equally be applied to Dante: 'he delighted in new modes of existence'. If there is less human interest in this *cantica*, there are some exceptions such as Cunizza and Solomon who come over as distinct characters, and Dante never fails to humanize even his heavenly figures — such as the irefully blushing St. Peter, although this has an inadvertently comic effect. The figure of Cacciaguida is problematic, spanning the poem's central cantos. His is a belligerent, masculine presence, perhaps a counterweight to Beatrice: he is Dante's great-grandfather, a crusader and a representative of what we come to realize are for Dante the ancient and vanished Florentine virtues of honesty, simplicity and integrity. Almost the best thing about him, to my mind, is the way he arrives, leaving the constellation of the cross like the play of lights on a spaceship's dashboard: 'Nor did that gemstone leave its bezelled rim, | but ran a length along the radial beam | as fire behind some alabaster screen' in Kirkpatrick's version. Though Cacciaguida begins with Latin, his speech is vigorous Tuscan vernacular (and includes very earthly itches that need scratching). His account of the dilution of Florentine blood by the arrival of neighbouring folk looks unappealingly like an argument for a homogenous state. In the Hollander translation:

> but the city's bloodline, now mixed
> with that of Campi, of Certaldo, and Figline,
> was then found pure in the humblest artisan.

In his essay 'Dante and Florence', John M. Najemy maintains that here Dante is at least partly sympathizing with the *popolo* Federation of Guilds ('the humblest artisan') and taking belated account of the devastation wreaked on Florentine society by the warring aristocratic families — a reading which allows for a more subtly shaded politics.

Cacciaguida's long speech has a brusque, lurid and heraldic force when delineating sections of Florentine history. With some generosity, its roll call of families has been compared by Attilio Momigliano to Homer's list of ships. As Dante's pent, atavistic excitement in meeting Cacciaguida, for which he unconvincingly reproaches himself, is unlikely to be shared by his readers, so this list of Florentine families may appeal more to his contemporaries and co-nationals. As Coleridge says of Spenser's list of kings: 'There is a magic in national names [...] Unknown names are non-conductors, they do not communicate.' But still, it's hard to find anything in Cacciaguida that makes him more admirable than Ulysses, who is stuck in hell among the Evil Councillors, and a contemporary reader might think justice better served by having them swap places. After all, despite Kirkpatrick's valid claim that Ulysses's quest is destructive both to himself and others, he went on exploring for the sake of discovery, not to kill the infidel; and he belongs to the world, not to a restricted, antique Florence. An even fitter candidate for eviction from Dante's *Paradiso*, though, would be Folco of Marseilles, the Provençal poet-turned-Bishop who in life spurred on the Albigensian crusade, and in the afterlife reproaches the Pope for not being pro-active enough in the 'terra santa'.

It may seem odd that this long discourse on Florence should occupy the middle regions of heaven, but Dante's bitter relation to his lost city was not to be erased by a visit to the *civitatis dei*. The poem is far from being all sweetness and light: after St. Peter Damian concludes his tirade against the corruptions of the Church, the souls of the contemplatives unite in a heaven-shaking, angry shout. *Paradiso* is not just the abode of bliss but is full, too, of vituperation and anger — principally against Florence and the Church. In a famous passage in the next canto Cacciaguida prophesies Dante's exile, and the griefs that he had already tasted at the time of writing: '...Tu proverai sì come sa di sale | lo pane altrui, e come è duro calle | lo scendere e il salir per l'altrui scale...' In the Hollanders' translation:

> You shall learn how salt is the taste
> of another man's bread and how hard is the way,
> going down and then up another man's stairs.

There is, I think, a deliberate echo of this in Milton's lament for his blindness at the beginning of Book iii: 'Taught by the heavenly Muse to venture down | The dark descent, and up to reascend, | Though hard and rare...' This sense of the hardness, sharpness and steepness of exile, embedded as it is in the middle of heaven, oddly makes heaven itself a site of exile, with its own steep staircases belonging to Another. And *Paradiso* is full of moments of acute homesickness, as for instance when Dante recalls the 'ovile' [sheep fold] where he was born, and the church where he was baptized. One of the most astonishing of these moments is that image of earth seen from outer space — the 'aiuola' already mentioned. Despite the emphasis being on earth's puniness, there is a frisson, here too, of nostalgia, where the small scale plays off against the magnificence of heaven. Much of the most memorable imagery of *Paradiso* is drawn from the earthly — the bird simile at the beginning of Canto XXIII is a case in point: 'Come l'augello, intra l'amate fronde'. Here, as with most of the epic similes he treats, Kirkpatrick substitutes a pedagogic imperative for the slow unravelling of tenor and vehicle: 'Compare: a bird, among her well-loved boughs'. Elsewhere, Solomon's reference to the speech of infants is similarly infused with nostalgia. The critic Manuele Gragnolati has shown how this nostalgia in Solomon is also for the bodies which the blessed will only resume after the final judgement.

One of the most loved and celebrated lines in the whole *cantica* is the poignantly childlike 'tin tin sonando con sì dolce nota' (translated by Kirkpatrick as 'its "ting ting" sounding with so sweet a note') which brings the heavenly choirs back down to earth and the local clock tower. When, on the threshold of the modern age, Baudelaire attempts something similar in his late poem 'L'Imprévu': 'Le son de la trompette est si délicieux, | Dans ces soirs solennels de célestes vendanges', the effect is comparatively remote and grandiose. Only Antonio Machado in his 'Alboradas', and then by imitation, gets close with his 'Tin tan, tin tan,| las campanitas del alba | sonando están.'

Paradiso is, itself, an inexhaustible source of light for future generations of poets. In its pages 'legato con amore in un volume']bound up with love into a single book] we keep meeting our own future: in English poetry alone from Chaucer (whose Troilus looks down from 'the eighth spherė' upon 'This little spot of earth that with the sea | Embracėd is') to T. S. Eliot, from Milton to Shelley (in whose 'Triumph of Life' Eliot rightly saw 'some of the greatest and most Dantesque lines in English'). Within Italian poetry the debt is incalculable, and continues. As just one example, surely Canto XII, with its 'nostre muse, nostre sirene' and its 'due archi paralelli' ('twin rainbows' in Hollander), lies behind 'la sirena [...] ai nostri mari, | ai nostri estuarî' and other details of 'The Eel', one of Montale's finest poems.

If heaven is where the human reaches beyond itself and the divine begins, where time ends and eternity begins, the challenge for Dante is to write about a state of fulfilment and yet to keep the account moving, in both senses, and interesting. Simone Weil touches on the difficulties of the enterprise when she writes: 'Imaginary evil is romantic and varied; real evil is gloomy, monotonous, barren, boring. Imaginary good is boring; real good is always new, marvellous, intoxicating. 'Imaginative literature', therefore, is either boring or immoral or a mixture of both.' Dante's *Paradiso* must be the nearest thing we have to a refutation of this aphorism.

Dante reaches, several times within the poem, heights of joy beyond which he feels it impossible to go, and yet the poem moves on and he with it to further reaches. There are versions of a clockwork universe, all in harmony, that are offered as definitions of its shaping principle but they are far less satisfying than the earthly images that are their vehicles. And yet, the final cantos deliver a spectacular and more challenging vision. Virgil's Lethe is transformed into Dante's technicolour river which, even if allegoric, with its sheer vividness breaks out of the bounds of its theological referents. From this point on the writing has such intensity and power that the final canto's image of Neptune staring up to see the keel of the first ship, the Argonaut, passing overhead, could stand for the reader's experience . This image of wonder brings to a climax all the *Commedia*'s ship imagery, and the many images that in *Paradiso* deal with vision through water, and it marries the Classical with the Christian world-views. Where we expect a crescendo Dante is rapt staring at the 'semplice parvenza' [the simple appearance] of the light. This word 'semplice' most likely has behind it Thomas Aquinas's complex arguments of God as 'simple', in his disputation *On the Divine Simplicity*. But the reader doesn't need this theological prompt to feel the intensity of a vision that has shed, or rather condensed, all the complexities of light in the intervening heavens, all the machinery of their rotating spheres, the vertiginous intricacy of Dante's own construction, with its numerological and geometric coordinates, and dissolved them into this mysterious simplicity, a single point of light, which moves him and his poem into the same circular pattern of the final lines

> sì come rota ch'igualmente è mossa,
> l' amor che move il sole e l'altre stelle.

Hollander:

> like wheels revolving
> with an even motion, were turning with
> the Love that moves the sun and all the other stars.

The speed of movement in the celestial machine — its lightness and its fluency — is in deliberate contrast to the fixity and immobility of the damned, most evident in Satan, wedged into icy darkness, his only movement that of his three mouths, each gnawing a traitor, and the beating of his bat-like wings. The figures in hell are themselves ever more immobilized. The storm-tossed lovers in Inferno's Canto v, like Brunetto Latini running on the burning sands and the voyaging Ulysses, are all images of movement but futile, thwarted and without progression. Even Purgatory imposes its long wait on human souls (though there is some preparation for the speed of heaven). It is Dante, the pilgrim, who is constantly in motion, constantly learning. But unlike in the other two *cantiche*, in Paradiso it is the still human Dante who is slow, slow in his movement and in his learning, by contrast to the swift apprehension and motion of the blessed.

Dante set out in his poem to go beyond human experience, to 'transumanar', but the process has not just been one-way. He didn't arrive empty-handed. He came to heaven armed with the vernacular, with an image of the woman he loved and of the city he grew up in, and also with an attachment to Classical literature that he wasn't going to let Christianity deprive him of. Putting his own people there, he came to heaven to humanize — and Tuscanize — the place.

London Review of Books, 26 March 2009

— 10 —

Botticelli's Dante

In *Purgatory*, Dante briefly assumes the role of art historian, observing how Cimabue's fame has been eclipsed by Giotto's. The same goes for poetry: one Guido gives way to another (Guinizelli to Cavalcanti) and both may well be 'chased from the nest' by some new poet, perhaps — who knows? — Dante himself. But instead of offering a treatise on stylistic evolution in the arts, or even an advert for his own talent 'That with no middle flight intends to soar', aptly enough as this is where the proud atone for their sins, the passage turns into a humbling reflection on the transience of human fame with regard to eternity. One of Dante's crucial meditations on the plastic arts occurs in the preceding canto, Purgatory x, where, also on the terrace of pride, he encounters God's own handiwork, in the form of three didactic relief sculptures carved into the rock wall. The images, Dante tells us, not only leave Polycletus's work far behind, but even that of nature. This example of God outstripping his former creation, improving on his own (botched?) first draft, is a troublesome one, and one which is well treated in an essay by Andreas Kablitz, a member of the impressive team of scholars responsible for the exhibition catalogue.[1]

The three friezes, more cinematic installation than sculpture, have such a quality of verisimilitude that they continually cross over the sensory threshold proper to a work of visual art. Dante refers to them as 'esto visibile parlare' [this visible speech] and so they make the seen heard, make the visible come closer than is possible, in the merely human realm of art-making, to the art of poetic narrative. The German philosopher Lessing wrote about the limitation of picture-making vis-à-vis poetry's narrative by defining the 'co-extensive' nature of the pictorial image as opposed to the 'consecutive' nature of the poetic, the contrasting realms of space and time. In his description of God's artwork, it's as if Dante has anticipated that shortcoming in the (silent) visual arts and propelled them ever closer to his own, emphasizing the auditory, and having the sculpted characters engaged in a continuing dialogue which the imagination overhears. In a sense, Dante has also anticipated the kind of problems of narrative continuity within the single image that his illustrators will face.

Apart from the lugubrious Doré, Botticelli is the most renowned of Dante's illustrators, but the tradition of illustrating his *Commedia* dates back to within fifty years of his death, and testifies to the quasi-biblical status his work had already achieved. The pictorial solutions the artists found for the problems of illustrating

1 Sandro Botticelli: *The Drawings for Dante's Divine Comedy*, ed. by Hein-Th Schulze Altcappenberg (London: Royal Academy Publications, 2001). Exhibition: Royal Academy of Arts (March–June 2001).

the poem, such as aspects of narrative sequence, are numerous, and Botticelli's pictures, especially those from the *Inferno*, are indebted to his predecessors. One of the most intriguing, and pictorially complex, of the Inferno sequence is his Canto IX depiction of Dante and Virgil arriving via the Styx at the gate of the city of Dis, where the devils abusively refuse them entry whilst already an angel armed with a slender wand is both on its way *and* subduing the threatening devils. We can glimpse the higgledy-piggledy graves of the next canto beyond the gate, and already see the two pilgrims doing their rounds. In Dante's account, the demons on the tower who have called for the Medusa, causing Virgil to shield Dante's eyes, are interrupted by the arrival of the angel. Unwilling to forego the dramatic opportunity, Botticelli has a devil on the parapet brandishing the snaky head with the sinewy, triumphal gesture of a lead-guitarist at a roof concert. Another element in the picture, outside of Dante's telling, is the ferry-demon's return journey, suggesting the passage of time. The illustration is not only dense in detail, just a small fraction of which I've accounted for, but adds the onward (and backward) sweep of narrative, fighting the freeze-framed status of its form, and reinforcing the sense, as Hein-Th. Schulze Altcappenberg convincingly argues in the catalogue's introduction, of the continuing torments of the damned after Dante's spotlighting presence in their circle has moved on.

Botticelli's additions, like the inclusion of 'flashbacks' (views of what is still happening in the previous canto) and proleptic views to the next (such as the corner where the gravestone of the heretical Pope Anastasio can be seen) are all devices which allow the painter a more dynamic — and less servile and illustrative — relation to the poem. He has chosen inclusiveness over dramatic concentration: instead of focusing on one signal incident in each canto as most later (and some earlier) illustrators have, and dwelling on its implications, he decided, especially with the *Inferno*, to go for the whole narrative (plus, as noted, extras). Which means siting the travelling pair in several — as many as seven — places across the same picture. Earlier illustrators, such as the Siennese painter in the Yates Thomson manuscript have used the same device though without Botticelli's compositional intricacy. It's a choice that essentially plays to the weakness of the pictorial art — trying to do what the picture is least capable of, that is, returning to Lessing's co-ordinates: to work in the medium of time rather than space. And yet in this illustration the almost insurmountable difficulties of doing so have elicited from the painter solutions which are original and, in their own way, subtly narrative.

His drive to inclusiveness inevitably sacrifices almost everything that makes the *Inferno* a masterpiece — exactly what God's sculptural relief allows — the emotional power and compression of 'visible' and audible speech. To take one example from the poem, what's most impressive in Canto X is Dante's encounter with the awesome Farinata; and most moving, his brief conversation with Cavalcanti's father. The canto is concerned with time, with the damned soul's knowledge of the future but ignorance of the present, revealed by the equivocation of the past tense that makes Cavalcanti think his son has died. Because the canto is so crowded with incident in Botticelli's handling (though time *is* marked by the movement of the two travellers)

Farinata has none of the cavernous, impenitent dignity Dante invests him with and Cavalcanti *père* is barely visible. Nothing is visible, understandably, of the narratives of Ulysses and Ugolino in later cantos, but in the former all there is to mark one of Dante's most lyrical extended similes, of the hovering flames as fireflies, are some schematic tufts of flame. One of the few small question marks over an exemplary catalogue is the disservice done by the choice of this feeble image for the cover and the editor's description of its 'masterly freedom [...] as bold as it is sparing'.

The unfinished state of nearly all of the illustrations, including this one, leaves the viewer uncertain as to how Botticelli would have proceeded. Because of the painstaking process of first scratching outlines with a sharp nib on vellum, then pencilling-in, and then inking the lines preparatory to painting, some of the illustrations lack even the gestural freehand of the finest sketches and beg for the completed coloured state they were never given. What we can see (from the nearly complete Canto xxviii) is that Virgil and Dante are to be draped in their respective, fetching purple-and-blue and red-and-green toga strips in clear contrast to the team of flame-bronzed demons and the damned in raw flesh, with unpainted vellum for highlights. The drawing of the devils is often conventional — dog-faced, big-eared, taloned, tusked, hirsute, hermaphroditic creatures — but occasionally rises to the inspired in, for instance, the gurning, carnivalesque posse who corner the two travellers, in Canto xxi's illustration, which brilliantly captures Dante's menacing slapstick. The canto of the centaurs, a pagan topic evidently close to Botticelli's heart, also shows excellent draughtsmanship.

The choice to include the entire narrative may have been conditioned by Botticelli's reverence for the poem, but I think there's also a subtler design at work, which can be seen by comparing the illustrations to the three *cantiche*. The cluttered compositions of hell: the multi-perspectival chaos, the fractured rockfaces, the multiple 'simultaneous' encounters, the disordered graves, say, of the Canto x illustration, the skirmishes of the centaurs, or the spiky intricacy of the Suicide's Wood all emphasize, in Botticelli's handling, a kind of consciously medieval, regressive, non-perspectival approach. *L'enfer, c'est le passé.* In other words, the pre-Renaissance pictorial devices are all very well, and right too, for the description of hell, but wouldn't do for Purgatory, let alone Paradise. And it can be seen that each of these realms has its own compositional language in Botticelli.

Although none of the Purgatory illustrations are close to being finished, we can sense immediately that Botticelli is more at home in this zone whose air Dante, on arrival, celebrates for its colour of oriental sapphire which 'agli occhi miei ricominciò diletto' [restored delight to my eyes]. There is a choreographed and spacious feel, a rhythmic fluency to the drawing and a relishing of patterns. The canto with God's carving, especially, spurs Botticelli to feats of competitive brilliance, and we can see behind the frieze of David dancing that God uses Renaissance perspective — the first instance in the whole sequence. The illustrations to the last cantos, especially Canto xxx, showing the griffin-drawn chariot in the Earthly Paradise, combine a sweeping movement and dizzying complexity of design with absolute clarity of execution. It's perhaps most of all with this processional material that the visual, and Botticelli himself, is on home ground and can most successfully compete with Dante's descriptions. The use of a varying breadth of inked line and of cross-hatched modelling in the penwork for the illustrations to this and the next canto suggests the artist's belief in the autonomy of the sketch.

In the more severe, lit, geometrical *Paradise* illustrations, nearly all of which are contained in compass-drawn circles, the figures of Dante and his guide Beatrice are suspended in their unheard dialogue of heavenly things. Despite the absence of incident, you sense the philosophic passion of the painter, and Beatrice's oval face and the folds of her dress excite his talents far more than Virgil ever did. The larger scale of the figures, and the exclusive attention they call to themselves in their circular settings, are responsible for an extraordinary increase in the communicativeness of expression and gesture. In Paradiso XXI, we find the pair about to ascend via Jacob's ladder to the Heaven of Saturn. Consistent with his earlier-established conventions of narrative, the artist has sketched them also climbing the rungs and then, it seems, erased them. In heaven, apparently, the less bustle and narrative the better, though we may still be grateful for the ghostly drapes that complicate the design.

Modern Painters, Summer 2001

— 11 —

Bourdichon: The Big Miniature

Almost like Christmas itself, paintings of the Nativity carry with them a kind of numbing familiarity, with the emphasis on family. It is such an obsessive theme in Christian art that any representation of it has to struggle out of its swaddling bands or wrapping paper to make an impression on us. For this reason perhaps I've often found village art, the clumsy clay figures of Italian *presepii* or Spanish *belenes*, more engaging than the stock images in art galleries. This delight in the primitive can be heard in a recent Seamus Heaney poem which celebrates 'The solid stooping shepherds | The stiff-lugged donkey [...] And an out-of-scale, | Too crockery, kneeling cow.' In such cases the 'too crockery' skills of the artist can be perfectly suited to the subject matter of an impoverished rustic manger. Bourdichon is by contrast a sophisticated early Renaissance French court painter, decorator of royal tents and master miniaturist. And yet he has brought a freshness and striking intelligence to this conventional scene.

What a work this Book of Hours must have been. There are another eleven known vellum leaves from it in various sites, among them a superlative painting of 'Bathsheba Bathing' in the Getty Museum. In this is shown, against a background of formal gardens and palatial architecture, the naked figure of Bathsheba, up to her waist in a transparent veil of water with lacy calligraphic ripples — one of the strangest and most tactile descriptions of water in painting. The delicate restrained sensuality of the woman's portrayal as well as the opulent landscape are in marked contrast to this Nativity scene. Here the sturdy wooden architecture of the barn, the stone wall in the foreground, with its air of small cinder-blocks, belong to an entirely other world than that of the court. And yet the Virgin, clothed in a traditional blue mantle, if not sensuous, still bears a family resemblance to Bathsheba. Her diaphanous neck scarf with its undulating blue stripe recalls the flecked threads or wavelets in the water round the bathing Bathsheba.

A whole set of contrasts is brought into play within the painting: the rustic and the refined, the rough-hewn and the delicate, the divine and the human — and, on the smallest level, we see the golden light picking up the wood grain of the beams and even lying in hatched fibres on the stone wall. Everything is minutely textured and transfigured. Trinity and triangle — there are three sources of light: golden in the star-beaded rays that fall through the roof and that radiate upwards from the Christ child, and silvery white from the lantern that Joseph carries. The first and the third, the divine and the earthly, meet and seem to fuse on the Virgin's shoulders and back whilst her face and front are illuminated by the child's light. The textual source of these competing lights is St Bridget of Sweden's account which stresses how the lamp Joseph carries couldn't hold a candle to the divine light. But whilst Bourdichon follows this pictorial tradition, he also interprets it in his own way: Joseph's light is not altogether eclipsed — it has its place in the composition which would be poorer and less balanced without it.

The composition also echoes the two panels of light in Joseph's lantern. The wood-framed opening at the back of the barn gives onto a hillside village and on the left a huddle of heads (shepherds?) peeping in through the window frame. The whole picture is placed within a *trompe l'oeil* gesso frame (a characteristic of all the surviving leaves from this broken book) with the first line of a prayer inscribed on it. Frames within frames recede through the picture in a *mise-en-abîme*. It is as though the mystery of the child is circled by rings of beholders. In the inner circle are the donkey and cow still somewhat in the dark, but with their wide nostrils lit up, and also Mary. Joseph stands behind at one remove, and then the shepherds outside and finally the dormant village. Unusual too is the interior setting, albeit open to the outside, and the skill with which the artist has balanced both the sense of shelter and exposure.

In many Books of Hours the illumination includes a substantial part of the text as well as the kinds of scrolls and foliage that can be found on the verso of this sheet. Here precedence is given to the painting. There is also the question of its size. This is a very large miniature, itself a declaration of confidence on behalf of the commissioned painter. The effect of this is not what Heaney calls the 'out-of-scale' but it is another conflict that the painting internalizes and confidently resolves.

Tate Magazine, 2007

— 12 —

Michelangelo the Poet

Michelangelo: The Poems, ed. and trans. by Christopher Ryan (London: Dent, 1996); *The Sonnets of Michelangelo*, trans. by Elizabeth Jennings (Manchester: Carcanet, 1998)

It's odd to say so of the man who covered the Sistine Chapel ceiling with the history of the world, but the sensibility at work in Michelangelo's poems is a narrow one. There's a pent-up, crabbed quality to the writing that is an enemy to any consolatory music in language. Michelangelo feeds himself on an implacable diet of suffering in his love poems, and confesses that he enjoys this sense of devastation: 'Pur godo il mie gran danno' [I even relish my great injuries].

He is driven to channel his powerful sensuality into rigid Neoplatonic transcendence, and yet remains acutely aware that his impulse to enjoy and extol beauty is at war with his desire to spiritualize it: 'My eyes, eager for beautiful things, and my soul no less for its salvation' (in Christopher Ryan's prose version).

The self-lacerating wit of the tailed sonnet which portrays the painter as begoitred and harpy-breasted from the effort of painting the Sistine Chapel, and of a late poem mercilessly cataloguing his physical decrepitude, suggests the earthier poet Michelangelo might have become. These elements do recur elsewhere. Many of the poems hinge on the contrast between his own age and ugliness and the beauty of the addressee, since his most productive period of writing, between the encounter with Tommaso Cavalieri and the death of Vittoria Colonna (along with the so-called 'cruel and beautiful woman' the chief recipients of his love poems) only began in his late fifties.

But it's the very narrowness of his poetry which gives it such a singular intensity. Luckily, Michelangelo as a poet (and artist) pays no heed whatsoever to the pious sentiment with which he concludes an early poem: 'The soul [...] commits no sin in loving the things of nature, if it does so with balance, restraint and measure' (again in Ryan). Although his sonnets and madrigals are freighted with a conventional imagery of flight, flint, fire, phoenixes and Phoebuses (and an unconventionally insistent alliteration), his manner turns the suave Petrarchan traditions he inherited into something roughened and intransigent. The frequent elisions, contractions and inversions of word-order change language into an almost physically resistant medium.

In a poem attacking the Petrarchans of his day, his contemporary Francesco Berni praises Michelangelo by claiming 'ei dice cose, e voi dite parole' — he says things while you (merely) say words. Though idolized by his own age as an artist, his characteristic posture in the poetry is of the unschooled peasant with his 'rozza rima' [rough rhymes]. Whether this modesty is feigned or unfeigned, his poems show a reverence for the art of writing which is sincerely felt, as when he compliments Vasari on having laid aside the visual arts for this 'più degno lavoro' [worthier work].

Rather than perceive his awkwardness as dilettantism, as Benedetto Croce did, or his stylistic contortions as an excess of artifice, it makes more sense to consider them as deliberate aesthetic choices, as attempts to find an equivalent for language in its raw state and for the jagged, compacted way the mind actually works before it transforms thought into articulate form. The sense of a line like 'nel mal libero inteso oprato vero', though arduous to unpack and more like dog Latin than Italian, is still oddly immediate as well as memorably abrupt. (Ryan glosses it as 'for my having, in freedom, badly understood and acted on the truth'). The robust artisan sinew which Elizabeth Jennings catches in her translation of the opening of one sonnet — 'Only through fire can the smith pull and stretch | Metal into the shapes of his design' — can be felt throughout his work.

For all these reasons, though, the problems of translating what is most original in his poetry are almost insuperable, especially as English is so much less hospitable than Italian to the inversions that Michelangelo favours.

Carcanet have reissued Jennings's translations of Michelangelo's sonnets, first published in 1961. She follows C. Guasti's Italian edition (1863) which arranges the poems according to genre, or else follows John Addington Symonds's English translation (1878), which was based on it. Some of the phrasing shows Symonds's influence on her translations; and between his line 'The whole wide world would be a prize to scorn' and hers 'For this, the world would be a prize to scorn', Symonds's version should be preferred, if for no other reason than that the style may possibly have seemed less quaint in the 1870s than in the 1960s. But it would be unfair to suggest that Jennings's versions are generally so dependent on Symonds's. She has a distinctive clarity, often missing in the original, and evident in some fine endings.

In her 'Translator's Note', Jennings confesses that 'it has sometimes been necessary to simplify his argument in order that the poems may be more accessible to the modern reader. Nowhere, however, has the meaning been deliberately suppressed or altered.' Deliberately or otherwise, the meaning of her first sonnet 'On Dante Alighieri' has been both altered and suppressed; the invective against Florence caught in Symonds's 'the undeserving nest where I was born' is nowhere to be found in her 'the humble place where I was born', and the direct pronoun 'la', which refers to the star to which Dante is likened, and therefore should better be rendered as 'him', she translates as 'it', referring to Florence. In her Sonnet XXIII, Michelangelo's knotty (and admittedly futile) conceit about his feet being unable to bring the loved one within reach of his hands is rendered by the weirdly inappropriate and conventual 'let your demeanour shy and quiet appear | And walk with hands held both together close'. And, like the above lines, her last line 'And let no part of me uncouth appear' (which Ryan cumbersomely renders 'and may there then be no part of me which does not rejoice in you') loses the sense and inverts the word-order only, it seems, to preserve the anodyne iambics. Despite weaknesses like these, however, there are some notable successes (such as XVII, XVIII, XXIX and XLV) and, given the difficulty of the task, I doubt whether her translations will be bettered for some time to come.

Ryan has followed the superb, chronologically arranged, critical edition of E. N. Girardi (1960) for his text, and has supplied clear, or clarificatory, English prose versions parallel to it, as well as useful notes and introduction. The prose versions are an invaluable aid, although by their nature they lose the compacted force of the originals, about which Ryan himself justly observes 'they pulse with a dense energy', and it's perplexing to find that the English, naturally more terse than Italian, is here often more polysyllabic.

The history of Michelangelo's poetry has been one of deliberate suppression, from the first edition made by his great-nephew, Michelangelo the Younger, which combed out many of the stylistic irregularities and effaced the homosexual content of his love poems to Tommaso Cavalieri — even Symonds, in this respect, insists on translating 'Signor' as 'Lady'. So Girardi's edition, which allows us to see, as far as possible, the order and the entire span of Michelangelo's poetry, as well as including the fragments and incomplete sonnets, is of immense value, and Ryan's venture to establish the same for an English readership is especially welcome.

Times Literary Supplement, 1998

— 13 —

Velázquez: Epiphanies of the Disregarded

There's a passage in Lessing's essay *Laocoon* — a meditation on the arts of sculpture, painting and poetry — which is richly suggestive and immediately brought to mind, among other things, Diego Velázquez's painting known as *Old Woman Frying Eggs*. He writes:

> Pyreicus, who painted barbers' rooms, dirty workshops, donkeys, and kitchen herbs, with all the diligence of a Dutch painter, as if such things were rare or attractive in nature, acquired the surname of Rhyparographer, the dirt-painter.[1]

The confident judgment here, that there are elevated topics for art and ludicrously base ones, that there is a hierarchy of subject matter, is likely to make the contemporary reader dissent. And not just the contemporary reader. And not just as regards the visual arts. This view also recurs in reference to poetry, the novel and drama. 'Kitchen-sink', an (initially) disparaging moniker for a style of drama, is a telling instance. In recent avant-garde poetic discourse the terms 'domestic' and 'anecdotal' are often used as a shorthand to describe belittlingly a whole school of undesirable verse, as though the avant practitioners only lived in yurts or caravans, and as though any personal experience of the everyday were beneath regard. At some level they are the heirs of Lessing's idea of the elevated.

Intriguingly, as recorded in Norbert Wolf's concise book on Velázquez,[2] Francesco Pacheco, at the time one of Seville's leading artists, with whom Velázquez was serving his apprenticeship and whose daughter he would marry, often referred to this same Greek painter Pyreikos, but in a very different spirit to Lessing's dismissal. Not as an example to avoid but rather as one to follow. He will have come across 'the dirt-painter' in an account by Pliny the Younger, most likely also Lessing's source.

Lessing's reference to the ancient Greek dirt-painter suggests how long this war has been waging, and how often it breaks out anew. It recalls the Impressionists dislodging history painting as the acme of genres, and incidentally, with those 'barber's rooms', reminds us that Turner's father was a barber, and that Velázquez's mythological painting *Vulcan in his Forge* indeed depicts a 'dirty workshop'. But first

1 Gotthold Ephraim Lessing: *Laocoon: An Essay on the Limits of Painting and Poetry*, trans. by Ellen Frothingham (New York: Dover, 2005) (originally published by Little, Brown & Co., Boston), p. 9.
2 Norbert Wolf: *Velázquez* (Cologne: Taschen, 1999), p. 12.

of all it made me think, as I said, of Velázquez's *Old Woman Frying Eggs* which was painted in 1618, almost exactly a hundred and fifty years before Lessing published his essay, in 1767.

When Velázquez painted it in Seville, the city of his birth, he was nineteen, and still apprenticed to Pacheco. It's unquestionably a virtuoso work, a demonstration of mastery within the popular Spanish genre known as *bodegones*. The word refers to the *bodega* — tavern — so literally a *big* tavern, but the genre not only includes scenes of what art historians call 'low life' — in contrast, one assumes, to the high life or the life of the court — but it's also close kin to the genre of still life, *stilleven*, that Dutch painters were exploring at the beginning of the same century, along, there too, with tavern scenes. A famous Spanish example, though minus the tavern, is Juan Sánchez Cotán's *Quince, Cabbage, Melon and Cucumber* painted sixteen years earlier, in 1602 — one of the great still lifes. Manet, who would learn much from Velázquez, refers to still lifes as 'the touchstone of the painter' and it's a genre, however sedate and conventional it may now seem, that has frequently been the engine of revolution in the visual arts. We need only think of Manet himself, of Cézanne, and of Picasso and Braque's Classical Cubism, to see a prophetic truth in Manet's remark.

Velázquez's work is one of several *bodegones* he painted around the same period — the same boy can be seen in *The Waterseller* of 1620 and possibly also in *Three Men at Table* of 1618 — and is arguably the most impressive. In no small part this is due to the prominence and brilliance of his portrayal of the old woman who takes centre stage. As with his portraits of dwarves in the court, especially Don Diego de Acedo and Don Sebastián de Morra, and his portrait of his African servant, Juan de Pareja, 'sympathy' is an inadequate word. Absolute attention and absorbing curiosity come closer, a sense that she, like all of these other figures, is no less worthy of respect than the Pope or the members of the Spanish royal family he portrayed. In none of these figures does the painter see any reason for coarse levity or prejudicial caricature (of the kind Salvador Dalí would employ in his parodic reworking of the portrait of de Morra, turning the dwarf's hands into fried eggs). They meet his gaze and ours as arrestingly, proudly and engrossingly as any of his gods and royals, or even more so.

Lessing might well object to this depiction of low life: 'as if such things were rare or attractive in nature'. In a sense the *bodegon* is indeed a celebration of the commonplace, the quotidian, the disregarded — the tavern, the workshop, the kitchen, with its jugs and spoons, mortars and pestles, bowls and baskets and foodstuffs, its labour as well as relaxation. Velázquez would combine kitchen work and religious contemplation, the *via activa* and the *via meditativa*, in another painting of the same year, *Kitchen Scene with Christ in the House of Martha and Mary* (1618). This shows how deftly he was able to use the 'humble' material of his *bodegones* to figure the Biblical contrast between the sisters — Christ's words that 'Mary has chosen the better part' seem to cut little ice with the hardworking Martha in the foreground, and the painter by putting her labours *in primo piano* would seem to have taken her part. Velázquez uses the device of a mirror to inset the scene of Mary at the feet of Christ, and this same device the artist will use to brilliant effect again in his last great painting, *Las Meninas*.

Although many of his works were lost in 1734 when the royal palace was burnt, what remains is staggering in its diversity and quality. In his forty or so years of painting, Velázquez broaches and perfects every available genre of painting, and every element leads on to another that includes it and pushes forward. To give an idea of this range: *bodegones*; crucifixions; Madonnas; religious painting (*Joseph's Bloody Coat Brought to Jacob*); history painting (*The Surrender at Breda*); court paintings of the royal family; portraits — of dwarves and Popes (his portrait of Pope Innocent X and of his black servant Juan de Pareja, completed the same year, 1650); nude painting (*The Rokeby Venus*); mythological paintings such as *Vulcan's Forge*, *The Fable of Arachne*; and his *Bacchus* which combines mythology and the tavern, like a convivial version of a scene from Luis Buñuel's *Viridiana* which (supplemented by Da Vinci's *Last Supper*) it may well have inspired. A couple of mysterious landscapes or gardenscapes set in Italy's Medici Gardens have almost invented a new genre by bringing the background unashamedly into the foreground. The finest of the two, *View of the Medici Gardens* (probably 1649), Laura Cumming called 'one of the smallest paintings in the Prado and one of the greatest', adding that it is 'a painting that insists upon nothing, that appreciates something as mean as a wall, that makes a wall as beautiful as a painting.' Shorn of all narrative, Biblical or mythological, it depicts an untidily boarded-up arched entrance to a grotto but achieves a haunting portrait of the disregarded, the unheroic and the unpicturesque. This passage of landscape has declared independence, and already looks forward to the Impressionist's *plein air* canvases, but is in no way superseded by them. Although there is no evidence this oil sketch was seen by the Welsh painter, Thomas Jones, his dilapidated Neapolitan wallscapes, made on a parallel sojourn in Italy over a hundred years later (1780–82), are the Spaniard's true heirs. These extraordinary paintings share with Velázquez's work a frontality, an exquisite tonal clarity, and a foregrounding of the commonplace and the disregarded.

Velázquez's mastery of all these genres culminates in *Las Meninas* which unites like a dazzling *summa* so many elements that have figured elsewhere in his work. It includes a full-length self-portrait centre-stage: the artist at work, the ultimate self-reflexive meta-painting that the Neapolitan artist Luca Giordano referred to as 'the theology of painting'. This bold foregrounding of the artist will re-emerge in the nineteenth century with Courbet's *Artist's Studio*, which is surely indebted to the Spanish master, and in the twentieth in Picasso's series of witty, rickety, Cubist homages.

It's often remarked that in Velázquez's period in Spain the painter was considered a craftsman not an artist, occupying a lower rung than the poet (a situation very much reversed, in the present day, pretty much everywhere except the Middle East). Further, the Spanish painter lacked the prestige artists had gradually won for themselves in Italy. In 1614 or '15, three or so years into Velázquez's apprenticeship, the Cordoban poet Luis de Góngora y Argote wrote a sonnet about Domenikos Theotokopoulos, 'El Greco', which notes how the visual arts lacked the cultural status they deserved: Fame's clarions, 'los clarines de la Fama' should sound louder, 'aun de mayor aliento'. The painter is praised for elevating nature by art and art by learning, for giving colour to the rainbow, light to the sun and shadow to Sleep:

Heredó naturaleza
arte y el arte estudio, Iris colores,
Febo luces, si no sombras Morfeo [...]

This poem, 'Inscripción para el sepulcro de Domínico Greco' not only seeks to elevate the intellectual status of poetry's sister art but achieves a visionary celebration of the artist's work with a dazzling final image of the incense trees of Sheba exuding resin through their bark, a synaesthetic leap that conflates the odour of oils in the painter's studio with the odour of sanctity from the painter's tomb:

[...] lágrimas beba y cuantos suda olores
cortezá funeral de árbol sabeo.

The adjective 'sabeo', meaning of Sheba, inevitably evokes 'saber', knowledge, and hence the Tree of Knowledge. Góngora's poem, like Velázquez's paintings, lifts the profile of the art by fusing the studious with the mysterious.

The relatively lowly status of the art, however, doesn't seem to have particularly impeded Velázquez who on his arrival in Madrid, with the help of the Count of Olivares, the Andalusian powerbroker in the court of Philip IV, obtained a series of court positions (such as the comical-sounding but no doubt illustrious role of 'Master of the Wardrobe') and quickly won the favour of the king. His arduous clamber up the stairs of power till he finally became a Knight of Santiago, an honour requiring considerable research to check the recipient had no Jewish or Moorish blood, shows no small degree of worldliness on the painter's part. In Norbert Wolf's concise account, we learn that he diverted money due to his studio assistants who then went on strike. Regardless of the dignity he recorded in his portrait of Pareja, he did not permit his gifted servant, whom he eventually freed, to develop his painterly skills. Nevertheless he became a justly celebrated painter. The U.S. poet Natasha Trethewey's poem 'Thrall', with a finely balanced sense of an ambiguous legacy, follows Pareja's acquisition of both his freedom and his subsequent artistic vocation:

And so
in *The Calling of Saint Matthew*
I painted my own
likeness   a freeman
in the House of Customs...[3]

Whatever we might think about the artist's ruthless ascent, the paintings speak in another language, and almost persuade the viewer that the first shall be last and the last first. At the apogee of power, Philip IV clearly had a discerning eye, and filled his new palazzo, el Buen Retiro, with magnificent paintings by Titian and Rubens, and seemed happy with everything Velázquez produced, including what must have

3 Natasha D. Trethewey: *Thrall* (Boston, MA: Houghton Mifflin Harcourt, 2012), 'Thrall', pp. 59–65.

been a very odd upstaging of the royal couple by the artist himself in *Las Meninas*.

April 2017, talk delivered in Spain

— 14 —

The Herculean Labours of William Blake, Painter & Poet

William Blake, Tate Britain Exhibition, 9 November 2000–11 February 2001

In his poem 'The Forge' Seamus Heaney imagines a blacksmith's workshop, the anvil 'somewhere in the centre...an altar | Where he expends himself in shape and music'. An eighteenth-century rolling press, more or less like the one William Blake used, rightfully occupies this central position in the Tate's celebration of Blake — part anvil, part altar. It was at an infernal machine of this type that the poet and painter expended himself in shape and music until his death in 1827. The works in glass cases and on all the walls seem to ray out from the dark worn tapering spokes of its wheel. The figure of the blacksmith is not far removed from Blake's own self-image: in his so-called Prophetic Books, Los, who is forever labouring heroically at the furnace as well as defending Albion from various foes, is often closely identified with Blake. In the poem *Milton* Blake even claims 'Los had entered into my soul'. If ever heroic labour entered into any soul it was Blake's, and even his bitterest detractors would have to concede the Herculean work-rate — both in writing and in the visual arts — which this exhibition bears witness to. (Appropriately enough, no. 13, Hercules Buildings was home to the Blakes during some of his most productive years.)

One of Blake's influential detractors, T. S. Eliot, though he praised in the highest terms the naked honesty of the early lyrics, lamented the 'home-made limitations' of his later writings, the fact that, unlike Dante (and who isn't?) Blake had no adequate and ready-made mythology to exploit, and so was forced in his mad Protestant way to make up his own. And it's certainly true that Blake's major inclination was to cut free of everyone and everything that might trammel his impulses — conventional Christianity as much as alternatives such as Swedenborgianism. Even heroes like Milton needed to be saved from their own worse — moralistic — tendencies (in this particular case by being forced to enter the tarsus of Blake's left foot). Even about his well-meaning patron, Blake was wont to vent his spleen in doggerel:

> I write the Rascal Thanks till he & I
> With thanks & Compliments are quite drawn dry.

Not only did he have to reinvent the Book (rewriting his own Bible with a whole new cast of eccentrically named characters) but he also invented a method for printing his own books. Memorably, in Blake's account of the affair, his dead brother Robert returned to instruct him in a new method of relief printing (the intricacies of which it's one of the merits of this show to have clearly explained). This despatch from beyond set in motion one of the most original careers in English art.

In the visual arts, Reynolds is Blake's particular bugbear, but he generously doles out vituperation to Correggio, Rubens, Rembrandt, Gainsborough and, in another bit of spirited doggerel, adds in 'Dilbury Doodle' for good measure, seeing them all as savages apt with 'a smear and a squall to destroy Picture or Tune'. Any colourist inclination 'To blend & not define the Parts' Blake numbers among 'the Idiot's chiefest arts'. These prejudices, which Blake never disavowed, had a discernible, and evidently not always beneficial effect on his artistic practice.

The crime of these artists in Blake's eyes was their having abandoned, or never clearly perceived, the 'bounding outline' but instead bleared all with mixtures of colour. Smudgy Venetians like Titian are the enemy — *viva Firenze*, especially Raphael and Michelangelo, whose works visual and poetic, Blake never tires of citing. Though there are dazzling and delicate exceptions, Blake's colours have a subsidiary status. He has a tendency to fill in his form with rainbowy translucencies and blocked-in primaries, watercoloured over the printed lines. His print of Newton, which has unaccountably inspired a beetle-plated sculpture outside the new British Library, is an attack on what Blake stigmatized as the 'Single Vision' of the great mathematician. The athletic, youthful Newton is hunched over, almost encased in the rock, at work with compasses on a bare geometrical figure. The rock he has turned his back on is clad in gloriously iridescent lichen or coral streaming in underwater currents. It could be said that Blake as a painter has himself, for much of his work, turned his back on the possibilities of the colourists and, like the Newton he invented to criticize, turned away from the natural world.

Spared the boredom of school, Blake was apprenticed early to an engraver, and sketched the Gothic tombs of Westminster Abbey, thence deriving a severe, stylized notion of the human form. But as his work progressed, he substituted for their attenuated elegance a more dramatic musculature — titanic figures with pecs and six-packs, Lamarckian composites with fishlike sinews and veins like vines. It's as though his images are recapitulating the ontogeny of all life-forms. Sometimes the flesh turns to scales as in Satan's groin in 'Satan, Sin and Death', sometimes to feathers, as in 'Elohim Creating Adam', sometimes, as in the haunting 'Nebuchadnezzar' it becomes matted and thatched and speckled — a mixture of vegetable and mineral — ending in mole's claws for digging his underground tunnel. It's not surprising that he should remind us of 1960s Marvel comics, since these artists must have looked to Blake as a pioneer in the form — with his narrative strips and his own brawny, interstellar, world-saving super-heroes. One striking feature of Blake's depiction of the human face is that the eyes are too big by a ratio of two to one, giving his creations the spiritualized, over-expressive look of bushbabies caught in sudden klieg lights, though judging by the plaster cast made of his face, Blake's own peepers were spectacular orbs.

Many of Blake's most memorable images have a frieze-like quality which he shares with certain classicist artist of his age and acquaintance such as Flaxman and Fuseli. His scenes are enacted against a shallow background, almost a stage on which the lighting severely picks out the foregrounded human figures. With exceptions such as 'Newton' — and even there the flora were perhaps serving a mainly polemical purpose — Blake has little interest in Nature: 'Natural Objects always did & now do weaken, deaden and obliterate imagination in Me', he writes in an annotation to Wordsworth's *Poems*. Copying from Nature was his abhorrence. At a formal level, this often means he has copied from copies of those who copied from Nature. His 'Newton', as the exhibition catalogue points out, is based on Michelangelo's figure of Abias, and his 'Joseph of Aramathia among the Rocks of Albion' was 'Engraved when I was a beginner at Basires | from a drawing by Salviati after Michael Angelo'.

Unnourished by an interest in the phenomenal world, imagination is not necessarily the best guide for painters. The distressingly coy tempera portraits of Adam and Eve are examples of Blake's work at its least convincing. And yet as an illustrator to some of his own poems, and to Milton, the Book of Job and Dante, he creates unforgettable images. Blake is the most combative of readers, and his hilarious and often brilliant annotations in the margins of the books he had, constitute a formidable body of criticism. As an illustrator, he enters into the life of these texts, he interprets and quarrels with them. The Dante illustrations Blake was working on at the time of his death are more variable, but still tower over the lugubrious Doré engravings which have clamped themselves like barnacles onto the *Commedia*. Blake's 'Dante Running from the Three Beasts' is one of the least fortunate, the lion looking like a gonk with a perm, and no single detail convincingly imagined. But 'The Simoniac Pope' draws from Blake a powerful Protestant ire, and 'The Circle of the Lustful' is both a vivid and compact evocation of the whole Canto v and a criticism of the punitive spirit Blake perceived in it. The lovers, whom Dante describes as like cranes singing their lays — 'facendo in aer di sè lunga riga' [making a long streak of themselves in the air] — spiral across the picture in a diaphanous membrane. Blake rightly understood the spiral to be the central image for this infernal storm. Dante, who in the final line, falls in a dead faint — 'e caddi, come corpo morto cade' — in pity at Francesca's tale, is seen outstretched in the centre, at Virgil's feet. Blake is not, however, content to leave the lovers in Dante's hell, and shows them redeemed and embracing in the sun above Virgil's head.

In his 1793 etched *Prospectus*, Blake writes that his 'method of printing which combines the Painter and the Poet' enabled him 'to bring before the Public works (he is not afraid to say) of equal magnitude and consequence with the productions of any age or country'. Among these advertised works, *Songs of Innocence and Songs of Experience* (price 5s. apiece) and *The Marriage of Heaven and Hell* (7s. 6d.) are works that fully live up to his claims — at least as far as the writings are concerned. The illustrations are of a considerably lower order of creation but are among the earliest that use the technique of relief printing which he was to refine through the years. The way the illustrations vie with and sometimes intimate shadowy elements within the poems makes them of continued interest, and yet much of the attention they've attracted, particularly from literary scholars, has a solemnity which they barely merit. It's questionable whether, for example, the bathetic tabby accompanying the momentous poem 'The Tyger' does the latter any favours. Many of the poems such as 'London', 'A Poison Tree', 'Ah! Sunflower!', however, will be loved for as long as the language is spoken. 'Ah! Sunflower!', for one, is as perfect in its way as the Shakespeare sonnet 'When I do count the hours that tell the time' which may have suggested it:

Ah, Sunflower! weary of time,
Who countest the steps of the Sun
Seeking after that sweet golden clime
Where the traveller's journey is done.

Where the Youth pined away with desire,
And the pale Virgin shrouded in snow
Arise from their graves, and aspire
Where my sunflower wishes to go.

Blake prints this lyric alongside two other botanical poems, as though it were too slight to occupy a whole page. The poem uses its simple language and plangent melody to utterly subvert the conventional Christian view of the afterlife as a reward for abstinence in this one. He has fashioned a beautiful circular trap in which the Sunflower, the Youth and the Virgin will have to remain constantly seeking and aspiring and wishing, without ever arriving. The third 'Where', a 'weary' word, leads back round again to the first, reinforcing a sense that this *where* is nowhere to be found. If the promise of the afterlife is a gilded falsity, Blake still allows its allure to work on the reader. The poem is typical of the *Songs of Experience* in which a formidable political intelligence destabilizes, without abandoning, the language of Christian piety. Perhaps his greatest poem, 'London', condemns both Church and State for the misery of the city, for child labour, and for the death of soldiers. In its third stanza it rises to a pitch of intensity that equals Cassandra's vision of blood covering the walls of the house of Atreus:

How the chimney-sweepers cry
Every black'ning Church appalls;
And the hapless Soldier's sigh
Runs in blood down Palace walls.

But Blake also subtly observes how the 'mind-forg'd manacles' are forged from within as well, how the 'Marks of weakness' conspire with 'marks of woe'.

Arguably, in some passages of the Prophetic Books, Blake, still armed with this political passion, has ceased to be a poet and has become instead a writer of tracts. Even his language begins to ring with 'terrific' dinning effects, his sentences sprout redundant prepositions — 'down descending' or 'up ascending'. He harangues the reader: 'Mark these words — they are of your eternal Salvation', and confuses all but the most patient exegetes with his host of symbolic entities. Blake has this reply to hand in *Milton*:

The idiot Reasoner laughs at the Man of Imagination,
And from laughter proceeds to murder by undervaluing calumny

— himself being no slacker at laughter and calumny. And yet there's always a suspicion with Blake — call it credulity — that, despite the longueurs of his Biblical or Ossianic lines, his writings contain some vital perception about the human condition the world has forgotten, or never known, as though his philosophy was a Tantric offshoot he has had to evolve isolated, unassisted and in a totally inhospitable climate. Blake advocated unrestrained sexual pleasure like the Tantrics — 'Bring me my Arrows of desire' — and his splitting and warring emanations have much in common with their deities which proliferate and subdivide from the self. At times his prints resemble Tantric figurations of the Cosmic Man — notably the figure of Albion in *Jerusalem*, whose limbs are tattooed with sun, moon and stars. This cosmology was evolved over hundreds of generations in the East; Blake had only a mortal span. But if his poems sometimes deteriorate into prophesy, his pictures improve, as can be seen in some of the marvellous illustrations to his books *Milton* and *Jerusalem*.

Even though there's an imbalance throughout, one way or the other, between the two elements in Blake's combination 'of Painter and Poet', the books he created by his 'method of printing' are works of a radical and grand design. The catalogue records the heartfelt tribute of a writer in the Spectator on a visit to Hercules Buildings on the eve of its demolition in 1918:

> No one can stand before this blackened shell of a home, once alive with so much fire and passionate vision, without a sense of awe.

With all the evidence of that fire and passionate vision now re-assembled in the Tate, a sense of awe still seems the proper response.

Modern Painters, Winter 2000

— 15 —

Passing Strangers: Whitman and Baudelaire

I.

The first edition of *Leaves of Grass* — twelve untitled poems — was published in 1855. In the same year Baudelaire published eighteen poems in the *Revue des deux mondes* with the title *Les Fleurs du mal*, two years before the first edition of that book. At exactly the same time, then, we witness the first flowering of modernity from those poets of the new and the old world who will most shape the subsequent developments of the art.

Assembled under their respective botanical titles, throughout their lives both poets would keep expanding their works into an inclusive *canzoniere.* The French title declares at the outset an allegorizing intent, whilst the American one is stripped of anything but itself, stripped even of the definite articles which the French one includes. They share the possessives 'of' and 'du', which makes of them both a kind of balanced structure, a barbell or a pair of scales. Whitman's title *Leaves of Grass* differs from the more usual, and more martially symbolic, phrase 'blades of grass' — it demilitarizes the plant. Leaves are peaceable things — mundane, mild, multiform and multitudinous. By contrast *Flowers of Evil* are exotic, morbid, poisonous, mysterious. One grows anywhere and everywhere, the other, one supposes, only in the most peculiar hothouse conditions (although this supposition proves wrong: they flourish abundantly in the nineteenth-century metropolis).

Whitman was a compositor and his title also plays on the terminology of his trade: 'leaves' as is often noted, are pages. So his poems are offered to the reader as if they were products of nature, growing without effort, and his book is the harvest. But 'grass' also has a typographical provenance — another facet of Whitman's title till now, as far as I know, ignored, that was brought to my attention by the printer, Graham Moss. In his words: '"Grass" is an old printing term for the physical typesetting of matter when it was deliberately done in advance of it being needed for printing.'[1] This extra resonance seems to me convincing. Whitman was involved

1 Moss continues in an email: 'It ties in to a whole view of the pre-industrial organisation of printing [...] before the mechanization of typesetting from the 1880s onwards, but specifically it was a way of keeping the men on the job rather than laying them off at times when there was little work in that part of the day to day work of the printshop. "Grass" would be typeset and collected on Galleys, the trays that held completed work before or after printing. Thus it seems that Whitman is saying something about the episodic nature of the printshop end of the production of the book — he did the typesetting himself at first, and did it sporadically, at times to suit his own schedule and that of

in the design and the typography of the various editions of his poetry and would declare:

> I sometimes find myself more interested in book making than in book writing, the way books are made — that always excites my curiosity: the way books are written — that only attracts me once in a great while.

So grass was not only, as he elsewhere wrote, 'the flag of my disposition' but also the ensign of his trade.

The coincidence of the dates and the titles must have been wondered about before — I think T. S. Eliot, somewhere I can't find, makes a passing reference to it — and yet it's hard to imagine two more mutually *contradictory* poets. Whitman and Baudelaire would seem to embody two opposing temperaments — respectively, the optimistic and the pessimistic, the social and the anti-social, the gregarious and the egregious, the democratic and the hierarchical, the natural and the artificial. Formally, Whitman is the grandfather of free verse, his lines are as long as they take, taking their measure from the Old Testament and perhaps Ossian and the Mahābhārata (to which he refers in an essay), whereas Baudelaire employs rhyme and tight traditional forms — the quatrain, the pantoum, the alexandrine, and above all the sonnet. Whitman's poems reflect urban bustle, open prairie and democratic vistas; whereas Baudelaire's mostly reflect enclosed, nocturnal, interior and architectural shapes — narrow streets and vertiginous roofscapes and balconies.

Any attempt to unite them would seem doomed. Or so a critic like Malcolm Cowley would have us believe when he says of Hart Crane that 'he was a poet with the lyric sensibility of Baudelaire who thought he could write like Whitman.' Implicit in this, one of many monitory signs erected over Crane's career, is precisely the conviction that they are chalk and cheese.

Whether or not Crane, or any other poet before or since, has managed a musical synthesis of the two modes — Laforgue? Aimé Césaire? García Lorca? — I think most of us would agree with Cowley's implied premise: that they represent irreconcilable tendencies. Crane himself, early on, seems to have had an inkling of this predilection, writing of his 'love of things irreconcilable'. The crucial meeting point between the two traditions precedes Crane anyway by some years, in T. S. Eliot, and to an extent, in Ezra Pound. They attempted to fuse the French and the American traditions, while tending always to over-stress their debt to the European — to Dante, Baudelaire and Laforgue in Eliot's case, and to Cavalcanti, the Provençal poets and Gautier in Pound's. In their stated aesthetics the American tradition almost always appears upstart, raw, undisciplined. Pound in 'The Pact' needs first to register his detestation of his 'pig-headed' forebear before proposing a magnanimous truce with Whitman:

> It was you that broke the new wood,
> Now is a time for carving.

the establishment where he did it, collecting the set matter on Galleys until such time as he was ready to compose the pages and print it. So to me the title speaks to the nature of his mental approach to the whole book, that it was collected, and who knows, written or re-written in the process of setting the type, as well as to the practical way in which the work of compositing was approached.'

> We have one sap and one root —
> Let there be commerce between us.

Whitman and Baudelaire stand at the threshold of the modern age, and they indicate the opposing directions which the modern lyric has chosen and travelled. Formally, they represent a choice between an open and a closed form, a self-made irregular metrics and an inherited one. Even with regard to such an inestimable technical resource as the enjambment their practice could not be further apart. In Baudelaire's 'Recueillement', as just one outstanding example, we encounter a radical stride over the abyss of the octave and sestet, the place of the traditional *volta*: 'Ma Douleur, donne-moi la main; viens par ici, || Loin d'eux', where the 'Loin' mimetically and exactly measures the distance. Whereas in Whitman's poems a run-on line, let alone one with any purposeful function, is as rare as gold dust.

The two poets also mark an extreme spiritual divergence, between a pioneering, anti-historical perspective and a sense of terminal decadence and ennui. In Baudelaire a taste for the new comes from a heightened awareness of the old: his jaded palette is forced to seek 'toujours du nouveau'. It is a contrast between the Adamic in Whitman's case, and the Cain-like in Baudelaire's.

In 'Spontaneous Me' Whitman turns the Oath of Declaration of Independence into 'the oath of procreation I have sworn, my Adamic and fresh daughters', although the procreation he refers to is more metaphoric than literal, and we see his 'Adamic and fresh daughters' primarily as his poems. In 'Ages and Ages Returning at Intervals' he writes:

> Lusty, phallic, with the potent original loins, perfectly sweet,
> I, chanter of Adamic songs
> Through the new garden of the West, the great cities calling,
> Deliriate...

— lines which reveal quite how consciously he assumed this role of a new Adam for the New World. Even the neologism 'Deliriate' — not to be found in Noah Webster's *An American Dictionary of the English Language* (1828), or anywhere else for that matter — characterizes the poet as a wild original. By contrast in Baudelaire we have the corrupted world of Cain. In his poem 'Abel et Caïn', which swings back and forth in couplets between the anaphoras 'Race d'Abel...' and 'Race de Caïn...', Abel's offspring sleep, drink and eat under God's complaisant smile, whereas the race of Cain is condemned to a life of misery, cold and mud, but in the end is exhorted to mount to the heavens and throw God down to the earth. The smug and righteous hypocrisy of Abel is contrasted with the vivid authenticity of Cain's suffering, with which the poet clearly identifies himself.

Baudelaire's introductory poem acknowledges a damnable *fraternité*, a diseased complicity of ennui between writer and reader, an imminent shared yawn that threatens to swallow the world — 'hypocrite lecteur, mon semblable, mon frère'. This address is in the strongest possible contrast to the fraternal manner in which Whitman invokes the reader 'ages hence', in the tones of a rough, carefree Manhattan. The one is full of insidious aggression, the other of confidently shared humanity.

Regarding friends, Baudelaire's venomous aside in *Mon Coeur mis à nu*: 'Beaucoup des amis, beacoup des gants.' It's hard to imagine Whitman wearing gloves — never has a poet's skin to such an extent been his largest organ of perception.

And yet in that phrase 'mon semblable' there is a hint of an approach between the two poets, a similar contract with the reader, whom Whitman addresses at the opening in the 'Song of Myself':

> And what I assume you shall assume,
> For every atom belonging to me as good belongs to you.

The identity shared between poet and reader, however takes the form of an accusation in Baudelaire and a gift in Whitman.

So far the contrast would seem all in Whitman's favour. But even Whitman's most enthusiastic European advocates balk a little at his all-embracing, world-hugging fraternity. D. H. Lawrence, surely the most talented inheritor of Whitman's poetic forms and procedures, is appalled in his essay on the American poet by the undifferentiating, indiscriminate welcome that Whitman extends to all humanity. Lawrence's undemocratic, Nietzschean world-view would just not admit the corrupted multitude into his select *polis*.

The deepest opposition between these poets, who, it's fair to assume, knew nothing of each other's work, concerns the issue which the Christian tradition has called 'Original Sin'. Baudelaire prefers to call it 'the primeval perversity of man' and praises another American poet, Edgar Allen Poe, for having correctly apprehended this condition:

> It is pleasant that a few explosions of old-established truth should thus be detonating in the face of all those complimenters of humanity, all those coddlers and cajolers who never cease to repeat with every possible nuance and inflection, 'I was born good, and you too; we were all of us born good!', forgetting, no, pretending to forget, those topsy-turvy egalitarians, that we are all born marked for evil!' (Further Notes on Edgar Poe, my translation)
>
> [...oubliant, non! feignant d'oublier, ces égalitaires à contre sens, que nous sommes tous nés marqués pour le mal.]

Nothing will loosen Baudelaire's grip on this 'mark of Cain'. Wherever he catches a whiff of perfectability he answers with spleen: 'This primitive irresistible force [...] man's natural Perversity'. Evil is our element, and claims us. We are 'les fleurs du mal', the 'mal seme d'Adamo' that Dante writes of, but without his salvific cosmology. Everything suggests that, had Baudelaire read Whitman, he would have recoiled from the American's hearty embrace of an essential human goodness. For one of the most recurrent effects in Whitman is to consider himself in the light of what might seem to others shameful and to divest himself of shame, in the hope that others will follow him, indeed to show that 'we are all of us born good'. In his poem 'I Sing the Body Electric' (section 2) Whitman passionately declares: 'If anything is sacred the human body is sacred'. In its first section he argues:

> The love of the body of man or woman balks account, the body itself balks account.
> That of the male is perfect, and that of the female is perfect.

He goes further than those 'égalitaires' that Baudelaire loathed: not only are we 'born good', we are born 'perfect'. By that perplexing phrase 'balks account' Whitman seems to be saying that it cannot be *held* to account but also that it *exceeds* any account we might give of it. Webster's *An American Dictionary of the English Language* defines 'balk' in its first two relevant entries:

> 1. To disappoint; to frustrate. *Locke.*
> 2. To leave untouched; to miss or omit. *Drayton. Shak.*

I think all of these meanings are in play here. The feelings inspired by a body as well as the body itself are beyond even poetry's competence. They are ineffable. The French poet's relations with the body are typically a mixture of intense sensuality and a concomitant shame and disgust. He ends his 'Un Voyage à Cythère'

> Dans ton île, ô Vénus! je n'ai trouvé debout
> Qu'un gibet symbolique où pendait mon image...
> — Ah! Seigneur! donnez-moi la force et le courage
> De contempler mon cœur et mon corps sans dégoût!

2.

The coincidence of dates and titles between these two great modernists is reinforced by a further curious overlap. In 1860, Whitman published a poem called 'To a Stranger'. In the same year Baudelaire published 'A une passante'. The very same topic of a chance encounter in the street occurred to both poets almost simultaneously, and the extreme contrast of their treatment is signally revealing about both their deeply opposed temperaments and their shared experience.

To a Stranger

> Passing stranger! you do not know how longingly I look upon you,
> You must be he I was seeking, or she I was seeking, (it comes to me as of a dream,)
> I have somewhere surely lived a life of joy with you,
> All is recall'd as we flit by each other, fluid, affectionate, chaste, matured,
> You grew up with me, were a boy with me or a girl with me,
> I ate with you and slept with you, your body has become not yours only nor left my body mine only,
> You give me the pleasure of your eyes, face, flesh, as we pass, you take of my beard, breast, hands, in return,
> I am not to speak to you, I am to think of you when I sit alone or wake at night alone,
> I am to wait, I do not doubt I am to meet you again,
> I am to see to it that I do not lose you.
>
> — Walt Whitman (included among the Calamus section of the 1860 edition of *Leaves of Grass*).

À une passante

La rue assourdissante autour de moi hurlait.
Longue, mince, en grand deuil, douleur majestueuse,
Une femme passa, d'une main fastueuse
Soulevant, balançant le feston et l'ourlet;

Agile et noble, avec sa jambe de statue.
Moi, je buvais, crispé comme un extravagant,
Dans son œil, ciel livide où germe l'ouragan,
La douceur qui fascine et le plaisir qui tue.

Un éclair... puis la nuit! — Fugitive beauté
Dont le regard m'a fait soudainement renaître,
Ne te verrai-je plus que dans l'éternité?

Ailleurs, bien loin d'ici! trop tard! jamais peut-être!
Car j'ignore où tu fuis, tu ne sais où je vais,
Ô toi que j'eusse aimée, ô toi qui le savais!

— Charles Baudelaire (15 October 1860, *L'Artiste*)[2]

The number of affinities between these two poems is startling. The topic of an encounter with a passing stranger which provokes erotic longing is surely an experience common to everyone who lives in a big city, where most of the passers-by are not only unknown but unlikely ever to be seen again — a recognition which gives a kind of urgency and poignancy to a lost opportunity. (Walter Benjamin, writing about Baudelaire's poem, wittily calls this phenomenon 'love at last sight'.)

The four adjectives that Whitman uses to describe the passing stranger — 'fluid, affectionate, chaste, matured' — have a correspondence in the four adjectivized units in Baudelaire's description of the — or rather *a* — 'passante': 'Longue, mince, en grand deuil, douleur majesteuse', the first two of which describe the physical characteristics, the third the black dress, 'in full mourning' — the poet, in his imagination, has already disposed of his rival — and the fourth discerns a sexy

2 In the absence of any especially striking translation, I include my own merely functional version that adheres fairly closely to the French.

To a Woman Passing

Round me, the street was all a deafening roar.
Slim, tall, majestic in her widow's weeds,
a woman passed, her hand conspicuously
lifting and flouncing her dress's folds and hem.

Lithe and noble; with her leg like a statue's.
Grimacing like a maniac, I drank
from her eye — a livid sky where hurricanes were brewing —
the sweetness that lulls, the pleasure that kills.

A lightning flash...then night! — Fleeting beauty,
at the sight of which I was suddenly reborn,
will I see you again only in the afterlife?

Elsewhere, far from here! too late! or *never*!
For neither you nor I know where the other went —
O you whom I might have loved, O you who knew it!

and majestic quality to the ascribed grief. How strangely natural, almost innocent, Whitman's description is beside Baudelaire's. And yet this is a first signal difference in that Whitman's attributes are ones that the speaker seems equally to share, and this reveals an assumption of reciprocity which Baudelaire's poem, at least initially, withholds. At the same time, despite his sly havering over the gender of the passer-by, and despite the assertions of 'affectionate, chaste' we soon realize that Whitman's speaker's gaze is amorous.

The eye in both has a special status: in Whitman 'You give me the pleasure of your eyes, your face, your flesh...' a series of images that moves from the visual to the tactile and arrives at the strangely foreign locution: 'you take of my beard'. The passer-by seems to partake of the poet's beard as though it were food, or even to steal from it, as a tress of the beloved's hair might be kept in a locket. If something is taken, something is lost. For Baudelaire too the eye is the gateway to 'pleasure' or at least the promise of it:

> Moi, je buvais, crispé comme un extravagant,
> Dans son œil, ciel livide où germe l'ouragan,
> La douceur qui fascine et le plaisir qui tue.

Here the description which foregrounds the 'I' turns the poet into a caricatural being, one of those street-dwelling madmen — off the rails with desire — and the eye of the woman becomes a miniature hemisphere with its own dangerous weather system. Here for all the lure of 'douceur' the pleasure is fatal. But desire and pleasure, for all their different treatments, are the motors of both poems.

The unlikelihood of ever re-encountering the passer-by is again dealt with in the most contrasting manner imaginable (cf. Benjamin's slightly impatient dismissal of this theme in Baudelaire). Baudelaire asks: 'Ne te verrai-je plus que dans l'éternité?' — a whole other future life, an afterlife, must be invoked for this remote possibility to be envisaged. In Whitman this becomes a forceful claim: 'I am to wait, I do not doubt I am to meet you again, | I am to see to it that I do not lose you.' The pathos of the claim is weighed in the reader's mind by the all but sure knowledge that the stranger has already been lost in the crowd. So for the claim to have any truth value, we must infer that fantasy is already a kind of lasting possession, one that the speaker will have to safeguard, following some interior injunction: 'I am to see to it that I do not lose you', an alexandrine composed entirely of monosyllables. (Out of the poem's 162 words only sixteen are more than one syllable.) It is as though he has been assigned this task of *not* losing, of keeping safe, by the prompting of his own nature, or by Nature itself. It is even possibly implied that the writing of this poem is a mode of keeping, of safekeeping — a secretive and fugitive personal perception that has become a public declaration in the poem. This strangeness of phrasing is one of Whitman's triumphs: the idiomatic and prosaic 'I am to see to it' is linked to an unexpected, even an inappropriate task. As a sentence it has the air of naturalness combined with an awkwardness which is almost alien to the language. It is a feat that he pulls off again and again in the 'Song of Myself', even the title of which, with a century and a half of familiarity, still rings strangely in the ears.

Two further observations about 'A une passante'. The woman's glance (or the poet's glance at the woman?) has been the cause of a sudden re-birth — 'm'a fait soudainement renaître' — so this briefest and most fugitive encounter has occasioned a similar kind of conversion to that of Dante and Beatrice in *La Vita Nuova*, un coup de foudre — present in the poem as 'Un éclair' that opens up a vision of the eternal life on a Parisian street, and links Baudelaire's poem with the love poems of the Florentine and Provençal traditions. But the poem is also intricately linked within his own *oeuvre*, to 'Recueillement' (another late poem) by way of that earlier mentioned enjambement 'viens par ici, || Loin d'eux' which is here reprised in the last tercet: 'Ailleurs, bien loin d'ici' where the value of 'here' is reversed, valorized in the first instant (even if ironically) and regretted in the second, where the here and now is on the verge of a disappearance into a futile 'hereafter'.

In both the French and the American poem, there is an implied awareness that they are writing an unusual, specifically modern love poem — a poem that can only be conceived within the modern urban context where the love object is fleetingly glimpsed never to be seen again. This is not the case, say, with Dante's first encounter with Beatrice di Folco Portinari in the large city that thirteenth-century Florence was, where with relative ease he could find out the name of the young woman he had just seen: 'la quale fu chiamata da molti li quali non sapeano che si chiamare', although his next reported encounter is nine years later. At the time of writing these words, Beatrice was already dead 'nel grande secolo' or the eternal life. Baudelaire's question seems to take cognizance, even if with a sardonic twist, of this prototype of the medieval love poem.

The eternity of restitution (and loss) in Baudelaire is curiously converted in Whitman to the past 'I have somewhere surely lived a life of joy with you', a shared life which, even if the future, we may surmise, will never fulfil, has been retrojected and already enjoyed, in another world, the world of an imagined past. It seems as though longing leads Whitman to the promise of fulfilment and Baudelaire to the certainty of loss.

Where Whitman immediately offers a consoling myth of reciprocity and shared life, only at the end of Baudelaire's poem does the ghost of reciprocity appear: 'Ô toi que j'eusse aimée, ô toi qui le savais!' and we realize that in the micro-instant of a look, a look that we now understand has been exchanged, a whole eternity of longing and loss has been experienced, and possibly shared. The knowledge on the part of the woman, though, is not exactly reciprocal, but the poet claims that she has understood, by the intensity of his gaze, that 'he could have loved her'.

Another specifically modern aspect of both poems is an occasion that is so indeterminate and fleeting. It has barely occurred before it is over. And yet both poems determinedly dwell on its instantaneity and couple it in Whitman's case with a past life and in Baudelaire's with a future eternity. Both poems stretch out the instant, a momentary encounter of passing a stranger who 'flit(s) by' on the street, and make it not merely a prompt for erotic reverie but a revelation of desire set against deep time. They are love poems which have for their premise the impossibility of further meeting (though Whitman stubbornly asserts 'I do not doubt I am to meet you again') and at the same time explore a realm of erotic tension that is predicated on not knowing the other. In both cases the invocatory mood, the 'you' and the 'tu' are addressed with the familiarity of lovers, although Whitman begins with the vocative and Baudelaire moves from the third person in the octave, to the intimate second person in the sestet.

The modernity of both poems should not be overstressed. Baudelaire's own quest for 'toujours de nouveau' and Whitman's for 'The new life of the new forms' doesn't mean they work from nothing. As with the street encounter of Dante and Beatrice this is a perennial theme. Far closer in time we can find a direct precedent in Gérard de Nerval, written in 1832 (when de Nerval was a young man, though in his melancholia he sounds ailing and aged), and published in book form *Odettes* — little odes — in 1853, four years before Baudelaire's poem:

Une Allée du Luxembourg

Elle a passé, la jeune fille,
vive et preste comme un oiseau:
A la main une fleur qui brille,
à la bouche un refrain nouveau.

C'est peut-être la seule au monde
dont le cœur au mien répondrait,
qui venant dans ma nuit profonde
d'un seul regard l'éclaircirait!

Mais non, — ma jeunesse est finie...
Adieu, doux rayon qui m'as lui, —
parfum, jeune fille, harmonie...
le bonheur passait, — il a fui![3]

This poem must surely have been an influence on Baudelaire's 'A une passante' — it shares the urban background, the fleeting sight of a woman and a reflection on the poet's loss of erotic opportunity, and there is the parallel phrasing in both 'tu fuis' / 'il a fui'. And yet, its gently piercing regret and resignation seems to belong to an older world of 'où sont les neiges d'antan'. Bird, flower, song — the girl's symbolic attributes — and the four adjectives of the first stanza 'jeune ...vive...

3 A basic translation:

An Avenue in Luxembourg Gardens

She passed by, the young girl,
alive and alert as a bird:
in her hand a bright flower,
in her mouth a new refrain.

Perhaps she's the only one in the world
whose heart would answer to mine,
who coming into my deep night
would light it up with one look!

But no — my youth is over...
Goodbye, sweet ray that shone on me —
Perfume, young girl, harmony...
Happiness was passing...it has fled!

preste...nouveau' are listed wistfully and set up the *finale* of 'le bonheur passait — il a fui'. The ending beautifully balances the opening phrase 'Elle a passé' so the girl and happiness have merged into a single being — *elle* and *il* — that has gone forever with all the light imagery they have brought into the speaker's deep night.

3.

The improbable street encounter of these two towering and contrasting figures, which I've contrived within this piece, continues to reverberate in succeeding generations of poets. We find perhaps midway, Cesare Pavese, whose long inclusive lines show a debt to Whitman but who is also steeped in French poetry — in 'Due sigarette', the street encounter with a woman who asks the speaker for a light owes much to Baudelaire's 'A une passante': 'Ogni rado passante ha una faccia e una storia' [Each rare passer-by has a face and a story] though the outcome is more predictable, and though it's by no means sure that the woman is a prostitute, the predicament plays off the Italian slang — 'lucciola' [firefly] for sex workers and the lit cigarettes that signal their presence on the dark street.

It's no surprise that the revolutionary talent of Aimé Césaire should have found sustenance, in his own account, from both Whitman and Rimbaud, the Rimbaud for whom Baudelaire was 'comme un dieu'. C. K. Williams's *Flesh and Blood* with its Parisian encounters — in the best sense pedestrian, flâneur and 'loiterer' — employs the sonnet form but with Whitman's extensive lines. Even more recently, Terrance Hayes's *American Sonnets for My Past and Future Assassin*, though there are many other tributaries to the collection, marry the condensed form of the sonnet to an exuberant Whitmanian rhetoric:

> I lock you in an American sonnet that is part prison,
> Part panic closet, a little room in a house set aflame.
> I lock you in a form that is part music box, part meat
> Grinder to separate the son of the bird from the bone.
> I lock your persona in a dream-inducing sleeper hold
> While your better selves watch from the bleachers.

We might consider, then, that the 'irreconcilable' elements of Whitman and Baudelaire which, according to Cowley, Hart Crane was vainly seeking to yoke together were instead fused into a magnificent alloy. In *The Bridge* (though it's Poe who is invoked alongside Whitman, and not Baudelaire) these two poets are battling for supremacy. One of Crane's finest poems, 'At Melville's Tomb', although it deliberately enshrines an American master, alludes very clearly to a French tradition of tribute poems such as Mallarmé's 'Le tombeau de Charles Baudelaire', and Crane's six-part masterpiece 'Voyages' pays homage to the Baudelaire's eight-part 'Le Voyage'. However irreconcilable, these two elemental figures remain vivid, evergreen and inextinguishable forces that continue to seed hurricanes even now.

Unpublished, 2018

— 16 —

Dickinson and Duration

Because I could not stop for Death —
He kindly stopped for me —
The Carriage held but just Ourselves —
And Immortality.

We slowly drove — He knew no haste
And I had put away
My labor and my leisure too,
For His Civility —

We passed the School, where Children strove
At Recess — in the Ring —
We passed the Fields of Gazing Grain —
We passed the Setting Sun —

Or rather — He passed Us —
The Dews drew quivering and Chill —
For only Gossamer, my Gown —
My Tippet — only Tulle —

We paused before a House that seemed
A Swelling of the Ground —
The Roof was scarcely visible —
The Cornice — in the Ground —

Since then — 'tis Centuries — and yet
Feels shorter than the Day
I first surmised the Horses' Heads
Were toward Eternity —

What I most admire in this poem is its small compass and enormous span — a curve which links the everyday to forever. Emily Dickinson is one of the few poets who can give an abstraction like 'Eternity' a distinct physical presence. Especially here, where the subject is time.

Rhythmically the poem slows down then breathlessly accelerates time, elongates and foreshortens it, until by the final ' — ' any conventional idea of duration is in shreds.

* * * * *

Duration has, however, been consistently and disturbingly re-imagined in terms of space, a seismic shift on the spatio-temporal axis: 'We...drove...We passed...We passed...We passed...'; then 'We paused'. From passing to pausing, from movement to stasis, is where this mortal turn occurs. Or rather, it happens a stanza earlier in the line 'Or rather — He passed Us — '. Here what we have come to see as movement we now see as stasis. Time and space, and the sun that measures them, are passing the moving hearse, carrying the ('stopped' dead) person, whom the poet imagines herself to be. The small town the cortège passes through has shrunk to 'A Swelling of the Ground' and the 'Centuries' to less than 'the Day'.

* * * * *

In *Houseboat Days*, John Ashbery adopts that startling phrase in the third stanza for one of his poem titles — 'The Gazing Grain'. The use he makes of it is enigmatic. His end-stopped first line 'The tyres slowly came to a rubbery stop', however, recalls Dickinson's opening: 'slowly', as for her poem, sets the tempo of the poem, the unidentified vehicle (though we doubt it to be horse-drawn) is reminiscent of hers, as his 'stop' recalls her 'stop', 'stopped' and 'paused'. Perhaps the second line's reference — 'Alliterative festoons in the sky' — refers back to the title and the heavily alliterated third and fourth stanzas of Dickinson's poem, which may also be the prompt for Ashbery's own alliterations:

> this branchy birthplace of presidents was also
> The big frigidaire-cum-cow-barn where mendicant
>
> And margrave alike waited out the results
> of the natural elections...

The chiasmic arrangement of the two open vowels in the poem's final line — 'These days stand like vapor under the trees' — hauntingly replay the sounds of Dickinson's final stanza: 'Centuries... Day... Eternity'.

On reflection, and especially in comparison to the poem's final line, its first line is far from arresting: 'rubbery' adds little to tyres and consorts ill with 'slowly' and 'branchy', though the effect is characteristic Ashbery, a disarmingly low-key *incipit* that barely breaks the silence, as with such other first lines from the same book as 'Sometimes a word will start it, like' ('Variant') or 'There is no reason for the surcharge to bother you' ('Unctuous Platitudes'), though I prefer both of them. Still, I'm now wondering if in its sly way the poem isn't taking up where Dickinson leaves off, at the threshold of the afterlife. That 'big frigidaire-cum-cow-barn' then takes on the aspect of a cryogenics establishment. The 'mendicant' never felt like a real beggar any more than the 'margrave' was a real prince or defender of the Holy Roman Empire. And what are they waiting *out* for? The 'natural elections' sound more Darwinian than presidential, and maybe even takes on a faint shadow of a Final Judgement?

* * * * *

In Anne Carson's witty, desolate meditation on Proust *The Albertine Workout*, a pamphlet of 59 epigrammatic paragraphs and (supposedly, but not actually) 59 appendices, 'appendix 21 on nuns' ends:

> On the last page Marcel contemplates the task of writing before him and confesses: 'A feeling of vertigo seized me as I saw below me, and yet within me, as if I were miles high, so many years of time.'

In Proust, too, time is considered spatially, and Marcel's vertigo is close to what Dickinson's reader experiences at the end of her poem when she 'first surmised the Horses' Heads | Were toward Eternity — '.

The last of Carson's appendices 'appendix 59 on a bad photograph' describes a photograph in which Albertine's prototype, Proust's chauffeur Alfred Agostinelli, and the author are seated in a car, and notes how the angle of Alfred's head suggests the speed of the vehicle though in fact they are 'sitting stock-still in the car'. She wonders what they talked about during the long exposure in which he would have had to maintain this posture:

> as the photographer fiddled with his lenses and the cicadas sang in the hawthorn hedge and a summer afternoon at the farthest edge of human love extended itself before them into, apparently, eternity.

Carson seems to me one of the few contemporary poets able, almost, to follow Dickinson into the often bleak, 'furthest edge' of human experience.

(For the poetry anthology Lifelines 2 *(Dublin: Town House, 1994) numerous writers were asked to choose a favourite poem and to add some brief comment. I include the poem by Emily Dickinson and my comment, and to this 'condensed Despatch' have added some further thoughts.)*

— 17 —

Odilon Redon: Dreams Fit to Live

'Odilon Redon: Dreams and Visions', Royal Academy, London W1, from 17 February 1995
Douglas Druick, *Odilon Redon: Prince of Dreams* (London: Thames and Hudson, 1994)

'One should not,' according to *Galateo*, a sixteenth-century Italian handbook of courtly manners, 'weary others with such low matter as dreams, especially stupid ones, which most dreams are.' I hate to think what he would have made of Odilon Redon (1840–1916) — an artist whose *oeuvre* seems almost entirely devoted to dreams. Huysmans, an early promoter of Redon's work and the author of *Against Nature*, the manual of Decadent etiquette, dubbed him 'the prince of mysterious dreams'. He was paying a deserved compliment and one that suited Redon's tenebrous excursions into the subconscious; yet the near tautology of the phrase 'mysterious dreams' also puts the case against him.

Redon was born and brought up in the Gironde, in southwestern France, at a time when peasants in thick furs could still be seen perched high on stilts guarding their flocks. This paradoxical image, juxtaposing the earthbound and the airborne, is given a variety of obsessive, metaphorical twists throughout his work. As the scion of Peyrelebade, a wine-growing estate, his childhood should have been privileged but, perhaps because of his epilepsy, perhaps because of other tensions within the family, the young Redon was farmed out to an uncle and, as he remarked in his journal *A Soi-Même*, felt like an outcast from his bourgeois family; indeed, he was brought up beside the children of the peasants. His identification with 'the people' was fortified by a period of conscription into the army during the Franco-Prussian war of 1870.

His slow development as an artist, hindered both by misplaced literary ambitions and by persistent crises of confidence in his abilities, was given a decisive push forwards by the death of his father, who had acted as an inhibiting factor in Redon's life. His career began to flourish in his late thirties with the publication of his first lithographic album, *Dans le rêve* and he started to receive recognition from Huysmans and other writers of stature. At this point, Redon recorded, 'I then made lots of drawings, abundantly for myself, for myself alone, for the sole joy that their happening gave me.' Ultimately, it was his mastery of charcoal, and later of transfer lithography (a method of printing from stone) that accommodated tentative smoky effects, which allowed Redon to trust to the peculiarities of his vision.

The creatures he brought forth have a dual or divided nature: centaurs, sphinxes, winged horses, spiders or plants with human faces, decapitated Johannine heads.

What lifts these images above the merely macabre is the doleful humour and sympathy which Redon feels, and transmits, for his hybrids and monsters. His charcoal Cyclops, for example, as though unaware of its spiky mane, idiot grin and thick features, turns its lone eye poignantly towards the heavens. And Cactus Man is a typical Redon creation, a transitional life-form with its own grotesque dignity, part pot plant, part jack-in-a-box. Redon's interest in the microscope and in protozoic forms was much encouraged by his friend the botanist Armand Clavaud. It was especially gratifying to Redon that the great biologist Pasteur, to whom he sent *Dans le rêve*, responded by pronouncing Redon's monsters 'fit to live'. It's not that Redon turned dreams into art, but rather that he found an equivalent state in his art: an uncertain, suspended, floating consciousness out of which images unexpectedly appear.

Redon's themes are narrow and — with the exception of his landscapes and his later flower paintings and saccharine portrait commissions — they are drawn exclusively from mythology and fantasy. He produced thousands of black-and-white images — *noirs* as he called them — but his drawing lacks — whose doesn't? — the vitality of Goya and Rembrandt, two of his models. As he himself admitted, he was poor at modelling the human form and his heads often sit uncomfortably (if at all) on the bodies that carry them. His motifs, too, are narrowly circumscribed: the same or similar rocks with cloudy contours, the same cloud like a luminous boulder, the same tree with its thick trunk and spindly limbs haunt a succession of drawings and paintings throughout his career. Nonetheless, his cross-hatched and chevron lines build up intriguing textures like sooty lint. And even if the emblems are repeated, their power is intensified by repetition. Just as a book of poems can extend the significance of one poem's imagery through its interplay with other poems, so Redon in his albums pioneered the graphic equivalent: each single motif, repeated in this context, grew more potent and mysterious. This device was developed by the Surrealists, notably in Max Ernst's lithographic albums and in Max Klinger's incomparable etched sequence *The Glove*.

It's this intensity that has sustained the interest in Redon, among both critics and the public, while the reputation of the other Decadents, his contemporaries Bresdin, Moreau and Puvis de Chavannes, has plummeted. He himself claimed to have 'opened a small window onto mystery'. And while we may not be as drawn as he was to the concept of mystery, there's some truth in Redon's claim. He has supplied lasting emblems of the uncanny, unforgettable images of obsession, enslavement and psychological paralysis of the kind that dreams reveal and that consciousness forgets with a shudder. The bright colours of Redon's later painting seem almost unbearably intense compared with the darkness of his graphic work. It is as though the small window he had opened has been shut and the walls which enclosed him had swung open on to a landscape of vivid pigments. They are radiant, though they lack the brooding originality of his earlier, inward visions. But they, and that brooding originality, show how right Redon was to have faith in dreams as a legitimate subject for art.

Observer Magazine, 11 February 1995

— 18 —

Skulls and Flags: James Ensor

Between Street and Mirror: The Drawings of James Ensor, ed. by Catherine De Zegher, The Drawing Center, New York (Minneapolis: University of Minnesota Press, 2001)

His skulls, masks and lurid crowd scenes have won for James Ensor a surprisingly durable niche in a fin-de-siècle gallery of oddballs. He was born in Ostend, then a fashionable resort, to a cultured, alcoholic English father and a Belgian mother whose family ran a souvenir shop. In his usual tones of high-spirited self-delectation, Ensor describes its formative effects:

> I spent my childhood in a shop, surrounded by the curiosities of the sea, the splendours of pearly iridescent shells, weird skeletons, monsters and marine vegetation. These wondrous surroundings [...] doubtlessly contributed to my becoming a painter in love with colour, sensitive to the dazzling light.

The shop's colourful clutter, the crowding-in of curiosities, does indeed offer a kind of equivalent to what he achieves in his art, although clutter and curiosity are dangerous commodities for an artist. What takes such pains to inspire interest can soon induce its opposite. His fellow Belgian, René Magritte, in a deadly 'Hommage', argues that for Ensor 'The subject seems irrelevant: it merely serves as a pretext to compose works without order, addressing us in the decorative language of the colourist [...] His oeuvre presents us with a rather good idea of bourgeois happiness around the turn of the century.'

It is in the years 1885–98 that Ensor's finest work was produced, although, dying in 1949, arguably he was to outlive his gift for more than fifty years. (For an artist who habitually portrayed himself as a skeleton, it's only fitting that his obituaries preceded his actual death by several years when he was reported killed in a bombing raid on Ostend.) Those years correspond to the first period of Leopold II's destruction of the Congo, 'the most gigantic fraud and wickedness which our generation has known' as it was called by the Liverpool shipping clerk E. D. Morel, who worked tirelessly to expose it — an account of which can be found in Adam Hochschild's superb *King Leopold's Ghost*. Conrad's Marlow famously referred to Brussels as 'a whited sepulchre', and the skulls and masks of Ensor might seem, in this context, to be extraordinarily intuitive, and utterly in tune with his time and place: a work of witness rather than mere grotesquerie. Or are his crowd scenes and skull motifs only coincidence — a literary convention he'd adopted from Poe and Baudelaire, and to which he'd given his own hectic signature? Among all the banners and flags that wave over his death-haunted Brussels there's no ominous gold star on a blue ground, the flag of Leopold's company. And among the masks, no sign of the magisterial Kuba masks which were entering Belgium at this time and were to inspire several European artists in the twentieth century. Ensor expressed himself roundly on this topic in a 1937 newspaper article: 'I condemn without remission the incompetent masks from the hellholes of Africa [...] a plague on the features and the facile, outmoded charms of Negroid or gorilla-ish fetishism'. His actual expression 'des enfers d'Afrique', however well it might describe Leopold's Congo, merely serves as a jokey rhetorical turn, with perhaps a side swipe at Picasso. On one level the mask for Ensor, returning to Magritte's attack, is an image of carnivalesque exuberance, and recalls such events as the annual Festival of the Dead Rat in his native Ostend, a favoured resort of Leopold II. And yet it also remains an image of sinister duplicity, of hypocrisy, and in Ensor's paintings is explored both cryptically and with great expressive power.

There's no word about Africa in *Between Street and Mirror: The Drawings of James Ensor.* But if Ensor's politics entirely lacked an international dimension, the drawings and prints which are examined in the book demonstrate that local politics had his full and bitter attention. *Belgium in the XIXth Century*, a crayon drawing of little artistic merit, has the myopic Leopold II peering down from on high with an expression of lugubrious piety at a demonstration being viciously attacked by guardsmen, with the king's words printed below the banner appealing for UN PEU DE PATIENCE PAS DE VIOLENCE. Another shows an 1887 riot of Belgian fishermen against the import of cheap English fish (in which seven protesters were killed and two seriously injured). This crayon picture composed of twelve glued sheets is of more interest but technically still marks something of a retreat from his earlier, densely cross-hatched studies of interiors with phantasmagoric superimpositions, from the subtle, woven chiaroscuro of his *Visions: The Aureoles of Christ and the Sensibilities of Light* series and even from his first, deft landscape etchings, inadequately represented here. In this drawing, the figures are (intentionally) like wooden toys and the line merely serves the caricatural intent and has become oddly woollen — more darned than knitted. A particularly scurrilous and crudely executed print (touched up with gouache) is *Doctrinaire Nourishment* which has the heads of state and church, including Leopold II, with their breeches down, feeding the crowd below with streams of gilded excrement. After Ensor, already a Chevalier of the Order of Leopold, had been made a Baron by King Albert I, he did his utmost to buy back and destroy every copy of this print.

A case is made by all four contributing essayists for the autonomy and importance of Ensor's drawings — as one would expect. The longest essay, by Susan Canning, gives a valuable, well-argued account of how Ensor's satirical drawings drew inventively on popular culture to address the historical moment, and follows the development of his anarchist leanings and the internal quarrels of Les XX, the Belgian art movement to which he belonged. Only in the final paragraph does she lapse into cataloguese, commending Ensor's 'exploration of the drawing process' as 'seductive, yet oh so witty and sardonic'. Robert Hoozee's essay traces the three stages through which Ensor's drawing evolves. His prose, perhaps unhelped by translation, has a glazed air, as when he describes Ensor's early landscape etchings: 'A prudent, composed style lends the landscape a forceful, suggestive aspect', and at times his judgement is puzzling: 'One of Ensor's most macabre works, *My Portrait in 1960*, is also one of his most sensitive'. This mildly sensational but undistinguished etching shows the artist as a reclining heap of bones. One problem of translation certainly occurs in the otherwise informative catalogue index in reference to Ensor's illustration to a tale by Poe called 'The Revelatory Heart'. These Poe illustrations compare favourably with and even, in the case of 'Hop Frog's Revenge', seem to have directly inspired Arthur Rackham's chilling illustrations from 1935.

Marcel de Maeyer's essay is the best attuned to the work's formal properties and in the course of a study of the (problematic) dating and technique of *The Mystic Death of a Theologian* reveals how Ensor's later additions to various drawings deliberately parody and undermine the original work. Herwigs Todts, in the final essay, examines the development in Ensor's use of the mask motif. Despite the subtlety of De Maeyer's formalist approach, these writers rarely concede, or even notice, any unevenness or weakness in Ensor's drawing. When the same quality of attention is paid to a feeble effusion like *Ensor and General Leman Discussing Painting* or to the schematic, squirmy-lined, seaside-postcard effect of *Bathing at Ostend* as to an uncanny etching like *Peculiar Insects* or a masterpiece of tall space and crowdedness like *The Cathedral* (both oddly Kafkaesque), it begins to feel as if the reader has entered a domain of indiscriminate advocacy. It's ironic that an artist so uneasy at 'the transiency of the pictorial material', who wanted to entrust his survival to 'hard copperplates, imperishable ink', should be remembered almost exclusively for his painted works. For his most famous painting *The Entry of Christ into Brussels* Ensor even used cheaper, and far less durable, house paint to block in its large, bold areas of colour.

Times Literary Supplement, 12 July 2002

— 19 —

A Music of Hautboys: Plutarch, Shakespeare, Cavafy, Eliot

And all the way (a horn!) from fjord to fjell his baywinds
oboboes shall wail him rockbound...

JAMES JOYCE

Il est des parfums frais comme des chairs d'enfants,
Doux commes les hautbois, verts commes les prairies...

CHARLES BAUDELAIRE

If you say on the hautboy man is not enough,
Can never stand as god, is ever wrong...

WALLACE STEVENS

The Tragedy of Antony and Cleopatra is a play of astounding harmony and dissonance, of balance and imbalance, of contrary worlds and values. This set of balances is even audible in the prosody. Without having laboriously tested the idea, I doubt any other Shakespeare play, any verse play at all, has anything like its quantity of enjambments, has used the device to set up and subvert the balance of the line with such intensity and purpose. Exceptions can be found elsewhere, in *The Tempest*, for example, where Caliban's abrupt and disruptive run-ons ('You taught me language; and my profit on't | Is, I know how to curse. The red plague rid you | For learning me your language' (I. 2. 519–20) where the clumsy elision at the end of the first line stumbles into the premature caesura of the next, creating a haunting, broken music that challenges the authority and order of the play.

But in *Antony and Cleopatra*, the very first speech establishes this pattern of a line, a Nile, that overflows its banks:

PHILO Nay, but this dotage of our general's
O'erflows the measure. Those his goodly eyes
That o'er the files and musters of the war
Have glowed like plated Mars, now bend, now turn
The office and devotion of their view
Upon a tawny front. His captain's heart,
Which in the scuffles of great fights hath burst
The buckles on his breast, reneges all temper
And is become the bellows and the fan
To cool a gypsy's lust. (I. I. I–10)[1]

1 All quotations from the play are taken from William Shakespeare, *The Complete Works*, ed. by Stanley Wells and Gary Taylor, Oxford: Clarendon Press, reissued 1998), pp. 1001–36.

Without a single end-stop, these sinewy lines bend like bulrushes, turn on their axles and burst their buckles. As each line overflows into the next, the rhythmic propulsion of the whole play and its massive underlying harmony is set in motion. The same property of harmony and dissonance, and boldly enjambed verse, is audible throughout, most notably in the major speeches of Antony and Cleopatra themselves, often end-loaded with verbs. Even the measured Caesar, by the end of the play, seems to have caught a milder version of the bug:

> If they had swallowed poison, 'twould appear
> By external swelling, but she looks like sleep,
> As she would catch another Antony
> In her strong coils of grace. (v. 2. 339–42)

It may seem risible to make a play that spans the known world and centres on a crucial episode of classical history hinge on such a small technical device but it is, after all, as Giorgio Agamben makes clear, the very thing that distinguishes poetry from prose — the *possibility* of enjambment — and I want to consider the play with regard to the music of poetry.[2]

Though there's little that's English about *Antony and Cleopatra*, where better to look for the full gamut of English poetry, and for one of its pinnacles. Voltaire boasted of having only found a few jewels in the dunghill of Shakespeare's *oeuvre*, a kind of provocation thrown out later by Tolstoy and Bernard Shaw. But sticking with Voltaire, even the word 'dung' is used as a jewel at the beginning of the play and at the end: Antony's 'Kingdoms are clay: our dungy earth alike | Feeds beast as man' (I. 1. 35–36) is echoed by Cleopatra, contemplating suicide and death 'Which sleeps and never palates more the dung, | The beggar's nurse and Caesar's' (v. 2. 7–8).

It is a world of slime, mud, clay, and of 'immortal longings'. In *All for Love*, Dryden seems to have intuited the importance of this imagery, but overdoes it in Serapion's first speech:

> Here monstrous phocae panted on the shore;
> Forsaken dolphins there with their broad tails,
> Lay lashing the departing waves: hard by them,
> Sea horses floundering in the slimy mud,
> Tossed up their heads, and dashed the ooze about them.

Dryden brings his accustomed skill to the ordered end-stops as to the enjambments, and read without the looming precedent of Shakespeare there's much to admire in these lines.

In Shakespeare's play, the earthly is continuously set against the transcendent, and the four elements are in continual combat: 'I am fire and air', as Cleopatra with harrowed grandeur claims at the play's end. The ordered French literary mind of Voltaire's generation would have been hard-pressed to apprehend this breadth; though with Baudelaire, who said of Paris 'Tu m'as donné ta boue et j'en ai fait de

2 Giorgio Agamben, *The End of the Poem*, trans. by Daniel Heller-Roazen (Stanford, CA: Stanford University Press, 1999), p. 109 '...the possibility of enjambment constitutes the only criterion for distinguishing poetry from prose' is a thesis Agamben approves, and which leads him to the curious paradox that 'it follows that the last verse of a poem is not a verse', p. 112.

l'or', it's a different story. Mud figures extravagantly in the opening of Stéphane Mallarmé's 'Le tombeau de Charles Baudelaire' as the proper medium of the poet:

> Le temple enseveli divulgue par la bouche
> Sépulcrale d'égout bavant boue et rubis...

But with all three French authors, mud and pearl, mud and gold, even mud and rubies are seen in opposition, whereas for Shakespeare mud itself is generative and precious.

The critic J. F. Danby speaks perceptively of 'deliquescence' as a characteristic of the play. We could also add liquefaction, though of course that's almost a cliché in critical studies concerned with its imagery. In the first lines where Philo complains that Antony has 'o'erflowed the measure' and then dwells on the 'stale of horses, the gilded puddle', a baroque description of the horse piss that Antony was prepared to drink on campaign, we are introduced to both spiritual and bodily fluids. Antony's first sonorous speech 'Let Rome in Tiber melt...' would have the solidest thing in the world turn to liquid; but even the vaporous and aerial is subject to both solidification and liquefaction: 'Sometimes we see a cloud that's dragonish, | A vapour sometime like a bear or lion...' As the speech resumes, Antony finds the definitive image of the indefinite:

> That which is now a horse, even with a thought,
> The rack dislimns, and makes it indistinct
> As water is in water. (IV. 14. 9–11)

His next speech concludes with the prospect of suicide: 'there is left us | Ourselves to end ourselves'. The indistinctness of water in water seems to lead to the dissolution of the self in the parallel repetition of 'ourselves'. Antony's self, throughout a name to conjure with — as even Caesar says 'in that name lay | A moiety of the world' (V. 1. 17–18) — is simultaneously actual and historical, mythical and mercurial, shape- and role-shifting. The recursive is an emphatic feature of the play throughout and culminates in Antony's own penultimate lines: 'a Roman by a Roman | Valiantly vanquished.' (IV. 16. 59–60) with its vaunting alliterations balancing and tilting over the line.

That image of water in water is the kind of circular, self-referential trope that's often heard in the early poems of Valerio Magrelli ('as though a cloud where to assume | the shape of a cloud', cf. p. 281) and I can't help wondering if he'd read the play in translation. He could of course have found a parallel route to these images, for they are lyrical meditations on how the self perceives the self, where the play has similar concerns from a dramatic perspective.

These images of liquefaction are sometimes, however, reversed as we see in Antony's boast before his suicide: 'and o'er green Neptune's back | with ships made cities' (IV. 15. 58–59) so perhaps it's better to speak of the constant metamorphosis of the four elements — from Cleopatra's description of Antony 'his delights | Were dolphin-like, they showed his back above | The element he lived in' (V. 2. 87–89) to her final speech 'As sweet as balm, as soft as air, as gentle' (V. 2. 306).

Like mud and clay, water is a generative force: 'a courser's hair' — the hair of a horse that was meant to turn into a snake when added to water — and Nilus's mud which generates life are just two examples that are images of mutability but also of seething fertility.

The whole play is like an ingenious Renaissance fountain that uses the hydraulic head of a Roman viaduct to jet streams of water at the same time that one filled receptacle tips its contents into the next. The naval battle of Actium is one such moment in Antony's career as a Roman general. But the crucial tipping point is perceived, after a final illusory victory for Antony, as a ghostly music, in a stage direction: 'Music of the hautboys is under the stage'. These sounds, described by the First Soldier as 'Music i' th' air', by the Third as 'Under the earth', takes shape in the divination of the Second Soldier:

> 'Tis the god Hercules, whom Antony loved,
> Now leaves him.

The hautboy is an early version of the oboe, from the French *hautbois*: *high (-pitched) wood*, a reed instrument used elsewhere to announce important entrances (as of Duncan in *Macbeth* I. 6). It may be kin to the 'scrannel pipes' in 'Lycidas' but in this scene it is how Shakespeare *hears* and translates a passage in North's Plutarch. If the 'Flourish' which interrupts Philo's first speech, quoted above, is a Roman and military fanfare, this music is of another kind, hedonistic but eerie: the oboe has replaced the trumpet. The scales have turned against Antony, and the Alexandrian revelries are over. It is as though Shakespeare has externalized the phrase 'his courage deserted him' by embodying it in the god of war who 'Now leaves him'.

The relevant passage in North's Plutarch reads:

> Furthermore, the selfsame night within little of midnight, when all the city was quiet, full of fear and sorrow, thinking what would be the issue and end of this war, it is said that suddenly they heard a marvelous sweet harmony of sundry sorts of instruments of music, with the cry of a multitude of people, as they had been dancing and had sung as they use in Bacchus' feasts, with movings and turnings after the manner of the satyrs; and it seemed that this dance went through the city unto the gate that opened to the enemies. Now, such as in reason sought the depth of the interpretation of this wonder, thought that it was the god unto whom Antonius bare singular devotion to counterfeit and resemble him, that did forsake them.

Shakespeare's reworking of this passage is wonderfully concise — one stage direction and three brief comments, and yet it contains all that he needed: a music that melts away into the air or the earth, from a heavenly or an infernal source, and reduces North's 'marvelous sweet harmony of sundry sorts of instruments' to the singular reedy scrannel piping of hautboys.

* * * * *

Centuries later, the Egyptiot Greek poet Constantin Cavafy (1863–1933) heard this haunting music in both Plutarch and Shakespeare, and replayed it in one of the two poems he dedicated to Mark Antony. Cavafy's poems span four thousand years of Greek and Mediterranean culture from 2000 BC to the early nineteenth century. Those with an ancient setting treat that period as though it were the present on which the future (even if already past, even if we already know it) inexorably hangs. Some operate in three distinct time zones. Two Italian past tenses are named 'passato prossimo' and 'passato remoto' (recent and distant past); Cavafy's imagination has added a third tense which might be called 'passato antiquo', and some of his poems triangulate between a recent event that sparks an earlier memory which in turn is illuminated by another event in ancient history. This antique past tense suffusing his work often employs the present tense: a typical opening 'Phernazis the poet is at work | on the crucial part of his epic... ('Dareis') or 'The ageing of my body and my beauty | is a wound from a merciless knife' ('Melancholy of Jason Kleander, Poet in Kommagini, A.D. 595', translated by Edmund Keeley and Philip Sherrard).

All of these past tenses, however, are lit with a prohibited homoerotic passion: 'His erotic tendencies, | condemned and strictly forbidden | (but innate for all that) were the cause of it...' ('Days of 1896', p. 105). That deft parenthesis sweeps aside the enduring and blighting theories that homosexuality can be cured still held today by, among others, the victorious Brexit candidate and national treasure Ann Widdecombe.

Cavafy, after spending a part of his youth in Liverpool, was said to have spoken Greek with a vestigial English accent. So perhaps an Egyptian Scouse accent, like that of the great striker Mo Salah. He was certainly well-read with respect to Shakespeare, as apart from the Antony poems, one of his longest poems is a revisionary reading of *Hamlet* in which Claudius is presented as a gentle and peaceable monarch whom the murderous and unhinged prince falsely accuses. But while it deftly opens up a reversed set of sympathies, it's also susceptible of another reading in which the credulous speaker is unable to discern the hidden sequence of events that the Elizabethan play reveals. Cavafy is as aware as T. S. Eliot that 'History has many cunning passages, contrived corridors | And issues', most likely far more aware, as for no poet has ancient history been so much the living present.

* * * * *

Eliot is another poet who employs this brief, haunting passage in Shakespeare. 'Burbank with a Baedeker: Bleistein with a Cigar', in common with much of *Poems 1920*, is an echo-chamber or honeycomb of allusions. The echoes in the poem are from *Antony and Cleopatra* and *The Merchant of Venice*, as well as, en passant, that other Venetian play, *Othello*, and Eliot has transposed the action from Alexandria to Venice. In addition to the Jamesian epigraph, the final stanza's rhetorical question 'Who clipped the lion's wings | And flea'd his rump and pared his claws?' is, as R. C. Turner has argued, a reference to Jonathan Swift's ironic praise of Grub Street hacks in *The Tale of a Tub*.[3] The second stanza is a stylish reworking of the hautboys episode:

> Defunctive music under sea
> Passed seaward with the passing bell
> Slowly: the God Hercules
> Had left him, that had loved him well.

3 <https://www.tandfonline.com/doi/pdf/10.1080/00138387108597434>.

Eliot has fashioned a music that's at once solemnly elegiac and discreetly mocking, and the pluperfect tense accords with the sense of an irretrievably lost grandeur seen from the perspective of a squalid present. It's a characteristically Eliotic manoeuvre: the culture and inhabitants of the present are reduced with respect to the past — a guttering candle — so that the direction of time's arrow is always *rallentando* and downwards.

Here Antony's impending defeat is used as an encompassing image of the decline of the West even as the sun rises in the east in the next stanza: 'The horses, under the axletree | Beat up the dawn from Istria | With even feet.' The last phrase is itself another cunning echo, this time from Horace I, 4, 13: 'pallida mors *aequo pulsat pede*'. The entire poem insists on decline and descent and diminishment, from Burbank in the first stanza crossing 'a *little* bridge | *Descending* to a *small* hotel' then at the arrival of the vulpine Princess Volupine: 'They were together, and he *fell*' (my italics). The crucial preposition in the second stanza, quoted above, is 'under' picking up the Shakespearean direction 'under the stage', and again it's sounded in the third stanza's 'under the axletree'. That stanza ends with a further reference to the play: 'Her shuttered barge | Burned on the water all the day.' This alludes to Enobarbus's speech, 'The barge she sat on like a burnished throne | Burned on the water' and possibly threads the burning with ominous desire and frustration: the barge has become the site for a sordid sexual encounter. Of course this is only a reader's inference as everything is veiled or shuttered until, that is, the next three stanzas where the poem descends into a visceral and vicious series of anti-Semitic tropes in describing the Bleistein who shares with Burbank a double-billing in the title. At this point, the descent of man is figured in his ape-like mode of perambulation, 'A saggy bending of the knees', while his eye 'Stares from the protozoic slime': 'The smoky candle end of time || Declines', before rats and Jews and furs are bundled together in a crude finale with the repeated preposition 'underneath':

> On the Rialto once.
> The rats are underneath the piles.
> The Jew is underneath the lot.
> Money in furs. The boatman smiles

Only Princess Volupine, having presumably disposed of the tedious Burbank, *ascends* 'To climb the waterstair' and entertain Sir Ferdinand Klein, and in this case the climbing, we may guess, is social and financial. All of the names have significance: Bleistein meaning 'leadstone', hence base metal, Klein is German for small (again), and perhaps even the name Burbank is resonant. Luther Burbank was a commercially successful American botanist who cultivated the Russet Burbank potato, now the main ingredient of McDonald chips. He was also a eugenicist who advocated involuntary sterilization and promoted anti-miscegenation laws and racial segregation. Different rules, then, for humans than for tubers and the various hybrid species of fruit he cultivated. It may be an extra irony of the poem that an advocate of racial purity should 'fall' for a probably 'foreign' and Jewish aristocrat who has an unclear association with Bleistein, a Chicago/Viennese Jew, perhaps a pander or business associate. Such is the miscegenated corruption of contemporary

Venice in the poem's infernal descent: a case study in prejudice. The reader is caught between admiration for the subtle way Eliot has marshalled all these echoes and dismay at the ends to which they're made to serve.

* * * * *

As it happens, an essay by the Greek poet George Seferis,[4] which seeks to establish the affinities and connections of Cavafy and Eliot (not mutual influence, which he discounts, though they did know of each other's work) overlooks this point of convergence though he gives another — Dante's phrase 'colui che fece per viltade il gran rifiuto' [he who through cowardice made the great refusal], in reference, supposedly, to Pope Celestino V. The account he gives of Cavafy is brilliant and illuminating, so it discomforts me that I see the two poets he wants to bring together as so much at odds in their historical visions.

Cavafy's Alexandria is a melting-pot of peoples: Syrians, Jews, Greeks, Romans, Christians and Egyptians and none of his poems seeks to exclude any group whatsoever. He might prefer a hedonistic Greek approach to physical pleasure but there are also sympathetic considerations of Christian morality. And the one-way, downward gradient from glory to squalor that characterizes Eliot's stance is alien to Cavafy's complex and intimate relations with the past and the present.

'The god forsakes Antony' written in 1911 is, Peter Mackridge explains, 'the earliest of the poems explicitly set in Alexandria that he [Cavafy] later allowed to enter his "canon" of approved poems'.[5] Here another triangulation occurs as Cavafy situates himself between Plutarch and Shakespeare, more between than after, as his imagination has been nourished, unlike Shakespeare's, at the source in ancient Greek.

I quote the poem in Sherrard and Keeley's translation, the best I could find:[6]

At midnight, when suddenly you hear
an invisible procession going past
with exquisite music, voices,
don't mourn your luck that's failing now,
work gone wrong, your plans
all proving deceptive – don't mourn them uselessly:
as though long prepared, and full of courage,
say goodbye to her, to Alexandria who is leaving.
Above all, don't fool yourself, don't say
it was a dream, that your ears deceived you:
don't degrade yourself with empty hopes like these.
As though long prepared, and full of courage,
as though natural in you who've been given this kind of city,

4 George Seferis, *On the Greek Style*, trans. by Rex Warner and Th. D. Frangopoulos (repr. Limni, Evia, Greece: Denise Harvey, 2000), pp. 119–65.

5 C. P. Cavafy, *The Collected Poems*, trans. by Evangelos Sachperoglou (Oxford: Oxford University Press, 2007), p. xii.

6 C. P. Cavafy, *Collected Poems*, translated by Edmund Keeley and Philip Sherrard (Princeton, NJ: Princeton University Press, 1992), p. 33.

go firmly to the window and listen with emotion,
but not with regret, the whinings of a coward,
listen – your final pleasure – to the voices,
to the exquisite music of that strange procession,
and say goodbye to her, to the Alexandria you are losing.

This double source of Plutarch and Shakespeare has often been noted in Cavafy's poem, so rather than dwell on it I only want to underline the obvious but crucial deviation of Cavafy. Plutarch's Antony is abandoned by Bacchus; Shakespeare's by Hercules (perhaps a guess at 'the god unto whome Antony bare singular devotion'); and Cavafy's hero by an invented female deity, Alexandria. The city itself has assumed a feminine identity. Greek gender for city — πόλη — is feminine, as also in the Romance languages, so perhaps it's natural to fashion a goddess rather than a god out of Alexandria, especially in this case where the unmentioned queen and counterpart is Cleopatra. All three have chosen gods appropriate to the different facets of Antony's character.

North's Plutarch's 'marvellous sweet harmony' is here rendered (twice) as 'exquisite music' and seems to carry an echo of the swan song, whereas, as we've seen, Shakespeare's music is of bare unaccompanied oboes. The poem has a slow processional denouement, so that the final line, which almost repeats the eighth, but substitutes in the English, that follows the Greek, 'losing' for 'leaving', loss for departure. To an English ear it can't help evoking the sea shanty 'So Fare Thee Well, My Own True Love' with its line 'It's not the leaving of Liverpool that grieves me', a song it might be a bit far-fetched to believe Cavafy had heard in his youth, though one version goes back at least as far as 1885. In this case, though, it is the town that is leaving, floating away on the air, and not the sailor.

An interesting contrast, given my starting point, is the absence of any radical enjambment in Cavafy. This, with a few exceptions, is a characteristic absence in his poems. Despite his often extended sentences, Cavafy tends to break them in unostentatious fashion, along the grain or according to the phrasal pause. It's consistent with what the Russian poet Joseph Brodsky, in his essay on Cavafy, notes as the Alexandrian's habitual poverty of expression: simple adjectives, clear exposition, a scarcity of metaphor and simile.[7] He argues that these qualities make Cavafy eminently translatable. Without Greek, I've no way of knowing if this is true, but the force of Sherrard and Keeley's translations, which have made Cavafy into a major English poet, inspire confidence and tally with Brodsky's observation. A reader with knowledge of ancient and modern Greek would likely be better placed than me to piece together this aural mosaic but even those without can hear the way Plutarch's 'marvellous sweet harmony' (as North would have it) has travelled north, west and south again, over the centuries, and been transposed for

7 '...as early as 1900–1910, he began to strip his poems of all poetic paraphernalia — rich imagery, simile, metric flamboyance, and [...] rhymes.' Joseph Brodsky, *Less Than One: Selected Essays* (London: Penguin, 1987), p. 55. A propos of music, Brodsky's description of the timbre Cavafy's poems is also persuasive: 'that implacable note of ennui which makes Cavafy's voice with its hedonistic-stoic tremolo sound so haunting.' Ibid., p. 67.

ghostly oboe, then become ‘exquisite’ music in Alexandria, ‘defunctive’ music in Eliot’s Venice, and been heard throughout the Magna Grecia, from the Nile and then far beyond to the Avon and the Thames.

Athenaeum Review, May 2020

PART III

❖

In and Between Wars

— 20 —

Wassily Kandinsky

It is one of the paradoxes of Modernism that revolutionary practice goes hand in hand with reactionary theory and Kandinsky is no exception. A reader wishing to confront his theoretical work *Concerning the Spiritual in Art* (1912) needs to be willing to wade through a certain amount of Theosophical waffle, amply spread with what Twain called hogwash and soul butter, before reaching Kandinsky's intriguing though highly conjectural thoughts about form and colour. Even here, the writing is beset with contradictions. Within the space of two pages, we first hear 'there is no "must" in art, because art is free' and then that 'we are faced with the [...] principle, which is to set art free, the principle of the inner need' and wonder why what has already been declared free should need to be set free. Yet despite the hieratic tone, there is an impulse to work out principles of pictorial harmony and discord, and a thoroughgoing attempt, step by step, to explore the consequences of a 'revolt from dependence on nature', which is how he saw the nascent movement of abstraction of which he was one of the founders and pioneers. He is also wary, even at this early stage, of the dangers of abstract art declining into 'mere decoration [...] suited to neckties or carpets'.

Kandinsky began his artistic career at the late age of twenty-nine, abandoning a secure post as an academic in Russia to study painting in Munich. The two decisive experiences, recorded in his *Reminiscences*, were the sight of Monet's *Haystack* in which, perhaps with some fond hindsight, he sensed the potential of colour to be autonomous of content, recognizing that 'unconsciously the representational became discredited as an unavoidable element of a picture'. The other was a performance of Wagner's *Lohengrin* at the Moscow Royal Theatre which induced a visual/acoustic hallucination: 'Wild lines verging on the insane formed drawings behind my very eyes'. This synaesthetic experience is entirely credible and had a shaping impact on the whole of Kandinsky's development. A correspondence between the arts was a cornerstone of Symbolist aesthetics and in Kandinsky's case became an article of faith, especially the deep affinities between music and painting. Gifted with eidetic recall, colour continually presented itself to him with a musical accompaniment. One famous passage from *Concerning the Spiritual in Art* describes colours in terms of musical instruments — vermillion, for example, 'is a sound of trumpets, strong, harsh and ringing'. Although synaesthetic associations are notoriously arbitrary, this is interestingly close to the philosopher John Locke's seventeenth-century account of a blind man who described scarlet as 'the sound of a trumpet'. And if it still lingers some way short of consensus, surprising areas of overlap in the experience of synaesthetics have been noted. A *New Scientist* article records how in one recent controlled test the nine synaesthetics, when asked to describe the colours of 130 words and sounds, were over 92% in agreement. Kandinsky's conviction that an underlying ('spiritual', if you like) language of correspondence exists shouldn't be too briskly dismissed.

'Every form', Kandinsky writes, 'is as sensitive as a puff of smoke, the slightest breath will alter it completely'. This observation catches the vertiginous and unsettling possibilities of an art liberated from conventional representation and also suggests how in his finest paintings the tensions and counter-tensions within the pictorial space are held in such delicate balance. It also reveals a motive for the rapidity of brushwork in his art. Although the selection of watercolours and prints gathered together in the Royal Academy is an exceptionally fine one, there are inclusions which (usefully perhaps) show how fragile, vulnerable and chancy this balance was in Kandinsky's career. Least convincing are the three watercolours (1915–16), painted during a three-month visit to his long-term partner, the gifted painter Gabriele Münter, in the security of neutral Stockholm, which seem to shy away not only from the World War but from the world at large, even from the abstraction which he had already achieved in some of the great 1913 canvases from the Blaue Reiter period such as *Composition VII* and the study for that painting (*Draft 2*), held in Moscow and Munich respectively. Here instead he took refuge in saccharine mythological 'figures of Old Russia' and picturesque landscapes of peaked hills and lakeshores and rainbows. Münter referred to them, politely enough, as *bagatelles*. Rather than marrying her, as she had long expected him to, Kandinsky no sooner returned to Russia than he married the student Nina Andreevskaya. In the words of the Guest Curator Frank Whitford, 'She was younger, less intelligent and physically more attractive than Münter, a combination irresistible to a fifty-year-old male no doubt worried by his flagging libido'. (Why, you wonder, is the curator so sure that the artist's libido was flagging?)

Represented at the beginning of the exhibition are several of the stylized early Munich gouaches (to which the *Bagatelles* revert) such as *Night* (1907) where the small irregular blobs of colour float like iridescent seeds or stars on a black ground. These works are full of a folkloric nostalgia which seems tailored for export, with figures out of fairytales or ballads, peasants in costume and bearded Old Believers in settings scattered with birch trees and redemptive onion domes. Yet the colours do have emotional force and intensity. More impressive are the earlier woodcuts such as *The Singer* (1903), in five colours. Perhaps guaranteed by Kandinsky's feeling for music, this woodcut has a rhythmic assurance in the bold ivory striations of the singer's dress and in the poised silhouette of the pianist. The colour woodcuts of 1911 are radical shifts towards abstraction and where, as in *Large Resurrection*, the figurative prevails — with the angel and trumpet at top left crossed by a hurtling red apocalyptic star and the striped demonic snake at the bottom — the sense of confident and dynamic patterning shows how well suited Kandinsky is to this medium.

Kandinsky returned to Russia at the outbreak of the war, and after the Revolution found employment in the Moscow Institute for Artistic Culture (INChUK) where the Constructivists Rodchenko and Malevich were also teaching. Although Kandinsky learnt much from the latter especially, as his later more assured use of isolated geometric shapes makes clear, his own theories were treated with increasing hostility by his fellow painters. He left for Berlin in 1921, and within a year had taken up a teaching post in the Bauhaus at Weimar. A school which sought to unify the applied and fine arts was an ideal environment for Kandinsky, with the added advantage of a close association with his friend Paul Klee. Soon after his arrival he created for Propylaen Publishers the graphic print sequence *Small World* which consists of four colour lithographs, four woodcuts, and four, predominantly drypoint, etchings. Each of these prints has a tremendous self-contained explosive vitality, employing a bewilderingly complex but integrated set of markings: combs, bars, lattices, rings, threads and needle-shapes which float across and intersect one another as though in response to an individual and unrepeatable set of dynamics. This is especially impressive in the black-and-white woodcut *Small Worlds VI* and in the coloured woodcut *Small Worlds VII*. This last (and for that matter also *V*) are erroneously called colour lithographs in the catalogue index.

Kandinsky's paintings during the Bauhaus period shows the benign influence of Klee (though Klee referred to him as his 'friend and mentor') technically in the use of delicate stencilling and of an atomizer or watercolour spray diffuser, but also more significantly in their humorous, dreamy and childlike clarity and inventiveness. The structure of *Supporting Circle* (1929) for example seems to play off the metal base of a globe map of the world. But out of the globe with its lifted crescent lid a series of precariously balanced figures have hatched, including, on the right, some distressed triangles, the largest of which suffers from a crease in its already bent hypotenuse. Each of the figures as well as the broken circle is given a darker aura of sprayed orange on a fainter speckled orange ground.

Gloomy Situation (1933) is a wonderful valedictory watercolour to the Bauhaus period in the same stencilled and spray-painted idiom. The title is a rare instance of some external or political reference in Kandinsky. Like protozoic hieroglyphs, two dark figures confront each other separated by a slot of light which is the point of overlap of three stencilled rectangles. The only other break in the dun brown (the colour of the Brownshirts?) which covers the page is a band of glowing magenta in the left-hand figure which looks like a pen topped with a dark eye. 'But there remains brown,' as Kandinsky had written in *Concerning the Spiritual in Art*, 'unemotional, disinclined for movement'. Even in this gloomy picture there is a flicker of grim humour. In response to local right-wing attacks, the Bauhaus had moved from Weimar to Dessau in 1925 — in Felix Klee's delightful *Recollections*: 'In the midst of gloomy industrial sites (sugar, gas, Agfa, Junkers), this little capital drowsed like a sleeping beauty'. But in the early Thirties the atmosphere within the school had become politically polarized, and under the new directorship of Mies van der Rohe it had lost its dynamic character, while suffering from increasing Nazi hostility. In July 1933 not long after Hitler came to power, the Bauhaus finally closed.

In 1934, assisted by Marcel Duchamp, the sixty-eight-year-old artist moved to Paris. During the next ten years of his life (he outlived the liberation of Paris by only a few months) he moved into a phase which Hajo Duchting calls 'Biomorphic Abstract'. In these works there is some sense of Kandinsky having come full circle as he returns to the medium of gouache on black paper which he used in the fairytale-like Russian paintings of his first period in Munich. They have a similar intensity of colours suspended over the black ground and yet there is a far more rigorous formal design and balance. In *Line with Accompaniment* (1937) the line in question is a white scumbled serpentine figure that continues as blue where it loops over the lower black rectangle. It snakes in and out of eleven circles of different pastel colours and densities, itself a collapsed circle or ouroboros. There is a subtle sense of shallow spatial recession as it threads over and under the sides of these circles which are linked among themselves, and yet the fact that all the circles are true and show no ellipses (though they advance or retreat according to their colour, tonal value, relative size and thickness) has an unsettling *trompe l'oeil* effect. The rectangular pattern of the ground is intensified in the left-hand corner by a blue rectangle and a smaller pink rectangular outline directly below. The curving organic white line seems to set the rigid geometry of the rest of the composition into a state of vibration. These pictures explore the oxymoron of static movement.

Kandinsky wrote of his intention 'to let the viewer stroll around within the picture, to force him to forget himself, and so become part of the picture'. Many of the pictures brought together for this exhibition will reward anyone willing to do so. The choice of watercolours and prints gives a smaller scale, intimate quality to the experience of this, the first large exhibition of Kandinsky's work in London. Surely it's time a gallery here provided the chance to stroll around, and within, his oils as well?

Modern Painters, Summer 1999

— 21 —

Clown of Ocean: Jack B. Yeats

In a prose piece done for the *Manchester Guardian*, a fine example of the traditional Irish 'bull', Jack B. Yeats describes a Shove Halfpenny contest in which the local pub champion Val Dance has been 'set up' by the incoming hustler Bill Boland, who 'did things to those halfpennies to learn which must have taken the practice of half a lifetime'. The accompanying ink and watercolour sketch has the seated crowd's attention skewered to the tabletop as undistractably as though they were witnessing the Fall of Troy, whilst the artist himself can be seen leaning rakishly at the back of the bar, observing it all, himself included. Despite the vigorous control of line in this early illustration, it was to take the practice of more than half a lifetime for Yeats, as an artist, to hit upon his own winning streak. Only around 1925, when he was already over fifty years old, did his characteristic palette of primary colours and his speedy, reckless manner of handling paint begin to emerge, and Yeats acknowledged that this was 'a land of new birth' in himself.

It came as a result of his breaking through and out of the strong outlines of his earlier, prolific illustrative work and of the first phase of his oil painting, which relied likewise on a dark bounding line, although he often achieves a Daumier-like freedom and boldness in its use, as in *The Barrel Man* or *The Circus Dwarf* (both 1912). But there is no break with his concerns and subject matter: horse-racing, circuses, boxing, orators, entertainers, singers, tinkers, travellers and sailors would remain in his repertoire of images. His circus animals, especially his horses, would never desert him.

Yeats's horses are generally of a different breed from his brother, the poet's, of a far less aristocratic demeanour. Jack Yeats's belong to the kind that would run in the meets called the Four-and-Nineteens because the betting being under £5 meant they stood beyond the law. For W. B. Yeats, in 'At Galway Races', the feats of the horsemen have usurped the attention that should have been the birthright of poets, and he looks forward to the future when 'the merchant and the clerk' will have been cleared away and when the poets will again 'find hearteners among men | That ride upon horses'. By contrast, Jack Yeats's paintings refuse an exalted posture in relation both to everyday Irish life and to popular art; rather they have a natural affinity with the ballad-singers and the melodrama actors, and seem to draw their inspiration from the same clear source.

There are a great number of his paintings which celebrate the act of singing, and their titles often include the name of the song in case the viewer has failed to catch the tune from the singer's expression, as in *Singing the Dark Rosaleen, Croke Park* or *Singing 'Way down upon the Swanee River'*. One of the first of these, *Singing '(Oh)*

Had I the Wings of a Swallow' (1925), contrasts the dark red tones of the woman's rigid coat and the wooden drinking booths with her white outstretched throat and the underlit, ecstatically yellow wings of the ceiling and the white windowed skies on either side. Tom Paulin, who as a poet shares many of Jack Yeats's passions, including a commitment to the risks of the present moment, rightly argues that Yeats 'seems to be sketching in oils to catch the intensity of the vocal moment'.

This idea of the moment, or 'the happening', is at the heart of Yeats's vision: the intense drama of the unrepeatable moment is as much the meaning of strangers meeting on roads in the empty landscapes of his paintings as it is of his luminous tattered Atlantic skies. Though he was on the whole secretive about his procedures as a painter, painting 'sub rosa' with a paper rose on his doorknob to stop any intrusion, nevertheless his recorded remarks are always pithy and illuminating, as when he claimed:

> The true artist has painted the picture because he wishes to hold again for his pleasure — and for always — a moment, and because he is impelled by his human affections to pass on the moment to his fellows and to those who come after him.

It was perhaps this commitment to the integrity of the moment — joined to the recognition that his later style would be ill-served by them — which made him so opposed to the reproduction of his work where formerly he had supported it. John Berger, in a pioneering essay, claims that this did little to help Yeats's international reputation and that the painter argued 'The better they are the worse they are'. In Hilary Pyle's superb *Jack B. Yeats: A Catalogue Raisonné of the Oil Paintings*, despite the quality of the reproductions — or because of it, as Yeats might say — this problem remains. The colour plates only give clues to the bold impasto and the sidewinding nervous signature of his palette-knife, whilst the black-and-white plates are sometimes, through no fault of their own, scarcely legible.

In a later prose work, *And to You Also*, Yeats returns to this theme when considering the filming of sports events: 'The substitution of the celluloid memory of an event for a chancy, human and private memory weakens the event itself.' This 'chancy, human and private memory' is what none of Yeats's paintings is prepared to sacrifice, and 'the event itself' is precisely what they struggle to keep whole.

Yeats's marvellous sea paintings are again expressions of an unsheltered human predicament and his refusal to escape from it. As Samuel Beckett wrote in an early review:

> he brings light as only the great dare bring light to the issueless predicament of existence, reduces the dark where there might have been, mathematically at least, a door.

His *Under Bare Poles* has a two-masted ship as flimsy as cardboard dwarfed by the mass of sea, whilst *The Clown of Ocean* shows a hapless, quixotic figure armed with a punter's pole propelling his raft a mere fraction from the shore. I can't help thinking that in these paintings Yeats was looking ironically over his shoulder at Turner's imperial seascapes with their similar predilection for primary colours. In *A Storm*, the sea is a mere stroke of Prussian blue behind the man seated reading with his feet on the lustrously peach-coloured sandy path. All the painting's energy seethes and sparkles in the red flames of the fuchsia hedge behind him and is picked up again faintly but menacingly in the scumbled light-blue clouds and the red above them.

Beckett, who abstemiously refused to offer 'reassuring notes on these desperately immediate images' in his *Hommage à Jack B. Yeats* wrote that 'The artist who stakes his being comes from nowhere. And he has no brothers'. Whilst Beckett was probably defending Yeats from some folkish appropriation of his work, and doing so in French to make his point, this Yeats from '*nulle part*' is only partly recognizable. Though the adult Yeats didn't leave his Devon home until he was forty, it was his childhood stay in Sligo and his travels around the west coast of Ireland, especially the Congested Districts of West Galway and Mayo with his friend and collaborator J. M. Synge, which shaped his identity as an artist. Yeats was probably not gulling the Mayor of Sligo when, in his eighties, he told him that every painting he'd ever done had 'somewhere in it a thought of Sligo'.

Although after the mid-'20s his exhibitions were titled simply 'Paintings', the early exhibitions were nearly all titled 'Life in the West of Ireland', a name which gave way briefly to 'Paintings of Irish Life'. His concern with the Irish cultural renaissance was also deeply political, as can be seen in his pale, restrained canvas set during the time of the Civil War, *Communicating with Prisoners* (1924), which shows Kilmainham Jail in Dublin, where the republican women prisoners are waving from the windows they have broken to the women on the street. But the Yeats that Beckett was responding to is still vividly present in his paintings, and is evoked by one of the characters in his play *The Deathly Terrace*, when he declares, 'Time has no meaning to me. I am embedded in time and floating in eternity'.

James Joyce, another earlier admirer, and buyer, of Yeats's paintings, claimed that they had the same method of working, and indeed a crude but intriguing parallel can be drawn between the shift from the taut, meticulous quality of *Dubliners* to the extraordinary, untrammelled style of *Ulysses* and that of Yeats's earlier, more documentary records of Irish life and his freer later work which has cast off its moorings in the actual only to enter it more resonantly through the passage of dream and memory.

Joyce, in a famous manifesto passage, has his Stephen Dedalus speak of wanting to 'forge [...] the uncreated conscience of my race', giving a Romance-language spin to the word 'conscience' — in the sense of 'consciousness'. And Yeats was more obviously confronted with an *uncreated* consciousness in terms of the tradition of modern Irish visual arts. The consciousness he brought to this parallel task was singular in its lack of self-importance and unswerving attachment to the spur-of-the-moment and the improvisatory.

John Berger interestingly observes that Yeats 'Like Giorgione or Delacroix [...] can cast his spell even on the foreground of his pictures', a remark which Yeats himself adumbrates:

> I generally begin a painting in the distance and come away forwards and let the people walk in... I'd like to think that you are able, as I can, to stand within the picture on the ground.

Where his early illustration for that pub contest portrays him as a background observer, Yeats increasingly made use of a stand-in for himself right at the forefront of the picture, as in his glorious late painting *The Circus has Come* (1952), where the youthful figure in profile directs our gaze backwards to the faint commotion of the circus in the distance. The painting has all 'the freshness of a moment's thought', to use his brother's phrase, and all the power and longing of a retrospective glance which takes in a lifetime's commitment to the vibrant event itself.

Modern Painters, Spring 1996

— 22 —

Castile via Caledonia: Antonio Machado and Don Paterson's *The Eyes*

Don Paterson, *The Eyes* (London: Faber and Faber, 1999)

Except for one quatrain that makes a ghostly appearance after the Notes, the final poem of Don Paterson's *God's Gift to Women* is a translation of Antonio Machado's elegy for his own heteronym, Abel Martín, a poem which, now shorn of its 'in memoriam', finds a new home in his collection of Machado poems, *The Eyes*. This skilful rendering of Machado's poem must have assured Paterson of a kinship with this poet of distances and absences who prays, in Paterson's version 'To the God of absence and of aftermath': 'let us honour Him who made the Void, and carved | these few words from the thin air of our faith'. The liberty he takes in the last line which substitutes 'these few words' for the Spanish 'nuestra razón' [our reason] gives a nice self-reflexive twist to the line, even if it loses the clash and opposition of Machado's two abstractions: faith and reason.

Don Paterson's Afterword to *The Eyes* is a declaration of independence, or at least of regional autonomy, from the claims of Machado's original poems. He writes with due caution about 'being true to the 'spirit' rather than a literal meaning' and that caution is 'one more reason to plead with the reader to forget the relation in which these poems stand to the originals'. But it's unclear why he should want to efface this 'relation' when his own versions rightly remember it (although the absence of Machado's name on the book's front cover *is* forgetful, to say the least). The reader who can follow the Castilian will enjoy this subtle, lucid and often re-inventive relation as an active element of the composition. His claim that 'It should surely, by now, be axiomatic that poetry cannot be translated in a way that will preserve anything of the flavour of the original' overstates the case so boldly that it helps the reader work out why the statement is untrue. And yet his scepticism about any literal rendering has equipped him to put his own resources as a poet to work.

In 'Recuerdo infantil', Machado's opening and closing stanzas are identical except for a prepositional shift from 'tras' [across] to 'en' [on] and the additional syllable of a definite article in describing the rain on the window panes of a school classroom. Charles Tomlinson in his version of this poem translates:

> The schoolboys are at work.
> Beyond the window panes
> where day is raw and light is weak,
> monotony of winter rain.

In his last stanza 'Beyond' is rendered with 'Across' which gives a sense of small encroachment. Paterson's version is a little freer:

> A winter afternoon. The sun
> has gone in, and the class begun.
> The students settle. Steady rain
> lacerates the windowpane.

His final stanza substitutes 'lashes at the windowpane' which catches some shift in Machado's verbless sentence, although the change registers no intensification, unless the weather is being made to embody the punitive 'ancient master'. In Paterson's penultimate stanza:

> The children rise at his command
> then intone the dismal lesson:
> A hundred hundreds make a thousand.
> A thousand thousands make a million.

Machado's children are being taught a less dismal lesson — with numbers that add up: 'mil veces ciento, cien mil'. This may be an example of the 'deliberate mistranslation' that Paterson confesses to but the effect ends up (more than numerically) as a reduction.

One notable triumph here as elsewhere in the book, though, is the rhythmic poise and the rhyming which arrives so naturally as to create the illusion that only an original impulse (rather than an original poem) has had to be grappled with in the writing. The lucid ironies, perceptual intensity and philosophically explorative nature of Machado's poetry (which Paterson describes in terms of 'moral instruction') have allowed him to extend his own voice in the process. The effects are barer than in his own poems, and if less contemporary never archaic. And the subtle changes, the additions and subtractions, are often to shed or to sharpen an abstraction with specific observation, a process of coming into possession of the material, and one that in the present circumstances needs little justification. In the sonnet 'Profession of Faith' the extended conceit of the sea as an image of God opens characteristically with a negative 'God is not the sea, but of its nature', a procedure that makes God paradoxically both more visible and more invisible. The sestet turns into a prayer:

> Let that pure source
> that pours its empty heart out to us pour
> through my heart too; and let the turbid river
> of every heartless faith dry up for ever.

The movement from 'pure' to the repeated 'pour', with the subtly inverted penultimate foot in the second line quoted that makes the line-break so dramatic, is, to my taste, a distinct improvement on Machado's lines 'Que el puro rio | de caridad que fluye eternamente, | fluya en mi corazon', good as they are. Paterson's own insertion of a paradoxically 'empty' heart which is the source of that outpouring is an example of him subtly resisting the rhetoric of the image. Many another translator would have found the original images of hearts and an eternally flowing pure river unworkable, or merely roughened up the surface. What Paterson has achieved here, and in a good number of other poems, is an essential sympathy with the original which has allowed him to enter deeply into the spirit of Machado's poem whilst at the same time maintaining the independence of his own voice and cast of mind.

Times Literary Supplement, 14 January 2000

— 23 —

Rilkean Thresholds

Rainer Maria Rilke, *Diaries of a Young Poet*, trans. by Edward Snow and Michael Winkler (New York: W. W. Norton, 1998)

In the years which these three diaries cover (1898–1900), Rainer Maria Rilke, the most inward-bound of poets, travels across Europe, to Italy and Russia, and then takes up residence in Germany; but the most strenuous journeying is internal. This is especially true of the first, 'The Florence Diary', ardently addressed to Lou Andreas-Salomé, a married woman and established writer fourteen years older than the twenty-two-year-old Rilke. It's curious that so soon after the beginning of the affair she should pack him off to Florence to study Renaissance art, setting him the task of recording his experiences in a diary for her. (The introduction suggests she may have arranged for an abortion during his absence.)

Her response to the diary fell short of the rapturous one Rilke expected: he records, with insight into his own motives as well as courtly self-abasement, that he 'wanted this time to be the rich one, the giver, the host, the master, and You were supposed to come and be guided by my care and love and stroll about in my hospitality. And now in Your Presence I was again only the smallest beggar at the outermost threshold of Your Being.' Whatever else she objected to, she must have found the transparent agenda behind the following entry unwelcome: 'A woman who is an artist is no longer compelled to create once she has become a mother. She has given her goal a place outside herself and from that moment on may in the deepest sense live art.'

The diary reveals an extraordinarily precocious, but also precious mind ranging over questions of Renaissance art and using such questions to advance his own poetic credo. There is, however, more métier than matter. A kind of religiosity of art, a hushed soulful veneration often overcomes him — especially when considering his own vocation and potential. Very few passages lead one to believe that Italy is populated by anything but landscapes, architecture and works of art. But, interestingly, some of the sharpest passages interrogate religion: 'God is the oldest work of art. He is very badly maintained, and many parts are later, approximate additions.'

Lacking anything raw and inchoate, the writing translates his youthful uncertainties into vatic exhortations and polished aphorisms. His remarks about other writers are surprisingly few and indistinct. When he does descend to detail, as in his trivial judgement that Leopardi's pessimism is 'inartistic and embarrassing', you can see why he should want to take refuge in the general. Throughout these diaries his discussion of the visual arts is far more specific and passionate. Like Greek

Art for Marx, the Renaissance for Rilke represents a discontinued springtime, and he looks to his own era 'to begin the summer of this far-off and festive spring'. Seasonal imagery overabounds in these pages as an emblem of the psyche: 'If behind our sadness a shimmering springtime flickers and moves about in high clouds, then our sadness will be more heartfelt, and our feeling dons purple robes when it forms wreaths out of falling leaves...' Here Rilke's prose frequently dons purple robes, with a preference for expensive materials like silk and damask.

Although the first two diaries are addressed to Lou, they have a calculated discretion about them. For any biographical information, the reader has to refer to the translators' clear and helpful introduction and notes. In terms of his own self-presentation, hardly a hair seems out of place. In the third, 'The Worpswede Diary', a number of pages have been ripped out following the painter Paula Becker's decision to marry Otto Modersohn, an event that we can only surmise was traumatic enough for Rilke to write something heartfelt and unembroidered. However, it's part-way through the second, 'The Schmargendorf Diary', where Rilke spends his time with a group of young artists which includes Heinrich Vogeler, Paula Becker and Clara Westhoff, that the prose ceases to worship what on page after page he calls the 'festive' and becomes warmer and more vividly social. His residence at Worpswede (a small hamlet near Bremen) amongst these friends is genuinely celebratory, and he begins to rethink his whole way of looking at the world as well as at pictures: 'this way of looking was foreign to me before my intercourse with these rigorous and excellent painter-people, who get so unbelievably close to their pictures.' Clara Westhoff was soon to marry Rilke and whenever she is mentioned Rilke's writing becomes more animated. But still Rilke's main interest in people is as a route towards his inner self. One love poem from 'The Schmargendorf Diary' pays the loved one the highest compliment: 'thus in your eyes I recognized myself'.

When his friend Vogeler confides his plan to marry, Rilke records: 'In that moment a sense of infinite partaking filled me'. This sense, when combined with the patient intentness of looking out, is what will lead to his first major work in *New Poems* (1907), where poetry vies with the visual arts in its desire to trace the contours and sound out whatever meets his gaze, and to return with what defines the object as well as the quality and nature of the gazing subject — 'in our gazing lies our truest acquiring'.

Increasingly the diaries give way to the poems which will later be published in *A Book of Emblems*, as well as his poems in French and Russian. Another feature of the second diary is the presence of stories, fragments of projected works — the most impressive is an incomplete story, set within a brutal military academy which has affinities with Robert Musil's *The Young Törless*. The translation reads well, though sometimes the English struggles Germanically with Rilke's compounds: 'I want to remain in this storm and feel all the tremors of this great being-gripped' or 'The two of us shall find through the paradise of having-each-other-regained the surest way into summer', where some surer ways might have been discovered. Only once does his prose reach the intensity of his finest poems, in this description of a successful archaeologist: 'Just as a diviner listens to the ground for some secret rushing, so every shining that is cloaked in darkness reveals itself to him, and all buried pasts have become for him bell-chimes swaying at the end of shafts as in the tops of towers turned upside down.'

For all that these diaries are often chillingly high-minded, and seem attuned only to the most exquisite and rarefied emotions, and occupy almost exclusively an aesthetic milieu (the one historical event they fleetingly chronicle is the death of Bismarck), there is a sense that only with this kind of elaborate self-preparation, these gradual exercises in perception, could Rilke have found his way to writing the poems for which he will be remembered.

Independent, 15 March 1998

— 24 —

Compass and File: The Poetry of Edward Thomas

Few other lyric poets offer such an unerring sense of the poem as a means, often by indirections, to 'find directions out', as though the poem itself was a compass, or a 'path, winding like silver'. It's as if Edward Thomas's poems are endowed with the magnetite that's said to help birds navigate over long distances by day and night. Each of his poems is like a miniature quest. Some, like 'The Glory', admit defeat in their quest: 'I cannot bite the day to the core.' Yet even that ending arrives with well-earned fatigue after lines of such richness — 'And tread the pale dust pitted with small dark drops' — that they negate any sense of defeat for the reader.

A poem like his 'Beauty' seems trapped in depression until, midway, the poet sees himself as a dark river, 'while | Cross breezes cut the surface to a file' — this beautiful, characteristic line is where the poem takes light, and flight. The file, an image for surface turbulence as well as for the craft of poetry,[1] seems to secure the accelerated movement of the poem's last half — mediated, as often, by bird imagery:

> There I find my rest, as through the dusk air
> Flies what yet lives in me: Beauty is there.

The poem's movement, which begins with him framing an epitaph for himself 'Here lies...', ends with the discovered reversal 'There...flies'.

Similarly in 'Adlestrop' the almost comic pointlessness of a train stop in the middle of nowhere becomes grounded — or whatever the aerial equivalent of that would be — with birdsong:

> Close by, and round him, mistier,
> Farther and farther, all the birds
> Of Oxfordshire and Gloucestershire.

The shift from disorientation to re-orientation is done entirely through sound. ('The train hissed. Someone cleared their throat'). If it were merely a contrast between the mechanical and human (bad) and the natural and avian (good) the poem would sustain little interest. What it does though, in a visionary way, is link place names, naming and language itself to a wider order. It's this almost epic scale of Thomas's small poems which makes him so irreplaceable.

Branch-Lines: Edward Thomas and Contemporary Poetry,
ed. by Lucy Newlyn and Guy Cuthbertson (London: Enitharmon, 2007)

1 See for instance Giacomo Leopardi's 'Scherzo': 'Musa, la lima ov'è? Disse la Dea: | La lima è consumata; or facciam senza.' (Muse, where is the file? The Goddess replied: | The file is worn away, now we do without.)

— 25 —

Amadeo Modigliani

Exhibition: Tate Modern, November 2017–April 2018

As popular as Picasso's saltimbanques, prints of Modigliani's curvaceous nudes and elongated oval faces have adorned countless walls for decades, and probably few artists have suffered so much from over-familiarity, so it's hard to approach this exhibition without a slight dread that his mysterious odalisques will have lost their mystery, and left indifference in its stead. Yet seeing so much of his work in different media, in proximity, and in chronology, both defamiliarizes his art and opens up further questions about it.

This ample retrospective immediately allows the viewer a chance to perceive the rapidity and depth of Modigliani's learning. He was born in 1884 into a relatively well-off Sephardic Jewish family in Livorno, left school early, was diagnosed with tuberculosis, and began training as an artist in Florence, then continued in Venice. Paris's fame as the centre of artistic innovation drew him there in 1906 and he soon installed himself in Montmartre, then something of a bohemian village on the Parisian outskirts. There he absorbed the influences of the earlier generation of painters including Cézanne and Toulouse-Lautrec and befriended the outstanding artists and writers of his generation — among the many artists who had settled nearby, he knew Picasso, Soutine, Rivera, Brancusi (who in 1909 would find him a studio nearby his own in Montparnasse) — and, again with notable speed, he was taken up by patrons and dealers. As that abbreviated list of his associates shows — Spanish, Byelorussian, Mexican, Romanian — Paris in the first decade of the last century was what Shelley called Italy a century before, a 'heaven of exiles', and especially so for artists.

When he arrived he was already a superb draughtsman, as the earlier sketches in pencil, crayon and graphite attest. One small regal black crayon sketch from 1911, 'Woman Dressed in a Low-Cut Gown Reclining on a Bed' depicts the Russian poet Anna Akhmatova, with whom he became deeply involved. The execution is decisive but also delicate, wittily employing a dotted line to describe the prominent bridge of the poet's nose, the floral design of her gown and a long foot extending from the bedclothes. (His friend Jean Cocteau described the artist's line as 'sometimes so delicate it seems the ghost of a line' while possessing 'the alacrity of a Siamese cat'.) Apparently the affair between the poet and painter began with long walks in the Jardin du Luxembourg and was fostered by their shared devotion to Verlaine's poetry, much of which Modigliani also knew by heart. They also spent much time together in the Louvre's Egyptian gallery, a passionate enthusiasm and important stylistic influence on the artist. While Modigliani is said to be recalled in at least one of her poems ('Heart to Heart is Never Chained'), she inspired numerous sketches and her tall, elegant form can be detected in the two frontal Caryatids, one in crayon (1911), the other in oil (1913), small masterpieces which look like studies for an imagined sculpture.

One of the first mature paintings on display is 'Self-Portrait as Pierrot' (1915), which employs the traditional French motif of the melancholy clown, and already we see a characteristic feature — the asymmetric handling of the eyes. One eye has a black iris against white, the other has no white but is the same corrosive verdigris that appears on the right side of the face, mottled to suggest shadow. This peculiar kind of ocular dimorphism is a repeated trait, and declares an interest in something other than representation, as though one eye is looking out, the other in. There will be many permutations of this odd phenomenon in later paintings — sometimes one eye is cross-hatched or 'harlequinned', the other blank. Even in his stylistically singular portrait of Picasso — a flattened pumpkin-head — one black iris, twice the size of the other, seems in ascension like a dark planet. In other pictures both eyes remain blank, and in this case his faces recall sculpture, which has special difficulties in representing the eye and its gaze. 'Son regard est pareil au regard des statues' as Verlaine wrote of his dream 'femme inconnue'. The statue's gaze is a speciality and an aspiration of Modigliani's portraits.

Sculpture had been from the outset a primary ambition of his, and before leaving Italy he had worked in the studio of the sculptor Emilio Puliti in Pietrasanta, close to Carrara. Modigliani's work in this medium was confined to the years 1909 to 1914, the latter date coinciding with when the dealer Paul Guillaume began to buy his paintings, which in all likelihood influenced his decision to abandon sculpting. Apart from the higher prices commanded by painting, and the considerable cost of stone, his tuberculosis may have made him sensitive to dust, and there is evidence his health began to decline during those years. Still, the nine heads are among the finest things here displayed, especially the two in limestone, which are the highlight of the exhibition and a revelation. All seem an astonishing combination of refinement and primitivism, brilliant relics of an ancient civilization that only existed in the artist's imagination.

There is also a substantial gathering of Modigliani nudes, again famous from prints and posters. The presence of pubic hair in some was apparently sufficient cause to provoke a police commissioner to have all the nudes removed from the artist's only lifetime solo exhibition, though now they seem mild and inoffensive. One of the least interesting of these 1917 nudes is to be found on the otherwise excellent catalogue's front cover. Half turned to gaze forthrightly at the viewer over her shoulders, she floats on a spongy-textured white sheet against a brown and black background, but despite the elegant distortions and emphases, the suggestive pinkish tones of her cheeks and flesh, the picture achieves little beyond the decorative; the face especially lacks any of the expressive detail that animates his best portraits. Art has no obligation to respond to the present moment, and may have a right to resist it, but somehow the date of this painting in the midst of the war adds a further false note. Given his ill health, though, the painter's commitment to a vision of sensual pleasure could be seen as dauntless.

In an attempt to alleviate Modigliani's ill health, much worsened by absinthe, and to avoid the bombardments of Paris, his Polish dealer Léopold Zborowski — who on the painter's generous advice also supported his impoverished friend Soutine — found an apartment on the French Riviera for Modigliani and his lover (and henceforth most frequent model) Jeanne Héburterne. The change did stave off his decline for a while. From this late period, 'The Little Peasant' (*c.* 1918) is one of his finest portraits, and its subdued greys and greens, and its monumental simplicity, suggest the resumption of a fruitful dialogue with Cézanne.

Barely six months after the end of the war, at the age of thirty-five, Modigliani died of tubercular meningitis. His huge legacy centres on his unmistakeable portraits, and as this exhibition shows, his remarkable talent as a sculptor. Even the nudes remind us of how out of step the painter was with the main tendencies of his time and of the twentieth-century artists that would follow him. What distinguishes Modigliani is a restless search for images of beauty — a quality that has been so insistently devalued, and its opposite so stressed, that his amorous homages to the female form and face seem like outposts of *quattrocento* and Renaissance ideals. It makes one aware that, despite the excitement that Parisian experiment and formal disruption had for him, Italian art from Cimabue to Titian, absorbed in his teenage wanderings around the museums of Italy, had left an ineradicable trace.

Times Literary Supplement, 26 January 2018

— 26 —

Luigi Russolo: Life and Works of a Futurist

The Estorick Collection of Modern Italian Art

The painter Luigi Russolo brought his own din and dissonance to Futurism's sound and fury. The son of a cathedral organist, with two brothers who were musicians, Russolo was one of the founding members of Futurist painting, and went on to invent a series of noise machines — among them howlers, growlers, cracklers — to enliven concert halls, 'those hospitals for anaemic sounds' as he called them in his tract *L'arte dei rumori*. Just as Futurism strove, against the grain, to impose movement on static pictorial forms, Russolo constantly tried to embody music and noise on the silent canvas.

Though a self-taught artist, he closely followed the classes of friends studying at Milan's Brera Accademia, but his apprenticeship was more eclectic and included restoration work on Leonardo's *Last Supper*, commercial posters and women's fashion design. By the time he met Umberto Boccioni, a meeting which soon gave rise to Futurist art, he was already an accomplished etcher in the Symbolist tradition. One of the finest of these early etchings is 'Bat Woman', an aquatint of a vampish figure sporting bat wings which could stand comparison with the graphic work of James Ensor or Max Klinger. He gradually sheds these fin-de-siècle concerns for sombre visions of Milan's expanding industrial periphery, its factories and chimneys. A similar view appears in the window of one of several portraits of his mother sewing. Quiet, delicate, domestic, these etchings stand at the furthest remove from the masculine furore of his subsequent Futurist productions.

Although Russolo abandoned the medium in 1910 (with one known exception), his etchings deserve the prominence given to them in this exhibition, a first inclusive retrospective, expertly curated by Franco Tagliapietra and Anna Gasparotto. For, despite his application of Divisionist theories, colour was never his forte, and it's no coincidence that his most impressive paintings are those in which a restricted palette means that less can go wrong. His famous canvas 'Solidity of Fog' (1912–13) is composed entirely in blues. The streetlamp sets off gradually darkening concentric circles which invert their contours as they ripple through the dark blue figures in the street. The effect is as much liquid as solid, as though light has been filtered through a dense medium, or turned into muffled waves of sound.

Russolo uses this motif of blue concentric circles in several canvases, notably in his early Futurist work, *La Musica* (1911), where it again forms the percussive, organizing principle of the composition, here overlaid with a darker blue serpentine shape that twists up from the shadowy pianist in the foreground through an opened fan of scarlet, green and yellow masks. The colours lurch and jolt — the whole effect as garish and giddy as a fairground Waltzer.

Alongside other Futurists and his friend Boccioni (killed in 1916), Russolo fought in the First World War in the Volunteer Cyclist and Automobilist Battalion, and suffered from a head wound which entailed a long convalescence. In the aftermath of the war he worked on his invented instruments and performed concerts in Paris and elsewhere. His conception of noise as an integral part of modern music has been credited as an influence on electronic music and on composers such as John Cage, and his acoustic work was used by two French avant-garde filmmakers, Jean Painlevé and Eugène Deslaw. Another artist intrigued by synaesthesia, Kandinsky, took note of Russolo's ideas of sound and noise in his Bauhaus classes.

During the twenties he maintained his contact with Futurism's leader Tomasso Marinetti and was briefly drawn into the orbit of Margherita Sarfatti, the influential art critic and mistress of Mussolini. He exhibited with a new wave of Futurist painters such as Sironi, but unlike the latter drew away from a commitment to Italian Fascism, and spent time in Paris (1928–32) and in Tarragona (1932–33). His letters from Spain attest to a growing disenchantment with politics, speaking of the unbreathable air of Italy, 'too poisoned by politics, rhetoric, nationalism and war.' The only notable canvas from this decade is his 1926 'Impressions of a Bombardment Shrapnel and Grenades'. Even if this can't be placed beside the great pictures of the First World War like Paul Nash's 'Menin Road', it still carries an original and haunting recreation of noise transcribed into geometrical forms: three bright red crescents intercut by blue and white wedge-shaped shrapnel bursts.

Russolo's last years in Cerro di Laveno, until his death in 1947, were dedicated to the study of psychic phenomena, occultism, yoga, acupuncture, magnetism and ethereal bodies. The author of the 1920 manifesto 'Against all Returns in Painting' returned, however, to painting, in a style he called 'classico-moderno': mainly placid vesperal landscapes, amongst which are homages to Bach and Beethoven. The latter landscape is divided into three weather zones, or *tempi* — *agitato, adagio andante* and *allegro finale* — all overseen by the composer's marble-like head set in the storm clouds. In these late paintings which continue to celebrate Russolo's involvement with music, the ex-Futurist has finally become both pastoral and pastist.

Times Literary Supplement, 1 December 2006

— 27 —

Kurt Schwitters: Merzfest

A poster by the Seine announcing 'Enfin à Paris — Kurt Schwitters' showed the artist's impish, burgherly face in the act of performing his phonetic poem *Ursonata*. On the fifth floor of the Beaubourg's Perspex galleon, you could hear a recording of this poem — a baleful stuttering like an elocution lesson for porpoises:

Tata tata tui E tui E
tata tata tui E tui E...

Whatever the evidence, I'm willing to believe Hans Richter's epic account of how Schwitters would triumph over the 'orgy of laughter' that his recitations provoked in the public:

> But all that was no match for Kurt. He did not stop his *Ursonata* a second. He just raised his trained, enormous voice, till it dominated the hurricane, which blended with his well-articulated sounds, as the sea might have counterpointed Demosthenes' words two thousand years ago on the Aegean seashore.

Poetry was only one among many forms which Schwitters's artistic quest assumed: 'the pursuit of diverse forms was an artistic necessity for me', he claimed. 'The reason for it was not any desire to expand the field of my activities, but to be an artist.' For him, the role of artist excluded the possibility of guarded frontiers between the various arts: what he sought were the laws that would unify his work in a type of *Gesamtkunstwerk*, a total artwork.

This is not to say that his excursions into collage, assemblage, sculpture, typography, poetry, graphic design, industrial draughtsmanship, architecture, theatre, performance, landscape painting, portraiture, photography, magazine design, editorship and so on were all of equal success and importance, but that these activities were essential to the all-embracing cultural regeneration Schwitters envisaged. He made each different activity feed into, enrich, and reinforce the others. His poetry, for example, in its use of overheard scraps counterpointed with other assembled verbal elements, including non-sense, anticipated and laid the foundations for the finer work he was to achieve in collage.

The first room of the exhibition shows a tentative, conservative eclecticism — drab expressionist canvases suddenly chancing on the edge of a medium or, better, an atmosphere which he was to make his own. The nonsense and rubber-stamp drawings of 1918, with their childlike pastel shades and open spaces begin to incorporate lettering. It is this non-denotative lettering (like the phonemes of *Ursonata*, banished from any feasible context) which brings the pictures alive: the letters make diagonal compositional lines, or circles which are drawn on to form cogwheels. Suddenly the spaces are filled with infinitesimal activity, part whimsy, part machine.

Within a year of these preliminary studies, Merz had been born and Schwitters had launched himself unstoppably into twentieth-century art. As he was later to boast with his inimitable chutzpah: 'I know I am an important factor in the evolution of art and that I will always remain important. I say this in the clearest manner so no one later will claim "The poor man didn't even know how important he was".'

Richard Huelsenbeck, who blocked Schwitters's attempt to join the Berlin Dadaists, referred to him as a petty-bourgeois sentimentalist committed to a vision of art that had no room for political activism: 'the abstract Spitzweg, the Kasper David Friedrich of the Dada revolution'. He seems, however, to have been far more like a kind of Good Civilian Schwejk, preserving himself, as he said, 'for the fatherland and the history of art by bravery behind the lines' by wangling his exemption from active service in the First World War through a mixture of ill-health and bribery. Besides his rejection by Dadaism was possibly a mercy in disguise. Dadaism was to be declared dead by both Breton and Tzara in 1922, and anyway Schwitters was free to collaborate with and learn from those Dadaists like Raoul Hausmann and Hans Arp, with whom he felt a marked artistic affinity. And it fuelled him with the energy to found his own movement — MERZ. Another four-letter word thumbing its nose at Dada, Merz was, as Michael Hofmann puts it in his haunting poem 'Kurt Schwitters in Lakeland', 'withdrawn from *Kommerz- und Privatbank*' — as if it were a suffix that would now become an all-purpose prefix: *Merzbild*, *Merzzeichnung*, *Merzbau*, *Merzbühne*, to cover Schwitters's plethora of projects. Adjective, verb and noun of undecided gender, it is as polyvalent as its creator.

Schwitters's remark about poetry — 'words are torn from their former context, dissociated and brought into a new artistic context, they become formal parts of the poem, nothing more' — are a key to his procedure in every artistic field. The same aesthetic of dissociation is a consistent and continuous discovery of his work in whatever medium, and helps explain his absolute mastery of collage and relief assemblage, which he designated respectively *Merzzeichnung* (Merz-sketch) and *Merzbild* (Merz-picture).

There is really nothing in twentieth-century art like Schwitters's joyful discovery of collage in the early years of the '20s. The form seems to have been invented especially for his manipulation, for his minute sensitivity to colour, shape and texture. The effect of the smallest quantities — print-size, lettering font, numerals, the ribbing of cardboard, torn or cut edges, overlaps and underlays, and so on — all seem to be exactly weighed against each other without in any way reducing the atmosphere of tenderness, humour and spontaneity. Werner Schmalenbach, in his pioneering study of the artist, now unreasonably out of print, responds movingly (despite a slightly weird translation) to the intricate constructions and rhythms of these collages:

> The stimulus, the inspiration that life sent him emanated from the pieces of paper. But he must have been 'an inspired one' intrinsically to be capable of being touched by these faint voices...

Collage was 'invented' in 1912 in the great experiments conducted by Braque and Picasso in Auvergne and Céret. It opened the illusionistic box of tricks, but as a painterly adjunct — newsprint and chair-cane representing themselves. The discovery rapidly spread beyond the visual arts. T. S. Eliot's *The Waste Land* (1922) employs a collage technique of juxtaposing and offsetting scraps of pub conversations with excerpts from Buddhist scripture and sawn-off quotes from famous works of literature. The apocalyptic end to which he gathered this material is suggested in the line: 'These fragments I have shored against my ruin'. Schwitters had an altogether less gloomy end in view. While the destruction of the Great War gave a special meaning to the concept of fragments, Schwitters's use of the torn and discarded is not marked so much by the sense of loss as by that of the happy find. His Merz is delightfully free of *Weltschmerz*. Collage itself was an art of poverty, given the expense and scarcity of artist's materials in the wake of the war, but Schwitters embraces this poverty as if it were a treasure trove.

Schwitters generally renounces the illusionistic potential of the medium, instead exploring the abstract drama of the surface and admitting a far more vivid palette than Analytical Cubism allowed. *MZ 601*, for example, includes a ticket for a Manet exhibition at the top of a triangle, or rather a ziggurat of rectangles, which ends in a hemispherical postmark on the right, and among the other fragments are a Dutch tram ticket, a cloakroom ticket, squared notepaper and graph paper. The organization is straightforwardly along vertical and horizontal axes. The dot after the numerals 23 is just off-centre, a black circle around which this delicate construction of squares and rectangles arranges itself. There is a used-up, urban feel to the material; the one natural form, centre right, is a leaf skeleton like some wormed or foxed paper, more something crushed on a pavement than pressed within a nature album. While the colours are subdued buffs, beiges and grey-greens, the red squares and the black are able to dominate, creating the two triangles, one inverted, which subtly balance the picture. It's worth noting the tiny square of cerulean, a typically lyrical touch, as well as the spiky rhythm and slant given by the handwriting. But even an exhaustive analysis of its elements would be far from accounting for the beauty of the collage. The form itself, made out of scraps which draw attention to their separate provenances, is one in which their separateness must be made into a new whole — something more than the sum total of its parts, and it was Schwitters's gift to have such a responsiveness to both the personality of each composite part and a sense of their potential to be transformed, or 'Merz-ed'.

Schwitters claims that all the materials used in his works were on 'an equal footing' and, disregarding Huelsenbeck, I don't think it's wrong to deduce a political engagement underlying his aestheticism. The democracy of elements redeems and frees scraps, labels, tickets, wrappers and packaging from the life of drudgery which consumerism had consigned them to. Although Schwitters in his theoretical writings insisted on the non-referentiality of the pictorial elements —

'a consistent work of art can never refer to anything outside of itself without loosening its ties to art' — this self-contained status is both contravened by his practice and by the medium itself. In *Mai 191* the collage is reminiscent of a wall covered by torn posters, the gothic script making fragmentary reference to the electrical and metal workers' strike in the Bavarian Soviet, brutally suppressed on 1 May 1919. In this case the torn elements enact, like the final *9* lost from the date, the violent truncation of what occurred. The three primary colours have a worn, elegiac tone — referring perhaps to the black, yellow and red flag of the Soviet established in 1918 — which suggest the artist's sympathy for the strikers.

For an artist who declared art's independence from politics so forcefully, Schwitters's own artistic life suffered constant and severe disruptions from politics. His work was vilified by the Nazis and he lost his graphic design job for Hanover Council. He finally fled Germany in 1937, leaving his beloved *Merzbau*, a construction built into his house, for Norway, where he lived until the German invasion in 1940. Another flight through northern Norway took Schwitters eventually to Britain, where he was interned for seventeen months, mainly on the Isle of Man. Subsequently he lived in Ambleside until his death in 1948. Hanover, Lysaker and Ambleside are the three sites where he undertook his *Merzbau* architectural constructions. Waldhausenstrasse 5, Hanover, in which the living space had been cannibalized by the strange process of cave-making, enclosure and accretion, so that the 'Cathedral of Erotic Misery' grew like a column through the bedroom floor, was destroyed in an Allied bombing raid in 1943. Schmalenbach writes of it as unique, 'an unparalleled example of the irrational shaping of space, all the more striking because the stylistic means employed were those of rational Constructivism'. The *Merzbau* in Norway was destroyed by fire in 1951, and the Ambleside project was left unfinished at his death. In the middle of the Pompidou exhibition there is a plaster reproduction of the initial *Merzbau*, its space faceted by geometric stalagmites, and yet the effect is somewhat hygienic, its aura evacuated. What made the original so bizarre, with its fetishistic grottoes, dedicated to various friends, enshrining a bottle of urine, a stolen key, strands of hair etc., has now been lost forever. Though these losses are irreparable, there is something about the whole *Merzbau* enterprise that was always work in progress, always destined to be uncompletable. Indeed all of Schwitters's best work has this ongoing freshness and experimental lack of closure. John Elderfield refers perceptively to his collages in terms of an 'almost diaristic method, forming the materials that surrounded him into miniature epistles of everyday experience'. The larger-scale relief assemblages as well as the collages speak of his tireless foraging among the detritus of his time. These creations vary from urban to rural to maritime in the forms and materials they reflect and salvage, as contemporary history dictated his whereabouts, but continue to show the way he transformed anti-art into art. This wonderful Parisian *Merzfest* fully justifies the second part of Schwitters's statement: 'I prefer to distance myself from contemporary events [...] But I am more deeply rooted in my time than the politicians who hover over the decade'.

Modern Painters, Spring 1995

— 28 —

War Paint: C. R. W. Nevinson

Michael J. K. Walsh, *C. R. W. Nevinson: This Cult of Violence* (New Haven, CT: Yale University Press, 2002)

C. R. W. Nevinson was an unlikely English outpost of Italian Futurism. Famously he beat the big drum in a backroom for one of F. T. Marinetti's cacophonous recitations at the Dorée Gallery during the Italian's 1914 London tour. Nevinson's temperament is summed up poignantly in his letter to Dora Carrington, with whom, alongside of his friend Mark Gertler, he was involved in an evidently galling, three-sided relationship: '& why is a crowd always happy & individuals always unhappy'. He was drawn to the noise and group-identity of Futurism, but his own insecurities often pushed him to the edge of the collectivities to which he strove to belong.

In his own words 'I, who was born for Oxford and the army in a hotbed of intellectualism, religion and the classics, found refreshment in ugliness and the uncouth'. The titles of some of his early, lost works — 'Gasometers', 'Carting Manure' and 'Cement Works' — testify to a robust dislike of the picturesque and sound a note of challenge. The challenge proved less radical and thoroughgoing than it promised to be. In an early draft of *The Waste Land*, 'the young man carbuncular' in the Café Royal, 'London's only café', tells the secretary he wishes to impress 'with a casual air | Grandly, I have been with Nevinson today', but in the final version, after Pound's editorial lacerations, all that remains is the 'silk hat on a Bradford millionaire'. For a time during the First World War he was one of the best-known living artists in England. In a recent book on Futurism, he merits only two brief mentions.

His father was a renowned reformer and political agitator and (although this remains unacknowledged in Nevinson's autobiography, *Paint and Prejudice*) used many of these skills in tirelessly promoting his son's work. On the eve of the Battle of the Somme, Michael J. K. Walsh tells us, he was dining with Sir Ian Hamilton, veteran of Gallipoli, securing the old soldier's consent to write a catalogue introduction for what was to be his son's most successful exhibition. Nevinson's parents' enthusiasm for Futurism seems to have preceded his own and their artistic, social and even military contacts underwrote his career. The artistic rebel was guaranteed an unusual degree of establishment interest and patronage.

The early paintings which survive have a wavering promise and offer a kind of Camden School Impressionism — 'The Towing Path' (1912), for example, sentimentally offsets the menace of its towering factories by foregrounding an embracing couple. His trips to Paris, miserable according to his letters and glittering in his autobiography, were stylistically inconclusive, but his meeting with the Futurist Severini was to prove decisive. He adhered to this movement with tenacity and fell under the spell of Marinetti, to the extent of co-authoring with him an English Futurist Manifesto called 'Vital English Art'. This was to prove the occasion of his falling out with a group of avant-garde artists including Wyndham Lewis, Gaudier-Brzeska, Epstein and Bomberg, some of whom he had generously named as the leading spirits of the age. Several of them used this pretext to distinguish their own movement, Vorticism, from Italian Futurism, and Lewis especially, despite his earlier enthusiasm, seemed to resent playing second fiddle to 'wops', given that the English, in his account, had been the inventors of machines and didn't need to be instructed how to live with them. Nevinson was spurned by the artists with whom he had hoped to join forces.

To his partial credit, Nevinson never aped Marinetti's crass and criminal glorification of war ('War is the hygiene of the nations') nor was this included in the English manifesto. When war was declared he showed no eagerness to enlist, and with the help of his father and his own ailments — pericarditis, rheumatic fever and a limp — he eventually joined the Friend's Ambulance Unit, achieving the uniquely contradictory status of Quaker Futurist. But even this brief spell of six weeks at the Front, as lorry driver and nurse, would have shown him how hideously unhygienic war could be; his autobiography comments:

> I had seen sights so revolting that man seldom conceives them in his mind, and there was no shrinking even among the most sensitive of us. We could only help, and ignore shrieks, pus, gangrene and the disembowelled.

His harrowed, sepulchral canvas 'La Patrie', painted in 1916, showing rows of the dying in an improvised field hospital, is a testimony to this experience. Nevertheless, no sooner had he returned to London than, striking the vainglorious Futurist note, he declared to the press:

> All artists should go to the front to strengthen their art by a worship of physical and moral courage and a fearless desire of adventure, risk and daring and free themselves from the canker of professors, archeologists, cicerones, antiquaries and beauty worshippers.

This list of enemies is parroted almost verbatim from a 1913 Marinetti declaration. In another article he distances himself from his Italian friends by saying that 'I do not glory in war for its own sake, nor can I accept their doctrine that war is the only health-giver'. War, then, is only one of several salubrious things. This partial volte-face was gleefully mocked by Lewis in *Blast 2*. (Incidentally, Nevinson claimed to have supplied Lewis with the name of his magazine.)

Walsh offers the reader a rich selection of contemporary verdicts on, and subsequent discussions of, Nevinson's work in an attempt to account for the way this artist whose pre-war work had been treated as madcap antics gradually found himself in the position of respected war artist. What happens is that an adapted Futurist technique, a chromatically challenged, khaki-and-mud palette, simplifications of form and broken, interlocking planes, provides Nevinson with an effective illustrative medium. The air of technical radicalism, the brutal, mechanized anonymity of the marching French Infantry in 'Returning to the Trenches' or of the wounded in 'La Patrie' dispenses with a heroic tradition of war painting and achieves a workable fusion of modernist technique and descriptive intent. Renouncing Futurism's engagement with speed and movement, and its multi-perspectivism, Nevinson's paintings of the war years are, with a few exceptions such as 'Bursting Shell', notably static. Walsh seems undecided whether Nevinson's manoeuvres — half-retaining, half-abandoning Futurism — are a kind of 'balance, or compromise', but the unwitting effect of his descriptions is to lend weight to the negative connotations of the second term.

In general, Walsh's advocacy of Nevinson's work seems to furnish the case for the prosecution. His defence of the war paintings can be something of a liability, as when he argues 'In the light of the ensuing "rappel à l'ordre", on a European-wide basis, the moderate shift to the right is neither surprising nor dubious'. Surprising it may not be but the 'rappel à l'ordre' is more than dubious. It might have been worth a closer look at the Italian Futurists whose own 'richiamo all'ordine' led many of them to accommodate themselves eagerly within the Fascist regime and took some painters, such as Soffici and Sironi, as far as its sinister dénouement in Salò.

Nevinson's accommodations have none of this quality, but they certainly leave an impression of opportunism which hasn't escaped Walsh's commentary: in 1916 'with time to concentrate on his work, Richard could identify and cater for the critical tastes of the era'. The commercial tone of the phrase 'cater for' haunts innumerable passages throughout the book — 'his military credentials fresh and as up to date as any artist living in Britain, to say nothing of his patriotic stock rising in value too'. Walsh's collusive language oddly highlights something more than distasteful about Nevinson 'cashing in' on his brief spell as a non-combatant in the gory context of the Western Front. 'It was precisely the time to make the most of any military credentials available', Walsh comments, and briefly you wonder if he is being bitterly ironic rather than admiring. In the end this way of writing reduces artistic endeavour to a series of shrewd career moves and erodes any sense of the war paintings as either powerful witness or as formal development, or both. I suspect Walsh is right that in Nevinson's case there is a fair degree of 'catering' going on, but it's odd that in a book apparently intended to rescue the painter from his declined reputation that a more vigorous, and less mediated, defence isn't offered. Even Walsh's quotations from Nevinson's autobiography stress his careerism and strident self-promotion rather than the warmer side of his character which can be found there — for instance, his generosity to other painters such as Gertler (whom he continues to revere even after the latter brusquely dropped him) and his dead friend Modigliani (whom he describes with vivid affection).

It's not surprising that in the context of war the message prevails over the medium, and that an artist like Nevinson should tailor his vanguardist leanings towards a more illustrative aesthetic. Even if this won for him the opprobrium of a critic like Pound (who recommended he 'leave off trying to please everyone at once') some of his First World War canvases have a force that is more than merely documentary. His dreary mud-coloured paintings, with their ominous, mechanical-looking soldiers, such as 'La Mitrailleuse' remain powerful. In this modern Golgotha, if the barbed wire above the three soldiers forms a kind of crown of thorns, and the wooden stanchions in the foreground suggest a cross motif, the effect is achieved without over-insistence. Even the limitations of his colour sense are turned to impressive effect in war paintings such as 'Shell Holes' (1917) where the silvered, tan puddles and slag-grey craters evoke a poisoned monotony. Oddly the height of his fame as a war artist coincided with the beginning of the decline of his talent. Even his influential backers noticed a failure of nerve. Walsh understandably excludes the paintings after 1920 from consideration, although it might have been useful to see how his style faltered and fell apart. The cartoonish file of wounded and stretcher-borne troops in 'Harvest of Battle' (1919) as an example seems already to have lost sight of the structural rigour that made his earlier war paintings memorable.

Times Literary Supplement, 4 April 2003

— 29 —

Paul Nash: Modern Artist, Ancient Landscape

Exhibition: Tate, Liverpool, July–October 2003

A late watercolour by Paul Nash called 'Landscape of Ancient Country' must have prompted the exhibition's title. An instant poetic reflex is built into that word 'ancient'. It evokes Coleridge's Mariner and Blake's 'Jerusalem': 'And did those feet in ancient time | Walk upon England's mountains green?' This poem, much favoured as a hymn for weddings and funerals, through no fault of Blake's, has become the trigger for a bracing, slightly weepy atavism. Yes, we want to reply, it was right here on the village green that those thundering feet went by, causing acorns to fall and sprout into mighty oaks which shade the beasts of the field and the fowls of the air. Apart from those synecdochic feet, for the human figure is pretty well absent, these associations — Blake, Englishness, pleasant greens, small birds, big trees, most especially the trees — are seminal to Nash's art. He was much exercised as a painter in how to reconcile this ancient Englishness with the art movements of European modernity. In one 1932 article, he asks 'whether it is possible to "go modern" and still "be British"'. (Even to frame such a question would suggest a negative response.)

His own answer to this question is wavering and intermittent. He will often regroup into a Palmerish landscapism after forays into Surrealism or Abstraction. He feels an obligation to come to terms with the alien and progressive whilst being drawn back to the familiar and the conservative. It may be for this reason that, left to his own devices, his art has a tendency to stagnate. It's when he is not left but has his devices intruded upon, as was the case in the First World War and also in the Second, that his most magnificent pictures come into being.

Although this generous exhibition devotes a whole room to World War I, there are many crucial paintings of that period missing (but at least available as postcards downstairs) such as 'Void', 'The Mule Track' (both 1918) and 'A Night Bombardment' (1919–20). But 'The Menin Road' (1919), which dominates this room, makes up for a lot of omissions. It would hardly be worth saying how much greater this painting is in the flesh than in any reproduction, in its scale and peculiar delicacy of colour, if the opposite wasn't sometimes the case with Nash. (With some guilt I have to admit to disappointment at finally seeing his 'Battle of Britain, August–October 1940'). 'The Menin Road', to use Nash's antithesis, is neither British nor Modern, at least neither in any significant proportions, but epically his own work and subsequently one of the inescapable images of human history.

To my mind, nothing in the rich archive of visual art from World War I touches its bare *and* cluttered, devastated majesty — neither Nevinson's effective, muddy witnessing, nor the Italian Futurists' festive and fragmented images.

The two pairs of dwarfed figures in the middle ground and the distance are badly painted and look like toppling toy soldiers — so much for the Slade's focus on figure drawing. But that doesn't seem to matter. As always with Nash, the trees are the real human figures and the ultimate barometers of something easeful or amiss in the human sphere. And here the trees, that compose the middle-ground and the right distance, are splintered columns. The only green they carry is a sickly green on their left flanks which should have been where the light fell. The foreground and the sky which they imperfectly join are what dramatize the canvas. The sky is riven with searchlights and disrupted by the luxuriant foliage of two explosions. The foreground is silvery-green deadwater in which float the reflection of the stumps as well as a German helmet and a red ration tin. Crimson weeds grow on the mud islets. Loops of blood-red wire and salmon-coloured corrugated iron mimic a listless, otherworldly vegetation. The metallic greens, tans, pinks and yellows of the foreground have a boldness and confidence unprecedented in any of his pre-war work. In fact little that Nash did before the war (the exhibition's first room) would make you sure the man was an artist at all. The admittedly precocious Nevinson, born the year after Nash, had already painted 'The Towing Path, Camden' in 1912 and within a year would be starting to grapple with Futurism when Nash was content to paint 'Vision at Evening' — an undistinguished landscape with a Pre-Raphaelitic woman's face peeping from the clouds. Another case perhaps of Nash 'going Ancient' at an early age is a more unusual, and more intense scene from 1912 of the pyramids engulfed in stormy waves. A painting of Wittenham Clumps signals an Oxfordshire subject he will return to again and again but nothing anticipates the force of 'The Menin Road' — a painting that describes an apocalyptic wound in nature and in consciousness.

That the wound was also internal became clear when he was diagnosed as suffering from 'war strain' after falling into a five-day unconsciousness. His recovery was slow and took place in Dymchurch, Kent, the site of many fine, bleak drawings, engravings (Nash became an exceptional engraver and illustrator), lithographs and paintings, culminating in his masterpiece 'The Shore' (1923). Its colours are less than promising — sandy beige, orange, two shades of blue and an unappetizing lilac for sky, sea and land. Its structure is bare and notional — some sketched breakwaters and a black-and-white concrete groyne; the horizon has a hint of rondure. But the whole thing works miraculously, with an air of endurance, frailty and convalescence that one can sense without knowing anything of Nash's condition. Perhaps we see in the concrete structure the shape of a bird's head and outspread wings or that of an aeroplane, but it's more likely that the picture has its power from the starkness of its components and its eerie, restrained, inward quality.

The next decade is not a good one for his painting. He and his wife, Margaret, move to Iden, where he paints, and tends, his garden. One spectacularly, and for that reason almost likeably, bad garden painting from this period is 'Landscape at Iden' (1929). It has a sinister, folkloric woodpile and on either side an out-of-place, ancestral wicker-fence and what looks like a propped reed-screen. Behind is a sterile, enclosed orchard of leafless apple trees and a high horizon of English hills capped with banal meringuish clouds — a sort of sad idyll, part-de Chirico, part-Garden Centre display. Perhaps with Nash, it's a question of trusting the trees not the teller: and so this neat pile of chopped wood is not to be read as a homely, Heideggerian metaphor of dwelling but as an image of nature as *mutilé de guerre*. And yet it's hard to believe this is the work of the same painter who created 'The Menin Road' or even 'The Shore'.

The following decade, the Thirties, in which he struggles to incorporate Surrealist and Abstract tendencies into his work, is not much better, but at least it's more engaging. Despite worsening health — he suffered from severe bronchial asthma — it is a time of engagement in the art world. With Moore, Hepworth, Wadsworth, Nicholson and others he founds Unit One to promote modernism in the visual arts. The spirit of de Chirico, alongside other strands of Surrealism, enters his work with a vengeance. There's none of the joyful embrace of this imagery and the freedom of invention that can be found in the paintings of Eileen Agar, an unjustly neglected painter with whom he had an affair. With Nash the conventions seem imposed from without, as he puts on display the meshes of internal scaffolding. Perhaps the most compelling work of this period is 'Harbour' — a queerly spliced and tilted interior/exterior. The interior of ox-blood striped Georgian wallpaper and marble fireplace is split open by the enclosed harbour waters — it profits from its situation in the Liverpool Tate where the view from the window grandly extends the scene.

The mid- to late Thirties also saw Nash employed by Shell in a campaign to promote Britain's landmarks and motoring as a leisure pursuit. Though Nash himself never had a car, it coincided with his growing obsession with megaliths, menhirs, and planet-like spheres parked on ancient landscapes. 'Event on the Downs' (1934) has a monolithic blasted oak weighed next to a huge tennis ball whose yin-yang, isotropic seam is reworked as a split track over the next knoll. The background is a chalk cliff national monument brooded over by a chalky-looking cloud. The effect is paradoxically static and precipitant.

At the onset of the Second World War, Nash was for the second time commissioned as a war artist. Whilst Nash's famous 'Battle of Britain' and his more abstract 'Battle of Germany' are both impressive paintings, neither so productively embodies the tensions of his whole artistic career as does his 'Totes Meer' (1940–41).

This painting occurs in the unlikely setting of Oxford: the Cowley dump for shot-down German aircraft. A dead sea of ripped aluminium and shattered wings under a seamed half-moon employs much of the imagery of his Surrealist ventures but with superb pictorial means and absolute conviction. The way, for example, the moon's circle is picked up by the blue circle of the plane's wheel creates a strange planetary or gravitational axis in the picture. He employs the same doubling in 'Pillar and Moon' (1932–42): there the Cotswold stone sphere atop the pillar is exactly the same dimension as, and mirrors, the moon. Though this picture has a haunting quality the double disc effect seems a coincidence, a painterly device. In 'Totes Meer' the dynamic triangles combine to make the wheel and the moon, the flying and the finally grounded, the natural and the mechanical, into acrid antagonists and strange allies. The Surrealist tropes of the last decade have finally found a place of residence where there is nothing forced about their idiom, where the nightmare of history has broken in on them with its own imperatives, and Nash was ready to record them.

Modern Painters, Autumn 2003

— 30 —

Stuart Davis: Reality's Ouch

Taking a jab at Abstract Expressionism, Stuart Davis wrote of his 1951 painting *Owh! in San Pao:* 'It has been scientifically established that the acoustics of Idealism give off the Human Sounds of Snoring, whereas Reality always says "Ouch"'. The Owh and Ouch of his brash, abrasive colours, and of the jarring, strewn-about elements of his geometry have kept the sound of snoring safely at bay throughout his long career as a painter. This splendidly curated exhibition (which I saw at the Peggy Guggenheim Collection in Venice), the first European retrospective of his paintings, has assembled Davis's work from his earliest canvases in the Ashcan School idiom, and from the first impact of Cubism on that style through four decades of confident excursion, to the dazzling, culminating abstracts of the early '60s. His work profits greatly from being seen in force, and chronologically, as the strands and intersections of his development both reinforce each other and reveal the range of his achievement.

Davis not only overlapped themes, structures and words in paintings which were made concurrently ('diads'), but also to a dramatic degree reworked images from his own art, sometimes over a period of decades. His basic egalitarian ethos regarding subject matter legitimized the use of commercial wrappers, labels, billboards, household utensils, shopfronts, and, by extension, the recycling of the forms within his own paintings, as can be seen for example in the semi-abstracted *Percolator oi* (1927), which reappears structurally unchanged though jazzily heightened in colour and with the addition of words in *Owh! in San Pao* 24 years later. The premise that essentially nothing is unacceptable as material for the painting, so long as it comes from the surrounding environment, obviously also includes his own paintings which have entered that environment. It was also Davis's nature to be reflective about his work as well as self-reflexive, and reabsorbing the structures of his own painting was a natural opportunity to explore and extend the frontiers of his art.

There are certainly lulls and dissatisfactions to be met with. The series of canvases, for example, set in Paris during the late '20s have a thin, decorative, Dufy-like quality, as though the creative air of the artistic capital had reached him pre-digested in the manner of London tap water. Léger, on an exchange of studio visits, found them 'too realistic', but to Davis's delight commended his earlier, crucial 'Egg Beater' series, abstracts grounded in the everyday, whose geometry has assumed a life of its own. It's odd that this self-confessed exile in the 'American Art Desert' should so deeply need the urban air of America to fire his imagination. Karen Wilkins begins her perceptive catalogue essay with the claim that Davis is a 'homegrown Cubist whose irreverent paintings resemble no one else's'. His early works do markedly resemble the paintings he saw at the Armory Show in 1913, displaying an initial predilection for Expressionism — van Gogh, even Munch — then proceed, as though in an accelerated learning curve through Cubism to Léger's tubular forms and Matisse's cut-outs. And yet by 1921, he was already producing work which was undeniably his own.

The so-called 'Tobacco Still Lifes' of that year, including his famous canvas *Lucky Strike,* live up entirely to the latter title, representing one of the most fortuitous moments in his career, where he chances on a manner and subject way in advance of his own artistic certainties, as subsequent movements in his work expose his retreat from this radical and innovatory series which, with its emblazoning of brand names, predates Warhol's *Campbell's Soup Cans* by some forty years. Throughout his life as an artist and heavy smoker, tobacco brand names, cigarette packets, cigar adverts, etc. have a talismanic presence in his work, but never more centrally than in this 1921 series. Frontally addressed, these oil paintings on canvas give the impression of collages, though on an exaggerated scale. The strong colour contrasts of *Lucky Strike,* the complementary red and green stripes broken by waves and circles to which the lettering conforms, have a dense rhythmic unity, and yet we simultaneously recognize the flattened packet become strangely and serendipitously monumental.

In the year following this series, Davis doubles back as if unsure of the underlying premises of his own lucky strike, and produces crude apprentice work in the manner of Synthetic Cubism, some ill-carpentered versions of Braque's *guéridons.* It seems as though he was as yet unsure that he could give himself the go-ahead without securing the pictorial lessons of the European masters. And yet these experiments lead to the bold, black-outlined, bright-coloured still lifes of 1923 and 1924, of utensils and light bulbs which look remarkably like Patrick Caulfield's canvases of the 1960s. These mundane household objects culminate in a repellent masterpiece, *Odol*, which depicts a product for oral hygiene ('It Purifies'), perhaps the remedy for a smoking habit and the Tobacco series. Framed by black and purple, the Odol flask with its squatly sloping top and nozzle is a mass-produced odalisque transposed from the Turkish bath to an all-American bathroom — or so we guess from the neat background of chequered white and green tiles and a slanted cube of lines (white against purple, black against white) which represents either a medicine cabinet or the bevelled edges of a bathroom mirror. Never again would Davis be quite so uninhibitedly full-frontal in his approach to the picture-plane or so joyfully vulgar in his colour scheme.

This, like many other Davis paintings which feature labels and brand logotypes, raises the obvious but still perplexing question of what exactly the artist's relation was to the machine-age products his art is celebrating. Almost forty years on, Davis took little pleasure in being seen as a precursor to Pop Art's deadpan reproductions of the industrially produced, insisting that his procedure and aims were entirely different. Is there in Davis a provocation which conflates high art and commercial design or is he asserting a belief that any subject is equally interesting (or for that matter equally boring) from an artist's standpoint? As a painter steeped in Marxist theory, and committed as an activist during the Depression, Davis undoubtedly felt these were questions that mattered:

> An art of real order in the material of paint doesn't say 'Workers of the World Unite', it doesn't say 'Pasteur's theory has many beneficial results for the human race' and it doesn't say 'Buy Camel cigarettes'. It merely says 'Look, here is a unique configuration in colour-space'.

Davis's *Visa* (1951) perhaps pushes his interest in brand names and his lifelong obsession with lettering to the furthest point. It reworks a canvas of the previous year called *Little Giant Still Life* which consists almost entirely of the word CHAMPION taken from a matchbook (smoking again) which advertises spark plugs. (There may be a buried allusion here to Picabia's '*Portrait d'une jeune fille américaine*' as spark plug, just as in the 'Egg Beater' series there is a possible reference to Man Ray's *L'Homme* (1919) figured as an egg beater.) Why is Davis, who doesn't want to sell Camels, content to reproduce the lettering which the graphic designer has used to sell Champion Little Giant spark plugs? Davis claims that he used words 'because they were part of urban subject matter [...] the design of this matchbook was singularly uninteresting and it was the challenge of the lack of interest [...] rather than the direct stimulus of a subject' that spurred him.

The catalogue entry for *Visa* shrewdly speculates that Davis was aware of art (his own included) as a passport and commodity that crosses frontiers — *Visa* itself was intended for the São Paulo Bienal, and the next year Davis would represent America in the Venice Biennale. There's a smug glint to the painting in this respect, though clearly it also alludes to the American product destined for a global market. Does this mark a moment of self-doubt as well as self-satisfaction? What makes the artist so different from the graphic designer whose original (and boring) logotype he is content to exploit for his own not uncommercial ends? And how, given the above, is the artwork distinct from the commodity whose advertisement the artist appropriates when both pass into the international market place? The painting fabricates a teasing visual conundrum, with the self-referential phrase *The amazing Contin-uity* (note the discontinuous hyphen) added to the right border in Davis's unique ribbony or crêpey script, perhaps referring to the way his work is recycling with admirable parsimony the earlier canvas; but equally it draws attention to the problematic continuity between the industrial product's advertising design and the artwork itself. Despite the knowing verve of this work, and of others from the '50s, there seems something schematic and over-determined about it, which makes me prefer the period through the '30s when, despite the demands of his political activism, he painted his great American cityscapes.

If the Parisian cityscapes are disappointing, they nevertheless helped Davis develop a pictorial language (and in his case the word is only partly metaphoric, since script — including the ever-more conspicuous motif of his signature — continues to operate in his paintings as a key compositional effect) which was responsible for some of his finest paintings. *Landscape with Garage Lights* manages to make an intriguingly dissonantal harmony out of the maritime jumble of Gloucester,

Massachusetts's industrial waterfront. Its childlike inclusiveness is astonishing — a fish-processing plant, a coal tower, factories and warehouses, boat, telegraph poles, petrol pumps with curly proboscises, and a café awning on the far right like a limp hand reaching for a row of bottles underneath. There's even (unusually for Davis) a faintly scumbled human figure at the railings looking out seawards. The large, flat, bright areas of colour, broken up by angular sections of black and by parallel lines, curves and crosses, delight in their angles and contingencies and toy with the actual, find a composite equivalent for it, rather than feeling obliged to *describe* it. The CO. of one sign echoes the COAL of another. The word FISH has a fishbone I, perhaps because it's occluded by a mast, while the last upright of the H seems to have slithered out beyond the wall it adorns as though leaping back into the black sea underneath.

Although the exhibition is exclusively of paintings, it would have been interesting to see some of Davis's lithographs from this period, a medium which must have assisted him greatly in this new and bolder use of black.

The arrival of Abstract Expressionism would displace Davis somewhat from the vanguard of American painting. Although he found the Abstract Expressionists too introspective, nevertheless that period saw his own increasing commitment to abstraction. But it was during the '30s, when the plethora of urban life impelled him towards an abstraction which he both enjoyed and resisted, that he achieved some of his finest work. Perhaps most successful of all is *New York under Gaslight* (1941), which is like a summa of this stage of his career, putting together all his favourite urban elements in a gaudy stage set; though the colours are garish under a whitened chrome green sky, we understand that it is night time by the black hulk of one pier of Brooklyn Bridge in the background and by the white illumination from windows and shopfronts, which compete for attention with their signs and (mainly smoking) advertisements. The lettering is as playful and varied as ever, the M in ROOM curtailed as if there wasn't enough room, the D in DENTI[ST] itself dented or chipped like a tooth. Its mood is valedictory, as if Davis sensed he was about to move on to the bold abstract variations of his final two decades. And yet the improvisatory, jazz-like quality of this painting, and the extraordinary classical intelligence that shapes an order from inner city clutter and from clashing non-representational colour, is what makes Davis one of the finest twentieth-century painters of urban experience.

Modern Painters, Spring 1998

— 31 —

Chaim Soutine: The Hunger Artist

Invigilated by butchers, Kafka's 'Hunger Artist' performs his long fasts before an ebbing crowd; the secret of his ability, he finally confesses, is that he has never discovered a food which will satisfy him. Chaim Soutine was a hunger artist of a different kind — one for whom hunger was involuntary. He was born in a small Lithuanian village in 1893, the tenth child of an impoverished 'mender' at the lowest level of the *shtetl*'s social scale. His earliest efforts in painting were rewarded by violent disapproval on the part of his own brothers and of the Jewish Orthodox community, which, in the light of the Second Commandment against all graven images, considered painting a crime. When, at the age of sixteen, he asked a pious Jew to sit for a portrait, Soutine was savagely beaten by the man's sons. With the compensation of 25 roubles which his mother helped him to win for his injuries, he and his friend Kikoine left Smilovichi to study painting in Minsk. The story is revealing about Soutine's tenacity, and in part explains the determination with which he held on to a 'recognizable' motif in his paintings, insisting, as he did, on painting what was in front of him — something he had had to struggle so hard and so transgressively in the first place to paint. It also helps explain how Soutine's paintings never lose sight of insult and injury.

Soutine experienced gnawing poverty (a cliché particularly apt here) throughout his youth and the years in Paris before being taken up in 1923 by the American collector Albert C. Bames. And this literal hunger is enacted in the still lifes of dead animals as much as in his portraits of butchers, pastry cooks and waiters. Even later, as Esti Dunow observes, when Soutine had the money to eat what he wanted, he was prevented from doing so by the stomach ulcers which were to cause his death in 1943. He was instructed not to eat the very foods he obsessively painted at that time: fowls, hares, beef. Yet his hunger wasn't exclusively forced upon him. His dealer Zborowsky recounted how well he painted meat, especially when he was hungry:

> Well, he buys a piece of raw meat and fasts in front of it for two days before he starts to paint it. Look at that red: hasn't he put all his cannibalistic appetite into it?

As with Kafka's creation, there is something ritualistic and performative about Soutine's hunger.

In the 1982 Arts Council catalogue, David Sylvester rigorously argues that in the Céret landscapes (roughly 1919–22) Soutine grapples with Cézanne and Modernism, and wins through to his most original work. After that: apostasy — the date more or less coinciding with his discovery by Bames and his sudden prosperity. Sylvester's arguments rest, almost convincingly, on the next period of Soutine's landscapes at Cagnes, with their curly forms and saccharine palette — the only moment where he approaches the folkloric sentiment of Chagall. Those Céret landscapes were the victims of a self-lacerating fury on Soutine's part; he frequently, and at the slightest provocation, shredded any canvas that displeased him, but these paintings he even bought back from the dealers so as to erase all record of them. Though Sylvester is right to suggest that they represented a special impasse for Soutine, I think the reasons he gives for this are misleading. The Céret landscapes are of an unusual violence, even by Soutine's standards: runged and excavated, full of splitting seismic confusion, they record vertigo and panic. I think Soutine instinctively understood that to follow their logic further would be to sacrifice the expression and the presence of the subject for unrecognizable distortion and mannerism. Sylvester sees the psychological root for Soutine's defection in his culturally deprived background — a parvenu with a parvenu's insecurities in relation to the Old Masters. But who isn't an upstart in relation to tradition? What different class background would have guaranteed Soutine a more urbane and confident stance?

What marks Soutine's work throughout is the purposeful and direct quality of his encounters with the few painters who engaged him — Fouquet, Chardin, Courbet and, most lastingly, Rembrandt, whose *Slaughtered Ox* Soutine passionately recreated in his series of the *Carcass of Beef*, closer-up, as always with Soutine, and, especially in the 1925 paintings, more iridescent and animate in its rawness, with cadmium yellow and red thickly dragged across black. Soutine commented on Courbet's ability to catch the whole atmosphere of Paris in his nude women: '*Moi, je veux montrer Paris dans la carcasse d'un bœuf*'. This statement speaks eloquently about the narrowness of Soutine's subject matter and the extent of his ambitions — how much he intended to compress into each of his canvases. Soutine is not, as Chagall called him, a 'morbid Expressionist', though the stories that circulated about him would suggest otherwise. He is said to have kept pouring fresh blood over one beef carcass to ignite the colours, until his neighbours became so disgusted by the stink of decay they called in the Department of Health, at which Soutine shouted in dismay: 'Art is more important than public sanitation!'

Aside from the anti-bourgeois nature of this remark, Sylvester's idea that Soutine crossed back over the Rubicon of Modernism (Cézanne) at the same time as he sought refuge among the solid bourgeois values of his new patrons seems inappropriate in considering a painter whose finest portraits are of those in positions of service, anonymous valets, waiters, bellhops (and, by extension, choir boys), an underclass invisible in everything but their functions, and the uniforms which signal them, to the bourgeoisie, and of no interest at all to a parvenu. There's nothing sweetened about Soutine's depiction of these servants, nothing parallel to Picasso's Blue Period. These are not paintings of hunger which make their appeal to the surfeited. John Berger saw in Gericault's paintings of the mad the terminus of a tradition of portraiture which had emphasized wealth and bearing, possession and self-possession, seeing in them studies of another kind of 'possession', or rather dispossession and exclusion. The insight is eye-opening but too unwilling to concede that there's always a *plus ultra*. Though Soutine perhaps draws back from madness as a subject — with the powerful exceptions of *Mad Girl* and *Village Idiot*, if the titles have any authority — his portraits of 'menials' challenge that tradition as thoroughly as Gericault's lunatics, perhaps all the more for having drawn back from Romantic extremity.

Degas, with greater compositional sophistication, depicts the labours of laundry women and ballet dancers and women bathing from the perspective of an aesthete. These activities, at first glance demystifications of beauty, are finally the drudgery that beauty exacts. Everything, even ugliness, is in the service of beauty, and stands for the pains the artist himself takes in the studio. Soutine strips his servants of their activities, of their setting, of any props of their trade except their uniforms, in a radical exclusion that is common to his still lifes. Soutine sees through a 'narrow chink', to adapt Blake's expression about the senses, but that narrowness gives him an extraordinary trenchancy. His Parisian servants have achieved a lasting status, like Gogol's petty councillors or Kafka's clerks, surveyors and court officials.

It is significant that Soutine painted only one surviving nude, a painting in which both the artist and sitter seem to be recoiling from the exposure of seeing and being seen. Soutine's seeing — 'gaze' is too quietistic a term for his nervous, jolting perceptions — renders his clothed figures more naked than most paintings of nudes. His thin figures try to fill out their uniforms or clothes, and the pictorial space, with an intense discomfort, sometimes with wariness, sometimes bravado. Distortion is at the service of the particular and the unrepeatable qualities of each anonymous sitter — as de Kooning perfectly expressed it, 'Soutine distorted the pictures but not the people'. The astigmatic tug of a shoulder towards the top corner of the canvas, the enormous extension of one ear in the earliest *Pastry Cook* to croissant-like dimensions, or the twisted nostrils of a head-waiter are the physical signs of fragility as well as of adaptation to their work. *The Cook of Cagnes*, with its jaundiced cream, brown and violet streaks across the white uniform, is a wonderfully understated study in fatigue.

Soutine's work divides exactly into three parts — Portraits, Still Lifes, and Landscapes — and is presented under these headings in the superb *Catalogue Raisonné* prepared and introduced by Maurice Tuchman, Esti Dunow and Klaus Perls with exemplary commitment and clarity. The only pictures not in colour are the twenty-one from the Barnes Foundation, which forbids colour reproduction of its collection. Infuriating as this is, these black-and-whites are instructive in the way they show how utterly indispensable colour is to Soutine. Collision and collusion in pigment, as well as the elasticity and mobility of paint, are at the heart of his work. Among the still lifes, there are a few slightly morose and clumsy flower paintings (apart from some incandescent gladioli) which are clearly not to his purpose and soon abandoned. One of his most serene still lifes, with an unusually stated background, is *The Hare against a Green Shutter*, where the green shutters have the lyrical intensity of landscape, only they serve to shut out the landscape and the light. Suspended by its hind legs, the hare's stasis is an image of movement: shift the vertical axis to a horizontal and the hare could almost be running through grass. This mobility in death is a common property of his still lifes. The vivid panic and flurry in his upended *Yellow Turkey* is an unforgettable image of terror and insult, and may, as Tuchman suggests, have much to do with the scapegoating ritual of whirling a fowl which Soutine would have witnessed in his youth. Soutine's own recollections of a kosher slaughter touch on the conflict which his paintings enact:

> Once I saw the village butcher slice the neck of a bird and drain the blood out of it. I wanted to cry out but his joyful expression caught the sound in my throat... This cry, I always feel it there. When as a child I drew a crude portrait of my professor, I tried to rid myself of this cry, but in vain. When I painted the beef carcass it was still this cry that I wanted to liberate. I have still not succeeded.

The slaughter, the butcher's 'joyful expression' and the choked cry belong to the same world as the final page of Kafka's *The Trial*, just as the hunger and conflict of Soutine's paintings could he glossed by Kafka's diary entry of 10 February 1922:

> Attacked right and left as I am by overwhelming forces, it is as plain as can be that I cannot escape either to the right or the left — straight on only, starved beast, lies the road to food that will sustain you, air that you can breathe, a free life, even if it should take you beyond life.

It's only perhaps in his late landscapes painted during the German occupation, where the wind is made visible in the trees, and his roads lose their earlier steep and dizzying gradients, that Soutine glimpses this 'air that you can breathe'. Having lived in concealment through this period, registered as a Jew ('*Connu comme Juif*'), Soutine died of a ruptured ulcer on 9 August 1943. It was the delay in coming to Paris for hospital treatment, due to fear of arrest, that was to prove fatal.

Modern Painters, Spring 1994

— 32 —

Alberto Giacometti

Exhibition: Tate Modern, May–September, 2017

Solitude is the usual condition of Alberto Giacometti's sculptures and paintings, which tend to isolate the individual human form, and occasionally an individual feature such as a nose or an arm, so it's disconcerting to confront, as the viewer does in the first room of this exhibition, some two dozen sculptures clustered in such sociable proximity. Vertical, sometimes vertiginous — as in his *L'homme qui chavire* [*Falling* or *Capsizing Man*] (1950) — the format of his work is nearly always 'portrait' not 'landscape' and his most characteristic figures are spindly and tapering, the head usually smaller than the feet, which though proportioned like carthorse hooves seem to offer only minimal security and balance. The poet Yves Bonnefoy plausibly suggested that this sculpture is connected with an accident Giacometti suffered after being run down by a car, when his foot was badly broken, but the figure with its arms flung out to grasp at nothing seems poised between the acutely physical and the metaphysical. His witty *Limping Figure* begun in 1931, a thin wooden sheet intersected by three prongs, one bent, shows how early the idea of imbalance attracted him. It seems to play off the Sphinx's riddle '...what goes on three legs in the evening?' and brings to mind a character in his friend Samuel Beckett's *Watt* whose limping is described as 'a series of abortive genuflexions'.

The poet André Breton in his 1928 article 'Surrealism and Painting' hailed 'the inspired sculpture of Alberto Giacometti', and the Surrealist years were formative and productive for him. In the late Thirties, the poet decided to expel the artist for what he took to be a retrograde interest in the merely representational, and thereby lost for the movement their only talented sculptor. And what talent. Just how far Giacometti's direction was contravening Surrealist tenets remains an open question. Certainly, Breton's proposed experiments for 'Automatic Sculpture' in the same article could hardly be further from Giacometti's working methods where every mark, incision and hollow is designed and purposeful. His sculptures and his paintings are full of *pentimenti* that are not repented but meant. An archival film by Ernst Scheidegger and Peter Münger, showing in the exhibition, lets us see the sureness and speed of every brushstroke as, starting with the eyes — according to Giacometti if they could be got right everything else followed — he weaves together a darkening gossamer web of telling and increasingly complex lines. Observation and repeated study of a model, which he called 'copying', did indeed became his *modus operandi* and yet some of the artist's most brilliantly volatile and explorative work emerged under the banner of the movement that expelled him.

Woman with her Throat Cut, 1932, supposedly prompted by a study of praying mantises, has a splayed segmented form, the spine curved and the limbs contorted — a nightmare of exposure and vulnerability. Its horrid spiky shape has exploded the calm smooth curves of the Brancusi-influenced sculptures of only five years earlier such as *Spoon Woman*. Unlike many sculptors from Brancusi to Moore, the rounded forms of whose works seem to be an invitation, an inducement to touch, from early on Giacometti's sculptures have the opposite effect — they repel or discourage touch. The series of sculptures entitled 'Unpleasant Object', a hybrid between a magnified protozoa and a thorny phallic cudgel, is a celebration and study of the disagreeable and the repellent. The early Surrealist works in bronze share with the later dented and rough-textured figures in plaster this quality of being chafing or discomforting to the touch.

One of the marked successes of the Surrealist years is *Invisible Object* (1934–35), which has a dual (preparatory?) existence as a delicate etching. This work, made after his father's death, follows a series of sculptures, drawings and etchings inspired by the mysterious polyhedron in Dürer's *Melencolia 1*. Giacometti's hieratic female figure seated or restrained in a sinister chair like an upright gurney is grasping an object that doesn't exist, whose form is only implied by the shape of the two hands that grasp it. The absence might suggest a geometric shape or a Madonna and Child, only with the child absconded. Its lineage is eclectic — with hints of Egyptian, Polynesian, and Siennese art, in addition to the more recent influence, as the catalogue argues, of Georg Kolbe's *Assumption* — but whatever its sources, the sculpture is undeniably original, and by making what is invisible the very focus of the piece it challenges the essence of this most solid of all art forms.

Giacometti questions the solidity of sculpture in many ways: with scale, material, proportion and texture. With regard to scale he creates distance. In painting we expect perspective and the recession of space, but not in sculpture where it would seem an impossibility. It's most perceptible here in one of the miniscule figurines he made on his return from Paris to his native Switzerland during the Second World War. 'To my horror my statues became ever smaller from 1940 onwards', he recalled. 'First I made the sculpture so tiny, to see the distance in which I had seen the model.' Although his description emphasizes perception and technique, it's hard not to consider this series as also reflecting a diminishing of the human subject during those years. But even in his larger works, the artist creates an uncanny sense of distance, of a figure coming in and out of focus.

Giacometti's increasing use of plaster as medium (rather than as intermediary cast) again makes sculpture less solid. Like the Plasticine he also used, it has an ephemeral, deliberately impoverished quality — the equivalent of his use of biro in sketching. With regard to proportion, the exaggerated thinness and elongation of his post-war figures make them appear fragile and tremulous. Even the friable texture plays a part in this — with the scored, eroded and sometimes faintly painted surfaces, rough as lava, there is always in his later work an air of frailty, as though the protective layer of flesh has been stripped or blown away from the form leaving only pocked clay clinging to an armature.

The serial quality of his paintings — endlessly repeated sittings, especially of his brother Diego and his wife Annette, and later of a woman known as Caroline — suggest a process that can never reach completion. Beckett's famous injunction 'Try again. Fail again. Fail better' could equally serve as his motto. (He provided a skeletal, haunting, one-leaf tree for the second production of *Waiting for Godot* — a play with a quantity of its own falling men though they tend to fall in heaps.)

By continually revisiting the same subject, Giacometti's paintings work against the traditional notion of portraiture which aims at a definitive representation. None of these paintings, where the figure is seated and often surrounded by the clutter of the studio, has any claim to be definitive but each is a station on the route to perception, each stands as a monument to the moment. Giacometti professed no interest in depicting the character of the model: 'I have enough trouble with the outside without bothering about the inside'. His obsessive reworking as well as the unfinished appearance of these portraits doesn't ever seem to be in the service of representation or likeness (*pace* Breton) but of something altogether more ungraspable — a quest to arrest, if only provisionally, the constant shifting of perception, to align those perceptions as truthfully as possible with the actual constantly shifting subject.

This superb exhibition which gathers together some two hundred and fifty works, including the artist's sketchbooks, designed furniture and memorabilia, reminds us of Giacometti's versatility, wit, variety, inventiveness, his twin mastery of sculpture and painting but also of his heroic commitment to the human form in all its menaced frailty.

Times Literary Supplement, 21 July 2017

— 33 —

Trakl, Celan, Goethe

The Poems of Georg Trakl, trans. by Margitt Lehbert (London: Anvil, 2006)
Poems of Paul Celan, trans. by Michael Hamburger (London: Anvil, 2007)
Paul Celan, *Snow Part /Schneepart*, trans. by Ian Fairley (Manchester: Carcanet, 2007)
D. M. Black, *Love as Landscape Painter: Translations from Johann Wolfgang von Goethe* (Blair Atholl, Perthshire: Fras Publications, 2006)

Anyone who translates poems will be aware of a kind of Zeno's paradox by which the nearer the text approximates to the original the further away it becomes. And nowhere can this law of diminishing returns be more keenly felt than with the German poets Paul Celan and Georg Trakl. Trakl would seem the easier of the two. Surely English could manage something like the weird and pregnant stillness of his lines — with their air of a curdled idyll? Yet without Trakl's music, his tone and sonority, translation falls into bathos and Gothic stage-props.

Berryman summed up Trakl's short, blighted career in one line: 'Drugs. Alcohol. Little sister.' — and his life indeed seems to have spun ever further from a stable axis until his breakdown in 1914, in Grödek where he was working as a military nurse, and his suicide in Cracow soon after from a cocaine overdose. There's a troubling sense, though, in which the personal catastrophe of Trakl's life figures, at least in the poems, as a portent of a larger, European crisis — cultural unease, loss of religious faith, an encroaching decay — which will come to a head in the First World War.

Margitt Lehbert's translations include all of the poems of Trakl's two books and the late poems he didn't live to publish. It's a shame that her understanding of the originals is not matched by her performance in English — too often her lines lack tension and music, are enervated or fall back into trite, sub-Tennysonian inversions: 'Over parkland grieved and pale | ...In putrescence sweet and stale...'. In 'Melancholy in Evening', the over-dubitative line 'And maybe stars, perhaps, are also shining' is just not feasible in English. (The original is not so doubtful and gains force from its alliteration.) In her version of Trakl's extraordinary early poem 'The Rats' we read: 'And a horrid haze of something foul | Wafts after them from the toilet | That ghostly moonlight shudders through'. Compare Robert Grenier's version of these lines in the long-extinct *Selected Poems* (Cape): 'A greyish dust-haze reeks | After them from the latrine, through which | The spectral moonlight shivers.' Flat as this is, there's at least a hint of something uncanny; and even though Lehbert's volume is far more inclusive, I would still recommend that slender, bi-lingual edition, translated by several hands (including Michael Hamburger), for those who want some idea of what makes Trakl such a haunting and singular poet.

Celan's poems are if anything even less susceptible to translation. Born in Bukovina in 1920, Celan escaped when Germany invaded but both his parents died in a concentration camp, his father of typhoid, his mother shot. This violence and the evil of those years mark everything he wrote until his suicide in 1970. The poet and translator Michael Hamburger, who died earlier this year, has toiled for several decades, gradually adding to his translations of Celan. This posthumous volume is the sum of that exacting and exhausting work. The results are uneven; although I'm not sure how they could ever be other than uneven. Best in English, it seems to me, are the poems from the first book. Their songlike rhythms (often amphibrachs as in 'Du füllst hier die Urnern und speisest dein Herz' [You fill up the urns here and nourish your heart]), which Hamburger skilfully reproduces, and their eerie juxtapositions reach a crescendo in his famous 'Death Fugue'. Thereafter Celan chooses to break up the surfaces of his poems, to create a language which turns in on itself, examining with the utmost scrupulousness its own formations, its cognates, its parts of speech, as if only in language was there any refuge, and even that refuge has to be secured with infinite care. In the beautiful version here of Celan's poem to Mandelstam 'things lost were things not lost, | the heart was a place made fast.' The poems turn inward, resist entry, and Celan freights every utterance with almost more weight and meaning than words can bear.

His difficulty, as he himself argued and as Hamburger repeats, is not hermeticism. Unlike some forms of experimental writing which might claim Celan as a precursor, his difficulty proceeds from a surfeit not a paucity of meaning. You can see why, consummate as it is, the poet repudiated 'Death Fugue' in his unwillingness to find 'solace in euphony' (Trakl's phrase).

These difficulties multiply with translation. In Celan's much-commentated yet still elusive 'Todtnauberg', which records a visit to Heidegger's forest retreat, medicinal flowers — arnica, eyebright — stand like hopeful witnesses at the threshold of the poem. 'Whose name' Celan wonders, precedes his own in the visitors' book? Celan's hope of some 'word in the heart' that will confront or revoke the philosopher's enthusiastic support of Nazi Germany proves unfounded. The poem ends:

> die halb-
> beschrittenen Knüppel-
> pfade in Hochmoor,
>
> Feuchtes,
> viel.

Hamburger: 'the half- | trodden fascine | walks over the high moors, || dampness, | much.' The word 'fascine' — meaning a brushwood faggot — with its sinister reprisal of 'fasces' is an ingenious solution but too *recherché*. The word lacks the consonantal, physical immediacy of 'Knüppel' (a stick — perhaps to beat someone with). It's an example of how in Celan, while the meaning is elusive, the German remains palpable; and of how, especially when it moves towards the Latinate, English can lose purchase on his poems.

Ian Fairley has translated *Schneepart* (1970) with Celan's late poems. Like Hamburger's accompanying essays, Fairley's introduction brilliantly illuminates many aspects of Celan's work, the intricacies of his language, as well as the challenge of translating him. His own versions defy my initial proposition: they adhere as closely as they can to the German, diction and compounds, and unearth a living stratum of German in English, translating, for example, 'setz Lee über Luv' as 'sets lee over luff'. This can lead him into barely construable lines like 'strewing things timeunderhallowed' or to a phonetically nonsensical enjambment such as 'the sack of mutter- | ed resolutions' (presumably here to register the un-enjambed compound 'Beschlußmurmeln') but these are risks he seems willing to take. Where Hamburger, more conservatively, tends to respect what is possible in English, Fairley tries to extend that possibility. Any English reader of Celan owes a debt of gratitude to both translators. Even if so much eludes English in both, enough gets through to leave a sure sense that the loss and tenderness which resound through Celan's poems are like nothing else on earth.

To read D. M. Black's translations of Goethe in this context is to find yourself blinking like an owl at a sunnier, hedonistic world. The poet defies the Gods to rival his lusty pleasures, or at a roadside inn curses his inability to consummate the seduction of the maid, or taps out hexameters on his Roman mistress's back. Although there are moments when the metre and the language slacken, Black's versions of the Roman Elegies, particularly, are spirited and entertaining and we sense the Nordic mind unwinding where 'the moon gives more light [...] than mid-day in the North!' and where a 'bundle of brushwood' that 'falls into cinders and fades' is presage of further sensual pleasures and not a chilling symbol of fascism.

— 34 —

Eugenio Montale: Two Jackals on a Leash

Eugenio Montale, *Collected Poems, 1920–1954*, bilingual edition translated and annotated by Jonathan Galassi (New York: Farrar, Straus and Giroux, 1999)

The entomologist Henri Fabre, in a chapter called 'The Song of the Cicale', tells how in Provençal folklore the source of the sound from their 'musical thighs' is referred to as *mirrors*, 'a dry membrane coloured like a soap bubble', though he points out that these actually dampen the sound. Still, in Provence a singer out of breath or a poet without inspiration is said to have his mirrors broken. Jonathan Galassi, in an essay 'Reading Montale' appended to this translation of the poet's first three books, pays attention to the ancient association, particularly strong in the Mediterranean region, of poet and cicada and to its recurrence in Montale's poems. 'Debole sistro del vento':

> Feeble sistrum in the wind
> of a lost cicada
> no sooner touched than done for
> in the exhaling torpor

This (as Galassi translates the first stanza) is an early Montale poem which embodies in the cicada's carcass — 'corrupted leavings | the void won't devour' — that Provençal notion of a poetry with its mirrors broken. It is, even by Montale's standards, an especially stark and unconsoling poem. The image of the sistrum, a metal-wire Egyptian rattle, is a reduction to its barest essence of the vast orchestra and range of sound that the poet has access to (figuratively and literally: his poems abound in musical instruments, a natural patrimony for a poet who was a professional music critic and who also himself studied singing for many years with the baritone Ernesto Sivori). But reduction in Montale is never *ad absurdum*, even here where it speaks of the absence of inspiration.

Montale returns to this image most poignantly in 'L'ombra della magnolia giapponese' written more than twenty years later, in his third book *The Storm and Other Poems* (1957), where he foretells that 'the empty husk of him who sang will soon | be powdered glass underfoot' and where, as Galassi observes, the self-identification is explicit. The cicada then has something for Montale of that Yeatsian place 'where all the ladders start', as the key word 'foce' [estuary, outlet] in the last stanza of the Sistrum poem suggests, and his 'corrutte/vestigie' is like Yeats's 'foul rag-and-bone shop of the heart'. The dead cicada makes us remember that his song, loud and monotonous, serves an amorous purpose which is not so different from Montale's own — for all the elaborate structures and plural identities of the Muse-like figures his poems address as 'tu'. It's not that his poems are simply mating calls, but that like the troubadours he learnt from, the attitude to the world that brings them into being is essentially erotic.

This *mythos* is present also, though less consciously evolved and subtilized, in the first book, *Cuttlefish Bones*, which the poet published in 1925 at the age of twenty-nine. Its terrain is almost exclusively the Ligurian coast of the Cinque Terre — not, as Galassi claims, the (adjoining) Tuscan coast. The cicada's dry persistent chirruping might be considered an acoustic analogue — and accompaniment — for this rocky coastline that is not just the setting for these poems but almost their very condition, their reason for being. The earliest work ('Meriggiare pallido e assorto') Montale included in *Ossi di seppia* introduces this motif. The poem is obsessed with sound. In its first stanza — 'schiocchi di merli, frusci di serpi' — the hard clicking 'c' sounds of the thrushes (double consonants are sounded in Italian) and the sibilant rustling of the snake are picked up later with the percussive 'si levano tremuli scricchi | di cicale dai calvi picchi' [cicadas' wavering screaks | rise from the bald peaks] whilst the sound has ridden through the rhyme words 'formiche' [ants] and 'biche' [heaps] of the intervening stanza. The poem's final line is perhaps too final in likening the whole of life to following a wall which is harled with jagged bottle glass — 'che ha in cima cocci aguzzi di bottiglia' — and yet the way the hard and soft 'c's alternate in it, with subtle menace drawing together the whole sound pattern of the poem, shows the phonetic complexity which Montale is capable of even at the outset, and it's these densely textured sound effects that present one of the most formidable challenges to any translator.

This sun-dazzled drought and inertia is described so insistently and precisely in *Cuttlefish Bones* that it takes on the colouring of an existential state, a state of entrapment but also one of tense expectation. In the proem, 'On the Threshold', he tells the reader or the addressee or himself (or possibly all three) to 'Watch this solitary strip of land | transform into a crucible'. The poem itself serves as a crucible which breaks down the vision into its constituent elements and moves beyond a merely naturalistic perspective. It's only at this point that the poem envisages the possibility of an escape for the 'you' of the poem from the walled 'orto' [vegetable garden] which 'was no garden but a reliquary':

> Look for the flaw in the net that binds us
> tight, burst through, break free!

If the meshes of the phenomenal world — of landscape and perception — is also the world that the poem has brought into being, the act of writing gambles on the slenderest chance of breaking through to an untrammelled realm beyond appearances. Montale's claim that all his poetry 'is a waiting for the miracle' is made with the full awareness that miracles hardly ever occur.

There is certainly a pessimistic cast of mind the reader meets in all Montale's work. From the first poems onwards, the tone of voice is resistant and rebarbative. No poet is as attached as him to the use of the negative. His collected poems have no less than thirty-three poems that begin with the word 'Non' and another thirty which employ it in the opening line, without reckoning the number of negative prefixes. He adapts Verlaine's remark in commenting on his own style: 'I wanted to wring the neck of our ancient courtly language, even at the risk of a counter-eloquence'. There is an implied rebuttal in the stance of his poems to D'Annunzio's dithyrambic posturing, but also to the Fascist party for whom D'Annunzio was such an exuberant propagandist. (Whilst Ezra Pound, with Fascist assistance, was lording it over a librarian in Ravenna, as Lawrence Rainey's article in a recent *London Review of Books* recorded, Montale was working as a librarian in Florence, and was dismissed in 1938 for not having Fascist party membership). But, as Montale himself confessed, and Galassi's notes amply demonstrate, he felt the allure of D'Annunzio's writing as well as resisting it. One characteristic refusal to be conscripted in any way occurs in a famous early poem 'Non chiederci la parola...'. In Galassi's version:

> Don't ask us for the word to frame
> our shapeless spirit on all sides
> and proclaim it in letters of fire to shine
> like a lone crocus in a dusty field.
>
> Ah, the man who walks secure,
> a friend to others and himself,
> indifferent that high summer prints
> his shadow on a peeling wall!
>
> Don't ask us for the phrase that can open worlds,
> just a few gnarled syllables, dry like a branch.
> This, today, is all that we can tell you:
> what we are *not*, what we do *not* want.

What this impressive English version lacks is the formal definition of the original, the rhythmic control of its predominantly hendecasyllabic lines, the powerful rhyming — all of which ironically contradict the initial statement, unless, in the second stanza, the hypermetric rhyme 'amico/canicola', which is something of a Montale hallmark, could be said to subtly reinforce it. English cannot comfortably reproduce the five 'non's in the poem, the last two italicized, and the way they add up to a word, however 'twisted', which is the opposite to an open sesame, rather a spell for closing off illusory worlds. The word '*squadra*', here translated as 'frame', means 'square (off)' with the sense of craftsmanship which seems especially applicable to the form of the quatrain. But the poem is at once very sure of itself in its untypically spokesmanlike use of the word 'ci' for 'us' and the first person plural 'possiamo' and therefore not as utterly distinguished from the 'man who walks secure' as it might at first seem. William Arrowsmith, who has also translated these three books, abandons this entirely by using the first person singular throughout:

> Don't ask me for words that might define
> our formless soul, publish it
> in letters of fire, and set it shining,
> lost crocus in a dusty field.

By retaining the 'lost' ('como un croco | *perduto* in mezzo a un polveroso prato' in the original) Arrowsmith does, however, allow another ambiguity to emerge. Galassi's 'lone' is an imaginative solution, but in the Italian that idiomatic 'perduto in mezzo' sabotages the self-proclaiming word from which Montale distinguishes his own poetry. There's a similar bitter humour in the idea that his (the confident man's or poet's) shadow should be 'printed' like some poster on a flaking wall. What are set against each other here are two botanical options — either be a word like a 'lost crocus in a dusty field' or be some 'gnarled syllables, dry like a branch' — neither of which are attractive, though the latter, the counter-eloquent one, is preferred by Montale.

Two other early manifesto poems use plants as metaphors — 'The Lemon Trees' and 'Bring me the sunflower' — and, in fact, from the first lines of 'The Lemon Trees':

> Listen to me, the poets laureate
> walk only among plants
> with rare names: boxwood, privet and acanthus...

('privet' unfortunately, perhaps not just for the translator, isn't so rare a sound in this part of the world) to the last line of *Ossi di seppia:* 'Rifiorire!' ('flower anew!' — another imperative) Montale employs plants as aesthetic — even political — argument.

His second book, *Occasions* (1939), after his move inland to Florence, to what he calls its 'terra firma of ideas, tradition, humanism', is far less declarative. It moves towards a poetry which is just as resistant in its impulse, but far more cryptic in its manner. Though Montale sometimes loftily denied the impact of external events on his aesthetics, the fact that *Occasions* was written under the worsening conditions of Fascist Italy (the Racial Laws were enacted in 1938) and under the imminent threat of war may well have radically shaped these stylistic choices, and given rise to an encoded quality in the writing.

Sometimes these poems resist the reader's interpretations. William Arrowsmith in his translations of these three books began the procedure of encrusting the poems with commentaries. Galassi's notes, 170-odd pages of small print, which quote from a range of eminent Montale scholars like Contini, Cambon and Luperini, build onto this already towering superstructure, give a balanced and lucid discussion of each poem, and provide for the English reader an astonishing recovery of the intricate mesh of allusions to Italian literature from the *stilnovisti* and Petrarch, through Leopardi and Foscolo, to Carducci and D'Annunzio. There are, inevitably, some allusions which are missed in favour of more recondite ones. I think, for example, that Dante's 'Così nel mio parlar voglio esser aspro / com'è ne li atti questa bella petra...' [In my speech I want to be as rough | as this beautiful stone [-hearted woman] is in her acts...] can be heard behind Montale's great opening — from the *Mediterraneo* sequence — 'Avrei voluto sentirmi scabro ed essenziale | siccome i ciottoli che tu volvi...' [I would have liked to feel harsh and essential | like the pebbles you tumble...]. Or in 'Clivo' and in 'Nell'ombra della magnolia giapponese' the file that appears, just before those lines about the cicada's husk I quoted earlier, is far more likely to be a reference to Leopardi's 'Scherzo' (where 'la lima' represents the poetic craft he upbraids his contemporaries for not using) than to the stone-grinders in Ecclesiastes, which is Arrowsmith's guess, reiterated here. I'm torn between gratitude for this tremendous labour which undoubtedly serves any interested reader of Montale and a nagging worry that the poems begin to suffocate under the weight of commentary. Only Christopher Ricks's *Inventions of the March Hare*, as an equivalent for a twentieth-century poet in English, offers any competition. Reading Montale in this way is like reading the *Commedia* in Sapegno's scholarly edition, but there with 700 years of scholarship and much necessary retrieval of historical events and persons the modern reader can't be expected to know, the need is more pressing. Montale himself, with a defensive reflex, seems to have anticipated this fate in a passage that Galassi includes:

> The obscurity of the classics, not only of Dante and Petrarch but also of Foscolo and Leopardi, has been partly unravelled by the commentary of whole generations of scholars: and I don't doubt that those great writers would be flabbergasted by the exegeses of certain of their interpreters. And the obscurity of certain of the moderns will finally give way too, if they are still critics tomorrow. Then we shall all pass from darkness into light, too much light: the light the so-called aesthetic commentators cast on the mystery of poetry. There is a middle road between understanding nothing and understanding too much, a *juste milieu* which poets instinctively respect more than their critics; but on this side or that of the border there is no safety for either poetry or criticism. There is only a wasteland, too dark or too bright, where two poor jackals cannot live or venture without being hunted down, seized, and shut behind the bars of a zoo.

That last reference is to the final stanza, too brilliantly surreal not to be actual, of one of the *Mottetti* in Montale's second book which ends:

> (under the arcades, at Modena
> a servant in gold braid dragged
> two jackals on a leash).

This sequence is especially problematic and elliptical, it moves in leaps and flashes, and yet my impression is that even the most riddling of his poems communicate directly, through what Galassi calls their 'nervous, astringent music', 'their harshness and abruptness' (though a suaver music is always at his disposal). His sometimes abstruse imagery, as with the jackals, is always rendered with precision, his voice is intimate though that speaking tone has an astonishing range and timbre, just as his diction — surely the most inclusive in twentieth-century Italian poetry — is as much at home with dialect as with the literary and offbeat. He leaves a trail the reader can follow, a thread that leads out of the maze — as he puts it in 'The House of the Customs Men', 'un filo s'addipana. || Ne tengo ancora un capo [a thread gets wound. || I hold one end still]. What's difficult in his poems comes from a desire not to make things which are obscure to him deceptively clear to others — hence the frequent use of images of light, usually flickering or fleeting, 'lampi', 'folgore', 'bagliore', 'barlume' etc., as well as the English word 'Flashes' which he uses in a sub-title to suggest not only the camera's magnesium flare and the resulting snapshot but also the fitful sudden illuminations and signs, again like that of the jackals — sometimes hopeful, sometimes infernal (as for instance the Lucifer matches in 'Little Testament' which Galassi has translated with great skill). In this sense he has something in common with Robert Frost who wrote of the poet in his notebook 'he will have clarifications but they will be momentary flashes like this: light shapes like poems [...] smoke rings'.

In compiling his notes, Galassi does not always avoid that shedding of 'too much light' which Montale fears. Admittedly following various hints by Montale himself, Galassi's claim that the poems can be read through like a novel tracing the writer's spiritual biography is seriously misleading. Anyone following this advice would be likely to faint with boredom or exasperation. The reader could easily do without some of the more speculative notes which record critics' endless ruminations on the identity and function of the various, deliberately vague, muse-like women — Clizia, Volpe, Arletta etc. — who populate his third volume especially. In fact one of the most tedious impulses within Montale studies has been precisely this anxiety to supplement criticism with tenuous biographical elaborations, and to raise this convention of the addressee to the status of a whole poetic system. For all that Montale could be said to have collaborated with these critical speculations, on another occasion he noted with apparent relief: 'Per fortuna la poesia non è la narrativa'.

Speaking to his biographer Nascimbeni, Montale compared himself to a wine that had grown old, adding that not all wines improve with age, 'some just go dry'. The general view of Montale's work is that it didn't improve with age, but went off not long after the three first collections. Whatever the justice of this claim — personally, I find the disillusioned wit and more humdrum tenderness of *Satura*, his fourth book, and some of his subsequent work appealing — there's a great deal of evidence that his poems travel as badly as wine is meant to. No twentieth-century Italian poet has been as widely, and disappointingly, translated into English. Vittorio Sereni and Attilio Bertolucci are, for example, far more adequately served by translation here. It's hard to explain why this should be, except with the hackneyed, and likely true, notion that the greater the poetry is the more limpet-like its attachment will be to its original tongue. Unlike the sunflower, that Montale wishes to transplant 'nel mio terreno bruciato dal salino' [in my plot of land burnt by the salt wind], his language and modes of perception refuse to be uprooted.

In reading Montale translations, I keep noting in myself a graceless tendency to find the more accurate versions too constrained and literal and the freer versions irresponsibly loose. I'm not sure that the *juste milieu* Montale recommends for critical enquiry exists for translation. The process inevitably entails losses, but should that exclude some compensatory gains? Taking an example too exceptional to be persuasive, Wyatt both translates *and* radically departs from Petrarch's 'Una candida cerva sopra l'erba' in 'Whoso list to hount I know where is an hind'. All of Petrarch's seasonal freshness, colour and descriptive specificity are wilfully sacrificed but the harsh northern climate of the English poem makes the experience of love even more like an exhausting psychic steeplechase, and advances the original by making it more trenchantly secular, political and erotic: 'for Caesar's I am | And wild for to hold though I seem tame'.

Of recent translators Arrowsmith and Galassi belong to those more faithful to the original, and Robert Lowell and Jeremy Reid to the licentious. Galassi's translations *sound* better than Arrowsmith's, and have a far more informed and reliable sense of the original than either Lowell's or Reid's, though only Lowell in the ten versions gathered in *Imitations* manages to make Montale read like a major poet in English. With Lowell there is an unmistakeable energy and panache in these lines from 'The Coastguard's House':

> For years the sirocco gunned the dead stucco with sand;
> the sound of your laugh is a jagged coughing;
> the compass, a pin-head, spins at random;
> the dizzy dice screw up the odds.'

The inaccuracies here, at least, are a small price to pay for the confident possession of the material.

A short early poem by Montale, which has a characteristically brilliant onomatopoeic effect at its outset, is:

> Cigola la carrucola del pozzo,
> l'acqua sale alla luce e vi si fonde.
> Trema un ricordo nel ricolmo secchio,
> nel puro cerchio un'immagine ride.
> Accosto il volto a evanescenti labbri:
> si deforma il passato, si fa vecchio,
> appartiene ad un altro...
> Ah che gia stride
> la ruota, ti ridona all'atro fondo,
> visione, una distanza ci divide.

which Galassi translates as:

> The well's pulley creaks,
> the water rises to the light, dissolving.
> A memory trembles in the brimming pail,
> an image smiles inside the perfect circle.
> I bring my face to evanescent lips:
> the past disintegrates, turns old, belongs
> to someone else...
> Ah, and already
> the wheel shrieks, gives you back to the black deep,
> vision, a distance keeps us separate.

The poem hinges on the precision of the noises within it and the vagueness of the image or mirage of a loved face — which grows old, and loses its remembered contours, its 'form', *in absentia.* Montale's regular hendecasyllables have turned into Galassi's pentameters (with two shorter lines) but his powerful intermittent rhyming has been abandoned, as has the repeated 'la' sound, especially marked in the first two lines and returning in the penultimate. The relative inflexibility of English word order has meant the overall effect of the phrasing is far more static and solidified, and yet there is a sense of consistency and formal intelligence in Galassi's version that places the momentary recognition between the two grating sounds — 'creaks' and 'shrieks' — that the pulley makes as the bucket rises and falls. Arrowsmith's translation reads:

> The windlass creaks in the well,
> the water rises, dissolves in light.
> A memory quivers in the brimming pail;
> in the pure circle an image laughs.
> I bend my face to fleeting lips:
> the past grows twisted, wrinkles with age,
> belongs to someone else...
> Ah, but then a screech,
> O vision, and the wheel slides you back to darkness,
> riving you from me.

Except for the unfortunate 'I bend my face', I marginally prefer this version until it reaches the seventh line's aposiopesis, after which it takes a turn for the poetic and the last line is a disaster. Galassi's 'black deep' gets closer to the more archaic 'atro' — which combines a suggestion of Orphic loss with a sense of dread. I think this fairly represents Galassi's general advantage over Arrowsmith — a surer feeling for the whole shape of the poem, even if the local details are sometimes less impressive. Reid describes his versions as 'independent satellites fuelled by the imagery and something of the dynamic of the original', so it's maybe wrong to expect too much accuracy there. Only I find ludicrous his claim that he tried to achieve 'a series of poems in which the poet's intentions are placed within a context of late twentieth century values', with its supposition that a recent poet needs a little gentle updating. Anyway, here for the purpose of comparison is Reid's version:

> The handle creaks in cranking the well-shaft,
> and water brims to spill into the light,
> memory's a rainbow in the bright pail —
> the image minted was once part of you.
> I bend to it, and my face polishes
> the interlinking shadows. Which is true?
> Things change upon the instant...
> The wheel hums.
> Its rage will deliver you to the pit.
> It's only for a moment that we're two.

His first line attends to the sound effect but leaves the question of how you can crank 'the well-*shaft*'. His imported 'rainbow', 'minting' and 'interlinking shadows' over-define and leave the impression of the poet flailing about for a suitable image. 'The wheel hums' sounds altogether too acoustically harmless, the penultimate line introduces a slice of Poe, or Hammer Gothic (late twentieth-century values?), and the final line delivers an unexpected happy ending, near as you can get the exact opposite of what Montale writes. Here — though this is not always the case with his versions — Reid leaves a serious doubt as to whether he has grasped the meaning of the original before spinning off on his own orbit. Galassi's translations never leave the reader with this doubt, and the notes, even if they can be exhausting to read, are hugely informative about Montale's practices and prosody, and also about the interconnections both between his own poems and between them and his predecessors. For making the qualities of Montale's poetry more generally perceptible and comprehensible than they've ever been before to English speakers, Galassi's volume is likely to be irreplaceable for a long time.

London Review of Books, 1 July 1999

— 35 —

More Montale

Over the last fifty years, no other Italian poet except Dante has been so often translated into English as Montale. Googling Amazon for book publications confirms this guess. And that's not to speak of the innumerable one-off versions by contemporary poets, or of the burgeoning critical industry in English, let alone the mountainous one in Italy. This kind of fame has the effect of flattening out the context his poems emerge from as well as crowding out the reputations of several remarkable contemporaries and successors. It's a monument that fills the whole piazza.

Writing about Edgar Allen Poe, Montale asked: 'Has he been favoured by his myth, the legend made of him? We have no difficulty in believing that, but the destiny of poets is also a part of their work.' Criticism should have some 'difficulty' with this belief, and should surely try to disentangle the work from its reception. Montale's reputation is distinct from Poe's in that his eminence abroad corresponds to his fame in Italy, even if, there, it isn't bestowed nearly so exclusively. The Nobel Prize can only have helped, though Salvatore Quasimodo, an earlier winner, hasn't taken over here (or taken over, here) to anything like the same extent. In Montale's case there may also be some kind of a return of favours: Italian critics often remark, sometimes rather vaguely, on the ascendancy of Anglo-American influences on his work, from Hopkins and Dickinson to Eliot. These claims are unconvincing, but there is a kind of muted irony, a use of barbed understatement, in his writing that might specially recommend him to an Anglo-Saxon readership. The fact that it comes accompanied by sun-baked Ligurian coastal views, by a sense of nature in midday, Dog-day extremis, especially in his first and most translated work, *Ossi di seppia* [Cuttlebones], only serves both to exoticize and to authenticate the mode.

Ossi di seppia, first published in 1925, when the poet was twenty-nine, must be one of the most astonishing debut poetry volumes of the last century. The earliest poem included, written when he was twenty, 'Meriggiare pallido e assorto', is a hymn to stunned inertia:

> To shelter at noon, pallid and rapt,
> back against a scalding orchard wall;
> to hear from in the thick of briars
> blackbirds' blatter, the slither of adders.
>
> To spy how over the tares' stalks, along cracks
> in the earth, lines of red ants that break
> and close ranks, intertwine
> atop miniature haystacks.

To observe through boughs the sea's
distant shimmering of scales
while from bald heights the cicadas
unleash their tremulous calls.

Then walking out in the dazzling sun,
to feel, grimly amazed, how all
of life and its drudgery is in
this act of following a wall
whose top is harled with jagged glass.

This translation of mine falls some way short of the complex acoustics of the original. Although Montale's poems will tend towards subtler and more oblique effects, the very stated moral in the original poem's last stanza is offset and facetted by an ingenious series of interlocking rhymes ('abbaglio /meraviglia / travaglio / muraglia / bottiglia). The poem's structure is basic: static infinitives organize each of the four stanzas — meriggiare, ascoltare (st. 1), spiar (st. 2), osservare (st. 3), sentire (st. 4). But the senses they call on, especially that of hearing, are vividly alert to a bristling panorama of small-scale activity. The 'k', 'g', (hard 'c') 'ch', and 'sh' sounds (schiocchi ... frusci... veccia... s'intrecciano... formiche... biche... scaglie... cicale... calvi picchi) are superbly orchestrated in the final line 'che ha in cima cocci aguzzi di bottiglia'. (It's worth remembering that in Italian the double consonants are sounded.) Though the form looks at first conventional, there are irregular lines, and even the rhyming has odd qualities such as the already noted final stanza and the hypermetric rhyme 'veccia / s'intrecciano'. The harsh consonantal quality of the writing and rhyming is reminiscent of Dante's 'rime petrose' [stony rhymes], which particularly in this section of the book (the actual '*Ossi brevi*') might be termed 'bony rhymes'.

This early poem also introduces the idea of the wall, a limit to perceptions, which will, in a number of transformations, be a signal motif throughout his work. It appears in the volume's proem 'In limine' as the 'erto muro' [sheer wall], as well as 'the net', a break in which will allow the addressee to escape. Elsewhere this image becomes a veil, a seal, a husk, and most famously 'un'aria di vetro' [literally, an air of glass], a glass screen. Though some of them are addressed to absent people, the poems are essentially self-communing, or rather enact an engagement of the self with the natural world, minutely and brilliantly apprehended, but always acknowledging some prohibiting veto, some wall that blocks human access to the primary and Edenic. Frequent bird, animal and plant imagery is constantly set against the defining backdrop of the sea. The risk of solipsism is not always averted, but the rewards of the poems are in their chaffing, percussive musicality, the precision of the imagery and the vast reach of language that blends the colloquial, even occasionally dialect words, with the offbeat and recondite (here, for example, the verb 'Meriggiare' is uncommon and literary).

The negative constructions that abound in his work are already fully present in this first book (most famously in those lines from another *Osso*, 'Don't ask us for the word...': 'all we can tell you today is | what we *don't* want, what we *aren't*') and announce a sceptical, resistant sensibility. Montale is a poet of resonant negatives, an anti-rhetorical stance probably taken with D'Annunzio in his sights. This cast of mind will equip him well for the years of Fascism, and *Le occasioni*, his second and perhaps greatest book, takes what was essentially a contract with the natural world and exposes it to the social world, to the *terra firma* of culture, as he was to call it.

Le occasioni was published in 1939, its composition more or less coinciding with the poet's residence in Florence. The move towards greater obliquity, or Hermeticism, can be seen in the sequence 'Mottetti', where single images, or 'flashes' (the English word is used by Montale) suddenly illuminate a whole psychological complex, and then, just as abruptly, vanish. The poems are more fractured, sometimes even febrile in their imagery. For all that the personal experience they record seems under increasing external threat, the writing itself has an unwavering assurance. Pasolini characterized Montale's poetry as the product of a wounded, bourgeois sensibility, but this unnecessarily limits the scope of the poems. The critic Glauco Cambon notes that though the First World War, in which Montale was a combatant, rarely surfaces in his poems, 'the repercussion of that first holocaust of the century is to be felt in the atmosphere of hopelessness which recurrently visits his poetry', and his refusal of any further ideological conscription is informed by that experience.

Another feature that emerges fully in these poems is the presence of a 'tu', often a woman, whom the poem addresses. As with the dedicatory poem of *Ossi di seppia*, these figures (who will come to be known as Clizia, Arletta, etc.) are often the repositories of the poet's fugitive hopes for an alternative to the increasingly sinister world the poems register.

Those years of, and leading up to, the Second World War might not seem the most auspicious of times for a poet to try to re-animate a Provençal or 'stilnovistic' convention, in which a departing or absent female figure becomes a crucial — both spiritual and erotic — governing principle of the poem. But this renewal of a tradition is what Montale undertakes. And, by anchoring this principle within the menace and finely observed phenomena of the times, in 'Dora Markus', 'News from Mount Amiata' and 'The Coastguard's House', for example, he achieves effects of extraordinary intensity.

For those wanting to learn more about this topic, and much else about the individual poems of the first three volumes, Jonathan Galassi's notes to his translation (Montale, *Collected Poems, 1920–1954*) offer an incisive summary of a range of critical material on the poet. When I reviewed the book, I objected to this long coda of footnotes the poems had to drag behind them, but have since been grateful for their existence. Still, the question remains as to how fruitful all the endless research into the symbolic properties of these addressees really is, and it's a question about which Montale himself remains playfully sceptical.

These absent presences, though they may involve actual figures such as Irma Brandeis, a Jewish friend and Italianist who returned to the U.S. in 1938, are also poignant residues of the poet himself, the 'signs' of life of a spirit that hasn't been deadened by the times it lives in. The 'tu' which, Montale himself joked in a later poem, has become a critical institution, is also something that belongs within the consciousness of the poem, a fugitive other. And so much of the finest of Montale's writing is pitched towards these curtailed impressions or flashes that vouchsafe a sense, however menaced, of a better life.

In *La bufera* (1956), the third volume which completes his major work, a woman addressee (probably Clizia) gloriously re-emerges in one of his greatest poems, 'L'anguilla' [The Eel]. Another, more earthbound, figure, La Volpe [the Vixen] — identified as the poet Maria Luisa Spaziani — provides a contrast to the ethereal and transcendental Clizia. Oddly, Robert Lowell's translation of 'The Eel' incorporates the next, untitled poem which is addressed to La Volpe ('Se t'hanno assomigliato...') as part of 'The Eel'. I suspect this was done inadvertently through his use of George R. Kay's *Penguin Book of Italian Verse* as the source. There, the second poem follows 'The Eel' without title, so that a reader not paying attention to the conventions of the book (first word in caps.; first letter in larger size for each new poem) might easily assume the two separate poems were two stanzas of the same poem. Had Lowell referred to an Italian text — or even looked more closely at Kay — the error wouldn't have occurred. Apart from links in the imagery, the two poems in the Italian have interesting formal similarities, each being thirty lines long without a full-stop and ending in a question. Though the two poems seem to be addressed to different women, the deliberate formal connections between them may have added to Lowell's conviction that the two belonged together, and may even account for the way Lowell has badly misconstrued the final question of 'L'anguilla'. (*Imitations* prints both Italian 'titles', separated by a semi-colon, after his translation, which would suggest that, by the time of printing, Lowell had been made aware of his initial mistake — but, by that stage, I suspect he was committed to the version as it stands.) Given the licence he claims for his versions, why shouldn't he call them (make them) '*sisters*', to reprise Montale's question at the end of 'The Eel'? I think the answer is that they aren't, and Lowell, for all the energy of his version, leaves 'The Eel' in a sorry tangle.

Several subsequent volumes followed in a far quicker succession that wasn't to be interrupted by his death in 1981. (He seems to have cannily arranged for a productive afterlife.) Beginning with *Satura* (1971) — effectively considered the cut-off point — these works have a drier, more casual tone. Their manner of de-mythologizing the earlier work has caused some dismay in critics such as the poet Giovanni Raboni, as if they were not just a falling-off but a betrayal. Montale himself acknowledges that the three first books constitute a complete entity, calling them his three canticles. Many of these later poems have the air of aftermath, of having outlived their occasions; and yet though they lack the pitch of intensity and the musicality of the earlier work, they can still call on his style of 'condensed despatch'. In contrast to the shadowy, supramundane, female figures that populate his earlier poems, the elegies for his wife, Drusilla Tanzi, nicknamed La Mosca, in *Satura*'s Xenia sequences, tenderly and ironically record a vivid, actual presence. Even the briefest of these work well within the sequence:

> Listening was the only way you had of seeing.
> Now the telephone bill's a damn sight cheaper.

(His wife's short-sightedness is a recurrent image.)

A poem like 'In the Window' could represents this late manner:

Birds that bode ill — say owls of one type
or another — only turn up live
in undernourished Kasbahs or else stuffed
in the glass cases of misanthropes. And if
a swallow should happen to build its nest
in a vent or flue and an incautious tenant
snuffed it from the fumes: that would be a one-off
and not enough to change the total picture.

Considering the abundance, one could say excess, of translations of his best-known work, mightn't these sinewy and durable late poems — relatively ignored in the English-speaking world — deserve more attention?

Poetry London, 52, Autumn 2005

Hart Crane: The Imaged Word

Hart Crane, *Complete Poems* (Newcastle upon Tyne: Bloodaxe, 1984).

The importance of Hart Crane's poetry has never been in doubt in America. In Britain, where his poems have only been intermittently available, his reputation is far less sure. One reason may be that Crane's richly metaphoric and flamboyant style is at odds with the prevalent idioms of British poetry. Certainly, the six poems of 'Voyages', interweaving rhapsody and menace, sound recklessly exotic:

> Bind us in time, O seasons clear, and awe.
> O minstrel galleons of Carib fire,
> Bequeath us to no earthly shore until
> Is answered in the vortex of our grave
> The seal's wide spindrift gaze toward paradise.

These poems celebrate Crane's love affair with the sailor Emil Opfer, but their achievement is to show that love placed vulnerably at the centre of his whole experience as a poet. Though lines such as 'All but the pieties of lovers' hands' are hard to like, there's a pitch of intensity about the sequence unmatched since Shelley's *Epipsychidion*, an astonishing energy of rhythm and metaphor that avoids dispersal only through a desperate centripetal impulse on Crane's part: 'Hasten while they are true, — sleep, death, desire, | Close round one instant in one floating flower.'

His poems often have the dubious distinction of making the visible almost impossible to see: 'Portending eyes and lips and making told | The chancel port and portion of our June.' (There, the pun on port-ending, beautifully placed as it is, tends to overshadow the actual 'eyes and lips'.) But Crane's essentially symbolist design is to catch the experience of a thing rather than the thing itself. He longs for 'an "interior" form', as he puts it in an early letter, 'a form that is so thorough and intense as to dye the words themselves with a peculiarity of meaning.' In his best work, Crane achieves precisely this 'alchemy of the word'.

A fierce internal conflict of celebration and self-doubt is at its most apparent in his last, flayed testament, 'The Broken Tower', but just as crucially underpins an earlier poem like 'Repose of Rivers', one of his finest lyrics. It closes with a remarkably vivid sense of restoration, the fragility of which is highlighted by the negative comparison:

> ...There, beyond the dykes
>
> I heard wind flaking sapphire, like this summer,
> And willows could not hold more steady sound.

Committed to charting fugitive moments of vision, Crane is drawn to words like 'steady' and 'level' for the promise they hold of some more lasting covenant:

> The imaged word, it is, that holds
> Hushed willows anchored in its glow.
> It is the unbetrayable reply
> Whose accent no farewell can know.

Do those double-negatives add up to a positive that's believable, or desirable? To a great extent, the poignancy of these effects depends on the reader's feelings about writing being so unashamedly about writing. I've a preference for the less vatic; the moments of fatigue, as in 'Voyages V' or the wonderful 'Harbour Dawn', whilst realizing the quieter cadences they induce in Crane are intimately bound to the upward momentum that is his hallmark. 'Harbour Dawn' is to a fitful urban sleep what Frost's 'After Apple-Picking' is to rural drowsiness, both steeped in the enriched and looming images of a half-awake state:

> And then a truck will lumber past the wharves
> As winch engines begin throbbing on some deck
> Or a drunken stevedore's howl and thud below
> Comes echoing alley-upward through dim snow.
>
> And if they take your sleep away sometimes
> They give it back again. Soft sleeves of sound
> Attend the darkling harbour, the pillowed bay;

These lines are as effortlessly sensitive to the fog-muffled harbour sounds as Thelonius Monk's piano music is to the lulls and crescendos of New York traffic. The skill with which the phrase 'pillowed bay' and the synaesthesia 'soft sleeves of sound' manage to make the outside happenings a part of 'This wavering slumber' suggests the kind of success Crane could achieve when he lowered his sights a little.

For all its historical sweep, the central theme of Crane's long poem *The Bridge* is the modern city. Here the marriage of the ancient land-based cultures of America with its modern urban destiny is given a poetic and supramundane warrant: 'Sustained in tears the cities are endowed | And justified conclamant with ripe fields'. The Miltonic echo of 'justified' conveys Crane's sense of a calling to interpret the city and wrest from it something other than the spiritual poverty portrayed in *The Waste Land*. The urgent need to humanize technology in the Ford era, to articulate its possibilities and those of America itself may be hard to swallow in the context of the space shuttle and recent U.S. foreign policy. To have Crane's 'sidereal phalanxes' prophesying Reagan's star wars is to show the way his optimisms collude with some of the less wholesome aspects of the American Dream.

Though the poet's ambition to be the 'Pindar of the Machine Age' leads, in the 'Cape Hatteras' section, to a resounding bellyflop from Brooklyn's parapets ('By Hatteras bunched the beached heap of high bravery'), *The Bridge* is full of lines of great lyric power. In its memorable opening stanzas, for example, the way 'chained' is played against 'Liberty' and the downward drag of office-work against the gull's aerial grace gives an idea of how the poem is much more than a hymn to the Coolidge Prosperity:

How many dawns, chill from his rippling rest
The seagull's wings shall dip and pivot him,
Shedding white rings of tumult, building high
Over the chained bay waters Liberty —

Then, with inviolate curve, forsake our eyes
As apparitional as sails that cross
Some page of figures to be filed away;
— Till elevators drop us from our day...

One problem of *The Bridge*, as poem and symbol, is that the sheer weight of religious feeling Crane brings to it turns the structure into something of a golden calf. For all its steel cables, you can hear it creak under the strain of apostrophes like 'O Thou steeled Cognizance'. If such lines as 'Sibylline voices flicker, waveringly stream | As though a god were issue of the strings', seem to keep tabs on their own mythologizing, the impulse of 'Atlantis', the first-written and last-placed section of *The Bridge*, is to drive on undaunted:

Onward and up the crystal-flooded aisle
White tempest nets file upward, upward ring
With silver terraces the humming spars,
The loft of vision, palladium helm of stars...

This ransacks the language of Christianity and antiquity to invoke the metropolitan god Crane sees manifested in Brooklyn Bridge. And yet the poem remains an extraordinary attempt to realize Blake's proverb that 'Eternity is in love with the productions of time'. With this new edition, a timely product, Bloodaxe has ensured that this dazzling and difficult poet will find over here the wider readership he deserves.

Poetry Review, 1984

— 37 —

Obituary: Attilio Bertolucci

Attilio Bertolucci, born S. Lazzaro di Parma, 18 November 1911, died Rome, 14 June 2000

Longevity for poets is nowhere considered a guarantee of continued readership — its opposite being more likely to shed a posthumous glamour on the work. But Attilio Bertolucci, who died last week aged eighty-eight, has received increasing critical acclaim from his youthful first volume, *Sirio* [Sirius] of 1929 to (and beyond) his 1991 collected poems, which won the Librex-Guggenheim Prize. His poems have quietly maintained their course at a slight distance from the numerous, often clamorous, poetic movements which have succeeded each other in Italy during the last seventy years. They have profoundly regional roots in the Parma hills where he was born in 1911 and (except for a post-war period of residence in Rome) has continued to live. Thanks to Bertolucci, the names of small places like Casarola, Cinghio and Montibello have become firmly inscribed on the poetic map of Italy. If this were all, he would have been respected as a regional poet, a kind of landscape watercolourist. What lifts his work above a conventional agrarian nostalgia and quiescence is the sense of a menace and fragility that hangs over his well-lit impressionism. His skies are frequently 'rent' or 'broken to the west by long wounds of light' and, a shadow of anxiety constantly falls over the natural world: 'in autumn the chestnut tree is ill | its spread of gold means death.'

Anxiety loiters at the edge of his compositions, though his reticence makes it hard to be sure how much it is due to a historical predicament, how much to a personal disposition. He suffered for many years from a nervous condition, but whatever the source, at his best this affliction prevents those moments in which his writing celebrates small daily pleasures from ever being too complacent. On a formal level this sense of menace and melancholia is perceptible in the syntax which achingly prolongs and even estranges what he describes. His sentences often extend description to the thinness of a veil so that paradoxically the solidity of the perceived world becomes suspect and almost subject to an unravelling, a desubstantiation.

From the outset Bertolucci's poems combined lyric candour with shadowy reserve. The poet Montale, who liked to barb his praise with musical analogies, wrote that 'his is a small voice, that of a comic tenor, but with a fine sound'. Luigi Malerba, remembering conversations with him over many years, never recalls his voice rising to the level of an exclamation mark, and the same quiet, intimate, conversational tone can be heard throughout his work. A poem like 'The White Rose' has the freshness and lightness of touch that characterizes his early work:

I will pick for you
the last rose in the garden,
the white rose that flowers
in the first mists.
The avid bees came to visit it
until yesterday
but it's still lovely enough
to make one tremble
— it's a portrait of you at thirty,
a bit forgetful, as you will be then.

But even here, the change of season, the sense of yesterday and the final accelerated leap into the future (for all that he turns it into a delicate compliment) have a premonitory ring.

His long poem *La camera da letto* [The Bedroom] published in 1984 and 1988, and winner of the Viareggio Prize, is a kind of autobiographical novel in verse which brings to fruition the narrative tendencies already discernible in earlier collections such as *La capanna indiana* (1951) — which also won the same prize — *In un tempo incerto* (1955) and *Viaggio d'inverno* (1971). This saga traces the settlement of his family in the Parma region and his own life story. It is a rare example of the long poem in twentieth-century Italian poetry, a poetry that has taken Edgar Allen Poe's and, later, Benedetto Croce's strictures about the long poem very much to heart. It looks back to Wordsworth's *Prelude* and even its examination of childhood unease harks back to that earlier model. Wordsworth's individual confidence, with its revolutionary scope, here assumes a quieter, domestic aspect, as though the rural middle class, from which both poets emerged, had been sidelined by history in the intervening years (a process already well under way in Wordsworth's 1850 revisions). Nevertheless what is striking about the book is the manner in which it resolutely sets up and insists on the integrity of the poet's personal story against the claims of history.

After abandoning law studies, he took up art history in Bologna under Roberto Longhi, and taught the subject in a Parma school until 1954. Still a teenager, he began writing film reviews for the Gazzetta di Parma, and his passion for cinema seems to have been passed on to his two sons, Bernardo and Giuseppe, both renowned film directors. Throughout his life Bertolucci collaborated with this and other newspapers, notably *La Repubblica*, reviewing films, theatre, visual arts and literature. A collection of his essays, *Ho rubato due versi a Baudelaire* [I Stole Two Lines from Baudelaire], which he gathered together before his death, has just been published. In 1938, the year of his marriage to Ninetta Giovanardi, with whom he has spent his life since, he also helped found and directed the important foreign poetry book series La Fenice. Since then, he has edited several magazines including *Paragone* and *Nuovi Argomenti* as well as directing the cultural section of the TV programme L'Approdo.

His *Selected Poems*, translated into English by Charles Tomlinson, were published in 1993.

The Times, June 2000

— 38 —

Giorgio Bassani: *The Novel of Ferrara*

Taking a break from the 2016 centenary conference on Giorgio Bassani in Ferrara, where scholars, editors and translators from all over Europe had gathered to celebrate his work, I found myself in Via Vittoria in front of a disused, derelict building. Its sombre façade of ancient brickwork was hard to distinguish from the other neighbouring houses, except for a white marble plaque next to the arched doorway. Erected by the Jewish Community of Ferrara on 20 November 1992, that, too, was commemorating a centenary: a quincentenary of the same date in 1492, when Duke Ercole I d'Este had welcomed the Jews exiled from Spain to the city. It also recorded how the Sephardic synagogue on this site had been destroyed by the Nazis in 1944. Its twelve lines spanned five hundred years of history, asserted the place of Sephardic culture in Italy, and recorded these acts of welcome and persecution.

Was this then, I wondered, the site of the third synagogue mentioned in Bassani's *The Garden of the Finzi-Continis* as the place of worship for a small section of the Jewish community, the 'Fanese', somewhat shadowy and intriguing to the narrator, whose family attended the main temple in nearby Via Mazzini? The inscription immediately recalled the use Bassani makes — throughout his work, but especially in *Within the Walls* — of the city's public memorials, its plaques, statues and funerary inscriptions, and of his impulse to flesh out the history hidden behind the public print with the story of the complex private lives of those who witnessed the recorded events.

In that book of short stories alone, apart from the commemorative plaque of General Diaz's 1918 victory speech in the school where Clelia Trotti teaches, two other public memorials take centre stage in the narrative. 'A Memorial Tablet in Via Mazzini' begins with a peasant boy affixing to the temple façade a tablet listing the names of the 183 Jews deported to the camps and murdered by the Nazis. His work is interrupted by the hesitant protest of a certain Geo Josz, a survivor erroneously listed among the dead. The second is a plaque erected on the wall of the Estense Castle moat that commemorates the eleven citizens rounded up by a Blackshirt squad and shot at dawn on 15 November 1943. These are crucial dates in Ferrara's history, and Bassani's stories explore their significance in the most unexpected ways.

Giorgio Bassani and Ferrara are as inseparable as James Joyce and Dublin or Italo Svevo and Trieste. Like Joyce, Bassani spent only a small but crucial portion of his life in the city of his major work. Though he was born — 'accidentally', he claimed — in Bologna, his whole youth was spent in Ferrara, and even when he studied at the University of Bologna, under the tuition of the eminent art historian Roberto Longhi, he commuted by train. Those journeys in third class are memorably evoked in several chapters of *The Gold-Rimmed Spectacles* as well as in 'Verso Ferrara', one of the high points of his first collection of poems:

> At this hour when through the hot endless grasslands
> the last trains make their way toward Ferrara,
> their languid whistles fade as sleep engulfs them
> along with the lingering red on village towers.

Despite the Racial Laws, he graduated in 1939 and taught in the city's Jewish school until he was arrested, in May 1943, for the anti-Fascist activities in which he'd been engaged since his student days. He was released in July, the day after Mussolini was removed from power by the Grand Fascist Council and Victor Emmanuel III. Immediately after his release, Bassani married Valeria Sinigallia, whom he had met in Ferrara's Marfisa tennis club — the model for his Eleanora D'Este Tennis Club, which in the early chapters of *The Garden of the Finzi-Continis* excluded Ferrara's Jews. Two months later, as the Allied forces pushed northward through Italy, the Germans reinstalled Mussolini in the puppet Social Republic of Salò, which, with their military assistance, controlled northern and central Italy and, therefore, Ferrara as well. With Mussolini back in power, the couple had to live under assumed names, first in Florence, then in Rome. After the war, Bassani never returned to live in Ferrara but remained in the capital, where among other jobs he worked as the editor of the prominent literary magazine *Botteghe Oscure* and later in the publishing house Feltrinelli, for whom he had the discernment to accept Giuseppe di Lampedusa's *The Leopard* after it had been rejected by all of Italy's other major publishing houses. Bassani died in 2000 and was buried in the Jewish cemetery in Ferrara, which he describes so vividly in the first chapter of *The Garden of the Finzi-Continis*.

Situated in the Po Valley in Emilia-Romagna in the northeast of Italy, Ferrara was a potent and flourishing city during the Renaissance. Since that time, it had gradually declined in power and influence, but it remained relatively prosperous. During Bassani's youth, the city's population grew from around 110,000 to 120,000. A small though civically prominent community of some seven hundred Jews lived mainly in the triangle formed by the streets Via Vignatagliata, Via Vittoria and Via Mazzini — the last being the site of the Jewish Temple, which included two active synagogues, one referred to as the 'German School', the other as the 'Italian School'. The presence of three distinct places of worship within such a small area already signals how diverse this community was. The diversity is also reflected in Bassani's warmly inclusive diction, which employs words, phrases and sentences from Greek, Latin, Hebrew, German, French, English, and Ferrarese, Veneto and Hispano-Jewish dialects, not to mention the peculiar family idiolect of Micòl and Alberto, referred to as *finzi-continico*. During the 1930s, Ferrara was a stronghold of Fascist adhesion; and notorious squads of Blackshirts controlled the city. In its earlier phase, many Jews, like their Catholic neighbours, were supporters of Fascism; by the latter part of the decade, however, with what became known as '*la svolta al razzismo*' — the turn toward racism — the well-integrated Jewish community found itself utterly isolated.

The six books that make up *The Novel of Ferrara* were published separately between 1956 and 1972, and each, with the possible exception of *The Smell of Hay*, is free-standing and self-sufficient. Yet Bassani chose to extensively and rigorously revise them in order to unite them under the title *Il romanzo di Ferrara*, published in Italy in 1974 and republished after further revisions in 1980. That complete *Novel of Ferrara* in its definitive, final revision now appears in English translation for the first time. At some stage in the writing, it became clear to Bassani that the six books shared not only time and place and a cast of characters but also an essential aesthetic unity. The seed of the entire work — its nucleus and donnée — is already present and apparent in *Within the Walls*, first published as *Cinque storie ferraresi* [*Five Stories of Ferrara*]. In the concluding piece of the whole *Romanzo*, the author steps forward *in prima persona* to give an account of the composition of that first book, and its title 'Down There, at the End of the Corridor' echoes a phrase stressed in the opening of the very first story, 'Lida Mantovani'.

The nearest English equivalent for the word *romanzo* is the generic term 'novel', but in Italian it also carries the echo of an older meaning, one that goes back to the medieval 'romance' — originally a poem that celebrated the chivalric adventures of a hero or group of protagonists. It's likely that for Bassani the term held some of these poetic resonances. After all, as he insisted in an interview, he was as much a poet as a novelist. That may help explain why he designated this gathering of four short novels and two collections of short stories by the *singular* title of *Romanzo*. But it's also important to remember that for Bassani the role of the poet is to 'return from the realm of the dead and speak of what he saw there', as he remarked in the same interview — explicitly referring to the character Geo Josz, who becomes a living record of a history that, during the Liberation, was in the process of erasure; Josz is therefore an increasingly uncomfortable reminder of what his Ferrarese neighbours are busily trying to forget.

Bassani's *Romanzo* has unforgettably put his city, and the Jewish community he belonged to, on the map of modern consciousness. While Ferrara is present in all its formidable weight throughout, it still had to be rebuilt in his imagination, and the birth of this imaginary city had a slow gestation. (In his first collection of stories, *A City of the Plain*, published in 1940 — with the Racial Laws prohibiting Jewish publications in full effect — under the nom de plume of Giacomo Marchi, Ferrara is referred to merely as 'F'.) Aspects of the city's history are adumbrated throughout the *Romanzo*, but the central and recurrent historical focus in most of the works is the Fascist era, and most specifically 1938, the year in which the Racial Laws were enacted. These laws followed the German precedent of the Nuremberg Laws and severely curtailed the lives of Italian Jews with regard to employment, education and intermarriage, making them, hitherto respected citizens, 'strangers in their own home', in the telling phrase of the Portuguese poet Tatiana Faia. This theme emerges again and again for the characters in Bassani's fiction. Both *The Garden of the Finzi-Continis* and, even more centrally, *The Gold-Rimmed Spectacles* observe the process of 'eviction' through the eyes of Bassani's first-person narrator, an unnamed alter ego, the 'I' of both these books and also of *Behind the Door.* Bassani declared that the 'I', which he came to realize was such an essential element in the narrative, was a figure who was not exactly himself, although 'very like' in numerous respects.

In *The Gold-Rimmed Spectacles*, the fate of marginalization that befalls the Jewish narrator is shared by the homosexual doctor Athos Fadigati, and it's an act of imaginative generosity that allows Bassani to explore the subtle and devastating parallels between the two figures in this compact masterpiece.

On his return from Buchenwald, Geo Josz finds his house occupied by the partisans and is forced to encamp in the attic, awaiting its delayed repossession. But there are various, less explicit forms of estrangement enacted in these novels. The schoolboy narrator of *Behind the Door* ends the novel alienated from his family and his own well-being because of the treachery of a school companion — a unique case that, the narrator himself concedes, has for once little to do with his Jewish identity. The fiercely hierarchical and competitive school, however, foreshadows some of the cruelties and divisions that will soon become evident in the political sphere.

Perhaps the most profound treatment of eviction occurs in *The Garden of the Finzi-Continis*, where the narrator first experiences the increasing ostracism of the Jewish community; but then, in a turn that is even more psychologically devastating, he is expelled from the Edenic garden itself, which had offered a haven from this trauma. The loss of the garden is also linked to the loss of his first love, the radiant, precocious and elusive Micòl. Of the four 'novels' within the *Novel*, *The Heron* is the most atypical, not sharing the same first-person narrator of the other three, and being mainly set *outside* the city walls, in the nearby countryside. Yet it offers a particularly extreme and harrowing study of the corrosive effects of exclusion. Edgardo Limentani has returned from his Swiss exile and, in the compass of a single winter day of 1947, comes to know his full estrangement from his time, his city, his family, and finally his own life.

In his concluding essay, 'Down There, at the End of the Corridor', Bassani describes how, when composing his stories, he would find a geometric image taking shape in his mind. His account is oddly like the dream of the ouroboros that helped Friedrich August Kekulé resolve the chemical structure of the benzene ring. One such image that presides over 'A Memorial Tablet in Via Mazzini' is of two spheres circling one another, the two spheres being the irreconcilable entities: the city of Ferrara and Geo Josz. It's an image that could serve beyond the particular story's parameters for the entire *Romanzo.* If we see one orbiting circle as Bassani, or his various narrators, and the wall-encircled city of Ferrara as the other, we might have a simplified vision of the intricate construction and interlocking of these six books.

The geometrical images that guided Bassani — his visual imagination likely fostered by his study of art history — highlight a significant feature of his fiction. It is an exploration not only of time lost and time preserved but of space — especially architectural and urban spaces: cemeteries, gardens, streets, porticoes, and, foremost among these, the Jewish Temple described with such virtuosity in *The Garden of the*

Finzi-Continis. But even domestic interiors in Bassani are laden with significance. The cramped basement flat in 'Lida Mantovani', 'Professor' Ermanno Finzi-Contini's crowded study, Dr Fadigati's surgery, with its aspirational elegance, and the storeroom in Dr Elia Corcos's mansion are just a few examples of the way space shapes and impinges upon the lives of his characters. Perhaps the most intriguing interior description is of the chemist's room in 'A Night in '43' — the room from which Pino Barilari witnesses the massacre of Ferrara's citizens by the squad of Blackshirts and which Bassani approaches with an extraordinary circuitous tact. But none of these instances serve a merely decorative purpose; they are, rather, manifestations of time, or magnetic force fields for history.

The city walls — the '*bastioni*', as Bassani often metonymically refers to them — are both literal and metaphorical, and are not only the traditional place for romantic trysts but offer views out beyond into the flat countryside of the Po Valley; they are also the site of the first real encounter between the narrator and Micòl. The city walls are topped with a broad tree-lined avenue, along which one can walk or cycle almost uninterruptedly the entire nine-kilometre circumference of the city. (And Ferrara is still one of the few Italian cities where bicycles are the main mode of transport.) One frequently mentioned site, just within the walls at the south-east of the city, is Montagnone ('the big mountain'), which is actually a small hill built from the stone left from the construction of the walls and later turned into a garden. These walls, encrusted with history, are the verdant lookouts and the protective but also imprisoning circle for the many lives that Bassani's fiction illuminates, and there are walls within the walls — the inner walls encircle what was once the ghetto, walled in when Ferrara became one of the Papal States, which leads Bassani to describe his community as '*intra muros*'.

Time is not only factored into the tenses and structure of the narrative but is integral to the style and syntax. The characteristically long sentences, rich in subclauses and lengthy embedded parentheses — a translator's challenge, or nightmare — have a way of slowing up time, which is moving toward an ineluctable and fatal conclusion, and resembles those tennis matches played in the idyllic garden of the Finzi-Continis deep into dusk when the ball becomes all but invisible yet the play continues. A more declared sense of the passage of time is perceptible in *The Heron*, which begins when Limentani awakens to the insistent but discreet alarm of his Jaeger clock, and continues as on almost every page he anxiously consults his Swiss Vacheron-Constantin wristwatch to check the time as it elapses. The whole story takes a day (and Bassani speculated that the experience of reading it might be of the same duration) — a day we assume to be the last day in the protagonist's life, and so observing an inexorable Aristotelian unity. (The four sections of the novel, each comprising six chapters, amount, aptly enough, to twenty-four.) The only passage where this succession is suspended is during a mid-afternoon sleep, which disrupts the tedium of clock time with a bright and confusing dream time that accurately tells of the character's psychic disturbance, the way he is utterly out of step with his times. A well-off, land-owning Jew, he has returned from Swiss exile after the defeat of Fascism to find that he is hated by his tenants and effectively estranged from his home and his Christian wife, while the ex-Fascist Bellagamba, a bullying Blackshirt, has adapted perfectly to the new regime and has set up a prospering hotel restaurant in the neighbouring small town of Codigoro.

The actual places and factual dates — sometimes, as I've mentioned, the two combine on memorial plaques and monuments — are Bassani's material, and I can think of no other writer of fiction so concerned with factuality. He claimed to be 'one of the few, the very few, contemporary writers who places dates in the context of what he writes'. When Vittorio de Sica made his cinematic version of *The Garden of the Finzi-Continis* and had the narrator's father in the end transported to the death camps, Bassani indignantly withdrew his name from the film. That 'it didn't happen like that' would seem a strange objection from a novelist, but this gives us an idea of how significant historical veracity was to Bassani. Nevertheless — and this is where the overarching title of *Romanzo* needs to be kept in mind — only through the imaginative liberties he learned how to take, with the material he knew so intimately, could the novelist arrive, as he so convincingly does, at such a fierce and truthful evocation of the reality he, his community, and his city lived through.

Introduction to Giorgio Bassani, *The Novel of Ferrara*
(New York: W. W. Norton, 2018)

— 39 —

Stealing the Pumpkins: Cesare Pavese

Cesare Pavese, *Disaffections: Complete Poems, 1930–1950*, trans. by Geoffrey Brock (Manchester: Carcanet, 2004)

Cesare Pavese is one of those singular, disruptive poets, like Blake or Lawrence, who go against the grain — or the flow — of their culture, and for whom precedents would be as hard to find as successors. Poetry represents only part of Pavese's rich and compact achievement, which includes short stories and nine brief novels, as well as a compelling, often lacerating, journal that records his literary development from 1935 until his suicide in 1950 at the age of forty-two. His many translations of American novels and his critical essays opened a window during Italy's Fascist years onto another, more democratic, world.

His first poems, excluded here, are mostly flailing *cris-de-coeur* but in 1930 he completed a poem, 'South Seas', which pointed the way ahead, supplying him with an immense quarry for his future work, broaching a whole series of themes and, perhaps inseparable from them, a new form. Ousting the Italian hendecasyllable, it deploys a longer, flexible, anapaestic line, for which Geoffrey Brock has found a workable equivalent in English. The setting of 'South Seas' is Pavese's native Langhe hills in Piedmont — bare, hard uplands where peasants eked out a living from vineyards and smallholdings. Brock loses the two explicit references to the Langhe in this poem, universalizing them as 'hills'. Pavese's poems set these hills in tormented opposition to the neighbouring industrial city of Turin, one of several taut dialectics at work in his writings.

He kept adding poems to his first book *Lavorare stanca* [*Work's Tiring*] in the manner of *Leaves of Grass* or *Les Fleurs du mal*, two works he particularly admired. The title itself is a provocation to the Fascist regime that stressed the dignity of labour in its official art. (One contemporary postage stamp, in an issue to celebrate the Fascist Era, portrays a labourer towering over his plough with the stirring motto: 'Why Italy has bread for all its children'.) Pavese's poems address the indignities of labour — where it's to be had — and otherwise the bitterness of unemployment, and bread and sustenance are far from plentiful either for the peasants of the hills or the proletariat of Turin.

His poems select lives and stories that are anything but shining examples for the Fascist state, a cast of marginals and misfits — prostitutes, the unemployed, winos, drifters, prisoners, thieves. He portrays a dystopic Italy with blood on its streets, its homesteads ruled by incestuous fathers. That Pavese's first book should have passed so unscathed (only four of its poems fell foul of Mussolini's censor) is a testimony to how mildly, or else inattentively, that office was undertaken.

In his diary, Pavese describes the way he evolved what he variously calls 'poesia-racconto' [poem-story] and 'immagine-racconto' [image-story]. This last term takes us closer to his procedures. Often two images are constellated or merged, as in 'Atlantic Oil' where the first line 'The drunk mechanic is happy to be in the ditch' already suggests the two liquids — alcohol and petrol — which will govern the poem's progress. The mechanic dreams of producing his own wine in the future but his present is lived in the thirsty summer dust raised by the passing cars, themselves thirsting for petrol. At the poem's heart lies a typically sensuous perception:

> It's a pleasure to spend the morning in the shade
> where the stink of oil's cut with the smell of green,
> of tobacco, of wine...

once more bringing the two vital fluids into co-relation or exchange.

'Two Cigarettes' is another poem subtly articulated around a central image. It describes the meeting of a client with a prostitute under the streetlamps. In Italy prostitutes are sometimes referred to as 'lucciole' [fireflies] because their presence is signalled by the flare of a cigarette end. Although the word itself is never used, it is suggested throughout the poem: the wind in the opening lines is called 'lucido' and the conversation is punctuated by references to the cigarettes they smoke: 'Two butts, now, on the asphalt...'. The cigarettes give a promise of brief, creaturely pleasure, and there's a human warmth to this poem, rare at least among the earlier poems, as the two figures leave the scene, crossing 'the street, arm in arm, playfully warming each other.'

Pavese's language is a stark vernacular, sparsely flecked with dialect (as if to avoid too much literary 'colour') and resolutely bare like the hills he describes in poem after poem. He makes this connection himself in 'South Seas' in describing the speech of his returned friend:

> He told me all this, not in Italian,
> but in the slow dialect of these parts, which, like the rocks
> right here on this hill, is so rugged and hard
> that two decades of foreign tongues and oceans
> never scratched its surface...

His language and syntax would seem to offer few obstacles to the translator. Yet the irregular geometry of his dependent clauses tends to lay the phrases at odd angles to each other until the end of the sentence resolves or at least realigns them. Much depends also on the resonance of his final lines which often reinscribe the whole poem's trajectory, whilst deftly avoiding the epigrammatic.

Though much of his writing is obdurately opposed to the values of Mussolini's Italy, and though he was jailed and sent into internal exile in Brancaleone, Pavese is not a straightforwardly political poet. His tough, inclusive vision, however, and his refusal to turn away from human misery give his writings an additional, almost documentary, value. In 'Fallen Women' he begins:

People are right to treat them like that.
It's certainly better than pitying them
in your heart before you enjoy them in bed.

The poem returns to this idea: 'Pity was always a waste of time. | Existence is terrible, pity won't change that. | It's better to keep quiet, jaws clenched.' A tension is generated in his writing by a drive 'to keep quiet' and the urgency of his need to describe. Other elements in his writing, however, are not so fundamentally at odds with the regime, notably his misogyny. Paradoxically, his poems often investigate the actual condition of women's lives and even, in several cases, manage with terse empathy to depict the memories and the state of mind of prostitutes.

In Brock's translation some problems occur with what language teachers call 'false friends'. In 'Landowners', he turns the phrase 'la gente che rantola' into 'ranting patients', though the verb means gasp, as in death-throes. In the same poem 'le cure' of the priest attending the dying does not, in this case, mean 'his cures' but rather the things he has to do.[1] Elsewhere 'rubando le zuche' means ' stealing the pumpkins' not 'filling his gourds'. There are other slips of this order, but these don't detract from the solid merits of the translation, which is the best, and the most ample, in English to date.

Pavese's poems could be accused of a certain narrowness — a lack of humour and variety in tone and language. Even some of his images — his hills and streetlamps — can become over-insistent, whilst his favoured trope of dog and bitch to describe human sexuality is as bleakly reductive as late Tolstoy. And yet his marvellously peopled poems not only document the time — what Calvino called 'the Pavese era' — but also bear witness to a unique and restless intelligence.

Guardian, 2 October 2004

1 My bad! Brock uses the term 'cures' correctly, if a shade quaintly. Anyway, this kind of lexical, error-finding criticism is wearisome.

— 40 —

Pier Paolo Pasolini: *Affabulazione*. Introduction

The fame — and notoriety — of Pier Paolo Pasolini (1922–1975) as poet, filmmaker, intellectual, essayist, novelist and short-story teller is undiminished. His six works for the theatre, however, have been largely overlooked, even in Italy. *Affabulazione*, a play written in free verse, perhaps the best known of them, was published in 1966. In 1975, the year of Pasolini's murder, it was first performed in Turin by a group of young actors, and then two years later in Rome's Teatro Tenda, directed by Vittorio Gassman, who also played the main part.

The play proper begins with a cry and with an ominous dream which deeply unsettles the Milanese factory-owner, the protagonist, who is spending the summer vacation with his wife and son in their country villa. As the play progresses, the Father comes to unearth more about the nature of the dream: it leads to a sexual obsession with his son, a late adolescent or young adult. What follows is the unravelling of the Father's psyche, his position, his family, his world.

The driving force of the play is the problem of self-knowledge. Its Italian title *Affabulazione* — here rendered as *Fabrication* — which includes the Latin *fabula*: fable or story — highlights the nature of the Father's plight. He is continually fabricating stories which are intended to help him understand the predicament into which he has fallen. And yet, within this long quest of self-discovery, he continually falls short of self-knowledge, or at least of any understanding that can save him from destroying himself and his family. Even in the Epilogue, as an old tramp living rough in a railway station, twenty years after he has murdered his son, he is still indefatigably weaving a new synthesis, a new mythological account of his actions.

In *The Philosophy of History*, Hegel refers to the inscription 'in the sanctuary of the Goddess Neith: *I am that which is, that which was, and that which will be; no one has lifted my veil.*' Hegel comments that 'In the Egyptian Neith, Truth is still a problem.'[1] He sees this problem as something to which the Greeks offered a partial solution in the Apollonian creed 'Man, know thyself'. This could be seen as a version of the advice the Ghost of Sophocles offers to the Father after he has been wounded by his Son. Though the counsel is in some ways abstruse, he tries to get the Father to recognize the difference between the (Egyptian) Sphinx's riddle (the 'enigma') that was solved by his Oedipus, and a 'mystery'. The one can, if rarely, be solved; the other must

1 *Georg W.F. Hegel: The Philosophy of History*, trans. J. Sibree (Ontario: Batoche Books, 2001), p.220.

be left intact. It cannot be possessed as the Father wishes to, but only contemplated.

The problem, essentially a religious problem, of what remains mysterious in human life, of what cannot be grasped rationally, presents itself again and again in Pasolini's works in terms of sexuality.

All that we know about the Father would put him at the furthest remove from Pasolini's political sympathies. He is a successful industrialist from Milan. (Milan itself, for Pasolini, represented the North Italian hegemony of wealth and power over Rome and the South. Much of his fiction as well as his first film *Accattone* (1961) reveals his imaginative sympathy with the sub-proletariat of the Roman suburbs — the *borgate*.) And yet his sexual fixation on youth is Pasolini's own. That it takes the form of a ghastly intrusion on the son's sexual autonomy is an expression of the Father's accustomed sense of his own rights and importance that this doomed love has fractured.

The historically and personally specific nature of the Father's *agon* makes it hard for the audience to perceive its bearing on the universally human, if such a thing exists. More so because the Father's obsession is so idiosyncratic and repellent. Yet this is exactly what Pasolini attempts, and with good reason. If the historically and psychologically specific has any ultimate meaning, has any potential to reveal something essential about human nature, its specificity cannot be glossed over or evaded.

Theatre

From the opening speech, delivered by the Ghost of Sophocles, the play interrogates the medium it has chosen. Pasolini is intensely conscious of the theatre's history and potential. *Affabulazione* has been seen as a parody of Sophocles' *Oedipus Rex*, though a reversal might be a more useful description. It explores a Laius-complex rather than an Oedipal one, or refigures the myth of Cronus who castrated and kills his father Uranus with a sickle. The increasing consciousness of the Father also includes a political awareness, a sense of power and its purposes, which he had previously managed as it were *naturally*. His impassioned speeches which chart the way in which fathers are at war with their sons and plot their destruction are more fundamental and tragic than a mere generational conflict, which was the evident historical setting of the Sixties, the time of the play's inception. They touch on the recognition that King Lear, who is referred to in passing in the Father's last speech, comes to when he declares of the relations between power and the dispossessed: 'I have taken too little care of all this'.

In his 'Manifesto for a New Theatre' (1968) Pasolini argues for 'a theatre of the word' — 'a mixture of poetry read aloud and of 'theatrical conventions' even if they are reduced to a minimum [...] oral poetry rendered as ritual by the physical presence of the actors in a place reserved for such a rite.' This impulse is expressed far more potently in the Ghost of Sophocles' plea for the primacy of theatre:

> In the theatre, the word lives with a double glory,
> never elsewhere so glorified. And why?
> Because the word is both written and spoken out.

It's written like the word of Homer, but
it's also spoken out like the words exchanged
by two men at work, or by a gang of boys
or by girls at the launderette or women at the market
— in short, like the poor words we speak each day,
which fly away out of sight like life itself,
the unwritten words, than which nothing
is ever more beautiful...

Out of the devastating ugliness of this psychological drama, Pasolini has raised a restless enquiry into the nature of power as well as an example of a unique kind of theatre that is replenished by its dynamic engagement with the theatre's Greek origins.

Introduction to Pier Paolo Pasolini, *Fabrication*, trans. by Jamie McKendrick (London: Oberon Modern Plays, 2010)

— 41 —

Bishop's Birds

In a letter to the critic Jerome Mazzaro, Elizabeth Bishop writes that her poem '"Santarém" *happened*, just like that, a real evening & a real place, a real Mr. Swan who said that — it is not a composite at all.' She ends her reply by stating that 'The settings, or descriptions, of my poems are almost invariably plain facts — or as close to the facts as I can write them. But, as I said, it is fascinating that my poem should arouse in you all those literary references!'[1] In another poet this insistence on 'plain facts' might be disingenuous, but it's one of the virtues of Bishop's poems to convince us that they did indeed *happen* more or less as she said they did, even if they didn't, and to convince us that Bishop is a poet — the same could be said of her as a letter writer — for whom the 'real' takes precedence over the literary. And so for her to name another poet within one of her poems almost amounts to a breach of decorum. It makes sense, then, to take such references as signals that these poems are especially concerned with the art of poetry — though it's obvious that no poem is going to be truly unconcerned.

There's no shortage of explicit literary references in Bishop's poems — 'The Gentleman of Shalott', the wittily incomplete quotation from Wordsworth in 'Crusoe in England', the line 'The boy stood on | the burning deck' from Mrs Hemans, broken in half, in 'Casabianca', as well as some occasional poems, and the direct address to Marianne Moore, the unnamed Ezra Pound in 'A Visit to St. Elizabeth's' and so on. Bishop is not the kind of parochial poet who would subscribe, at least in her practice, to any kind of simple opposition between life and literature. But the only two occasions where she names other poets in her poems are to be found in 'The Bight' and 'The Sandpiper'. In both, the references, respectively to Baudelaire and to Blake (as though her own poems were sandwiched alphabetically between them) are affectionately mocking, and in both, I'd argue, for all their lightness of touch, their air of being *en passant*, the references alert the reader to an aesthetic quarrel within the poem: they serve poems which not only differentiate her own procedures from the poet named but also enquire into her own practice as a poet.

After its self-dedication in miniscule, bracketed italics '*(On my birthday)*', 'The Bight' begins:

> At low tide like this how sheer the water is.
> White crumbling ribs of marl protrude and glare
> and the boats are dry, the pilings dry as matches.

1 Elizabeth Bishop, *One Art: The Selected Letters*, ed. by Robert Giroux (London: Pimlico, 1994), p. 621. Henceforth referred to as *Letters*.

Absorbing, rather than being absorbed,
the water in the bight doesn't wet anything,
the colour of the gas flame turned as low as possible.
One can smell it turning to gas; if one were Baudelaire
One could probably hear it turning to marimba music.

Several critics (including Bonnie Costello[2] and David Kalstone[3]) have noted how, later in the poem, the line 'The bight is littered with old correspondances' , as well as referring to the foregoing 'torn-open, unanswered letters', takes on another meaning from its association with Baudelaire's signature poem 'Correspondances'. But why is Bishop conscripting the French symbolist for a poem which describes a stretch of Floridan coastline? 'The Bight' is wonderfully painstaking in its description — it also takes pain as being of the nature of the scene: the 'ribs protrude and glare'... 'Pelicans crash'... the boats are 'bristling with jackstraw gaffs and hooks', even the water itself, in one of Bishop's unobtrusively violent wrenches of perspective and of 'plain fact', is imagined as hard and dry. Nothing could seem further from Baudelaire's synaesthetic 'forêt de symboles', his taste for the exotic and his remembered voyages, which Bishop wittily sums up as 'marimba music'. Her use of the impersonal in 'One can smell it turning to gas' has a plummy formality she immediately sends up: 'if one were Baudelaire | one could probably hear it turning to marimba music' — that possibility depends on the improbable conditional of being the great French poet. But even if she makes fun of the exotic props of Symbolism, the poem is still troubled, it seems, by the need to come up with something, to be unlike the pelicans 'rarely coming up with anything to show for it' or like the dredge which, at the end of the poem, 'Brings up a dripping jawful of marl'.

The poem is Bishop's witty, slightly desolate ('awful but cheerful') birthday present to herself, and it scrutinizes, by displacing it onto the birds and the boats, the whole 'untidy activity' of writing at the same time as it observes the seemingly pointless maritime bustle of the bight. That this lies at a substratum of the poem (to extend the delving and digging similes she uses) and remains undeclared but for the Baudelaire marker is part of the poem's preference for reality, for the primary status of what 'happened'. This counters the symbolist aesthetic — even if the poem were to fail to retrieve anything from it, we sense that she would prefer 'the dry perfectly off-beat claves' of 'the little ochre dredge at work' to marimba music. But the irony that distances her own work from Baudelaire's is also a kind of homage.

From the first line's demonstrative 'this' Bishop attends to the here and now of the scene. Even the dry, short 'i' of the first line's 'this' and 'is' is sounded emphatically through the poem, especially in her similes, her own 'correspondances': *pickaxes, scissors, glinting like little plowshares, littered with.* The sound is heard deliberately at the end: 'Click. Click. Goes the dredge', followed in the last lines by 'brings up

2 Bonnie Costello, *Elizabeth Bishop: Questions of Mastery* (Cambridge, MA, & London: Harvard University Press, 1991), pp. 184–85.

3 David Kalstone, 'Elizabeth Bishop: Questions of Memory, Questions of Travel', in *Elizabeth Bishop & Her Art*, ed. by Lloyd Schwartz and Sybil P. Estess (Ann Arbor: University of Michigan Press, 1983), p. 14.

a dripping...' and 'activity continues'. The similes, unlike Baudelaire's, are largely drawn from the everyday, from a domestic setting or workplace — matches, gas flame, pickaxes, scissors, retrievers, plowshares, litter. If I'm right that the poem contains an uneasiness as to whether its descriptions are enough and that they suggest a drying up, a 'low tide', of the imagination, there is still a brave persistence in her method and a refusal to stray into a 'forest of symbols' for more heightened effects.

Aside from the bracketed self-dedication and an almost parenthetic personal appearance in the lines 'Pelicans crash | into this peculiar gas unnecessarily hard, | it seems to me, like pickaxes', the poem is scrupulously impersonal as we've seen also in her arch use of 'one'. The poem, for all that it suppresses the personal, is strewn with muted indications that the personal still subsists, like the birthday dedication and like the 'torn-open, unanswered letters' where the violent eagerness of 'torn-open' suggests loneliness whilst the 'unanswered' implies a degree of personal chaos. As Costello points out, Bishop describes the Bight after a storm in a letter to Robert Lowell, adding 'It reminds me a little of my desk'.[4] Her later prose poem '12 O'Clock News' which again links landscape and writing, only this time the other way round, elaborates its analogues in a far more stated and static manner.

Rather than serving the kind of maritime pastoral they easily might have, the poem's details (matches, gas flame, pile of stove-in boats, litter) amount to something closer to an imminent conflagration, a sacrificial pyre. Bishop doesn't seem to be a great enjoyer of her own birthdays, as indeed her letters record.[5]The reference to her birthday also makes of the poem an unobtrusive meditation on mortality, which is implicit in the clay of the second line's 'White, crumbling ribs of marl' and reappears again at the end in 'a dripping jawful of marl', framing the entire poem with a subliminal skeleton image, a memento mori with a formal equivalence to the anamorphic skull in Holbein's *The Ambassadors*. And the hard clicking sounds throughout, as well as particular details such as the 'blue-gray shark tails hung up to dry' and 'the little white boats [...] still piled up' do much to reinforce this image of the skeleton, a figure memorably present in several Baudelaire poems, notably 'Le Squelette laboureur'. For the marl itself, Costello adduces the 'burning marl' of *Paradise Lost* — 'Key West's marl being that black sediment of dead coral which Milton used to construct hell',[6] only here it isn't black but white. A more likely prompt for Bishop, though, is the derivation of the name Key West from the Spanish *Cayo Hueso* meaning Bone Key.[7] But even though the images of clay and bone inevitably evoke mortality, Bishop steers the poem away from anything lugubrious in the comic way that the 'jawful of marl' becomes acoustically transformed into the final line: 'awful but cheerful'. The word 'bight',

4 Op. cit. p. 186. (The letter can be found in *Letters*, p. 154).

5 See *Letters*, p. 182, 'After my 38th birthday I fell into a slough for a few days...', or p. 630, 'I HATE birthdays, or mine, that is...'

6 Op. cit. ,. 186.

7 This derivation is incidentally given by Robert Frost: 'Key West (Cayo Hueso, which being translated, should be Bone Key)', in *The Letters of Robert Frost to Louis Untermeyer* (New York: Holt, Rinehart and Winston, 1963), p. 251.

meaning a wide bay, is finally made to jostle with and suggest the homophonic 'bite' by way of the word 'jawful'. (In the only recording of Bishop reading this poem, she spells out the title so the audience doesn't confuse the word with its homophone.) Incidentally, the last line 'awful but cheerful' was Bishop's favourite line from her poems: she taught it to her mynah bird, Jacob, who seems, from the evidence of one of her letters, to have added a comma 'Awful, but cheerful',[8] and also asked for it to be inscribed onto her headstone. The line has a brisk stoicism to it, the jaw set behind that drab word 'cheerful'. The poem also lives up to this motto, and through its unflagging descriptions of 'untidy activity' finally comes up with something to show for it: not just a 'moral' but an extraordinarily precise account of *this* scene and also a disguised enquiry into an aesthetic.

★ ★ ★ ★ ★

The amused, slightly distanced perspective with which Bishop observes the labour-intensive pelicans in 'The Bight' is also employed in her description — characterization might be a better word — of the wader's antics in 'The Sandpiper'. A degree of self-identification, however, becomes more apparent as the poem proceeds. And, as often in Bishop's poetry, where a sense of scale is radically challenged, this distance of perspective is offset by the extraordinarily close-up optics of the descriptive effects. The first lines bring the reader into startling proximity with the sandpiper's view of the world:

> The roaring alongside he takes for granted,
> and that every so often the world is bound to shake.
> He runs, he runs to the south, finical, awkward,
> in a state of controlled panic, a student of Blake.

Many commentators on the poem have noted that the lines from Blake which have most bearing on the poem are from the opening of 'Auguries of Innocence':

> To see a World in a Grain of Sand,
> And a Heaven in a Wild Flower,
> Hold Infinity in the palm of your Hand,
> And Eternity in an Hour.

The sandpiper's microscopic scrutiny of the shoreline is ironically equated with that of the visionary poet who insisted on the 'minute particulars' of vision. The word 'state' is a peculiarly Blakean term — as in his description of the *Songs of Innocence and Experience* as 'SHEWING THE TWO CONTRARY STATES OF THE HUMAN SOUL'. Even the name 'Sandpiper' is reminiscent of the poet's vocation as it appears in the introductory poem of Blake's *Songs of Innocence*: 'Piper, pipe that song again'. (Sand, the other component of the bird's compound name, is the object of the bird's and the poet's scrutiny.) And yet the reference makes fun of both Blake and the sandpiper in their shared obsessive questing. I think Kalstone is right to draw attention to the differences between Bishop and Blake here: 'Bishop lets us know that every detail is a boundary, not a Blakean microcosm' and to see Bishop's

8 *Letters*, p. 504.

poem as 'a critique of Blake's auguries of innocence'.[9] Almost inadvertently, and seemingly unbeknownst to himself, the sandpiper at the end of the poem does chance on, or come up with 'something' — not too far from a 'World' or 'Heaven' — in 'the millions of grains of sand', though the effect occurs as a weird by-product to his act of 'obsessed' attention.

It is as though her poem were enacting the drama that, in a celebrated letter to Anne Stevenson, she noted in Darwin:

> — But reading Darwin one admires the beautiful solid case being built up out of his endless, heroic observations, almost unconscious or automatic and then comes a sudden relaxation, a forgetful phrase, and one feels that strangeness of his undertaking, sees the lonely young man, his eyes fixed on facts and minute details, sinking or sliding giddily off into the unknown. What one seems to want in art, in experiencing it, is the same thing that is necessary for its creation, a self-forgetful, perfectly useless concentration.[10]

Her phrase 'controlled panic' is seemingly a criticism of the whole visionary enterprise — the will to control the world through one *idée fixe*. But even here there may be more self-projection than the tone would suggest. Panic, we remember, is derived from Pan, the god of music and wild places, as well as the instigator of fear. Bishop herself, in *Efforts of Affection: A Memoir of Marianne Moore*, defends Moore's poems by seeing panic as crucial to the making of art:

> Lately I have seen several references critical of her poetry by feminist writers, one of whom described her as a 'poet who controlled panic by presenting it as whimsy.' Whimsy is sometimes there, of course, and so is humor (a gift these critics sadly seem to lack). Surely there is an element of mortal panic and fear underlying all works of art?[11]

Commenting on the poem, Seamus Heaney claims that it 'has about it a touch of comedy and a hint of self-portraiture'.[12] In a way, it is the comic distance that maintains the self-portraiture at the level of a hint, and it is typical of Bishop that the bard should take a back seat to the bird. Yet, as with the Baudelaire reference in 'The Bight', the presence of Blake in the first stanza of this poem alerts the reader to the ways in which the poem is concerned with the art of writing. The poem continues:

> The beach hisses like fat. On his left, a sheet
> of interrupting water comes and goes
> and glazes over his dark and brittle feet.
> He runs, he runs straight through it, watching his toes.
>
> — Watching, rather, the spaces of sand between them,
> where (no detail too small) the Atlantic drains
> rapidly backwards and downwards. As he runs
> he stares at the dragging grains.

9 Op. cit., p. 12.

10 Quoted in *Elizabeth Bishop and Her Art*, p. 288.

11 Elizabeth Bishop, *The Collected Prose*, ed. by Robert Giroux (London: Farrar, Straus & Giroux, 1984), pp. 143–44.

12 Seamus Heaney, *The Redress of Poetry* (London: Faber and Faber, 1995), p. 175.

The world is a mist. And then the world is
minute and vast and clear. The tide
is higher or lower. He couldn't tell you which.
His beak is focussed; he is preoccupied,

looking for something, something, something.
Poor bird, he is obsessed!
The millions of grains are black, white, tan, and gray,
mixed with quartz grains, rose and amethyst.

The seismic presence of the Atlantic alongside is heard rather than seen — its 'roaring' in the first and hissing in the second stanza. The ocean's edge is then perceived as 'a sheet | of interrupting water' which 'glazes over his dark and brittle toes'. Subliminally, this sheet with the implied marking of bird tracks recalls the act of writing. The presence of the ocean, or the macroscopic, is 'taken for granted' and the bird, and by extension the writer, or this particular kind of writer, couldn't tell whether 'The tide | is higher or lower'. It is as if, insofar as the bird stands for Bishop, the poem is reproaching the writer's craft for its massive exclusions, its insensitivity to external events. The peculiar kind of seeing that the bird is capable of is at once a miraculous magnification and a comic occlusion. The exact admixture of these two elements crucially depends on how the reader interprets the poem's last lines:

Poor bird, he is obsessed!
The millions of grains are black, white, tan, and gray,
mixed with quartz grains, rose and amethyst.

These lines have a diminuendo quality characteristic of Bishop's endings. Another striking feature is the way the poem's rhyme scheme which has been in a consistently *abcb*, full-rhymed pattern turns slant-rhymed only in this final quatrain with 'obsessed' and 'amethyst'. The acoustic effect is to make the ending less clinching and sounded. At the same time, the lines subtly weave together two sound patterns which have been created earlier in the poem: *awkward... backwards and downwards... (black, white)... quartz* and *hisses... mist... vast... focussed... obsessed... amethyst.* The penultimate line with its more or less monochrome and monosyllabically itemized shades 'black, white, tan, and gray,' (the Oxford comma after 'tan' slows down the verse and emphasizes the separateness of the shades) is quietly infiltrated in the final line by the mineral splendour of 'quartz grains, rose and amethyst'. The bird who has been 'looking for something, something, something' — presumably food, though the poem pretends not to have thought of this obvious fact — may well be unaware of the 'something' that the poem has made visible to the reader, and yet these semi-precious grains are all the more dazzling for the drabness of their setting. That vertigo of numbers that we sense in 'The millions of grains' (which Baudelaire visits in 'Le Gouffre': 'Je ne vois qu'infini par tous les fenêtres, || Et mon esprit, toujours du vertige hanté | [...] | — Ah! Ne jamais sortir des Nombres et des Êtres!'), a queasy sense of Blake's 'Infinity', seem finally to be sifted and ends up with the beautiful specificity of 'rose and amethyst'. The word 'rose' is so often in Bishop erotically charged (as in her extraordinary, unpublished 'Vague Poem',[13] which, again, employs a crystalline image) that it may account for a residue of this emotion in the final line.

Everything in this poem validates a remark which Kalstone makes in another context: 'all of Bishop's poems about seeing are critiques of the act of seeing'. There is something self-delighting but never self-congratulatory about the precision of Bishop's observations — and certainly, here, the sandpiper's excluding focus is problematic. The ambivalence of the ending and the humour directed at the 'Poor bird' — which includes the poet to the extent to which we allow Bishop's identification with the sandpiper — as well as the shift from full to slant rhyme make the ending muted and unemphasized, but the effect is paradoxically the stronger for that.

★ ★ ★ ★ ★

If Blake is invoked at the outset with irony, the poem may well have delivered more in the way of 'minute particulars' and found more 'detail' in each minutely observed grain of sand than Blake himself achieved with his more symbolic and visionary approach to the exterior world. Although the poem puts Blake *in primo piano*, there's reason to consider that Baudelaire's 'L'Albatros' is at least as much to the fore of Bishop's mind in composing it. In this poem, also in quatrains, Baudelaire describes the albatross on the ship's deck and contrasts its clumsy floundering there with its majestic flight. And then, in the fourth and final stanza, he explicitly makes a comparison with the role of the poet:

> Souvent, pour s'amuser, les hommes d'équipage
> Prennent des albatros, vastes oiseaux du mer
> Qui suivent, indolents compagnons de voyage,
> Le navire glissant sur les gouffres amers.
>
> A peine les ont-ils déposés sur les planches,
> Que ces rois de l'azur, maladroits et honteux,
> Laissent piteusement leurs grandes ailes blanches
> Comme des avirons trainer à côté d'eux.
>
> Ce voyageur ailé, comme il est gauche et veule!
> Lui, naguère si beau, qu'il est comique et laid!
> L'un agace son bec avec un brûle-gueule,
> L'autre mime, en boitant, l'infirme qui volait!

13 This poem whose last lines are:

> Rose-rock, unformed, flesh beginning, crystal by crystal,
> clear pink breasts and darker, crystalline nipples,
> rose-rock, rose quartz, roses, roses, roses,
> exacting roses from the body,
> and the even darker, accurate rose of sex —

can be found in Brett C. Millier, *Elizabeth Bishop: Life and the Memory of It* (Berkeley: University of California Press, 1993), p. 437.

Le Poëte est semblable au prince des nuées
Qui hante la tempête et se rit de l'archer;
Exilé sur le sol au milieu des huées,
Ses ailes de géant l'empêchent de marcher.

[Often for their amusement, the crew take hold of albatrosses, those large birds of the sea who follow, indolent fellow voyagers, the ship gliding over the bitter gulfs. No sooner are they put on deck than these kings of the azure, clumsy and shameful, let their great white wings trail beside them like oars. This winged voyager — how awkward and spineless he is! Formerly so beautiful, how droll and ugly he is! One pokes his beak with a clay pipe; another, limping, mimics a sick man flying! The poet is like this prince of the clouds who haunts the storm and scorns the archer; exiled on the earth in the midst of the hooting (crowd), his giant wings prevent him from walking.]

The two poems, Bishop's and Baudelaire's, apart from the quatrain form and the bird-as-poet analogy which they share, seem in other ways remote from each other. The greatest distance is perhaps in the method of analogizing — where Baudelaire's fourth stanza makes the comparison explicit, Bishop's comparison is both implicit and subsidiary. The effect of the crew's cruelty to the bird — these deckhands are indulging in a bit of Shelley-baiting — invokes a kind of pity, which finally seems close to self pity as well as being a triumphant assertion of the poet's storm-tossed grace. Their mimicry of the bird's clumsiness is something that Bishop does on a formal level with the repetition of 'He runs, he runs' — the phrase is like a refrain or a tic, occurring five times, and imitating the bird's stop-start, hasty movements. The repetition of 'something' serves a similar function and gives the impression of obsessive, repetitive, almost involuntary movement. It's notable how daring, and effective, these repetitions are in such a short poem. Though different in kind, the comic element in both links them, as does Bishop's epithet 'awkward' which is emphatic in Baudelaire in the two words 'gauche' and 'maladroit'. In Bishop's poem we've seen already how a sound-pattern almost alchemically transforms 'awkward' into 'quartz'; which in a way is equivalent to the albatross who is the butt of jokes on dry land but, in the air, 'se rit de l'archer' (laughs at the bowman). Both poems make large claims for the poet, Baudelaire's overtly and Bishop's far more cagily.

But it's perhaps in the contrasts that we can see the affinity, or at least the kind of engagement, Bishop has with her predecessor. Baudelaire's albatross, with its Coleridgean ancestry, is ultimately a stand-in and justification for the poet — socially ridiculous, but empowered in his own element. Bishop's bird, on the other hand, hardly even seems to have wings, and far from being a prince of the clouds is utterly earthbound, hugging the shoreline. Baudelaire's explicit 'semblable' makes a symbol of the bird, where Bishop resists this kind of allegorizing, and, though the poem is richer for its seam of associations with the poet's role, never lets the bird itself leave the foreground of the poem, never, as it were, lets it leave the ground and doesn't make it subservient to its symbolic properties.

Like 'The Bight', it seems to me, the poem is both a homage to and a criticism of the French poet's procedures. Bishop states in one letter that, alongside Herbert, Baudelaire is her favourite poet, and in another, to Robert Lowell, that 'The Swan' is 'one of my favourite Baudelaire poems'.[14] 'La Cygne' is another bird poem which takes Baudelaire's symbolist strategies to far subtler and more explorative extremes than does 'L'Albatros' and includes his declaration that 'Tout, pour moi, devient l'allégorie', a personalized version of Goethe's 'Alles ist Symbol'. The central image of the swan spawns a series of recursive variants on the theme of exile, change and loss — a series that includes Paris itself as setting and source, Andromaque, a tubercular 'négresse' and so on, as the poem itself concludes: 'Je pense aux matelots oubliés dans une île, | Aux captifs, aux vaincus!... à bien d'autres encor!' — whoever, in short, has lost what can never be regained: 'A quiconque a perdu ce qui ne se retrouve | Jamais! Jamais!'. The plangent repetition of 'jamais' implies that the poet himself shares the suffering of his examples. This repetition is reminiscent of Bishop's bird which is 'looking for something, something, something' — an obsessive search which implies the lack of an essential, if not necessarily an essential ever possessed. Again the first person pronoun which structures the entire poem ('je pense à...') highlights the plight and primacy of the poet who assembles these images of his own sense of exile, whereas Bishop's presence in her poem is left delicately unstated and indeterminate. (As an indicator of the enduring modernity of this poem by Baudelaire, it's interesting to see Paul Muldoon's affectionately exaggerated and parodic, and this time passive, re-working of its 'je pense à' format in his poem to the French symbolist poet Gérard de Nerval 'Something Else': 'he hanged himself from a lamp-post | with a length of chain, which made me think || of something else, then something else again.')

The presence of the words 'something' and 'quartz' alerts the reader to another allusion, this time to Robert Frost's poem 'For Once, Then, Something' (first published in 1920). If this kind of intertextual triangulation seems too suppositious, I can only say that Bishop started it with her reference to Blake. Frost's poem is even more evidently than Bishop's a kind of manifesto and justification as well as both a poem about seeing and an exploration of what brings a poem into being. Frost lets his critics mock him for his poetry's narcissism — of staring into wells, and seeing his own reflection deified:

> Others taunt me with having knelt at well-curbs
> Always wrong to the light, so never seeing
> Deeper down in the well than where the water
> Gives me back in a shining surface picture
> Me myself in the summer heaven, godlike,
> Looking out of a wreath of fern and cloud puffs.

This image allows the poet to appear as at once 'always wrong' and 'godlike', and (jokingly) allows the anxiety of 'never seeing | Deeper down' to attach itself to his writing. This is a comic way of going along with what 'Others taunt' him with, of showing them that they may be right and that he doesn't care if they are. Or else it could be seen as someone who exaggerates a fault, of which they stand accused, in a nonchalant self-parody which is meant to disarm further criticism. The poem continues:

14 *Letters*, p. 395.

Once, when trying with chin against a well-curb,
I discerned, as I thought, beyond the picture,
Through the picture, a something white, uncertain,
Something more of the depths — and then I lost it.
Water came to rebuke the too clear water.
One drop fell from a fern, and lo, a ripple
Shook whatever it was lay there at bottom,
Blurred it, blotted it out. What was that whiteness?
Truth? A pebble of quartz? For once, then, something.

The three 'something's here scattered through the poem are reprised all together in Bishop's poem. If Frost's poem begins with a taunt to the writer it ends up with the writer teasing the reader, teasing the reader's urge to find at last 'something' substantial to settle on which would validate the attention of writer and reader. This 'something' is uncertainly glimpsed by the poet, like the boasted catch of a fisherman '– and then I lost it'. That the whole poem should be constructed out of something so fugitive, and possibly inconsequential, is too disappointing a prospect for the reader to be at ease with, and therefore the poem encourages the reader to invest this 'uncertain' something with meaning — again, part of Frost's play is to put the abstraction and the actuality ('Truth? A pebble of quartz?') in the reverse order of expectation, and both in an interrogative form. Richard Poirier who, in his fine study *Robert Frost: The Work of Knowing*,[15] devotes very little space to this poem about the nature of 'knowing', enlists the sinister whiteness of Melville's whale to explain the effect of 'What was that whiteness?' — and in doing so enacts the way the poem toys with the reader's need to alight on larger meanings. Frost's readers also bring to this 'whiteness' the explicitly sinister and tainted whiteness of his later poem 'Design', in which the whiteness is that of a sepulchre and where the Thomist argument from design is deliberately subjected to the part Satanic, part Darwinian stresses of a vicious 'design of darkness to appall'. Certainly there is something unsettling here about 'something white' which is 'more of the depths', as though the darkness we would associate with the deep has entered into the white. But those two proposals — 'Truth? A pebble of quartz?' — which veer between the abstract and the concrete, the absolute and the particular, are left hanging and only seemingly resolved by the final phrase which also supplies the title — a phrase that leaves the reader no closer to 'knowing' or understanding anything. Though to some, the critics that 'taunt' him, this games-playing might seem too pleased and coy, the way the poem has been constructed out of (almost) nothing — a glimpse, an uncertainty — reveals much about poetry's interest in inklings and intimations and, beyond that, the way the mind latches onto the insubstantial and gives credence to the fugitive. Frost is characteristically drawn to the indefinite, starting three poems with the word 'Something' which here he ends on — notably 'Mending Wall' with its famous and unexplained opening 'Something there is that doesn't love a wall' — plus another which begins 'Some things are never clear'. It's possible that both Frost's and Bishop's 'something' hark back to the ending

15 Richard Poirier, *Robert Frost: The Work of Knowing* (New York: Oxford University Press, 1977), p. 252.

of George Herbert's 'Prayer' where in its final appositional phrase 'Something understood', the exhausted contentment of the voice seems sure of some counter-response available neither to the playfully sceptical Frost nor to Bishop's questing and fidgety bird. However the presence of quartz and three somethings in both poems suggests a deliberate reference on Bishop's part, though Bishop might well reply with polite discouragement, as she did to Mazzaro, 'but [...] it is fascinating how my poem arouses in you all those literary references!' Even if it's unconscious here, which seems to me doubtful, there is a sense in which poems may enter into critical dialogue with their predecessors without their author's express permission.

Whereas in Baudelaire the albatross had served as a symbol on which to hang the handicaps and consolations of the poet's vocation, Bishop's 'Sandpiper', whilst subtly introjecting the concerns of the poet, nevertheless gives primacy to the bird itself, and the poem could be appreciated well enough, even if incompletely, without the allegoric running alongside. I'd say that there's also a conscious element of reference to, and of self-differentiation from, Frost which enters into Bishop's poem. What is found at the end of both poems has an element of ambiguity. In Frost, it may be truth (but then we wonder what the poem which has 'lost' sight of it amounts to and how the poem might have grasped it) or it may be quartz (and would that give the poem a quality of artistic durability like Horace's 'aere perennius' or would the stone just be an image of natural beauty?), but is it really, then, something? In Bishop's poem it is uncertain whether the bird — and so the poet also — gets much joy from the quartz and amethyst, but at least the poem, and therefore the reader, does. By contrast with the Frost poem in which the poet's presence permeates, or supersaturates, the whole structure ('Me myself'), Bishop's presence in her poem is elusive and disguised, and far from 'godlike'.

* * * * *

The muted effect of the off-rhyme at the end of 'Sandpiper' is not an isolated example of Bishop subverting the formal structures she employs, making it a device to explore a dialectic between order and chaos, liberty and determinism. In 'The Map', the first poem of her first book with its geographer's title *North & South*, Bishop sets up for the first and last stanza a regular *abbacddc* rhyme-scheme (where *a* and *c* are identical rhymes) whilst leaving the middle eight-line stanza unrhymed. So the enclosed rhyme scheme (*abba*) itself encloses an unrhymed stanza. Rigid enclosure, or order around what continues to break out from it, is very much the subject of the poem. The continent described in the middle stanza is not without its order but it is one which resists human schemata or mapping. It runs over its edges (and line-endings): 'its edges | showing the line of long sea-weeded ledges' as she notes in the first stanza — 'The names of sea-shore towns run out to sea...'. The order here is more susceptible to touch than to sight: 'where the oily Eskimo | has oiled it' or 'These peninsulas take the water between thumb and finger | like women feeling for the smoothness of yard-goods'. And this discriminating subtlety of texture and perception is what makes her finally commend one kind of mapping over another: 'More delicate than the historians' are the map-makers' colors'.

In 'Sunday, 4 A.M.' — a poem which from the title alone, diary-like in its particularity, we would guess to be about insomnia — Bishop has contrived an unusual alternation between masculine and feminine rhymes which is maintained (with slight variants) until the final stanza, where it changes into alternating feminine rhymes in the same *abab* structure. The poem is a strange confusion of conflicting thoughts and voices ('Dream dream confronting') with a sense of increasing menace and sudden hypnagogic clarities. The penultimate stanza ends with the tone of a curdled fairy-tale:

> The cat's gone a-hunting.
> The brook feels for the stair.

Only in the last stanza does the threat finally diminish:

> The world seldom changes,
> but the wet foot dangles
> until a bird arranges
> two notes at right angles.

The alternation of masculine and feminine rhymes is the temporal equivalent of the spatial image of 'two notes at right angles'. The final change to all feminine rhymes in the last stanza is something of a resolution to the pattern, particularly two rhymes so close visually, the 'g' hardened by the addition of the 'l' in the second and fourth lines. The bird's notes, like the arrival or at least the promise of dawn, offer at once a reprieve from the rising water of the dream landscape and a consolatory music. This rhyme of 'changes' and 'arranges' is the same one Bishop uses at the end of 'North Haven', her elegy for her friend, the poet Robert Lowell, a poem that we would expect to be concerned with the craft of poetry, and those two words in both poems have to do with artistry, the bird's and the poet's, between which, again, she makes an equivalence:

> You can't derange, or re-arrange,
> Your poems again. (But the Sparrows can their song.)
> The words won't change again. Sad friend, you cannot change.

In that additional rhyming word 'derange', it's hard not to hear both a reference to Lowell's intermittent manic condition as well as to his obsessive rewriting — and underneath both, connecting them, that phrase from Rimbaud's 'lettre du voyant' which speaks of a 'un long, immense et raisonné *dérèglement* de *tous les sens*' (To Paul Demeny, 15 May, 1871).[16] 'North Haven' begins with another harbour view:

> I can make out the rigging of a schooner
> a mile off; I can count
> the new cones on the spruce. It is so still
> the pale bay wears a milky skin, the sky
> no clouds, except for one long, carded horse's-tail.

These natural observations are framed by the auxiliary verb 'I can' which seems

16 Rimbaud, *Complete Works, Selected Letters*, ed. by Wallace Fowlie (Chicago, IL, & London: University of Chicago Press, 1966), pp. 306–07.

oddly redundant, a rather listless declaration of power, until the last stanza highlights the contrast between what Bishop, being alive, *can* still do and what Lowell, now dead, 'can't'. Bishop even imagines the islands 'drifting... | a little north, a little south or sideways', pretending that they are endowed with a mobility implicitly denied to her friend. The third and fourth stanzas record the names of flowers and birds — all capitalized like the 'Sparrows' of the final stanza as though they were the names of fellow poets, or else the works of Nature:

Nature repeats herself, or almost does:

Repeat, repeat, repeat; revise, revise, revise.

This ongoing repetition and revision — for better or worse — both in life and in literature is what her friend Lowell 'can't' any longer take part in.

* * * * *

Although I've been amassing the kind of 'literary associations' which Bishop quietly discourages in her letter to Mazzaro, I don't mean to suggest that to make sense of her poetry it must be refracted through the work of other poets or, for that matter, that only these poems which mention other poets are poems which scrutinize the process of writing — what purpose the poem serves, its *raison d'être.* A comparable ending to that of 'Sandpiper' — a last minute adjustment or reversal (in this case a vocal one) — can be found, for example, in 'Under the Window: Ouro Prêto'. Its status as one of her 'Uncollected Poems' may betray some doubts Bishop had as to whether it was truly finished. And at a first reading, the poem would seem merely to describe the jumble of events taking place 'Under the Window' and around the fountain in this Brazilian gold-mining town, with that air of continuing 'untidy activity' which 'The Bight' records. In this case: conversations, gossip, the various animals that come for water, the black boy under a pile of laundry and the lorries, with their stickers, in their way as 'talkative | and soiled and thirsty' as the townsfolk. One truck 'grinds up | in a blue cloud of burning oil' — a stray image which prepares us for the transformation of oil at the end of the poem. Tom Paulin, in his essay 'Dwelling without Roots: Elizabeth Bishop', traces the original and charged uses to which oil is put in her poems — blending the natural and the industrial in unexpected ways, and challenging a traditional hierarchy of values: 'Oil is a sacral symbol of dwelling in her poems [...] an emblem that is insistently artificial, unnatural, technological, commercial'.[17] Here too spilt oil instead of being a pollutant takes on an almost redemptive, celestial quality, not the antithesis of water but its complement. If the water supplies a human and animal thirst, the oil quenches, it seems, at least momentarily, another thirst, a symbolic and transcendent one. Ouro Prêto means, in Portuguese, 'Black Gold' and was originally called Villa Rica de Ouro Prêto ('Town Rich from Black Gold') in reference not to the slave trade — another valence of the phrase — but to its mining history: the town grew around the discovery of alluvial gold and when that was exhausted they mined from

17 Tom Paulin, *Minotaur* (London: Faber, 1992), p. 201. See also his challenging discussion of Bishop's 'The Bight' in the same essay.

the ground gold that was mixed with silver, the silver blackening on contact with the air. Something of this history may linger in the word 'soiled' which in turn both phonetically and by association suggests the image of oil. But the prominence of the oil imagery especially at the end may have to do with 'black gold' being U.S. slang for oil — a phrase that will be familiar to those who still remember the song at the beginning of 'The Beverly Hillbillies' in which petrol is described as 'Black Gold. Texas Tea.' These are the last two stanzas of the poem:

> The seven ages of man are talkative
> and soiled and thirsty.
> Oil has seeped into
> the margins of the ditch of standing water
>
> and flashes or looks up brokenly,
> like bits of mirror — no, more blue than that:
> like tatters of the *Morpho* butterfly.

Bishop, in that first line and a half offers up a résumé of the prolonged foregoing description. But instead of ending on this note, the poem takes another turn, breaks off mid-line by noticing a small, *marginal* detail, something at the edge both of the scene and of the poem, some fragment that can carry the weight of all the accumulated details. It is interesting that the oil 'flashes or looks up brokenly' in a kind of defeated aspiration. There are several different types of metallic blue Morpho butterfly in Southern Brazil, but this is most likely the *Morpho electra*. In *Beautiful Butterflies*, J. Moucha writes that this family of butterflies can be captured by waving small coloured flags or 'by flashing a mirror in the sunshine'. He describes their appearance: 'Their wings reflect the endless blue of the skies — they are jewels on the wing...'.[18] A poem which has been at such inclusive pains to describe what happened, that would seem essentially mimetic in its relation to the world, finally, and I'd argue typically, moves beyond the mimetic with that simile of 'bits of mirror'. The mirror that reflects the world is broken, but not in the debased manner of Stephen Dedalus's symbol of Irish art: 'the cracked lookingglass of a servant' — an image that Bishop would handle very differently, as when she writes about the black servant 'Cootchie' and her grave marked by 'pink wax roses | planted in tin cans filled with sand'. On the contrary, this mirroring oil, even though in 'tatters' which effectively ground the creature, takes on the colour of one of the most dazzling butterflies and so the final simile rather than being merely reflective is subtly transformative.

★ ★ ★ ★ ★

Bishop's absorption in and minute attention to the world she describes is one of the most striking characteristics of her poems. Bishop was delighted when Randall Jarrell compared her poems to Vermeer's paintings.[19] Though her own paintings include several interiors, by far the best are some of the landscapes, in which,

18 J. Moucha, *Beautiful Butterflies* (London: Spring Books, 1963), p. 36.
19 *Letters*, p. 312.

though without any of his technical virtuosity, there's an almost Adamic kind of pleasure in landscape for its own sake that's reminiscent of Dürer's watercolour sketches. John Berger's *Dürer* quotes the German artist's credo 'The more accurately your work represents life, the better it will appear'.[20] Berger comments on this 'key tenet' of Dürer's:

> it accounts for his love of seemingly insignificant detail, apparent not only in his studies of plants and his portrait sketches, but also in the muzzle of an ox, or the attempt at drawing a walrus.

Elsewhere Berger writes:

> Never before had anyone dared to paint anything as insignificant as a piece of turf. Dürer was later to account for his avant-garde sense of the real in his *Four Books of Human Proportions*: 'Life in Nature reveals the truth of things'.[21]

We've come to expect from artists after Dürer, at least up until the age of photography, this kind of attention to the details of the natural world. With poets, it has been often seen as an encumbrance and a failure to respect the boundaries between the arts. Most notably, Lessing in his essay 'Laocoön', sees pictorializing description more or less as a dereliction of the poet's duties. In poetry, he writes, 'the detailed pictures of physical objects [...] has always been recognized by the best judges as a frigid kind of sport for which little or nothing of genius is demanded'. This argument is based on his belief that 'the verbal delineations of bodies fail of the illusion on which poetry particularly depends [...] for the reason that the *co-existence* of the physical object comes into collision with the *consecutiveness* of speech'.[22] It is precisely 'the consecutiveness of speech' that Bishop uses to such effect at the end of 'Under the Window: Ouro Prêto' with the interrupting qualification of 'like bits of mirror — no, more blue than that: | like tatters of the *Morpho* butterfly'. It has the same quality which M. W. Croll noted in the writers of Baroque prose, and which Bishop copied out in a letter she wrote at the age of twenty-two: 'Their purpose was to portray, not a thought, but a mind thinking...'.[23]

The *consecutive* nature of experience as a poem transmits it — as opposed to its spatial extension in painting — is a recurrent concern in Bishop's descriptions. Her strong pictorializing impulse (her 'settings' as she puts it in her letter to Mazzaro) frequently come up against the passing of time — not just in the formal sense that in a poem phrase follows phrase, as in the case of the ending of 'Under the Window: Ouro Prêto', but also conceptually. We've already seen how in the last line of 'The Map' time is set against space in the comparison: 'More delicate than the historians' are the map-makers' colors', and how a temporal image of 'consecutiveness' has been converted into a spatial figuration at the end of 'Sunday 4 A.M': 'until a bird arranges | two notes at right angles'. 'At the Fishhouses', one of her most meticulously and beautifully descriptive poems, concludes with a Heraclitean image

20 John Berger, *Albrecht Dürer* (London, New York: Taschen, 1994), p. 90.

21 Ibid., p. 76.

22 Gotthold Ephraim Lessing, *Laocoön, Nathan the Wise and Minna von Barnhelm* (London and Toronto, J. M. Dent & Sons; New York: E. P. Dutton, 1930); p. 63.

23 *Letters*, p. 12.

of the water that the poem has so patiently depicted suddenly perceived as free and mobile in time:

> It is like what we imagine knowledge to be:
> dark, salt, clear, moving, utterly free,
> drawn from the cold hard mouth
> of the world, derived from the rocky breasts
> forever, flowing and drawn, and since
> our knowledge is historical, flowing and flown.

In 'Poem', a poem which is ostensibly about a painting but which, as its title reminds us, is aware of the difference of its own art form, again Bishop confronts the temporal via the pictorial. The poem begins:

> About the size of an old-style dollar bill,
> American or Canadian,
> mostly the same whites, gray greens, and steel grays
> – this little painting (a sketch for a larger one?)
> has never earned any money in its life.
> Useless and free...

The poem records a sudden recognition ('Heavens, I recognize the place, I know it!') of the Nova Scotian scene within the painting made by her great-uncle, and the strangeness and intimacy of meeting the spirit of place in this 'minor family relic': 'life and the memory of it so compressed | they've turned into each other. Which is which?'. She ends by returning to the question of scale that she began with, only this time 'the size' has become duration, and 'Not much' at that:

> the little that we get for free,
> the little of our earthly trust. Not much.
> About the size of our abidance
> along with theirs: the munching cows,
> the iris, crisp and shivering, the water
> still standing from spring freshets,
> the yet-to-be-dismantled elms, the geese.

But in those last five lines the size of that 'Not much' has become infinitely expanded to include the cows, the flowers, the trees and the birds alongside the human — time being their common element.

There ought to be a rhetorical term to describe this central (and, as far as I know, uncommented-on) trope in Bishop's poetry, in which a pictorializing impulse cedes to a sense of time, what Lessing would call the 'consecutive' nature of experience as it's perceived in a poem. There is — at least for the reverse effect in 'Sunday, 4 A.M.' — where the sound of the bird's notes are translated into a visual (or geometric) image which could be termed 'synaesthesia'. But essentially Bishop has expanded the reach of this device to shift perception not just from one sense to another but from one axis or dimension to another, from time to space, or, in the other examples, vice versa. It is a recurrent figure, often signalled by the word 'free', whereby Bishop manages to conflate space and time, picture and poem, and so escapes beyond the determining limits of Lessing's categories.

* * * * *

Bishop's poetry, as we have seen, has one foot in the Symbolist camp, but her attitude to nature is essentially distinct from that of a poet like Baudelaire, for whom nature, despite his odd respectful reference to 'the temple of nature', is there to be improved on by art. But to say this risks making her descriptions belong to a mimetic, representational tradition that is prominent in painting, whereas her poems question how we perceive, not only through language, but through the whole spectrum and gamut of the senses. They are not content with mere representation — they push through towards that sense of mystery she noted in her passage about Darwin.

In her introduction to *The Diary of 'Helena Morley'*, Bishop quotes at length a letter by Hopkins to Robert Bridges about the book *Two Years Before the Mast* of which he writes:

> a thoroughly good one and all true, but bristling with technicality — seamanship — which I most carefully go over and even enjoy but cannot understand; there are other things, though, as a flogging, which is terrible and instructive *and it happened* — ah that is the charm and the main point.' And that, I think, is 'the charm and the main point' of *Minha Vida de Menina*. Its 'technicalities', diamond digging, say, scarcely 'bristle'...
>
> But — *it really happened*; everything did take place, day by day, minute by minute, once and once only, just the way Helena says it did.[24]

This passage is such a close repetition of the phrasing — down to the italics — of her letter to Mazzaro, that there's no mistaking its importance for Bishop. Here she is writing of a diary (a form she was fascinated by and taught as one of her courses) and this is the kind of expectation a reader would naturally bring to the form, whereas from a poem we might legitimately expect something more.

Her poem 'In the Waiting Room' which charts an inner event begins 'In Worcester, Massachusetts' and ends repeating the place, adding the date 'it was still the fifth | of February, 1918'. The statement of the external place and time have a talismanic importance as though the gulf into which the girl that she was falls could only be re-approached through the actuality of its setting — that 'everything did take place [...] once and once only'. Only thus could the poem be adequately equipped to confront the internal journey with its ontological vertigo, its questions of belonging, of gender, of identity, that make the world she started from and returned to something henceforth dangerous and unfathomable. The waiting room and the solid world of separate facts, dates, places and identities have slid 'beneath a big black wave, | another, and another'. This aesthetic of what really happened is at a considerable remove from both Symbolist practice and from reportage and straight description. As Kalstone suggests, 'She would use observation as a kind of tentative anchorage, as a way of grasping for presence in the world'. Her attitude towards the actual, far from consuming it, or turning it for consumption, is marked by a reverence, sometimes an appalled delight (awful but cheerful), that what

24 *The Collected Prose*, p. 99.

happened happened. Though that, perhaps, isn't 'the charm and the main point' of her poems.

Elizabeth Bishop: Poet of the Periphery, ed. by Jo Shapcott and Linda Anderson (Newcastle upon Tyne: Bloodaxe, 2002). The version of this essay published there was inadvertently the penultimate one, with minor errors and without its footnotes: the text here is restored as originally intended.

— 42 —

Singing to the Marvellous Stove: Elizabeth Bishop's Artwork

Elizabeth Bishop, *Exchanging Hats: Paintings*, ed. by William Benton (Manchester: Carcanet, 1997)

Only someone who perceives colour as a kind of absolute could dwell on it as emphatically and as unhurriedly as Elizabeth Bishop does in her poems. Entire lines are devoted to colour: 'blue, blue-green and olive'; 'pale blue, blue-green and brick'; 'black, red and white, and gray'. These examples from different poems could be joined by scores of others in which an exact shade is registered. Her paintings, painstakingly tracked down and gathered together by William Benton, originally for her first (and posthumous) exhibition at Key West and now for this book, show — in the appropriate medium — just how distinguished and subtle a colourist she was.

With the exception of two Cornell-inspired boxes and a watercolour of a dream machine like a portable juke-box, all of the paintings are from the life — interiors, exteriors, landscapes, cityscapes, flowers. And nearly all are watercolours (sometimes with ink and gouache) on paper which is of poor quality. They are records of the seen, which have, as Benton notices, a taste 'for patterns, for tasklike clarities'. The flower paintings are delicate, observant studies, but her paintings of landscapes and buildings are powerfully atmospheric and original works.

Of the landscapes, two are outstanding — a crop-quilted 'Brazilian Landscape' and 'Nova Scotia Landscape', which floats on a yellow wash three horizontal strips for water, earth and air. The water is composed of brief flicks of mauve and milky-violet which link it compositionally to the roof slates and the fir tree branches. It has exactly the same luminous, weirdly archaic atmosphere as her poem 'The Moose', and could describe the scene from the bus window:

> clapboard farmhouses
> and neat, clapboard churches,
> bleached, ridged as clamshells.

Architecture and decor are considered at length and often in her prose — for example, in the introduction to 'The Diary of 'Helena Morley' she describes Ouro Prêto's church as 'small too, but with her baroque facades trimmed with green soapstone, their heavy curves and swirls and twin mustard-pot towers, they are opulent and sophisticated, while the little churches of Diamantina are shabby, silent and wistful'. Her paintings, too, manage to blend the anthropomorphic with the exact. Her buildings have aged askew, their given features moulded not only by weather but by personal mannerisms, although the paintings themselves are translucent and impressively free of mannerism. In 'County Courthouse', there is something affectionately mocking about the way this fine but pompous civic structure becomes the sport of nature and dysfunction. The painting is organized in a series of triangles, and even the power lines from the tower to the pylon, which look as if they had been unstrung by a storm, make a rickety isosceles in the sky. The wedge of an energetic, drenched-green, tropical shrub seems to be dislodging the facade, while palm trees encroach on either side, the effect like an image of Justice shoved from her plinth with scales flying. The building looks so exhausted it's surprising the two clocks on the tower are still synchronized.

Her interiors — whether hotel room or cabin, since most give the impression of being in transit — celebrate the flowers, tablecloths, wallpaper patterns and lights (chandelier, candelabra, even a tacked-up extension cord) that make where we live more liveable-in. In her poem 'Filling Station', the plant and the paper doilies have this role. As with her poems, so also in the paintings the question of where we live is transformed into the question of how we live. In 'Santarém', the wasp's nest — the solid ghost of its former residents — has, for all the poem's humour, the same talismanic presence for Bishop that the Grecian Urn had for Keats, the basis for a whole aesthetic. Those who find such things trivial are represented by the Dutch burgher, who is given the last word: 'What's that ugly thing?' The structures she paints often appear lightweight and provisionally glued together, like 'The Armory, Key West', or unsteady from the pressure of remaining vertical, like 'Grey Church', most likely painted in Ouro Prêto. This has something to do, no doubt, with Bishop's inability to draw a straight line, but I'm sure she would not have wanted to, even if she could.

I suspect that it is Bishop's own orphaned childhood, and a life of moving from place to place, that invests her pictures of houses and buildings with such a sense of yearning and childlike intensity. Responsive to work as various as that of Vermeer, Schwitters and Delacroix's Algerian watercolours, Bishop is sophisticated and knowledgeable about art in a way that separates her from a primitivist like the Cuban Gregorio Valdes, whose work she celebrated and promoted. And yet she is capable of that primitivist attention to every detail which challenges the hierarchy of values implicit in perspective. Shakespeare's claim 'And Perspective it is best Painters art' is one which Bishop's paintings, as well as her poems, undermine. In 'Twelfth Morning; or What You Will' she writes of a white horse, 'bigger than the house', and asks if it's 'The force of | personality or is perspective dozing?' The same question might be asked of her 'Red Stove and Flowers', where the brick stove is dwarfed by a jug of flowers beside it, but tilted (without regard for perspective) so that the pans of beans and rice are proudly displayed beneath a tomb-shaped cheese-grater and a flower-like sieve. Her poem 'Sestina' ends:

> The grandmother sings to the marvellous stove
> And the child draws another inscrutable house.

Bishop's small-scale paintings commemorate marvellous stoves and inscrutable houses (which for that reason ask to be scrutinized). Unlike art by poets such as

Montale and Lorca, her paintings are not 'interesting' forays into an essentially alien form, nor are they divorced from the central intelligence of the poems but, even if technically less sure, they come from the same extraordinary source and make a justified claim to attention in their own right.

Times Literary Supplement, 20 February 1998

— 43 —

Curios in Paradise: Elizabeth Bishop's Letters

Elizabeth Bishop: *One Art: The Selected Letters*, ed. by Robert Giroux (London: Chatto & Windus, 1994)

At first it's hard to reconcile the sheer abundance of these letters with Elizabeth Bishop's poems — that mysteriously compact body of work which is almost without its equal in the last fifty years. The letters, though, bear the same signature of a personality which refuses to dull its primary gift of perception. Apart from some desperate times, most terrible of all the illness and suicide of her partner Lota de Macedo Soares, Bishop's letters are impressively frugal with their laments, and meet her many afflictions — asthma, allergy, alcohol — with laconic restraint. In the face of often heart-rending difficulties, she maintains an interest in everything around her.

One unflagging interest, both for her poems and letters, is geography — a peopled geography of two continents: cities, towns and villages from her native Nova Scotia to Brazil ('perhaps the only home I ever had') where she lived for fifteen years. Neither a travel writer nor an anthropologist, she has a faculty for empathy which draws her quickly past barriers of race or class or culture, though for some time in Brazil the language hampered her. Anyone who has suffered this fate will leap with recognition at her account of 'bleak stretches in which I wonder, my God, what am I doing here? — who am I, anyway? — did I ever have a personality?'

Perhaps because it enacted the movements of her orphaned childhood, travel for Bishop was a kind of internal necessity. Being abroad was her only home, and the act of travelling was like a moulting of all stale reflexes, a way of staying supple. In her elegy for Robert Lowell, the recipient of some of her finest letters, what she regrets most is that death has become fixity both for him and his poems: 'Sad friend, you cannot change'.

Late in her life she travelled to the Galapagos Islands, describing them as 'like one's idea of Paradise'. Besides toucans, seals, kittens and so on, on the evidence of these letters, Bishop's Paradise would have to have room for Herbert and Darwin, and everyone would sing Baptist hymns, Blues and Samba. Of Samba, she writes 'I suspect they're some of the last folk poetry to be made in the world.'

Another feature that links the letters to the poems is what Lowell called 'the minuteness and splendor of her descriptions' — 'no detail too small', as she writes in her poem 'Sandpiper'. She insistently speaks of herself as a 'literalist', prizing, above all, truth and accuracy. This quality of the imagination is distinct from, but in perfect sympathy with, 'primitive' painting, as her shrewd essay on the painter Gregorio Valdes shows. And as with some primitive painting, it's the way the tiny particulars belong inside an enormous panorama — in Bishop's case both Americas — that weirdly brings two conflicting scales of perception into harmony.

Bishop is at her most joyfully descriptive in her letters to Marianne Moore, sending back curios from her travels and vying with the older poet's otherwise incomparable palette. The parrot fish is 'all iridescent, with a silver edge to each scale, and a real bill-mouth like turquoise'; a crab's 'enormous claws, bright red and blue, fit around the body like parts of a puzzle together'. The natural phenomena she describes render Bishop's interior world semi-visible — like the waterspouts which are 'translucent and you can see the water or mist or whatever it is going up inside in puffs and clouds, very fast, just like smoke up a chimney — and the top of the chimney is lost in a storm cloud'.

At times there is a sudden, uncanny change of pressure in the writing which signals her chancing on a poetic subject. Twenty-six years after a letter that records an encounter with a moose in Nova Scotia, she will finally complete one of her masterpieces, 'The Moose'. But even before mentioning the animal, the atmosphere of poised wonder in the letter is unmistakable: 'It's the richest, saddest, simplest landscape in the world.' There are many other examples, such as the firefly 'that floats steadily towards you with a really big milky blue light — it can be quite frightening, like a burglar, or a distant train even' that finds another home in her great poem 'Manuelzinho' as

> a few
> big, soft, pale-blue,
> sluggish fireflies,
> the jellyfish of the air.

Only very occasionally is the direction reversed as when, homesick for the birds of Brazil, she buys a mynah bird and teaches it her favourite line from her own work 'Awful, but cheerful' ('The Bight'). You can almost hear the bird marking the comma with an exact pause.

Although the letters are not at all 'literary', her responses to contemporary literature are startlingly sure and concise. And beneath the frequently expressed doubts, there's an unwavering sense of her own direction. In her early twenties, she justifies a line in a poem of hers by writing 'sometimes I think about certain things that without one particular fault they would be without the means of existence'. Behind this remark lies a whole aesthetic.

Robert Giroux has selected a small fraction of her letters to make this huge volume. His difficulty has been solved, rather than resolved, by making frequent cuts (as many as eighteen in one crucial letter after Macedo Soares's suicide). This allows for more letters but is worrying, distorting the shape of them in a manner Bishop would have been unlikely to approve. His excuse of 'occasional longueurs' hardly fits the case. Alternatively, the impulse may have been protective of her privacy, and Bishop who was so upset by Lowell's use of Elizabeth Hardwick's private letters might have been grateful. Either way, in the absence of a collected letters, this is an utterly indispensable book for anyone interested in Bishop, as well a sure way of becoming so for everyone else.

Independent, 30 April 1994

— 44 —

Interior Landscapes and the Mind's Eye: Wilhelmina Barns-Graham

Ten years back, on the wall of my then landlady's attic studio, there was a slightly torn poster my eye kept returning to. A bony yellow granitic rockscape engrossed the whole foreground, like a huge petrified flower or a heap of elephant skulls. Behind, a promontory in the same ochre divided blue strips of sea and sky. Those two blues, a cerulean and an ultramarine, were pitched at odds with each other — somehow off-key and out of kilter. Even in poster form, the picture has a striking mixture of crudeness and delicacy, and a distinctive relationship to the seen: as though an actual landscape were in the process of being interiorized, and only because it had been chosen and made the painter's own could it then be rendered visible again in bold simplifications that remained attentive to inner structure and force. Asking about W. Barns-Graham, whose 'Retrospective 1940–1989' the poster advertised, I was told she was a Scottish woman painter who'd lived for years in St Ives. Why hadn't I heard of her? Pure ignorance, I suppose — but an ignorance which hadn't stopped me noticing and admiring a number of St Ives painters. I suspect that her reputation as an artist has been less forwarded by the usual mix of luck and promotional susceptibility — or even self-promotional agility, or even gender — than that of many St Ives painters of whom she is at least the equal.

For me, then, the current Tate St Ives show was a welcome opportunity to make some amends. The work represented spans sixty years, from the 1940 canvas *Island Sheds, St Ives, No. 1* to some outstanding pictures from the last decade. One room is filled with her work, and further examples are exhibited elsewhere through the Gallery, often helpfully placed beside paintings and drawings by other St Ives artists. The exhibition leaves the viewer wanting to see more: it represents the tip of an iceberg — a cliché which has some relevance here, given the selector's fondness for the theme of ice. If the selection is unsatisfactory, the catalogue is worse, with few illustrations, many of them undersized, and no list of exhibited works. The painting I referred to before, *Rocks, St Mary's, Scilly Isles* (1953) — probably the image by which her work is best known — lives up to and beyond the expectations the poster had encouraged. The large scale of the painting is perfectly fitted to its uneasy monumental serenity. The movement from crude and roughly textured foreground to finely pencilled forms of fields, walls and some buildings in the background is complicated by a diagonal movement of dark to light, lower right to upper left, but also by upward curvings in a series of darker crevices parallel to the horizon. Whilst the painting is representational, the foreground rocks are a celebration and a study of the abstract sculpture of natural form. There's something bare and telluric about the artist's encounter with landscape, not only in this painting but also in many of her landscapes, both painted and drawn, through the course of a long and astonishingly various career. These landscapes — Cornish coastal towns, the clay workings of Chiusure (Tuscany), the Swiss glaciers, the lava formations of the Canaries — have in common an interrogation of the complex drama of their structuring, a search for the internal rhythms and pressures that shape the exterior form.

Her superb drawings are, as she herself claims, a continuous kind of 'discipline', which she sets aside in order to paint her abstract pictures: 'I seldom work from my drawings. The discipline used releases me in my paintings, to work more freely...' They share some qualities of line with those of Ben Nicholson whom she frequently accompanied on drawing expeditions along the Cornish coast — notably a clean sinuous economy offset by intermittent pentimenti or softer thickenings of the line — sometimes accompanied by tempera or wash which gives a sense of rondure and ampleness to the forms which might otherwise be too stark or diagrammatic. Barns-Graham shares with Nicholson and other St Ives artists an interest in abstraction schooled by a painstaking attention to natural forms. One of the problems for many St Ives artists must be the way art history has arranged this community of artists — the English equivalent of Pont Aven or Céret — into the foremost names, Nicholson and Hepworth, Hilton etc., and then turned their collaborators, friends and associates into footnotes. To assume that artistic influence is always a one-way street from the more to the less prominent is often mistaken and oversimplifying, just as it was in the case of Gauguin and Emile Bernard.

If Barns-Graham's mastery of line has never been disputed, her status as painter has often been challenged on the basis of the stylistic diversity she displays. The first newspaper review of this exhibition perceived in her work the lack of a distinctive personal idiom — one not borrowed from the more famous artists associated with St Ives such as Alfred Wallis, Nicholson, Terry Frost and others. Again, this view underestimates the unique working environment of St Ives. Quarrels and rivalries aside, the post-war years for the artists there must have been a period of extraordinary ferment, of mutual encouragement and shared experiment in a number of different directions, with artists' work often overlapping, stimulating and reinforcing new efforts. Barns-Graham's stylistic variety can as easily, and more justly, be read as artistic vitality — of a kind not satisfied with a trademark style, and unimpressed by the imposition of personality or the achievement of a 'voice' — as it's called in the world of poetry. The absence of a demonstrable and triumphant stylistic progression in Barns-Graham's case may have severely disadvantaged her in terms of critical status. What we can see, rather, is a rigorous exploration, often circling and double-backing on itself to test out new technical resources on previously confronted problems. The thread that gives constancy to these endeavours, her abstract as much as her more representational paintings, is the study of movement in form and form in movement, and of the properties of form, its brittleness or malleability, its opacity or translucence.

Her drawings — another example of stylistic breadth — with the same expert handling can range from extreme simplicity to almost chaotic complexity. In *Eight Lines Porthmeor, No. 1* (1986), what looks to me like only six lines of increasing irregularity, down from the sea horizon's straight line (just lower than centre page), create the most minimal and cleanly effective study of the motion of waves. By contrast, any one of a number of her drawings from Lanzarote, which she first visited in 1990 — the white chalk on black paper, for instance, of *Lava Movement from La Geria* (1993) — show her equal gift for analytical seeing when applied to the vertiginously complicated shapes and conflicting directions of volcanic rock. This trip to the Canaries not only tests and extends her drawing skills, but also, it seems to me, coincides with the beginning of her finest work in colour. *Untitled 03/93* (not in the exhibition) is an example in gouache of this new joyful incandescence of colour applied in broad and dripping brushstrokes.

If there is a question about her paintings, it's related to her sense of colour. Like *de gustibus*, it's possible that *de coloribus non est disputandem*, or rather the whole topic is too wide open to dispute — one person's ideal colour scheme being another person's nightmare. When I asked an artist friend about the two blues which I claim are quarrelling with each other in Rocks, she said she had no problem with them at all. Well, nor do I; my feeling is that they work, but that they work, as it were, against the grain, against all expectation that they should. Her earliest paintings — for instance *Island Sheds, St Ives, No. 1* — show a wonderful colouristic harmony in a limited set of hues. This picture with its stormy blacks, whites and dark greens owes much to Wallis's palette. Another example in gouache — *The Malakoff, St Ives* (1942) — which I've only seen in a Jonathan Clark catalogue, shows exactly the same view, as though it were painted from the same chair in the same upstairs window as Stanley Spencer's oil *The Harbour, St Ives* (1937). Her painting, with its delicate beiges and umbers and almost primitive fretwork of blacks, has the flattened terseness of form and the simplicity of effect of a Lautrec lithograph, and compares favourably with the excellent Spencer. My suspicion is that the colouristic confidence she reached early in her training in Edinburgh Art School, may have been ousted or undercut by the formal challenge she encountered in the work of several of the St Ives artists, or else was sidelined by the more pressing problems of composition.

Whatever the reason, there's an impression that the colour has secondary status in her work and lacks the absolute sureness of her sense of line. A fine wartime pastel of a factory interior, the *Island Factory, St Ives* series (camouflage), for example, with its vigorous tonal contrasts, is weakened — but not disastrously — by the colours which seem superimposed rather than essential. Such is her gift of construction, in her canvases as much as in her drawings, that this fault, if that's what it is, is rarely damaging. The painting *Glacier Crystal, Grindelwald* (1950) — one of several works on this theme — is a case in point. The massive structure of the glacier is composed of translucent curves and blocks of varying blues, whitened greens and umbers, the darker colours more opaque, but the whites often transparent and dragged across a semi-concealed plane of colour. It's as though the predominating central greens

— 45 —

Keith Douglas's Desert Flowers and Repetition

> Living in the wide landscape are the flowers —
> Rosenberg I only repeat what you were saying —

The opening of Douglas's 'Desert Flowers' seems unsteady, and doesn't inspire confidence, and yet it turns into a poem in which the poet declares an unequivocal confidence in his calling. By no means the first enduring poem he wrote, it nevertheless stands as a kind of breakthrough. Still, the opening is troubling. That first line, beginning with a vague present participle, followed by the colourless auxiliary verb 'are' and the unspecified flowers — the whole thing twisted by an inversion — is then interrupted by the address to a predecessor, the First World War poet Isaac Rosenberg, who would appear to make the speaker, and what he has to say, redundant. Repeating what an earlier poet has said, as Douglas is only too aware, disqualifies his own poem from the originality that would justify it.

The flat, resigned tone may be taken to signal the fact that the soldiers in the Second World War are now reliving the experience of those of the First. Though a different terrain is suggested by the title — Egypt as opposed to the trenches in France — the predicament is unchanged and the perspective is therefore repeated.

As it happens, Douglas himself makes the same argument insistently and explicitly in a prose piece called 'Poets in this War', probably written in May 1943, less than a month before he sent off 'Desert Flowers' to Tambimuttu, the Sinhalese editor of *Poetry London*, who, along with John Hall and Edmund Blunden, was effectively the lifeline extended to his poems while in the Middle East, at least with regard to a literary scene that must have seemed far away. Like Arthur Rimbaud, another extraordinarily youthful poet, Douglas finds himself in North Africa, utterly remote and estranged from the literary circles he frequented, only in Douglas's case he hasn't quite severed the links. (He translated some of Rimbaud's poems and makes reference in *Alamein to Zem Zem*, his prose account of the war, to Rimbaud's 'Le Dormeur du val'.) Here, in a briskly dangerous manner reminiscent of Rimbaud's letters, Douglas is discussing why the poets in this war have made no advances on the work of the First World War poets:

> They do not write because there is nothing new, from a soldier's point of view, about this war except its mobile character. There are two reasons: hell cannot be let loose twice: it was let loose in the Great War and it is the same old hell now [...] Almost all that a modern poet on active service is inspired to write,

have been composed, via the refractions of the ice, out of the blue above and the yellow below. The overall colour effect has an efficacy and a *raison d'être* without any great power or impact. What impresses most is the tangle of crystalline dark lines at the centre, the way a facetted and recursive pattern of curves and pentagons, like fractals, is deftly suggested in the larger contours of the glacier's ovals and angles. This painting is also a masterly study of how, in a theatre of natural forms, the curved line and the angle can be combined and pictorially resolved.

Less successful pictorially, however interesting to observe as part of her development, are the two large *Variations on a Theme, Splintered Ice* (1987). These represent a return, almost thirty years later, to the theme of curves and angles, picking up some of the grid-work motifs from the abstracts of the intervening years, but however admirable and acute her observation of the planes of fracture in the ice, the milky sapphire blues and greens edged by the white lines of the light hitting off them show too little interest or variation in colour.

Which is perhaps why the (unfortunately) few later works exhibited here, with their explosive and fiery colours, seem such astonishing and unprecedented events. When little, at least colouristically, has suggested anything of this kind of freedom before, it's hard to fathom where she found the confidence and vision to make these paintings. In the wonderful acrylic *Night Walk Porthmeor 5 (Scorpio Series 2, no. 10)*, dense and radiant slats of colour jostle against the bars of black they overlay in a risky contrast to the large calm field of violet with its moonlike orange ellipse. It's a vivid improvisation, speedy, ideogrammatic. *June Painting, Ultramarine and Yellow* (1996) has a boldness in its (acrylic) colours, especially those of the title, but also in the animating flame red brushed on irregularly in the bottom corners, flecks and strips of which seep upwards and seem even to underlay the topmost bar of yellow, just as the yellows descend in smaller, luminous stretches of outline to the darker central curves which appear as a greenish black composed of all three colours. In this painting, as in many others from the last decade, the relative absence of a lighter-toned ground — which is the norm for the draughtsman — seems to have opened up more dangerous and surprisingly resonant colour alliances. This distinguishes the *Scorpio Series* and subsequent work. Exact but untrammelled brushwork too, but most of all an extraordinary richness and depth of colour have helped the artist, on the evidence of this selection so much more wintry in her earlier years as regards colour, to enter into an Indian summer.

Modern Painters, Spring 2000

> would be tautological. And the mobility of modern warfare does not give the same opportunities for writing as the long routines of trench warfare.

It is no surprise to find this brilliant twenty-three-year-old poet trying to find an entry into the art, to figure out how the present relates to the past, but what strikes the reader is the uncompromising and almost pitiless way in which he analyses the disabling impasse. He wants at all cost to avoid the repetitious, the 'tautological'.

⋆ ⋆ ⋆ ⋆ ⋆

A contrary reading of this opening would see the invocation of Rosenberg as a sign of confidence or 'being in the confidence of' and therefore able to speak freely and openly to the poet who perhaps, with the possible exceptions of Georg Trakl and Giuseppe Ungaretti, wrote the most uncanny and unprecedented poem of that conflict — 'Break of Day in the Trenches'. This alternative may be more plausible when looking back at the opening from the poem's end, so we need the whole poem in front of us.

Desert Flowers

Living in a wide landscape are the flowers –
Rosenberg I only repeat what you were saying –
the shell and the hawk every hour
are slaying men and jerboas, slaying

the mind: but the body can fill
the hungry flowers and the dogs who cry words
at nights, the most hostile things of all.
But that is not news. Each time the night discards

draperies on the eyes and leaves the mind awake
I look each side of the door of sleep
for the little coin it will take
to buy the secret I shall not keep.

I see men as trees suffering
or confound the detail and the horizon.
Lay the coin on my tongue and I will sing
Of what the others never laid eyes on.

As the poem proceeds we meet the odd zeugma of 'shell and hawk' (two things that fly) and realize that the shell must be killing the men, the hawk the jerboas (perhaps the desert parallel to Rosenberg's 'droll rat') and the repetition of 'slaying', with the uncomfortable wait for the run-on across the stanza for the isolated phrase 'the mind', make the reader feel the poet's uncertainty. Are the shell *and* the hawk really 'slaying || the mind'? Or isn't it rather the whole predicament which murders minds (as well as persons)? A development of this idea would find a far better home in his final poem, 'On a Return from Egypt', with 'the sloe-eyed murderers | of themselves' where the line break is, by contrast, arresting and purposeful.

This plodding bit of prat. crit. is not intended to show that Douglas is an incompetent poet, or even to reveal someone still learning his craft but unfortunately floundering. That second option is of course feasible — he was a young soldier in an unfamiliar landscape two thousand miles from his home and recently wounded by a landmine. But it is not a poem that asks for or requires either sympathy or special pleading, and I'm more inclined to think that the slapdash manner of the opening is deliberate. It's a sketch, laying down the lines fast. And what it describes is his uneasy predicament, both physical and psychical — the latter Harold Bloom would call 'belatedness'. The poet's access to originality and primacy is stymied and blocked by a precursor. In this case, the candour with which Douglas acknowledges the fact has something about it which is more comradely than the antagonism that Bloom is wont to describe. After all, without diminishing Bloom's insight, the agon that both poets faced was not so much psychomachia as literal warfare — they had other less phantasmal enemies to face. Chances are, as both poets knew, their deaths were imminent. And 'Desert Flowers', even more than 'Break of Day in the Trenches', bears witness to this knowledge, and presents it in a flat, almost posthumous tone of voice.

But to keep reading: although the poem has warmed up with the strange 'dogs who cry words' as though the Egyptian jackal god Anubis has been let off the leash, as perhaps falcon-headed Horus had been earlier, at the end of the second stanza once again he reproaches himself: 'But that is not news.' Not the 'news that stays news' which Pound said a poem should be.

And yet by the end of the poem Douglas, albeit in a conditional phrase, confidently claims that he 'will sing | Of what the others never laid eyes on'. So between the stumbling opening and this assured and haunting finale something has occurred that allows the poet to feel his tongue has been freed from repetition, from the fear of merely parroting the poets who have preceded him. What has happened? Where does this eerie certainty come from? Almost the same matter-of-fact familiarity with the mortal, the uncanny and the otherworldly that will surface in his later poem 'Vergissmeinnicht'. The derivation of the word 'eerie' is from Anglo-Saxon *earg* meaning 'cowardly' but there is nothing cowardly about the stance Douglas adopts in this or any of his poems. It has something of an earlier classical world view: an encounter with and an acceptance of Fate.

Having said that the night has unveiled his eyes, the final stanza reveals what he *can* see rather than what he looks for:

> I see men as trees suffering
> or confound the detail with the horizon...

This image wavers, sounds both familiar and strange. Its familiarity, as William Scammell points out in his fine book on the poet, is because it echoes the gospel of Mark (8. 23–26) when Jesus heals the blind man: at first he says 'I see men as trees, walking'.[1] It is a telling shift. This time the poet *almost* repeats another writer but has transformed his words. Yet the image still declares that the eyes are not yet adjusted to vision: a state resembling hyperopia where the nearby is blurred and the far off seems near. At the same time the human trees are indeed 'suffering', so the

1 William Scammell, *Keith Douglas: A Study* (London: Faber and Faber, 1987), p. 186.

confusion is accurate. The poem hovers on the brink of clarity before the assertion of the final two lines.

Each night, then, the poet has told us, as if in a hypnogogic state, he looks on both sides of the door of sleep for the coin — obol or bullet or juke-box token — that will vouchsafe this knowledge, a secret he has no intention of keeping. Of this he will 'sing' in his poem, in the poems he'll write, and 'sing' also connotes the activity of an informer (and so, especially in this wartime setting, a spy). Poet and informer, Douglas assumes the role of witness to 'what the others never laid eyes on' and thereby his right to speak.

With this ending, Douglas strikes a Rimbaudian note, recalling the line from 'Le Bateau ivre': 'Et j'ai vu quelque fois ce que l'homme a cru voir!' This time, though, it is not the repetition of the earlier poet's visionary argosy, his 'horizon des mers', but an actual desert horizon with none of Rimbaud's vivid and brilliant palette. On the contrary, things are out of focus: 'I confuse the detail with the horizon'. But it is his own horizon, and he has broken 'through the looking-glass which touches a man entering a battle', as he wrote in *Alamein to Zem Zem*,[2] and now he is not repeating what others have said. He has found his own inimitable tone and the exact language of his finest poems. We hear it resonate in the last stanza of his final poem 'On a Return from Egypt' which again employs this brittle, vitreous and premonitory image:

> The next month, then, there is a window
> and with a crash I'll split the glass.
> Behind it stands one I must kiss,
> person of love or death
> a person or a wraith,
> I fear what I shall find.

Wild Court online, 2 February 2020,
<http://wildcourt.co.uk/features/Keith-douglas-desert-flowers-repetition/>

2 Keith Douglas, *Alamein to Zem Zem*, ed. by Desmond Graham (London: Faber and Faber, 2008), p. 15.

PART IV

Contemporaries — Home and Abroad

— 46 —

Larkin's Prose

Almost ten years ago, the publication of Larkin's *Selected Letters* provoked a small storm of protest against his racism and xenophobia. The critical response so far to this new gathering of prose pieces would suggest that the storm has subsided and all is forgiven. If these pieces represent a Larkin 2nd XI (his 1st being *Required Writing*, a team picked by himself) then most reviewers have claimed that it could still outplay anything his successors might care to send onto the field.

And certainly, his phrasing is as right and pungent and memorable as ever. Beneath the nonchalant tone, his evaluations of other writers have a keen aesthetic logic and consistency. His radio broadcasts are expertly pitched and arresting in their argument: 'I am always very puzzled,' one begins, 'when I hear a poem condemned as "mere personal emotion". It seems to suggest that emotion can be impersonal, can exist in the abstract with nobody to feel it...' The biographical vignettes have a wonderful sureness, as in this description of Hardy:

> The little old gentleman with the light waistcoat and auctioneer's hat puts away his bicycle and trots in for luncheon with the Prince of Wales, but behind him innumerable dark trees thresh and ply, moaning of concealment, of betrayal, of domestic Sophoclean atrocities.

He reviews his friends without favourable bias — arguing as eloquently against as for Kingsley Amis's anthology of light verse (1978). It would be hard to find this independent-mindedness among contemporaries reviewing their acquaintances, let alone one of their best friends — an effect, perhaps, of the subsidized poetry-biz Larkin rails against hilariously in his letters. Consistency there may be, but what about his judgements? Given that the pieces cover a period of over thirty years, we might expect a development or deepening, if not widening, of taste. This doesn't seem to be the case at all: rather a narrowing and a hardening.

His heartfelt advocacy of John Betjeman's and Gavin Ewart's poetry has a pathos about it, when we consider the frigid welcome that he prepares for Robert Lowell's *Life Studies*. Similar questions of judgment occurred in his earlier prose collection, such as his turning away from Sylvia Plath 'with shock and horror' and his whittling away of Emily Dickinson to about twelve poems. 'Poetry is an affair of sanity, of seeing things as they are', he writes in that essay, and if the sentence accounts for many of his strengths as a poet, it also suggests a limitation. That we don't really know how things are dawned on him as a poet less and less, and the more certain he became the less he wrote. The lemony oppositions he builds his poems around (self and others, marriage and singleness, sex and solitude, money and privation, youth and old age) and which he squeezes till the pips sing, begin to disperse as he stares, snow-blinded, at 'Extinction's Alp' — a sort of white-out of his talent. One of the last missives from this outpost is his tremendous 'Aubade', a stripped-down, latter-day version of Claudio's presentiment of death 'in thrilling regions of thick-ribbed ice'. But as he remarks in one of the interviews, 'People say I'm very negative, and I suppose I am, but the impulse for producing a poem is never negative; the most negative poem in the world is a very positive thing to have done'.

As a poet he was too honest to keep repeating himself; but these pieces of prose begin to sag with repetitions. His claim that Auden's work declined because he went abroad is at least an argument he backs up, but as a general — and frequent — formulation ('Foreign poetry? *No!*') it amounts to nothing more than parodic insularity and a personal preference to stay holed up by the Humber.

One of the most sadly entertaining passages is from the interview with A. N. Wilson in which each tries to out-ordinary the other. Wilson affects not to understand Larkin's claim that his own novels weren't really novels but poems: 'What does that mean? I mean... to an ordinary chap like me, they seem to be prose works that tell stories.' Larkin finally wins this little battle when he mentions the readers who respond with recognition to his poems: 'And they're quite ordinary people, they're not people who write for the weeklies.' Only in England could such a competition take place; and even among English poets, only Larkin could play this game so seriously, with such a lifetime of practice behind him.

The Independent, 2002

— 47 —

Hans Magnus Enzensberger: *New Selected Poems*

Hans Magnus Enzensberger: *New Selected Poems*, trans. by David Constantine, Michael Hamburger and Esther Kinsky (Newcastle upon Tyne: Bloodaxe, 2015)

In 'Confession', published in his seventieth year, Hans Magnus Enzensberger admits to a weakness: the stirrings of admiration.

> Harder and harder for me
> are hatred, envy, contempt,
> the youthful feelings.

The poem assembles a team of losers, 'almost all' of whom have won his respect, and we are left to guess which one hasn't. They are found at the end 'unstoppably | feeling their way and burrowing'. These figures include an abstemious eater of eggs, an imprisoned politician, 'that wife with her six face-lifts' and 'the dosser in his kraal of plastic bags'. The final word 'wühlen' (from the verb 'to burrow') suggests a kind of blind activity on their part, an attempt to make themselves at home in a comfortless zone. His admiration is described as 'A habit | sweeter than rage | and more dangerous than smoking.' Questions hang in the air. Is the poet abjuring his earlier, adversarial politics and settling into mellow old age? Are those youthful feelings more, or less, dangerous? Is the speaker really boasting of a strength while confessing to a weakness? Is he saying good riddance to youth, or worried that this new tendency may make him less vigilant, thus more susceptible to being hoodwinked? The tone is flat and ambiguous; the list of persons, however, is rapid and sparky, and comes across well in David Constantine's translation.

This *New Selected Poems* is a reprint of the 1994 *Selected Poems* with the addition of *Kiosk*, translated by Michael Hamburger and the poet, of *Lighter than Air*, translated by Constantine, and of *A History of Clouds*, translated by Esther Kinsky. In his introduction, also reprinted from the former *Selected*, Hamburger prefers 'hard-headed' to aggressive as a description of Enzensberger's tone. There are good reasons for hard-headedness in someone brought up in the Third Reich, who in his youth in Nuremberg had Julius Streicher as a next-door neighbour. Enzensberger is a poet naturally disposed to see mildness as collusive with tyranny, as sheepishly abetting the wolves.

Now eighty-six years old, not only one of Germany's greatest modern poets but Europe's too, he has earned the right to be mellow if he wants to be. He may no longer be the '*zornige junge Mann*' [angry young man] that one critic deemed him, but this poem doesn't quite convince us that he's become quiescent with age. Besides, there has always been a tolerance and warmth behind the cool, abrasive style.

In vain, I have been trying to think of an English-language poet with whom he could usefully be compared. (A friend who knows Enzensberger's poetry well suggested Louis MacNeice for his range and intelligence and *joie de vivre*. But even that inspired suggestion seems slightly astray.) Perhaps in Germany too he stands as a solitary eminence. Of course every good poet is *sui generis* but it's something else I'm trying to suggest. In Italy, the slightly older poets with a trace of Brechtian lineage like Franco Fortini (born 1917) and Giovanni Giudici (born 1924) share some of his qualities. Both, like Enzensberger (born 1929) are brilliant essayists, their imaginations at once ethically probing, urbane and internationalist. Elsewhere, at least west of Germany, there's nothing parallel that I can think of. The idea that Italian poets of that generation, he and perhaps other Germans such as the far older Günter Eich and the younger Reiner Kunze should have much in common is not entirely random. They have all had to dig, or burrow, their way out from under the ruins of fascism: politically, culturally, linguistically; and that entailed a deeper, more extreme distrust of culture than has ever been forced upon British or American poets. The need for 'a revaluation of all values' was even greater in Germany than in Italy. None of this can make a poet, but a poet of Enzensberger's gifts can, and does, make something out of it.

We can find any number of British poets distrustful of a compromised language and disaffected in politics, but no one like Paul Celan who has had to re-assemble the language out of fragments. Enzensberger is not as radical and fractured as that, but his poems have a sceptical and anti-lyrical tendency. In his lines, politics, philosophy and science often displace the literary. But all this makes his work sound far grimmer, as well as more professorial, than it is. Though sometimes formidable in intellectual reach and confidence, his poems are vivid in their images, unexpected in their movement, and immediately appealing. I mentioned Eich earlier not because, whatever his post-war declarations, his politics are similar but because the starkness of perhaps his best-known poem 'Inventur' (Inventory) which, in Michael Hofmann's translation, begins 'This is my cap, | my coat, | my shaving kit | in the burlap bag' seems to have had a telling impact on early Enzensberger, and can be heard, for example in 'Middle Class Blues':

> The grass grows,
> the social product,
> the fingernail,
> the past.
>
> The streets are empty.
> The deals are closed.
> The sirens are silent.
> All that will pass

Enzensberger's poem shares Eich's rawness and minimalism, though his imagery is more mobile and vagrant.

His 'Historical Process' from 1964 reads like a parable of the Cold War, the world frozen in an identity-less state of torpor: 'The ice-breakers will be here by morning. | Then the trawlers will leave | [...] | [...] | So what. | It doesn't matter about your name.' (The German line that corresponds to 'A fighter howls across the island' is missing from the text.) The repeated, shrugging phrase 'So what', set near the beginning and near the end of the poem, acts as a curious framing device.

One feature that is discernible throughout Enzensberger's long career as poet is an almost architectonic feeling for the structure of a poem. Refrain-like repetitions, motifs set at angles to one another, the lack of adornment — all these create an impression of spatial design. In his subtle poem about immigration, 'Old Europe' from *Kiosk*, the first two stanzas end with parenthetical questions which set up the expectation that the final stanza will follow suit, but instead the reader is confronted by 'the dark-green portal | of the Elephant Inn, built in 1639'. The asymmetry leaves the poem at a tilt, as if the ancient inn was another exotic, earlier immigrant facing the Guinean selling 'key-ring pendants' and 'the old Bosnian woman | stretching her stiff legs'. Sometimes an entire poem is composed by ringing the changes on a single word or word stem, as in 'The Force of Habit' where 'Gewohnheit' [habit] or its cognates appear 22 times in 38 lines. This causes understandable obstacles for Hamburger's translation which must deploy several words for the one German root: 'habit' and 'habitual' have to give way to 'ordinary', 'extraordinary', 'gets used to', 'usual', 'are used to': 'Ordinary people ordinarily do not care | for ordinary people'. The original's elegantly twisted logic and virtuosic wordplay founders in the English, through no real fault of the translator. In another such poem, which the poet himself translates, the name Dante occurs at least once in all but one of its seventeen lines. Opening 'This is not Dante', it ends:

> This is a man who believes he is Dante.
> This is a man everybody, except Dante, believes to be Dante.
> [...]
> This is a man nobody believes to be Dante, except Dante.
> This is Dante.

It's a kind of 'House that Jack Built' enacting a dizzying identity crisis that might be taking place at a border crossing or a police station. The title of this poem in German is a gobstopper of bureaucratese: 'Erkennungsdienstliche Behandlung'. The literal meaning of the phrase is 'official recognition treatment', basically identification via photo and fingerprinting. Enzensberger renders it as 'Identity Check', which suffers a considerable loss of syllables. Like the Marxian 'Historical Process', his titles abound in idiolects, dehumanizing jargon, philosophical flotsam: 'Model Towards a Theory of Cognition', 'Delete the Inapplicable', 'A Hare in the Data Processing Centre'. His poems have an insatiable appetite for language, and in the final poem of this selection, 'A History of Clouds', even include the mathematical formula of Kepler's Conjecture regarding the stacking of spheres: where the scientist 'saw the atomic grid, guessed | its rotational symmetry, | sixty degrees, calculated | its packing density: $\pi/3\sqrt{2}$'. This is way above my head, but I suppose for those, like Enzensberger, who can follow the thought (he has written a delightful book for children about numbers), these abstract symbols are a kind of poetry. More approachable and of wider appeal is his 'Ode to Stupidity':

> how you shine from the bloodshot eyes of the hooligan
> and trip along in upper-class arrogance clearing its throat,
>
> and how you waft at us with a bedraggled Muse's bad breath
> and as polysyllabic delirium in the philosophy seminar.

Even here, where you expect a Popean 'Universal Darkness' to descend, the poem unpredictably changes tack at the end, offering a merciful reprieve: 'only to the elect do you grant the rarest of your gifts, | the blessed simplicity of the simple.'

The introduction refers to Enzensberger's *Mausoleum* (1975) as a 'book of prose poems'. This is misleading: that collection does include some prose poems but is mainly of verse, and it is one of Enzensberger's most original works. It would have been worth including something from Joachim Neugroschel's translation, now out of print, but the *New Selected* is already a hefty 400 pages. Hamburger's translations are themselves hard-headed and versatile, and they ably play the idiomatic against the conceptual, but still it's a relief to come to Enzensberger's own translation of *The Sinking of the Titanic* — though it's vexing he should also be such an accomplished *English* poet. He's the exception to the rule that you can only be a poet in your mother tongue. These lines from 'Apocalypse. Umbrian Master, about 1490', one of many poems to explore the pictorial, may serve as an example:

> Destroying the world is a difficult exercise.
> Hardest to paint are the sounds — for example
> the temple veil being rent asunder, the beasts
> roaring and the thunderclaps. Everything, you see,
> is to be rent asunder and torn to pieces,
> except the canvas.

There's nothing showy about the writing, but the rhythmic variety, from the dactylics of the second line to the iambics and trochaics of the third, and the gradual pace and economy of detail are all effective. It gives the reader none of the unease that poetry in translation can sometimes induce, that feeling that the essential thing is 'subject to loss by evaporation', as packets of tobacco used to warn before they were emblazoned with scarier stuff. If, as Enzensberger says, admiration is 'more dangerous than smoking', this book should carry a health warning.

Poetry Review, 105.4, Winter 2015

— 48 —

Ted Hughes: The Deeps are Cold

In 'Poetry and Violence', his eloquent essay-reply to questions by Ekbert Faas, Ted Hughes refers to Blake's 'Tyger' and Yeats's 'Second Coming' in connection with his own two jaguar poems. Both Blake's and Yeats's creations are instinct with a physical, psychic and, as Hughes makes clear, political violence. As far back as we care to go, in poems, in dreams and in life, these big cats mean business and threaten our safety. Jeremiah's prophecy plays on that dread: 'Wherefore a lion out of the forest shall slay them, and a wolf of the evenings shall spoil them, a leopard shall watch over their cities.' And Dante employs these same animals to impede his pilgrim's progress, allowing for the small change of leopard to *lonza*, a creature wearing a 'gay pelt' and known only to medieval bestiaries.

Ted Hughes's poem 'Second Glance at a Jaguar' revisits the subject of his own poem, 'The Jaguar', in a darker and more urgent spirit, and is an heir to all these. It breathes the same kind of menace as Jeremiah. Where his earlier poem had annulled the cage — 'Over the cage floor the horizons come', implying the rondure of the whole earth — the later 'glance' reveals a kind of obsessive, fateful, almost thuggish fury. This poem seems to enter still deeper into, to get further under the skin of the animal as it tries 'to grind some square | Socket between his hind legs round'. The cumulative effect of all those verbs of grinding and wearing out ('he has to wear his skin out') and wearing down and swivelling and rounding is like a ghostdance performed in a primitive stone-tumbling drum. If we compare it to Rilke's 'The Panther', another poem with which it has some kinship, we see that it offers an altogether more disturbing, less aestheticized experience. One aspect of the disturbance is the way that the animal is made to mirror back to us various vicious forms of human behaviour — 'gangster', 'dream of murder', 'Rounding some revenge' are all anthropomorphically insistent , as is the — more culturally specific — reference to Aztec ritual sacrifice. It's this capacity to disturb that brings the poem far closer to the heat of Blake's 'Tyger'.

Hughes's jaguar is observed much more closely, naturalistically, and, if the word doesn't sound too cosy, empathetically than Blake's picture-book emblem that leaps at us with its incantatory rhythms and repetitions. Of Blake's poem, Hughes writes: 'Blake saw his Tyger in a "vision" and tried to make sense of it by controlling it, yoking it with the Lamb (Christ, its apparent antithesis) and the God of Job.' This idea of control, the taming of the tiger, seems to me to overlook the cruel-cunning intent behind Blake's poem, its polemical depth-charge that occurs in the line 'Did He who made the Lamb make Thee?'. Blake is questioning the bland nature of a particular Christian cosmology that excludes the terrifying evidence of the creation by lifting up the image of the lamb. But Hughes's poem shows how well he understands that intent, as, incidentally, does his account of his own poem 'Thrushes' in the same essay. The caged animal, although subtracted from the natural order still belongs to it, in a way that its captors, to their cost, do not.

'Second Glance at a Jaguar' can be seen as Hughes's 'The Second Coming', his own 'vast image out of Spiritus Mundi'. As Yeats's poem begins with the falcon 'Turning and turning in the widening gyre', Hughes begins with a perception of roundedness and velocity: 'Skinful of bowls he bowls them'. The whole poem worries at this internal anatomical geometry; it assumes something of the same 'urgency of his hurry', discarding in the process one shape after another just as the jaguar itself seems to be refining its movements towards a perfect, imaginary kill. The spherical and circular images give way finally to 'heavy ovals'. These egg-shaped, birth- and death-bearing bones, which the jaguar has worn himself down to, subliminally evoke Yeats's sphinx-like beast which 'Slouches towards Bethlehem to be born'. But what does the jaguar give birth to? Itself — its head is a whole other reproduction of itself, a smaller, carved, or rather honed-down version:

His head
Is like the worn down stump of another whole jaguar,
His body is just the engine shoving it forward,
Lifting the air up and shoving on under.

It has duplicated its overworld self in the underworld. This isn't so much the human, criminal underworld that the poem has also evoked, but a mythical underworld which is no other than the human psyche.

Hughes's tautological and hyperbolic imagination is at its most triumphant when dealing with this moment of self-definition, in which, as Hopkins puts it, 'each mortal thing' 'Deals out that being indoors each one dwells; | Selves — goes itself; myself it speaks and spells, | Crying What I do is me: for that I came'. It is one of Hughes's most characteristic tropes — the point at which a mortal thing 'Selves — goes itself', where it sheds all the approximations that the poem has used to approach or stalk it, the point at which Hughes can declare, as he does in 'Pibroch':

And this is neither a bad variant or a try-out.
This is where the staring angels go through.
This is where all the stars bow down.

At one level the naturalistic observation in Hughes's animal poems may camouflage the super-natural drive behind the writing. The poem demands that we read it both as perceived reality and as cosmology. 'He coils, he flourishes | The blackjack tail as if looking for a target' and that target is the human psyche which would prefer to shut out this image of power. The threat which the jaguar poses 'Hurrying through the underworld, soundless' is one which the reader has to answer, just as he or she must in reading 'Tyger' or 'The Second Coming'. With Jeremiah it says 'a leopard shall watch over your cities'.

Many have noticed that Hughes's natural world is over-red, his seas incarnadined:

> The deeps are cold:
> In that darkness camaraderie does not hold:
> Nothing touches but, clutching, devours.
> ('Relic')

Kropotkin might point out many examples of mutual aid among the species. Even moray eels can be stroked, as divers have discovered, without biting off the hand that does so. But if Hughes doesn't inhabit a Peaceable Kingdom, his poems insist on the need not to settle for a falsifying myth which gives us teddy bears whilst it devastates the habitat both of the actual jaguar and the mythical *lonza.*

The Epic Poise: A Celebration of Ted Hughes, ed. by Nick Gammage
(London: Faber & Faber, 1999)

— 49 —

Congeries of Emotion: Arun Kolatkar

> She feels contradictory sensations, freezes, burns, raves, reasons, so that she displays not a single emotion but whole congeries of emotion
>
> — Longinus (writing of Sappho) in *On the Sublime*

However little of her work remains intact, Sappho has endured as the definitive erotic poet, and Longinus, to whose criticism we owe the preservation of some of her best-known poems, offers good reasons for her primacy. The phrase 'congeries of emotion' (in Jonathan Culler's translation)[1] also describes a crucial element in the poetry of Arun Kolatkar, a body of work which if not always erotic is recurrently and subtly amorous. We know Sappho in small fragments, but Kolatkar's poetry often needs space to develop, his short lines to unfold within a large compass, and his poems typically have several sections, like jump-cuts in films.

It always seems lazy and back-to-front to apply cinematic terms to poetry because all of those technical devices have been employed by poetry long before, and then by prose — close-up, jump-cut, travelling shot, etc. A spectacular example of the travelling shot — with a cosmic as well as a geographic reach — can be found in *The Iliad*, Book 14 (lines 270 following):

> And Aphrodite the daughter of Zeus went home
> but Hera sped in a flash from Mount Olympus' peak
> and crossing Pieria's coast and lovely Emathia
> rushed on, over the Thracian riders' snowy ridges,
> sweeping the highest summits, feet never touching the earth
> and east of Athos skimmed the billowing, foaming sea
> and touched down on Lemnos, imperial Thoas' city.[2]

In Kolatkar's case, however, cinema *is* one among many feasible prompts for his work. His hugely eclectic list of influences, delivered with uncharacteristic abundance in one of his rare interviews, includes ancient Chinese poets, Indian poets, French Symbolists, Beat poetry, Blues and film.

Despite his prolific output, both in English and Marathi (sometimes leavened with Hindi slang) Kolatkar seems to have been extremely loathe to publish except in small presses, so for a long time his poetry was mostly restricted to his devoted circle of fellow poets and readers, or as Laetitia Zecchini puts it in her lucid essay on the

1 Jonathan Culler in *Theory of the Lyric* (Cambridge, MA: Harvard University Press, 2015), p. 62.
2 Homer, *The Iliad,* (London: Penguin, 1991), p. 377. The translation is by Robert Fagles.

poet and his milieu, 'His absolute reluctance to stand in the spotlight was matched by a stubborn cultivation of the same elementary, and in part private, space'.[3] His *Collected Poems in English* has the bonus of the poet Arvind Krishna Mehrotra's perceptive and moving memoir and introduction. If he is little known in the UK or the USA, beyond a restricted loyal band, in India he has sometimes been read with suspicion, and Amit Chaudhuri's essay in *The Hindu* considers this phenomenon with exasperated wit. The problem, as he presents it, is that Kolatkar's aesthetic of estrangement (he adopts and transforms Shlovsky's term) is misread as distance and superiority. The insistent charges of 'tourism' and 'exoticizing' with which Indian critics have reproached him (and in Britain as well, frequently enough, we hear the same rebukes directed at BAME poets by sociologically minded critics) are exposed in this case as spectacularly inappropriate and leaden-footed.

Kolatkar was born in 1931 in Kolhapur, but moved to Bombay (his preferred usage for Mumbai) at the age of eighteen and there he remained till his death in 2004. His poems, panoptic and casually incisive, are a celebration of the city's seedy and burgeoning sprawl. Almost anywhere you open the book there are troves of wry observation and breathtakingly inventive imagery. Just as one example, 'Lice', that happily stands comparison with Rimbaud's great poem on the same irksome creatures ('Les Chercheuses des pouces'), has the speaker envious of a newly released prisoner who is being deloused by a beautiful girl in the street. In three cinematic sections, it starts with a description of the girl 'like a stick of cinnamon [...] sitting on that concrete block | as if it were a throne', then dwells rancorously on 'her dirty no-good lover' ('Just look at him, the yob...') and in its final section enters the dreamy state of this undeserving youth as he drifts off, while her hands move through his hair,

> and dreams
> that he's holed up in a mossy cave
>
> behind a story-telling waterfall
> booby trapped with rainbows,
> and hears the distant bark of police dogs.

This extraordinarily mobile and seemingly inexhaustible imagination can be heard throughout his work, and it shares with many of his poems an ingenious eroticism.

Though Kolatkar is hugely eclectic in his borrowings from other art forms, and equally so with regard to poetry, situating him here within a tradition of ancient Greek poetry may seem misleading, because Indian poetry has its own powerful and playful traditions of the erotic. This is evident in the Marathi poems he translates into English but also infuses his work throughout. Though perhaps Sappho is not so far from the mark. Catullus, who imitated Sappho and used her metres, comes high on his list of favourite poets cited in that interview, and appears, lower-case, in an unpublished diary fragment which Zecchini quotes:

3 Laetitia Zecchini, 'Translation as Literary Activism: On Invisibility and Exposure, Arun Kolatkar and the Little Magazine *Conspiracy*', in *Literary Activism: A Symposium*, ed. by Amit Chaudhuri (Norwich: Boiler House Press, 2016), p. 29.

I'm afraid I've been a glutton
consumed poets of Europe living and dead...
only after they have first been eaten consumed
and regurgitated by translators
[...]
I've supplemented my diet at various times with canned catullus
smoked baudelaire reconstituted villon
pickled apollinaire salted mashed mandelstam
and cured tomas transtromer[4]

The exorbitantly wayward leisure of Kolatkar's approach to his subject can be seen again and again in his work. As one instance, 'To a Crow', could anyone else have penned such an action-packed and absorbing (87-line) poem about a bird picking up a twig,

executing
a perfect hyperbolic curve
with throwaway ease...

where the last phrase describes Kolatkar's manner as much as the crow's? By the end of the poem the mock-pedantic enquiries the bird addresses to the twig begin to assume a wittily metapoetic as well as a metaphysical aura:

Does it scan? Does it rhyme?

Does it make sense;
and if it does, what does it mean?

without in the least weighing down the swift grace of the writing.

Another poem such as 'Meera', which describes a woman sweeping the street, from multiple perspectives, from that of the palm frond she employs to that of the rubbish she has to stomp down in an ancient pram, a residue of the Raj, is making a ludic parallel with the Rajasthani saint and poet Meera, also known as Mira Bai, supposed author of many devotional poems of love and longing for Krishna. Though born into a royal family she is associated with a deeply democratic urge, so her embodiment in a street sweeper is appropriate rather than blasphemous — not that that would matter much to Kolatkar, whose temple sites in his long poem 'Jejuri', for instance, are more likely to be home to a stray dog and her pups than to devout pilgrims.

That pram of colonial and Victorian provenance which becomes a conveyor of rubbish is a characteristic example of Kolatkar's radical re-purposing of history, as well as urban bric-a-brac. 'Meera', again typically, is a poem in several sections and from its start goes its own sweet way according to its vagrant and promiscuous interests. Italo Calvino describes the poetics of Ludovico Ariosto, the Ferrarese Renaissance poet, as 'errant', delighting in the way a mood, a place, even a weather system can change radically within the space of a mere eight-line stanza, the *ottavo* he put to such diverse uses in his unending long poem *Orlando Furioso*. The erotics of Ariosto's poem Calvino sees as eternal foreplay and rarely, and then less

4 ibid. p.44

happily, as consummation. Kolatkar's erotics — the clumsy and theoretical plural will have to suffice here — are similarly errant and perpetually mobile, even if he dispenses for the most part with any regularity of form. Formally the chaos is deeper, irregularity being of its essence. Anything stray or insignificant can enter his poem and find residence there: chance encounters, a labyrinth of streets that pulsate with life and merge the febrile and fertile mindscape of the poet with the city that provides him with an inexhaustible correlate, the most populous city of India with its almost twelve and a half million souls. Not since Baudelaire's Paris has a metropolis found such an adequate, disreputable and ideal laureate.

Unpublished, 2019

— 50 —

The World's Violences: C. K. Williams's *The Vigil*

C. K. Williams, *The Vigil* (Newcastle upon Tyne: Bloodaxe, 1997)

The long lines and short poems of C. K. Williams's *Flesh and Blood* (1988) combined the leisure of a flâneur with the urgency of a frontline reporter. His next book, *A Dream of Mind* (1992), although it contained some poems of the same extraordinary quality, in the long title sequence, at least, turned inwards, quarrying the psyche, and was rewarded by grim, unwieldy slabs of abstraction. *The Vigil* is somewhere between the two. Here too, as in his last two books, there is a poem about a vagrant. In each of them the poet attends unflinchingly to infirmity and terminal squalor. In this latest example, 'Thirst', from the opening phrase, Williams's perceptions hold the foreground of the story: 'Here was my relation with the woman who lived all last autumn and winter day and night | on a bench in the Hundred and Third Street subway...' The 'shocking seethe of her stench' is a feral protest the poet recoils from but can't escape: 'how rich, I would think, is the lexicon of our self-absolving; | how enduring our bland, fatal assurance that reflection is righteousness being accomplished'. This goes further than the earlier poems by accusing consciousness, and implicitly his own poetry, of complacency for merely not having averted its gaze. The poem then lurches into an inferno of empathy: 'then holocaust, holocaust: host on host of ill, injured presences squandered, consumed. || Her vigil, somewhere, I know, continues...' If Williams sometimes hovers like a cleric at the deathbed, his calling as a poet of mortal anguish is not in doubt.

This collection also explores the distance as well as the proximity of the gazed-upon. His powerful version from Ovid records its belatedness: 'In our age of scrutiny and dissection we know Deinira's mind better than she does herself'. This distinguishes Williams from the Adamic imagination of Whitman, whose long lines Williams's superficially resemble — his work acknowledges the secondary manner through which, at least in part, we come to know the world and its violences with a knowledge that sometimes seems illicit. In this respect *The Vigil* exercises in its voyeurism a kind of vigilance. In 'Fragment' a murdered shopkeeper's last moments relayed on the video system are retold with excruciated empathy. 'In Darkness' re-enacts a violent scene from 'That old documentary about the miners' strike in Harlan County...'. Williams draws an explicit political analogy from the snarling strike-breaker who 'posed, strutted [...] the way, now, so many in power assuming that same stance of righteous rectitude and rage | snarl their contempt at those who'd dare hold differing notions of governance and justice'. Yet even for those of us in sympathy with Williams's political stance, both the language and the shift of perspective ('the way') have a kind of imaginative fatigue about them which suggest that his use of these longer lines may have outlived its creative purpose. This instant allegorizing is characteristic of the volume. In 'Fire', for example, the description of a burnt house is immediately translated for us: 'Like love ill and soiled; like affection, affinity, passion, misused and consumed'. Somehow the nouns are too cursory and indistinct to convince us, and the cadences too monotonously doleful. Williams has often been willing to sacrifice subtlety for intensity. The urgency and clamour of his style can be mawkish but it also makes available to him as a writer tracts of the psyche which are overlooked by other poets. What is unusual is Williams's visceral empathy with others, with moments *in extremis* when the civilized mask drops and the human face with all its psychic lacerations and marks of woe appears before us.

In 'The Game', another kind of vigilance is seen when, contemplating the outset of an affair, he asks 'What difference if she was married, and perhaps mad (both only a little, I thought wrongly)'? The poem's last line, however, abruptly switches from acute psychological observation to a vertiginous, cosmic perspective: 'beneath me a planet possessed: cycles of transfiguration and soaring, storms crossing.' Because of his almost forensic attention to detail, his heaping up of evidentiary images, the reader is inclined to believe these rhetorical shifts, and yet they also feel calculatedly intensified. 'The Hovel', though written entirely in this visionary register, finds an arresting emblem for the soul: 'Slate-scraps, split stone, third-hand splintering timber; rusted nails and sheet tin...' This is Plato's cave installed with the faulty plumbing of nightmares.

'My Neighbour' proceeds via an ungainly cortege of possessed gerunds that shelve into present participles: 'my holding the door, her crossing the fragmented tiles, faltering at the step to the street, | droning, not looking at me...' which all insist on the actual now of perception. And yet this poem which brings together the poet's repelled surveillance of his neighbour and the memory of a relationship requires of us a sudden leap of faith when, out of nowhere, 'the god of frenzied, inexhaustible love says, rising in bloody splendour: Behold me.' Many of these poems function as parables and exempla in which the meticulously recorded everyday occurrences are denuded and then hurtled into a realm where they become 'cycles of transfiguration'. The redemptive urge behind these poems makes them compelling but the manner in which their perspectives shift can seem like the arrival of a *deus ex machina*.

Times Literary Supplement, October 1997

— 51 —

Another Ten: *Sixty Poems* by Ian Hamilton

While hosts of 'professional poets' have turned out their regular triennial volumes, Ian Hamilton, at least in poetry, has been laconic in the extreme. His poems, as well as his collections, have always been characterized by the utmost economy of means — the essentials — as if anything more would just be embellishment or blather. Only one poem here, the devastating 'Larkinesque', struggles on over the page, and most of the others are shorter than sonnets.

These poems, new and old, have a wintry, bitter, potent presence that is not easily shaken off. Hamilton is a master of a plain literalness more shocking and striking than the most far-fetched metaphor. Consider 'Birthday Poem', in which a shaving mug has become the spittoon of a dying man, to discover how a whole life, and the history it witnessed, is stripped bare:

Tight in your hands,
Your Empire Exhibition shaving mug.
You keep it now
As a spittoon, its bloated doves,
Its 1938
Stained by the droppings of your blood.
Tonight,
Half-suffocated, cancerous,
Deceived,
You bite against its gilded china mouth
And wait for an attack.

Hamilton's skills are deployed in the way that word 'mug' resonates throughout the whole poem, taking up, one by one, its various senses: cup, mouth, dupe, attack. The blood 'droppings' consort uneasily with the 'bloated doves', 'Empire' with 'Deceived', 'stained' with 'gilded'. A little ripple of rhymes — 'Tight... Tonight... bite' — offer no more formal consolation than do the only two iambic pentameters, the second line and the penultimate.

This powerful book is full of insidious iambic openings such as 'The waiting rooms are full of "characters" | Pretending to sleep' or pentameters like 'The dead flies pile up on the windowsill', almost mundane, straight lines with crooked purposes. It's a more than welcome return to print of this fine poet.

PBS Bulletin, *Spring 1999, though I have added two sentences the strict word limit didn't permit. Far more could be said about the poem but brevity may suit the subject.*

— 52 —

Seamus Heaney: *Opened Ground*

'Their beat embalms them' was Robert Lowell's funereal phrase for how poets survive in their poems. Seamus Heaney's beat has been sounding now for more than thirty years, and shows no sign of abating, as the publication of this new, enlarged selected poems, *Opened Ground: Poems, 1966–1996*, makes clear. As crucial as the beat, but harder to characterize, is the vocal timbre — the tone and texture which carry the living voice and keep it alive. Almost anywhere the reader might chose to alight on in this book, the lines carry an unmistakable signature:

> That midge-veiled, high-hedged side road where you stood
> Looking and listening until a car
> Would come and go and leave you lonelier
> Than you had been to begin with... ('At the Wellhead')

The compound-laden, densely patterned acoustics of that first line move into a perceptual clearing in the next, alerting the senses. And the way, instead of writing 'Than you had been before' with its iambic, lacquered finish, Heaney ruffles the last line with a deliberate awkwardness — all these effects show both a steady vigilance and a continued receptiveness not just to the realm of the senses but also to what they open onto. 'Gleaning the unsaid off the palpable', as he writes in 'The Harvest Bow', might stand as a fitting motto for his entire work.

In Heaney's early poems there is an awareness of density and weight, both of the earth itself and of language, and he has never abandoned this perception of the earthbound and the creaturely: 'I grew out of all this | like a weeping willow | inclined to | the appetites of gravity'. And yet his poems have become increasingly susceptible to the airborne, or to the anti-gravitational force of the imagination. In 'The First Flight' he assumes the alter ego of Sweeney, the Irish king who was turned into a bird:

> I was mired in attachment
> until they began to pronounce me
> a feeder off battlefields
>
> so I mastered new rungs of the air
> to survey out of reach
> their bonfires on hills...

If Heaney were not so 'mired in attachment', weighted down by relationship to his community and to the history of place, the ascent would be less charged and far-reaching. Feathers — regardless of the expression — don't fly. The heavier the weight the further it goes, at least holds true for poems, or as Heaney puts it, employing the metaphor of a ploughshare, 'the more brutal the pull | and the drive, the deeper | and quieter the work of refreshment.'

Heaney has weighed the claims of heritage against the (sometimes counter-) claims of the art, and by fully acknowledging both he has managed to betray neither. He has never shed his 'attachment' — and even the word 'mired' doesn't entirely succumb to a negative valence in this poet who is drawn to the 'darkened combs' of what has sunk in the bog. Yet he refuses to be circumscribed or entrapped by these attachments. This is, at least in part, what makes the elegies of *Field Work* such formidable masterpieces. 'Casualty' especially, which records the murder by the I.R.A. of a fisherman friend, is one of the finest poems to emerge out of the Troubles. Its power is one that takes apprisal also of the Irish civilians murdered by the British Army on Bloody Sunday, but it lives in the evocation of this particular figure's sly, gestural, freewheeling life beyond the exigencies of community.

The imagery of weighing and of scales not only marks a dedication to sensory experience — of how we know the world — but also implies a concern with justice, with what the world might or ought to be. This can give rise to the self-mockery of a poetic stocktaking:

> As I sit weighing and weighing
> My responsible *tristia*.
> For what? For the ear? For the people?
> For what is said behind backs? ('Singing School')

Elsewhere, as in 'Station Island III', his reworking of an earlier elegy for Colum McCartney, in which the dead man accuses Heaney 'For the way you whitewashed ugliness and drew | the lovely blinds of the Purgatorio | and saccharined my death with morning dew', it leads to a genuinely mordant examination of conscience and yet, in its return at this point to *terza rima*, it still retains, intact and unapologetically, the powerful Dantesque consciousness of the former poem.

Heaney, in his Nobel lecture, 'Crediting Poetry', claims that he 'began a few years ago to try to make space in my reckoning and imagining for the marvellous as well as for the murderous'. The sestet of 'Fosterling', with its dialectic of weight, its lift-off and final pun on 'lighten' shows how such space was made:

> Heaviness of being. And poetry
> Sluggish in the doldrums of what happens.
> Me waiting until I was nearly fifty
> To credit marvels. Like the tree-clock of tin cans
> The tinkers made. So long for air to brighten,
> Time to be dazzled and the heart to lighten.

Heaney's poetry has, however, always allowed a space for the marvellous — as early on as 'The Diviner' whose 'forked hazel stick' picks up 'Spring water suddenly broadcasting | Through a green hazel its secret stations'. Or take the final image of the raindrops on the telegraph wires in 'The Railway Children':

> Each one seeded full with the light
> of the sky, the gleam of the lines, and ourselves

So infinitesimally scaled

We could stream through the eye of a needle.

The incisive clarity of these lines recalls an Escher engraving only to excel it in imaginative force.

These poems find — in the dowser's gift and the child's perception of the world — images of the marvellous that are also wonderfully grounded. They work deftly as images of the poetic act, but rather than being conscripted as such are given free rein to be themselves. There are many figures of traditional crafts throughout Heaney's poems which offer similar, unforced parallels with the art of poetry — the thatcher 'pinning down his world, handful by handful', the blacksmith who 'expends himself in shape and music' and the tailor: 'My Lord Buddha of Banagher, the way | Is opener for your being in it'.

It's entirely apt that the last poem of *Opened Ground* should close on the word 'open', which has a talismanic quality for Heaney:

You are neither here nor there,
A hurry through which known and strange things pass
As big soft buffetings come at the car sideways
And catch the heart off guard and blow it open.

This ending, that seems to catch something of the optimism of the ceasefire, has a Zen-like readiness for the unexpected and, despite its title 'Postscript', the lyric gift of writing through to, rather than after, the event. The book, which has the feel of work very distinctly ongoing, also includes the Nobel lecture. Heaney is a poet who deserves to be read in entirety — a remark often made and rarely true. Out of what's been omitted from even this fuller selection, another Selected could be assembled (just think of the excluded 'Freedman', 'A Postcard from North Antrim', 'An Ulster Twilight' and so on) that would still place him firmly at the forefront of contemporary poetry.

Independent on Sunday, 6 September 1998

— 53 —

The Locative: Seamus Heaney's *Electric Light*

Acknowledging a sense of origin, or prehistory, within the entanglements of history has always been a concern of Seamus Heaney's poetry. And origin with this poet is always place of origin — his poems grapple with the spirit of place, the 'where' in which what happens happens. It's appropriate then that the first word of this new book, in the natal, place-named poem 'At Toomebridge' is 'Where' and that the last words of the book should be 'in Derry ground'. This might seem the parameters of a fiercely local kind of writing, an assertive territorialism, but the actual case, although it doesn't entirely exclude that possibility, is far more rich and ranging.

In these poems, global history, a sense of otherwheres and other times, is often paramount — six sonnets set in (modern and ancient) Greece, a poet's festival in the Belgrade of the Seventies with its well-oiled cast of bards, a Spanish trip in 'The Little Canticles of Asturias'. This last three-part sequence is, as the title suggests, a miniaturized *Commedia*: in the first, the 'furnaces' and 'hellish roads' of a descent 'Into the burning valley of Gijon'; the second in Piedras Blancas is a lighter-skied, purgatorial 'home ground' associated with the Gaeltacht; the third a paradisal glimpse at San Juan de las Harenas — the whole pilgrimage ending with a play on the final word ('stella') of all three of Dante's canticles: 'In the great re-echoing cathedral gloom | Of distant Compostela, *stela, stela*'.

The ambitiousness of trying to box epic into lyric would have sunk most poets, but this sequence plays gracefully off its Dantesque model and at the same time, by making links with this other rural, Catholic world, finds its feet — and a feeling of powerful kinship — within a foreign culture.

Another poem that makes a surprising connection between the Irish-speaking community of Ireland and Dante is 'Gaeltacht' itself, a wonderful adaption of the sonnet in which Dante wants all his friends to gather in a boat:

> I wish, *mon vieux*, that you and Barlo and I
> Were back in Rosguill, on the Atlantic Drive
> And that it was again nineteen sixty
> And Barlo was alive
>
> And Paddy Joe and Chips Rafferty and Dicky
> Were there talking Irish......

More marked by loss than the original, the poem still has the speed and flow of late talk, turning Dante's joyful vernacular into *craic*, and ends with the wish that the sonnet itself be 'the wildtrack of our gabble over the sea'. Dante's maestro Virgil is also represented here by his ninth eclogue. The eclogue is traditionally the form of city folk who dress up in smocks to praise the simple pains and pleasures of country life, so it's surprising that a poet so well versed in rural actuality should be willing to countenance it. But Heaney gives the complaints of Virgil's swains about dispossession a local twist: 'An outsider lands and says he has the rights | To our bit of ground.'

Although there are some short poems like 'Perch' which stand comparison with the best of Heaney's lyrics, one novel feature of the book is the number of poems which overflow their occasions and proceed by asterisk-linked sections, angled, bulky, cumulative re-visions of the poem's premise. These big, roomy poems seem shaped by an impulse and pressure to remember more, to get more said than the smaller single poem would have allowed him to. Many of them, while tuned to what in 'Lupins' Heaney calls 'the erotics of the future', are grounded in childhood memory — for example the title poem 'Electric Light', 'Out of the Bag', or 'The Loose Box', the final section of which has Michael Collins's murder prefigured in his boyhood game of falling from a hayloft 'foreknowledgeably deep | Into the hay-floor'. Heaney writes here of 'an underworld of understanding', and the word 'understanding' sounds out urgently throughout the book, as for instance in the childhood remembered in 'Lupins': 'And none of this surpassed our understanding' — which both activates a prefixal play on 'over' and 'under' and the notion of 'standing' as in 'Standing their ground'. The interest in how our capacity to perceive is perfectly fitted to what's perceived has a Romantic lineage, and many of the longer poems bring to mind Wordsworth's praise for 'those obstinate questionings | Of sense and outward things, | Fallings from us, vanishings', only Heaney has the uncanny gift of catching them in their falling, of stopping them vanishing, and bringing the reader up against what he calls, in 'Electric Light', 'The very "there-you-are-and-where-are-you?" | Of poetry itself'. That 'Where' at the outset has remained obstinately questioning, an interrogative as well as a locative.

Independent on Sunday, 8 April 2001

— 54 —

Word Made Flesh: Seamus Heaney's Bivalves

Out from the 'darkened combs' and 'responsible *tristia*' of *North*, the first poem of *Field Work*, sounds a radically different note:

> Our shells clacked on the plates.
> My tongue was a filling estuary,
> My palate hung with starlight:
> As I tasted the salty Pleiades
> Orion dipped his foot into the water.

Is 'Oysters' Seamus Heaney's hymn to cunnilingus? If it is, it's also a poem that touches explicitly on history, geography, politics, astronomy, marine zoology, cuisine, sex and poetry itself. From its starry-mouthed opening to its closing invocation of the word, from 'tongue' in the second line to 'tang' in the penultimate, the poem journeys from north to south, and its language is emphatically erotic.

In the second stanza the oysters 'lay on their beds of ice', a word picked up in the next stanza 'Laying down a perfect memory' where the phrasal verb consorts perhaps with the 'cool thatch' in the following line. (When I first read the poem in 1979 I thought the phrase eccentric but now find it's a common expression for memory encoding.) Still, what I think most attracts Heaney is the open vowel that plays through the entire poem and returns resoundingly at its end 'I ate the day'. The descriptive language throughout carries an erotic charge: 'Bivalves: the split bulbs | And philandering sigh of ocean...' 'frond-lipped, brine-stung...'

'Oysters' brings the reader into the bracing 'starlight' and 'clear light'. The effect is akin to the first canto of Dante's *Purgatory*, in which the poet, emerging from hell, salutes the 'dolce color d'orïental zaffiro' and speaks of a renewed 'diletto' in perception (of starlight and sunlight) and in a resurgent poetry. The epigraph for one of *Field Work*'s masterpieces, 'The Strand at Lough Beg', is taken from this same first canto, and the whole book has a fruitful engagement with the *Commedia*. 'Oysters' is a threshold poem, an emergence from the depths, but the way, as for Dante, is far from clear. The oysters represent the 'frond-lipped, brine-stung | Glut of privilege' of the Roman, and so by extension, the British Empire: they are the spoils of the victors, and themselves victims of violence. (Incidentally within the poem's superbly varied rhythms, the only line that's a conventional iambic pentameter is 'The Romans hauled their oysters south to Rome', though Heaney mentions in an interview the book's 'rhythmic contract of metre and iambic pentameter'.) The poem's obvious concern is hedonism and what stands in its way: the sexual violence in the second stanza 'Alive and violated... Millions of them ripped and shucked and scattered' and the implied colonial violence in that 'Glut of privilege' in the fourth stanza. The poet wants to be able to savour sensual delight unobstructedly, without guilt (a near anagram of glut) and without joining the oppressors.

The poems which follow in *Field Work* try to keep this clear light alive but nevertheless re-immerse themselves in the Troubles. The British tanks that invade the poet's country lanes are held to account by a mythical centre 'the still untoppled omphalos' — which makes a daring, even Joycian, pact between Irish and Greek culture as against the Roman/British 'charioteers'; the 'acquisitive' culture of the Southern Irish economic boom is rebuked, the internecine conflict is seen as boding a 'saurian relapse' and yet the newly unearthed carrots at the end of 'After a Killing' are filled with colour and regenerative — both symbol and quotidian actuality.

It's a bitter irony that this opening poem of eating should be shadowed not just by the violence it rehearses but also, as many readers have noted, by the sinister feasting of Ugolino at Archbishop Ruggiero's skull in the final poem of the book, a return to the lowest circle of the *Inferno*. Here, however, the meal is of a decidedly different order:

> I ate the day
> Deliberately, that its tang
> Might quicken me all into verb, pure verb.

It's true that the 'verb', as Christopher Ricks remarks, 'remains indissolubly a noun', and the whole question hangs on a 'might', and yet the verb 'ate' is repeated in concealed form in the adverb 'Deliber*ate*ly' and completes the sound pattern begun with the opening line 'The shells clacked on the pl*ates*' and picked up as a slant rhyme two lines later in 'pal*ate*', and then again in the second stanza 'alive and viol*ated*' (with a nod perhaps to Molly Malone) so it arrives as a kind of consummation. The whole poem and its intricate acoustics is a paean to taste, to the tongue, and the 'pure verb' itself, which is also freighted with its Latin origin 'Verbum caro factum est', the Word made flesh. The purity of that verb, though, at the very least remains in question.

Poetry Ireland Review, Issue 113, September 2015

— 55 —

Derek Mahon: Earth-Residence

Derek Mahon's poetry has often seemed most at home when most evicted. From one of his earliest poems, 'The Death of Marilyn Monroe' — 'Stars last so long before they go scattering ash | Down the cold back-streets of the Zodiac' — to the title-poem of his 1985 slim publication *Antarctica*, which has Captain Oates trapped in a valedictory villanelle — 'I am just going outside and may be some time' — heat loss, entropy, a kind of interplanetary wind-chill have always been his element. His imagination has an unforced Beckettian drive towards the point of maximum exposure. Even the titles of his books, *Night-Crossing*, *Lives*, *The Snow Party*, *The Hunt by Night* and *Antarctica* have an exhilarated, icy, posthumous air.

The new book, *The Hudson Letter*,[1] is perhaps his least even achievement so far, but then evenness is not, it seems, what Mahon is after. Outstanding translations from Laforgue, Ovid and Nuala Ní Dhomhnaill are followed by some witty but slight 'shorts' and clerihews and by 'The Yaddo Letter', addressed to his two children, which is uneasily poised between the private and the public, as most letter-poems are and as the best letters aren't. True, Mahon faces this paradox head-on when he lets on that 'Maybe I'll read this letter at the "Y"', but the poem is still a disappointment by his own fiercely exacting standards.[2]

And yet 'The Hudson Letter', in eighteen longish sections, his longest poem to date, shows the poet once more coming into his own. Its first line, 'Winter; a short walk from the 10th St. Pier', is like a clarion call to Mahon's imagination: 'The fishy ice lies thick on Gansevoort | around the corner...' The tone of the opening has a conscious shakiness, a raw convalescent feel which colours the whole poem's record of New York, its night noise, its river views and its cultural and subcultural buzz and static.

Mahon's poems have addressed many forms of urban and imperial breakdown, being in at the kill as with 'The Kensington Notebook', or his Lowellian (and Stevensian) masterpiece, 'Another Sunday Morning'. If the writing here lacks the suave economy that Mahon's readers have come to expect of him, nevertheless his depiction of the sprawling metropolitan underbelly achieves a cumulative breadth

1 Derek Mahon, *The Hudson Letter*, Oldcastle: Gallery Books, Ireland, 1996.

2 Re-reading the poem more than twenty years on, now I'm considerably older than the poet was when he wrote it, this judgement slightly irks me. Whatever reservations I might still have about the letter-poem as a form, I now find the poem affecting in its chastened but playful mix of the intimate and the formal. It may look back to W. B. Yeats's 'Prayer for My Daughter' but has shed the grandiosity of its great predecessor and found a conversational style that's still compact and heightened.

of vision, as in this excerpt from a twenty-three-line sentence which surveys the growing numbers of the homeless:

> from the Port Authority Bus Terminal to JFK
> and further afield, in freight yard and loading bay,
> gull-screaming landfill, stripped trailer and box-car,
> the gap increasing between the penthouse tower
> and the desert of cinder-block and razor-wire...

Although 'The Hudson Letter' is by no means so keyed into destitution as this might suggest, including as it does a witty tribute to Fay Wray and King Kong and another to Auden, what is most courageous and moving about the poem is the way the images of urban dereliction are tied explicitly to a personal crisis, a hard-earned, fraternal feeling for the down-and-out.

Underpinning the poem is a kind of self-healing impulse, sardonic as it is about 'health fascists', which calls on *The Winter's Tale*'s dream of restoration (prefigured in a masterly translation of Ovid on Pygmalion earlier in the volume) and also on the interspersed images of the nightingale which evoke Keats's lyric symbol, as well as Coleridge's and Respighi's, while the eighth section gives a powerful version of Ovid on Philomel and Procne.

The relentlessly literary nature (or culture) of Mahon's imagination, his central concern about the complex occult relationship between a violent politics and a polished aesthetics, is nothing new, but here it is taken to extremes. The whole poem (and each section of it) is replete with epigraphs and bristles with inverted commas, with quotations from a host of sources, the literary interlaced with advertisements, news flashes and the laconic graffiti of a certain Miguel who exhorts us to 'FIND THE CURE'. It is as though Mahon had embarked on that project Walter Benjamin only envisaged, to compose a book entirely of quotations, an ambitious urban collage which spans the contemporary and the historical, the quotidian and the arcane. Hart Crane is one of the forebears whose ghost most haunts the poem, and in 'Key West', the sixteenth section, which also pays tribute to that other Key West resident, Elizabeth Bishop, Mahon seems almost to be re-creating the kind of poem which Crane at the end of his career was trying to forge a new language for. Crane's 'I stood a long time in Mack's talking | New York with the gobs, Guantanamo, Norfolk, | Drinking Bacardi and talking U.S.A.' is transformed, in the aftermath of a similar hurricane, into Mahon's:

> and sat in Pepe's drinking (rum and) Coke
> with retired hippies who long ago gave up
> on the land and settled on the rocks.

Mahon's deflationary last line and mock-guilty parenthesis also signal the ease with which he can ironize his own self-projection as another, later poet of the Hudson River.

The fact of Mahon's having another home to talk about allows his vision of New York an extra dimension, as his own sense of being adrift can be read into his fine evocation of two other Irish immigrants, Bridget Moore and the painter ('father of the painter') John B. Yeats, who 'lived and died | like all of us, then as now, "an exile and a stranger" '. Mahon has always had the bleak gift of fending off any tribal loyalty while not deceiving himself that that sets him free of a difficult Ulster heritage. Home is a word which obsessively reappears in his work, often rhymed in such a way as to offset anything remotely *heimlich*, as here in 'IV Waterfront':

> I hear no Jersey blackbird serenade
> this rapt friar on the Big Apple Side;
> yet, having come so far from home,
> I try to imagine our millennium
> where, in the thaw-water of an oil-drum,
> the hot genes of the future seethe.

This downbeat Second Coming has a weathered irony that recalls many of Mahon's earlier poems, and his sense of being 'an exile and a stranger' has paradoxically allowed his own exemplary body of work to become, as he says of 'A Garage in Co Cork', 'One of the milestones of earth-residence'.

Times Literary Supplement, 12 April 1996

— 56 —

Ticktock Cries and Tin Tents: Tom Paulin's *Walking a Line*

Tom Paulin's fifth book of poems follows a seven year pause after *Fivemiletown* — the kind of pause which most writers would welcome — in which he has published an adaptation of Aeschylus, an anthology of vernacular poetry and an extraordinary collection of critical essays, *Minotaur. Fivemiletown* was one of those rare books which knocks the coordinates of poetry such a distance beyond contemporary practice that all it can expect is irate incomprehension. Paulin had evolved a mercurial style that mixes the subjective with the political so as to make new shapes out of both.

Walking a Line has a more clement, meridian feel to it. Somehow Paulin has managed to jettison the internal coat hanger and wised-up downbeat disillusion which is characteristic of the 'well-made' poem to which in 'Air Plane' he refers as 'Foursquare | a dead duck':

> they want us to love
> their rigid waddle
> their ticktock cries
> the way they confront
> our square earth
> in its box of —
> I should say sky
> — in its box of air

The constabulary manner of that word 'confront' is well judged, as is the way the voice veers off from the clinching rhyme. This poem isn't content merely to satirize but invents a parallel reality where language is free to try out new forms.

Paul Klee, whose meditations on the art of drawing give Paulin his title, is a guiding spirit, not only for the three poems in which he appears in person. The first of these records Klee on guard duty ripping primed canvases off crashed German bombers. That improvisational 'throwaway permanence' is what these poems value. Set implicitly against Horace's 'perennial bronze', there is 'History of the Tin Tent' which is

> bowed into shape
> from rippling thundery
> hundredweight acres
> of sheet metal.

Here we find a conflict between the poem's delight in the material of the tents and the history that brought them into being — 'Europe became a desert | so these tents could happen'. It's not a conflict that is resolved, but then the whole book is built on the unresolved — several poems end with question marks, not as evasions or as rhetorical questions, but rather as a way of earthing within the poem the forces that are left outside. 'The Firhouse', a title which, said rather than read, is an ingenious bit of sexual slang ('the house is set next a clump of fir trees on a small hill') takes a wary reading of the social climate of middle England. Everything is left in an indeterminate state — even the biro plays up 'as if it knows this poem (if it is a poem) | will never quite get written'. The poem's speaker goes to the door to enquire after a Christmas tree and is turned away by the woman of the house. He asks himself 'but why should you want in? why should there be | some little puja room you have to come inside of?'.

The way in which this poem sparks off questions of national identity, of sex and politics, alongside a playful questioning of the act of writing, is representative of the whole book. Dispensing with conventional punctuation as Paulin does here requires exact judgment of tone and rhythm. What he has achieved is a powerfully oral, child-like immediacy of tone without sacrificing complexity of thought or design. The poems are tuned to register the most fugitive perceptions, catching 'more jizz more quickchanging brightness'. In 'American Light', which crosses Donegal with Cape Cod, the opening sets up an original play of the visual and the tactile:

> — the wild China roses paths of clam shells
> those little slights of fog
> stuck in the firtrees

And the poem ends around a campfire, the company drinking and 'laughing our legs off'. That final image surreally re-imagines the 'slights of fog | stuck in the firtrees' as well as teasing out notions of being grounded, of belonging somewhere.

Walking a Line may well be Paulin's finest achievement to date — it is a real event to find, among others, poems as good as 'The Sting', 'Cadmus and the Dragon', 'Soldier and Packman' and 'Basta' in one book. The end of 'Basta', which reprises the joyful exuberance of the 'Brit' chapter in *Moby Dick* conveys the spirit of the book and the experience of reading it:

> — so we waded right into
> that watery plain
> that blue blue ocean
> and started diving and lepping
> like true whales in clover

Independent, 3 September 1994

— 57 —

Peekaboo Quiffs and Eel-Spears: Paul Muldoon's *The Annals of Chile*

When Baudelaire claimed that a poet's head should be a dictionary of rhymes, except perhaps in an opium trance he hadn't dreamt of anything as intricate as Paul Muldoon. In his last book *Madoc* — aptly subtitled *A Mystery* — Muldoon employed consonantal rhymes with a dizzying sophistication and variety. The enigmatic prose poem which prefaced that book ('The Key') ends with his 'footfalls already pre-empted by their echoes', an image which perfectly describes the subtle disturbance of his way of rhyming.

In his new book, 'Yarrow', a long piece composed of 150 short poems, takes rhyming into new territory. Muldoon operates a kind of telescopic or long-distance rhyming whereby a poem rhymes not with itself but with another poem, usually adjacent to it. Where Muldoon speaks of the yarrow, a mock-pedantic plant-book description soon shelves into a teasing evocation of his own procedure, the way his rhymes have been placed just beyond the threshold of audibility:

> With its bedraggled, feathery leaf
> and pink (less red
> than mauve) or off-white flower,
> its tight little knot
> of a head,
> it's like something keeping a secret
> from itself...

The complexity of the scheme is mirrored by the poem's allusiveness — from Camões to Hart Crane, Ovid to O'Rahilly. This can be more playful than purposeful, and the fabric of references to adventure stories, chivalric romances and television westerns seems to have become an end in itself, hindering the poem's movement. Among the poem's fund of languages — Latin, Spanish, neologisms, place-names, etymologies — Gaelic shares the line with English more insistently than ever before in Muldoon's work.

The best poems, though, are all in the first part of the book. The long 'Incantata' for the death of the Irish artist Mary Farl Powers puts Muldoon's complexity to its most moving use. This extraordinary poem is impelled by a desire to name and include everything that has been lost with the loss of the person and achieves an uncanny restitution. It's an elegy unlike any other — intimate, humorous and heartbreaking.

A poem for the birth of his daughter ('The Birth') reveals a similar delight in language and in:

> the inestimable
> realm of apple-blossoms and chanterelles and damsons and eel-spears
> and foxes and the general hubbub
> of inkies and jennets and Kickapoos with their lemniscs
> or peekaboo-quiffs of Russian sable

into which 'Dorothy Aoife Korelitz Muldoon' is hauled by way of a Caesarean.

Muldoon has always considered the world through an Ovidian prism, so that something is no sooner one thing than it's become another. Here, his translation of Ovid, though the rhyming in couplets is more conventional than might be expected, is superbly skilful, as is 'Testimony', his version of César Vallejo's 'Piedra negra sobre una piedra blanca', which catches a tragi-comic tone no other translator has detected let alone caught.

In 'Monarch and Milkweed', another poem from the first part, Muldoon perhaps has in mind Frost's poem 'Pod of the Milkweed' where droves of butterflies are drawn to this 'drab weed'. If for Frost 'waste was of the essence of the scheme', there is nothing wasteful about Muldoon's poem, or his rhyme-scheme — essentially that of the extended villanelle, with one rhyme anagramatically transposed onto the other: 'He'd mistaken his mother's name, "Regan", for "Anger": | as he knelt by the grave of his mother and father | he could barely tell one from the other.' The conflation of name with emotion, of one grave with the other, and of the milkweed with the monarch butterfly is brought into being as much by the twin rhymes as by the play of his images.

It's this mixture of chance and fixity, or ordered chaos, that makes Muldoon's rhyming so exceptional. His rhyme-words seek each other out in the most unexpected places, finding a phonetic pairing which is the equivalent of the biological link between the butterfly and the milkweed: 'Then: "Milkweed and monarch 'invented' each other".' That Muldoon should see the graves of his parents as an occasion to meditate also on the nature of language and sound may strike some readers as curious. But his formalism is so thoroughgoing that rhyme becomes a principle governing the secret, powerful affinities between things and between people.

Independent, 24 September 1993

— 58 —

Corona, Corona: Repetitions and Strange Adjacencies

The title of *Corona, Corona*, Michael Hofmann's third book of poems, published in 1993, which sounds like a Mexican oath in a Western, is derived from the poem 'Hart Crane' and describes the American poet's histrionic habits of composition:

> A sufficiency of drink, the manic repetition
> of a mantric record — any record — and he typed.
> Corona, Corona, Victrola, and a Columbia loud needle.

— A prickly mouthful of brand names from the Jazz Age and the 1920s economic boom. Giving their own 'manic repetition' ('record...record'), the two Coronas refer presumably, I almost said respectively, to a cigar and a famous make of typewriter. Another suspect might be the Mexican beer — considering Crane's long sojourn in Mexico and the last section of the book dedicated to that country. In what looks like an embarrassment of riches, Hofmann's *Selected Poems* omits this poem (along with several others including 'Biology', 'Dyptich' and — most regrettably in my view — 'Shivery Stomp') so the book title has a somewhat orphaned air as it now stands in the *Selected*'s index.

Corona, Corona is echoic in its ideas, its shapes and its sounds. Another meaning of *corona* is 'crown' and indeed the word appears in his poem 'Kurt Schwitters in Lakeland':

> Kurt Schwitters's tombstone was hewn in straight lines,
> *klipp und klar*, in the shape of a hat, brim — crown.

That line's alliteration makes its own corona. Repetition on a temporal as well as a spatial level is very much the theme of 'Guanajuato Two Times', the whole poem organized around a repeated conditional tense:

> I could keep returning to the same few places
> till I turned blue; till I turned into
> José José
> on the sleeve of his new record album,
> 'What is Love?';
> wearing a pleasant frown and predistressed denims;
> reading the double-page spread ('The Trouble with José José')

the poem begins, and goes on to explore pairings, doublings, ghostings, repetitions, and near repetitions of many kinds. Another example can be found in 'Shivery Stomp', a poem that traces 'a strange adjacency' to the novelist Malcolm Lowry:

> to have visited so many of your sites, Ripe and Rye,
> Cuernavaca and Cambridge, and by fifty-nine days,
> never to have done time — a term — together

where again the alliteration and the phonetic slippage of 'time' and 'term', with their shift from prison to school, plays on the theme of identity and near identity. A later line from the poem describing the England that Lowry 'fled and died in' — 'Brick and lichen, pruned willow, prunes and the WI' — makes an even more intricate play on sounds.

In Hofmann's first book, *Nights in the Iron Hotel*, there were already some remarkable 'lives of the artists' poems — on the Expressionists, on Kirchner — but it's really in *Corona, Corona* that he gives himself free rein to explore biography. Seven years after his intensely autobiographical second book, *Acrimony*, which tracks the painful relationship with his own father, the novelist Gert Hofmann, it could be thought that in these poems biography is autobiography by other means — 'It surely isn't me, pushing thirty, taking a life a night...' — as the question is not quite conclusively settled in the book's first poem, 'Lament for Crassus'. Most of the first section is devoted to poems on writers and artists, as well as the musician Marvin Gaye. Like the last, many of these seem to have had serious trouble with their father — Dadd kills his own dad, Gaye is killed by his — and so the book in a conscious and curious way projects filial conflict onto a wider screen. And yet the artists and writers whose lives Hofmann 'takes' are as often also taken as examples — Lowry, Schwitters, Beckmann are all tutelary spirits to whom the poems pay warm tribute, 'a strange adjacency'.

The book has, roughly speaking, a tripartite form — the first section biography, the second autobiography, and the third travel writing — three literary genres which the poems both regard askance and reinvent. Amid a generally chilly reception — or so I remember it in the immediate (and continuing) enthusiasm of my own response — one of the few reviewers that responded appreciatively and intelligently to the book was the poet Mick Imlah in the *Independent*. Noting the 'phenomenally rich vocabulary', he also speaks of the way the poems exploit 'diseased lexical harmonies akin to rhyme'. This is certainly a quality that distinguishes the collection from Hofmann's previous work which for the most part had fastidiously avoided conventional rhyme and metre; although his poems allowed for subtle word-play, they appeared largely indifferent to 'music' — any acoustic effects that might be considered adornment. Here poem after poem admits a complex play on sound, repetition and assonance, and their arguments sometimes seem to advance through phonetics.

My only reservation about Imlah's suggestive phrase is that 'diseased', though it perfectly fits his first example from 'Biology' — 'all pocked, opaque, Venetian, venereal' — gives scant acknowledgement to the more vital and vigorous part sound plays in these poems. Even where the speaker has a defeated or lassitudinous air, these phonetic effects act as a kind of counter argument: language is alive with patternings and possibilities.

A short poem such as 'Pastorale' may offer an example of how and why this is the case:

> Where the cars razored past on the blue highway.
> I walked, unreasonably, *contre-sens*,
>
> the slewed census-taker on the green verge,
> noting a hedgehog's defensive needle-spill,
>
> the bullet-copper and bullet-steel of pheasants,
> henna ferns and a six-pack of Feminax,
>
> indecipherable cans and the cursive snout and tail
> of a flattened rat under the floribund ivy,
>
> the farmer's stockpiled hayrolls and his flocks,
> ancillary, bacillary blocks of anthrax.

'Pastorale', bearing a dedication to Beat Sterchi, the Swiss author of *The Cow*, which Hofmann himself translated, is mordantly anti-pastoral, but arresting in its display of both colour and harmonics. From the first image of the cars that 'razored past', the poem bristles with militaristic terminology, and with a dark irony insistently presents the bucolic in terms of the martial — the hedgehog's 'defensive needle spill', the beautifully observed 'bullet-copper and bullet-steel' of the pheasant's plumage, the 'stockpiled hayrolls' and so on. It reaches a sinister finale with an alphabetic chiasmus, literally *abba*: 'ancillary, bacillary blocks of anthrax.' (A similar corona-effect can be heard in the title of another poem from the book: 'From A to B and Back Again'.) Anthrax rhymes jarringly with that 'six-pack of Feminax' — itself an unhappy collision of gender attributes (the brand-name being a now discontinued codeine-based drug for period pains). Even the word 'bacillary' from Latin *baculus*, meaning 'rod', has an aggressive air in contrast to 'ancillary' from Latin *ancilla* for 'handmaiden' — though in this case perhaps a handmaiden of war. The sounds become buzzing and armoured. If for the first time in Hofmann's work an almost Keatsian richness arrives in the language, here it's to subversive or uncomfortable effect. While these poems bask in the release of acoustic energies, it would also be true to say that they subject a long English tradition of *melopeia* (Pound's term) to a kind of critique.

The 'slewed census taker' — as Hofmann introduces himself in the first lines — walking against the traffic flow 'unreasonably, *contre sens*' (where the English puns on the French) is a singular take on the figure of the *flâneur*, whom Baudelaire dubbed 'le botaniste de l'asphalte'. This urban figure is given a comic twist by being exiled to an unspecified stretch of the countryside. No wonder he's 'slewed', and yet he collects his data, mainly roadkill, with an extraordinary determined precision and a dazzling palette.

Although Walter Benjamin saw the demise of the *flâneur* in the age of consumerism, Hofmann finds in this figure a continuing point of leverage. Characteristically a stroller around the metropolis, the *flâneur* has an inbuilt radar — lost in the crowd, he (a 'he' it is in all historic accounts) never abandons a sharp, perceiving eye and a leisurely sense of his own apartness. What Hofmann adds to this traditional figure is a set of very particularized character traits — the perceiving

'I' is at odds, disaffected, marginal, stripped of any external authority or even of the vatic tone that we might associate with a prototype of the *flâneur* in Blake's 'London': 'I wandered through the chartered streets, | near where the chartered Thames doth flow...' and yet the poet remains a witness, whose trustworthiness is earned, at least in part, by descriptive virtuosity. So while the tone of the poem chips away at any sense of stable authority, the performance on the level of language re-instates it.

Something in the compression and compounding of elements in that last line of Hofmann's recalls a similar effect in Blake's poem's ending 'And blights with plagues the marriage hearse'. For all that the speaker plays ironically on his doom-predicting role, and the poem moves to its macabre end with exaggerated emphasis, there is a reality which the poem reveals — anthrax (*bacillus anthracis*), a bacterium that affects livestock and soil, was tested on the Scottish island of Gruinard which remained contaminated for almost fifty years and has indeed been stockpiled by various countries, although Britain in 1956 renounced its use. Even in the land of the lamb the tiger's claws are visible.

Polluted, menacing pastorals are a strong feature of this collection, perhaps most definitively in 'Dean Point'. The poem which follows 'Pastorale', 'On the Beach at Thorpeness', begins:

> I looked idly right for corpses in the underbrush,
> then left, to check that Sizewell was still there.
> The wind was from that quarter, northeasterly, a seawind,
> B-wind, from that triune reliable fissile block.

Like '47° Latitude' which precedes 'Pastorale', making a kind of atomic and chemical triptych, this poem catches the jittery feel of the time after the Chernobyl disaster in April 1986, the sense of likely irreparable ecological damage, which has — or at least should have — re-awakened with the meltdown at Japan's Fukushima Daiichi nuclear reactor in 2011. If the opening plays on a jokey paranoia, there is — as in the tired old joke — a great deal to be paranoid about, so the comic persona, if persona is the right word, has history on his side, and the comedy is of a decidedly uneasy kind.

This opening splices a pedestrian's traffic code with a detective *noir*, and has the strolling subject again at his data-gathering. By surveying a stretch of beach he comes up against what used to be called 'the military-industrial complex', and arrives at the blunt Churchillian final line: 'Jaw jaw. War war'. Another repetition to recall *Corona, Corona*. Sizewell comprises three A and two B reactors, so I take the 'B-wind' (which otherwise refers to a film printing technique) to be a suggestion of the emissions from the Magnox block. The stanza's last line, with its run of three adjectives linked by assonance 'triune reliable fissile', picks up the preceding poem's 'ancillary, bacillary blocks of anthrax'.

In the third stanza, nature itself seems to be complicit, or entangled, in the nuclear threat:

> A set of three-point lion prints padded up the beach.

> The tideline was a ravel of seaweed and detritus,
> a red ragged square of John Bull plastic,
> a gull's feather lying down by a fishspine.

The writing is densely allusive — the first image may come from Elizabeth Bishop's 'The End of March', another walk-on-the-beach poem — 'a track of big dog-prints (so big | they were more like lion prints)' — and the last line, with a desolate wit, transforms Isaiah's vision of the Peaceable Kingdom into a marine landscape of *disjecta membra.* (Another reference to Isaiah (5. 29–30) is perhaps audible here: 'Their roaring shall be like a lion [...] And in that day they shall roar against them like the roaring of the sea'.)

In the poem's penultimate stanza, the acoustics intensify:

> The North Sea was a yeasty, sudsy brown slop.
> My feet jingled on the sloping gravel,
> a crisp musical shingle. My tracks were oval holes
> like whole notes or snowshoes or Dover soles.

Another feature that Imlah's review praised was 'an imagination whose way of thinking in shapes often brings geometry to mind: not just in incidental diagrams [...] but in the materials and organisation of whole poems' — this has indeed been a quality of Hofmann's work from the outset, from, say, an early poem like 'Shapes of Things', and it is a gift that has evolved dramatically. Here in the o-haunted sequence of images, that lay down near identical tracks on the ear, as in the last stanza's description of the tide that 'advanced in blunt codshead curves', an auditory as well as a visual imagination of a rare kind can be seen.

The prominence of the first person in this opening 'I looked idly right [...] | then left' is a frequent element in these poems: '[...] where I walked' — line 2 of 'Pastorale'; or 'I arrived on a warm day, early, a Sunday' (line 1 of 'The Day After'). See also from the Mexican section: 'I leaned round the corner in a Gold Rush town — ' ('Las Casas'); 'I walked on New Year's Eve from Trotsky's house' ('The Out-of-Power'). Then there are poems by contrast that open in sedentary or supine mode: 'Picture me | sitting between the flying buttresses of Cuernavaca Cathedral' ('Postcard from Cuernavaca') where the participles wittily contend. Or 'I eat alone in a room with a net' ('No Company but Fear'). Or in '47° Latitude': 'I was lying out on the caesium lawn | on the ribs and ligatures of a split deckchair'. This poem comes round full circle, a kind of corona, to end:

> as thick as pebbles
> on the beach. I lay out on the caesium lawn.

The cunning enjambment allows the title of Nevil Shute's 1957 nuclear apocalypse novel *On the Beach* to appear stranded. (The film of the same title had already figured in Hofmann's 'Shapes of Things' — so a repetition of a repetition.)

Each of these openings ostentatiously places the speaker very much in the foreground as if to rile an aesthetic espoused by the 'Cambridge School' poets in ascendance when Hofmann studied there, for whom this use of the 'lyric I' was, and is, a kind of taboo, and a sure marker of intellectual backwardness untinged by Modernism: 'the empirical derivation of poetry from exclusively personal experience', as Andrew Crozier put it sternly. Maybe it's wrong to conscript Hofmann into a battle in which he has no stake and probably little interest, but the question remains as to why the first person pronoun is so prevalent, central and insistent. In all of the openings quoted above there is little doubt about the irony, sometimes bleak, sometimes caricatural, with which the first person pronoun is surrounded. The 'I' is certainly not an unmediated construction: for all its continuity, it has to be made up afresh for the peculiar purposes of each poem, but there are unmistakeable traits in common throughout his poetry. It is worth noting, further, that the very distinctly located and personalized 'I' of *Acrimony* in which the first person pronoun is seen *in primo piano* is no longer a necessary convention for these poems, but still remains as steadfastly insistent.

As has often been noted there is no mistaking a Michael Hofmann poem: it just couldn't have been written by anyone else. For all that this hyper-distinctive 'I' might destabilize the convention, he refuses to abandon a lyric tradition that has characterized more than two thousand years of European poetry and can be found in lyric traditions elsewhere that go back much further. Try as we might, we do not see through others' eyes, and admitting the partiality of perspective is a kind of basic honesty rather than a tyranny of the self. Quirky as the 'I' is in Hofmann's poems, it seems to be an un-excludable given, a declared perspective — the avoidance of which would by no means guarantee any greater integrity or objectivity.

The performance is always on a high wire, and the risk of solipsism is always there. The poet's self-portrait at forty in 'XXXX', an appealing poem from Hofmann's last book *Approximately Nowhere* (1999), takes this risk to its limits. It begins 'I piss in bottles, | collect cigarette ash in the hollow of my hand....' and ends:

> I am quarrelsome, charming, lustful, inconsolable, broken.
> I have the radio on as much as ever my father did,
> carrying it with me from room to room.
> I like its level talk.

After his father's death, this poignantly recalls a poem from *Acrimony*, 'My Father at Fifty': 'Wherever you are, there's a barrage of noise: | your difficult breathing, or the blaring radio'. Though even here, in what looks like an entirely recursive moment, there's the ghost of an echo, from Gérard de Nerval's 'El Desdichado':

> Je suis le Ténébreux, — le Veuf, — l'Inconsolé,
> Le Prince d'Aquitaine à la Tour abolie :
> Ma seule *Etoile* est morte, — et mon luth constellé
> Porte le *Soleil noir* de la *Mélancolie*.

The unconsoled speaker in Hofmann's poem *carries* a radio rather than a star-spangled lute but the implied Melancholia bears a history that is not 'merely' personal. It's a shade antiquarian to suggest that a poem which begins 'I piss in bottles' needs an arcane allusion as ballast, but what I'm suggesting is that the 'I' used in poems as challenging as these comes with a dense history however fleet and insouciant the manner might seem.

In its repetitions of sound and shape, its plethora of echoes, ghostings, and pairings, however, *Corona, Corona* seems to me to have found the most satisfyingly complex way of exploring both identity and the world beyond the self — a world more inclusive than could easily be found in any other contemporary poet.

The Palm-Beach Effect: Reflections on Michael Hofmann, ed. by André Saffis-Nahely and Julian Stannard (London: CB Editions, 2013)

Selected, Selected: Michael Hofmann and Bernard O'Donoghue

Michael Hofmann, *Selected Poems* (London: Faber and Faber, 2008)
Bernard O'Donoghue, *Selected Poems* (London: Faber and Faber, 2008)

These two Faber *Selecteds* are in such contrast to each other that the only advantage I can see in reviewing them together is the proof they offer of real biodiversity within the poetic 'mainstream' — a term mostly, and lazily, meant to stand for 'homogenous'. One an early bird, the other a late starter: Michael Hofmann brought out his first book in his twenties, Bernard O'Donoghue in his forties. Hofmann's language is intricate, darting, laid with tripwires; O'Donoghue's is plain speech, rarely embellished. Hofmann's poems can be unflinchingly autobiographical when they are not unflinchingly biographical, or both at once; O'Donoghue's poems are, with a few exceptions, intensely reticent.

Hofmann's first book, *Nights from the Iron Hotel*, was published in 1981 and must be one of the most striking debuts of the last quarter century: he seems to have just vaulted over the whole messy ditch of juvenilia and known what he was about from the start. There's a striking contrast of the block-like, brickish look of them and the exceptional mobility of mind within. 'Gruppenbild ohne Dame', a fourteen-liner from an August Sander photograph, moves with sureness from the panoramic opening of '1923, Gathering Depression' to the clinching close-up of its ending: 'skinny boys | with their mother's big eyes and hurt mouth.' The figure of the father ('The maculate conceptions of his bald head') in this poem and in others point towards his second collection, *Acrimony*, where the relationship to his own father, the German novelist Gert Hofmann, comes under scrutiny. But that is only a part of the story. These poems offer panoptic, multi-levelled surveys of contemporary life, both British and Continental, interspersed with quirky excursions on the literary life, past and present, affectionate and disaffected portraits of others as well as of himself, but what is most indelible and inimitable is the style.

An epigrammatic element ('Time isn't money, at our age, it's water' or 'Familiarity breeds mostly the fear of its loss') vies with an unmatched eye for detail. By *Corona, Corona*, his third book, Hofmann's poems have grown denser, the effects more textured and more acoustic: 'my tracks were oval holes | like whole notes or snowshoes or Dover soles'. In the dazzling and sinister 'Pastorale', the poet notes 'a hedgehog's defensive needle-spill, || the bullet-copper and bullet-steel of pheasants, | henna ferns and a six-pack of Feminax...' This heightened visual sense inscapes his poems about artists — rather than 'picture poems' they offer a compact 'life', or even a demonstration. Perhaps best of these are the poems on Richard Dadd and Kurt Schwitters, the latter ending with a stone the artist had left: 'It had an air | of having been given a spin, | a duck, a drakkar, a curling stone'. I don't believe anyone else could have written that collage-like, last line: 'duck' gives way to 'drakkar', a Viking longship, which takes us into the artist's Norwegian exile, whilst the icy image of a curling stone leaves the poem in a state of ghostly, perpetual motion. The selection loses the tripartite form of the original book, which took on the genres of biography, autobiography and travel writing and made something original out of each, though this impetus behind the poems can still be sensed.

His last book, *Approximately Nowhere*, is well represented, and includes a number of the poems written after his father's death, including 'Cheltenham', which achieves the nigh-impossible feat of being an excellent poem about a literary festival. Starting with a lightning sketch of 'the old water town, spook town, old folk's town', it recounts a question-and-answer session which is both hilarious and moving. Among other extraordinary poems is 'Scylla and Minos' a dramatic monologue which replays Ovid through the voice of a majorette: 'I started cheering him on as he skewered our guys'. The seven new poems at the end are an intriguing bonus that show Hofmann's talent raw and inventive as ever.

O'Donoghue's *Selected Poems* have a different kind of consistency. Many of the poems look back to rural West Cork where he was brought up and make reference to Medieval Literature, which he teaches. This might seem a formula for reminiscence and antiquarianism, but one of the achievements of these poems is to establish such frontiers only to unsettle them. The voice is so consistently even and mild that the most inhuman moments it recounts can creep up on the reader unawares. 'This was his big day, and he was glad | His Dad was dead...' begins the tremendous 'The Fool in the Graveyard'. The sympathy held in check through the poem becomes audible in its last lines: 'It was like being loved, | And he'd always wondered what that was like. | It wasn't embarrassing at all.' Another from his first book, *Gunpowder*, 'O'Regan the Amateur Anatomist' tells of a local figure who tortures animals. The narrator responds with a smile:

> Knowing what grown-ups do, whatever breeds
> About their hearts is always for the best.
> Worms are cold-blooded; babies learn in the night
> By being left to cry...

The allusion to *King Lear* in the phrase 'whatever breeds | About their hearts' is retrospectively added to the appalled child's world-view, but is nonetheless right. His name recalling Lear's daughter, O'Regan's last act of cruelty is performed on himself: 'Down a darkening road he drove his car | Under a lightless lorry, cutting his head off. | I wonder what he thought he was doing then?'

Again and again these quiet poems are haunted by inhumanity. 'Stealing Up' is a witty and desolate confession of inadequacy in the face of life's demands, but it's also a secret manifesto, a statement about how his poems work. With unobtrusive tact, his best poems steal up on his readers, and confront them with the uncanny. Even those poems that remain with the everyday, like 'Passive Smoking', make strangeness apprehensible: each morning the speaker's father needlessly warms up the engine to look out on the countryside at 'the inexorable | Brown-green rain-infected mound' which is a drab, landlubber's version of Yeats's 'that dolphin-torn, that gong-tormented sea' but still carries a Quakerish epiphany.

From his last book represented here, *Outliving*, 'The Company of the Dead' shows just how much O'Donoghue can do in a short space:

> It's natural that they would feel the cold
> much more than we do; but that is partly
> what makes them such good company.
> They draw closer, rubbing their hands
> and praise the fire: 'That's a fine fire you've down.'
>
> Also, they've no unrealized agendas,
> their eager questions no barbed implications.
> They're no trouble round the place, their only wish
> now to get warmer: apart, that is, from wishing
> that they'd kept warmer while they had the choice.

The prosaic elements — 'but that is partly'; 'Also'; 'apart, that is' — which could easily have been clumsy are essential to the music of the piece. The tone is perfectly judged. As the title of his third book, *Here Nor There*, suggests, O'Donoghue's poems keep crossing over borders, not just of place but of time as well.

Poetry Review, Volume 98.2, Summer 2008

— 60 —

Mornings in the Grayzone: Durs Grünbein

Durs Grünbein: *Ashes for Breakfast*, translated by Michael Hofmann, Faber and Faber, 2006

In a late poem, John Berryman has his alter ego Henry grumble about the fate that befalls his work abroad:

> Translation will cast the whole thing down, like bins.
> They've tried it in Polish, Italian, German, lots,
> & it all came out a lump.

'Henry's thought, in Henry's original words', he goes on, '[...] was the point'. Though few poets are as translation-proof as Berryman, there's still a great deal in Durs Grünbein's poetry that could have been cast down. 'The whole thing' may never be available to translation, but Michael Hofmann's ample selection of Grünbein's poems consistently reads as though it was. In his preface, a searching and candid document in its own right, Hofmann contrasts his own 'small scale' English predilections with Grünbein's 'frontality and [...] abundance'. Whether or not one agrees with this self-characterization, and its national attribution, it's precisely on the level of small scale conductivities, of intricate linguistic connection, that most translated poetry fails to work, and it's here that Hofmann again and again makes his versions live.

Born in 1960 in the former East Germany, Grünbein's *Grauzone Morgens* [Mornings in the Grayzone] (1988) is a startlingly assured first book. These poems have a nonchalant grace, and shine against their settings of Stalinoid concrete, drabness and dreck. What makes them especially appealing are their volatile shifts of perspective, a sardonic wit and the way they seem to limn out a whole series of potential directions. The first could be representative: 'A Single Tin':

> of sardines flattened
> between the tracks &
> the orange sauce
>
> squeezed out the sides
> the colour of propane bottles
> (& pretty
>
> lacking in significance) alone
> among so much flotsam and jetsam
> so far inland keeps

whatever this morning promises
by way of beauty.

The translation gives the same deceptively sketchy, or even skeletal, impression of the original. But each of its elements is securely in place: 'propane bottles' recall the flame-coloured sauce, and 'pretty', dangled at the end of one stanza, deflated in the next, is redeemed or at least upheld by the poem's final word 'beauty'. The humdrum, marine phrase 'flotsam and jetsam' (like the original's 'Strandgut') leads on cunningly to an image of the sardines' stranded state 'so far inland', where the poem toys with a more plangent effect of exile, only to refuse it . We are left unsure how ironic this decision to aestheticize a bit of rubbish is — that shrugging 'whatever' suggests 'not much', but the last line is given surprising weight. It has the air of a manifesto and could even be a deliberate re-working of W. C. Williams's 'The Red Wheelbarrow', but it strips away the American poem's engaging faux-naiveté, and posits an aesthetic that has none of the consolations of the functional.

Grünbein's later poems (odd adjective to use of a poet who is still relatively young) consolidate and develop many of these openings and potentials, even if perhaps they never quite achieve this freshness of the outset. Individual poems increasingly give way to sequences, in a drive to include both the breadth and multifacetedness of experience. One sequence, that might have been spirited out of 'A Single Tin', places a different dead animal in a different European landscape, as if to conflate and wittily reinvent the two genres of *paysage* and *nature morte*, or to contrive a crash between them with attendant roadkill. Perhaps the most brilliant, at least in the English translation, is 'Variations on No Theme'. This sequence has a formidable range of material as well as tone. Within a few lines he can move from the Rilkean: 'What else is it but magic, that chasm | Between things and their names' to *Neue Sachlichkeit*: 'A bare fishbone on the plate | Resembles a hairclip in a pool of grease'. That these transitions are so effective in English is a tribute to the deftness and mobility of the translations.

The volume's overall title, *Ashes for Breakfast*, the sort of food one would expect in the Grayzone, is entirely apt — the poems being so often concerned with beginnings and endings, with terminus at daybreak — although in Grünbein's hands ashes turn out to be a surprisingly nutritious fare. In a poem about birth, the cutting of the umbilical cord is described as 'Die Zerreisslust der Parzen von Anfang an', and translated by Hofmann as 'The Fates love of sundering at the get-go.' The subtle variations on this trope — putting the Fang in Anfang — which are played on throughout the book are far from formulaic, and are part of a consistent worldview. 'Untitled', another early poem, which describes what seems to be the poet's own Registry Office wedding (on the anniversary of Lorca's murder) begins 'Ein neues Gedicht hat | begonnen' and ends with 'ein besonders kühler | Nieselregen begann.' These last lines in the English effectively reinvent the poem's atmosphere:

a particularly cool drizzle
Started to fall.

There the particles in 'particularly' are activated by the word 'drizzle' and the last casual phrase, both a beginning and an end, has in equal parts foreboding and celebration.

Human warmth was not foremost among the many gifts the gods showered on Grünbein's poems. They are more likely to make the reader suspicious of the easy comfort of the phrase. What they do have is a bruised, ranging appetite for experience — a kind of curiosity that includes otherness, even, in one sequence, the otherness of a dog's life. The dog that moves through this sequence, crossing borders — both internal and external — also permits Grünbein the occasional moment of self-portraiture:

> As for me, I was my own dog
> In the suicide strip, equidistant from East and West.
> It was only here that I sometimes performed
> My *salto mortale* in the gloaming between dog and wolf.

The unhoused quality of these poems has found as permanent and well-constructed a home in English as anyone, even Berryman, could wish.

Times Literary Supplement, 31 March 2008

— 61 —

Luc Tuymans: Belgium and the Congo

Luc Tuymans casts a cold, forensic eye on the world. His domestic settings have the air of crime sites. His use of enlargement, of abrupt cropping, and his apparent indifference to any painterly allurements, all add to an overwhelming sensation of unease. His 1994 painting *Pillows*, which describes an almost shapeless off-white plain with faintly lit heights and stained shadows, is an example of one of his comfortless interiors. The angles the pillows lie at are at odds with the frame. Where we might expect an image of pillows to be a challenge to the traditional painter's ability to detect subtle gradations of tone and to convey the texture of white linen, Tuymans offers an almost disdainful nod to the painterly in a few tonal shadings, a perfunctory, Cézannish touch of blue or purplish brown to offset — or perhaps increase — the monotony. *Pillows* leaves the viewer with a baffled sense that though the image itself is of importance to the painter, its aspect is only marginally so.

He makes, in Wallace Stevens's phrase, 'the visible a little hard to see'. At the same time as he negates the specificity of the seen he holds on, almost fetishistically, to the power of the image. Stripped of any ornamental attributes, the image is left in the glare of rawness and bareness. 'Meaning and necessity', he claims, are what drive his painting, and not aesthetics. He describes himself as being an analytic rather than a gestural painter, and values the anonymity of the elements of his painting which he associates with that of folk art, though his sophisticated avoidance of any painterly expertise and pleasure brings his work closer to an anti-art. His faces are dipped in a wash of anonymity — types, masks, coverings, effacements — so that just as any painterly expectations we might bring to his canvases are bitterly disappointed, so this cold vacancy within his figural elements cheats us of the reassurance of familiarity and recognition.

Is it important, or even legitimate, to know that the source for *Pillows* is a detail from a porn mag? Does the viewer have to process and apply this extrapictorial information or does it somehow suffuse the image itself? However we answer these questions, the unsettling presence of the painter's intelligence is sensed behind the picture. The curdled flesh tones of the pillows generate the same kind of faint dread that the pallid skin does in his paintings from a medical textbook in the 1992 series 'Der diagnostische Blick'. Because his paintings have the air of broken-off narratives, or at least elicit questions of a narrative kind without any intention of satisfying them, there is a way in which the viewer is led to consider each painting in relation to the *oeuvre* to try to make sense of them. This quality has inevitably drawn Tuymans towards the series. And yet instead of using this as a way of amplifying narrative potential, in his hands the series intensifies the fragmentary or incomplete nature of his narratives.

The Belgian Pavilion at this year's Venice Biennale is given over to a retrospective of Tuymans's paintings, the main part of which is a series made in 2000 concerned with the events surrounding the torture and death of the Congolese leader Lumumba, connived at by the outgoing Belgian administration, the CIA and the United Nations — the sleight-of-hand involved in the conferring of independence whilst ensuring a continued economic enslavement. Set in the Biennale's ever busier promotional bustle, it's a shocking experience to enter a national pavilion whose space an artist has dedicated to the exhumation of an episode of terrifying bitterness in the national — and international — archive. If the paintings had been merely documentary evidence they would have had undoubted importance as an act of recovery, or of uncovering. But these pictures do more: they interrogate the poisoned ambiguities of our way of knowing what happens, of how any visual reconstruction remains opaque and what still implicates us in its occlusions. These are history paintings of a most original kind, in which the impalpability of history is rendered as a kind of threat.

The whole exhibition is entitled *Mwana Kitoko* which means 'Beautiful Boy', an ironic epithet, as the catalogue explains, describing the Belgian Prince Baudouin during his visit to the colony in the 1950s. The phrase was changed for Belgian consumption to *Bwana Kitoko* meaning 'Beautiful Master'. Amongst the exhibits two of the most immediately striking paintings are *Mwana Kitoko* and *Sculpture.* They act as an oddly symmetrical axis for the series. Though they are of different sizes (208 x 90 cms and 155 x 64 cms respectively) — Tuymans never paints canvases of the same dimensions — they are strikingly close in their proportions (2.3 to 1 and 2.4 to 1 respectively), both almost full figures in a markedly vertical format. But they are linked in subtler and more subversive ways than their mere proportions. They are like mirror opposites or like spiritual adversaries. Paradoxically the Prince descending from his aircraft in his white uniform onto Congolese asphalt for his state visit is a stiff puppet of a figure, an official function in full military regalia, without any personalized or distinguishing individual features. His face is a blur and he wears shades against the bright midday sun. The Prince's appearance suggests something secretive, even underhand. He is the 'Beautiful White Man' of the exhibition's title, a kind of walking 'whited sepulchre', to recycle the biblical turn of phrase Conrad employed to describe Brussels in 'Heart of Darkness'.

The picture *Sculpture,* which is hung on a different wall, at first looks like and then troublingly continues to look like a black man in tribal dress, but in fact represents a polychrome statue in an Antwerp cafe. By contrast with the beautiful white man, this statue is aggressively individual, with a muscular naked torso and a direct gaze which challenges the viewer. With deliberate but still unresolved irony, Tuymans has animated the inanimate, and reified the animate (a strategy markedly similar to Conrad's treatment of the dead Verloc and his still rocking hat in *The Secret Agent*). The paradox that these two pictures present in themselves and in relation to each other casts an uneasy pall over the whole exhibition.

The painting called *The Mission* is a sinister-sullen 'outpost of progress' dropped like a police station into an equatorial forest clearing. Its spiky cross is like a bad omen. Its modern architecture slightly smug and irrelevant. Its mission might be the same as that thin philanthropic front Leopold II himself proclaimed in September 1876 to the delegates to the Conférence Géographique Africaine:

> Ouvrir à la civilisation la seule partie du globe où elle n'a pas encore pénètré, percer les ténèbres qui enveloppent des populations entières, c'est si j'ose le dire, une croisade digne de ce siècle de progrès.
>
> [To open up to civilization the only part of the globe where it has not yet penetrated, to pierce the darkness which envelops whole populations, that is, if I may say so, a crusade worthy of this century of progress.]

The painting is symbolic but in a static, almost stagnant way; it is symbolic like the leopardskin, but unlike that image it is schematic. These two images also confront each other as adversarial stereotypes: tribal (and 'natural') spoils versus modernistic Western architecture with a Christian proselytizing subtext.

Tsjombe, painted in glum grisaille, deliberately evokes a kind of documentary and photographic atmosphere: it purports to record a meeting of the Katangese Secessionist leader Tsjombe, puppet of the West, with three other Congolese figures including a military figure. Tsjombe, with finger raised in mid-flow of a speech, would seem to be offering directives or instructions. The military figure leans forward attentively. None of their faces have any recognizable features, the paint strokes have a furry, blurred indeterminacy. Out of the right frame protrudes an empty chair, cut off at its arms and legs. This has the sinister presence of Banquo's empty seat, whilst the cropping perhaps suggests Lumumba's body which was reportedly cut up after his torture. It may be that Lumumba's death was planned at a session such as this, which the picture records. The lack of any particularity, the sort of menacing anonymity which these figures display is reminiscent of the face of the Prince in 'Mwame Kitoko', and is in marked contrast to the actual portrait 'Lumumba', which is uncharacteristically expressive and particularized. In this portrait, the spectacles he wears, unlike the Prince's sunglasses, reveal his eyes, and his features are clearly portrayed. His expression has a touch of sardonic humour and seems at once determined and reflective. The grisaille technique of 'Tsjombe' is here enlivened subtly with warmer touches of red, pink and ochre though it retains a cool, slightly sepia'd, photographic quality.

Tuyman's brushwork has about it a feathery approximate character, as though avoiding the temptation of competence or professionalism. It's not merely that he insists — as he apparently does — that each picture, whatever its size or content, must be completed in a day. The paintwork has no poetic frenzy or rapidity about it. Quite the opposite: it seems abnormally lethargic, and where it's meticulous rather than indifferent the care offers no sensory rewards, rather a further glumness and distance from painterly skill.

The series of ten paintings of *Mwame Kitoko* constitutes a powerfully interactive whole; the relations between them as well as the individual paintings accumulate meanings as well as uncertainties, accumulate a sense of dread as much as either. Tuymans's paintings are repeatedly drawn to the sites of human helplessness and to the tainted sources of memory — Nazi medical experiments, the concentration camps, child abuse. In this series his peculiar gift to create unease, to use the visual to sound the depths of what can never be adequately visualized, is at its height.

Modern Painters, Autumn 2001

— 62 —

Arturo Di Stefano: *Lasting*

Doors, windows, arches, colonnades — but especially doors — have long been signal presences in Arturo Di Stefano's paintings. Thresholds and entrances are fateful, and the stuff of cultural as well as personal memory. Like the eye, doors open and close; they hide and disclose. The Italian adjective *socchiuso* links the two senses: of a door being ajar, and eyes and windows being half-closed. 'The Doors of Perception', Blake's resonant phrase might, if it weren't now creaky from over-use, be an apt subtitle for this exhibition.

An entrance rather than a door, to a cave rather than a house, the Cumaean Sibyl's traditional site is a gallery cut into the tuff near Lake Averno, which itself was thought to open onto the underworld (easy going down, as Virgil says, but not such a breeze to return). It can still be seen today, a few miles west of Naples: a keyhole-shaped aperture, a primitive opening. There, according to legend, the sibyl wrote her prophecies on oak leaves, and if the wind scattered them, they had to be laboriously reassembled. That entrance might even be a locus for a Di Stefano painting, though his settings are predominantly modern and urban. This patient re-assemblage of fugitive elements also seems like a description of his working method. The Sybil herself first appeared in one of his student canvases, and again in a formidable oil and wax painting of 1988–89, *The Cumaean Sybil.* Here once more, in more youthful form, is the Sibyl herself, encircled by leaves. The leaf, in the legend, is a symbol of both what's most ephemeral and enduring. As though free-floating, a similar scattering or constellation of leaves can be seen in front of *Door,* the sunlit entrance to the exiled Russian poet Joseph Brodsky's New York flat in Greenwich Village. Of all the doors that Di Stefano has painted — that of Max Beckman's Amsterdam apartment, of the painter's own studio and many others — this must surely be the brightest and most inviting. It has a neo-classical composure, a beneficent, sunlit clarity and balance.

A twin to this door is *Door L. A.* that belongs to the Westwood house where the artist R. B. Kitaj settled after he left London in the wake of the vituperative response to his 1994 Tate retrospective. The house was formerly the home of the actor Peter Lorre, and its redbrick and mortar arch seem to hark back to the series of paintings of brick walls Di Stefano created some ten years ago. Here the arch is partly broken by a dense flurry of leaves. It is characteristic of Di Stefano's work that these two tutelary figures — a poet and a painter — should be celebrated *in absentia.* The titles themselves give no clue. Like stations of a pilgrimage, the tributes are of the most reticent and tactful kind, as though not wishing to disturb or impose on the shades who were the former residents. Even disclosing this information feels slightly intrusive, but these are specific and not generic doors and so their identity is pertinent.

This succession of doorways is an interwoven feature of Di Stefano's *oeuvre.* In conversation, he once referred to an artist's shows as a sort of 'imposed punctuation, artificial stoppages in time', and that remark reveals something which will be evident to anyone familiar with his work — how extraordinarily continuous, rather than merely consecutive, his concerns are. There are poets — Petrarch, Whitman, Baudelaire (the last portrayed in his 1986 *Sudarium* sequence) — whose work naturally forms a *canzoniere*, an accumulating total work rather than a sequence of individual collections, and Di Stefano is a painter of this kind. His doors are not repetitions because each is *sui generis*, and has an unassailable individuality. Each is a meditation on the particularity of an entrance that opens onto an utterly distinct life.

These doors are shaped, as it were, or imprinted by the figures that have passed through them. Architecture as character, as history, as fate. These are not the buildings that you might find in, say, a John Piper print, that makes organic puns on Gothic motifs, that plays botanical games with architectural features; they are altogether more gravid and weighted with human presence, a presence usually implied rather than stated.

A vivid exception is the *grisaille* 2010 painting *Cézanne (II)* which vouchsafes a full vision of the occupant, the artist himself, who emerges carrying a chair — to sit in the sun or to use as a painter's stool. There's even the anachronistic possibility that he might be taking the chair to the kind of village open-air cinema which Di Stefano would have witnessed as a child in his mother's native Bonito, in Campania. The figure has a grandfatherly air, a shy, almost Chaplinesque aspect, discreetly achieved by the tilt and curve of the walking stick leaning against the stone jamb, a tilt repeated in the held chair as well as in the figure itself counterbalancing the weight. It is the most disclosed and affectionate of all Di Stefano's doors, perhaps due to the status and significance of Cézanne as source in his, as indeed in Kitaj's, art. Cézanne is the subject of a masterly lecture Di Stefano gave last year at the National Gallery — one that teases out the mysterious elements in Cézanne's portrait of his father by way of history, art history, biography, language and technique. The patient and forensic intelligence of that essay is a perfect accompaniment to his own work, and is suggestive of the ways in which it might most profitably be read.

But stone — including brick and mortar — is not the only material that Di Stefano keeps questioning. Linen is its opposite and equally stressed companion — in his veronicas, veils, shrouds, palls, sudaria and indeed in the linen canvases he paints on. Canvases, of course, are cut from different cloths — cotton duck, burlap, hemp, flax and so on, but Di Stefano's choice is pre-primed, écru-coloured Belgian cotton. The exhibition's title 'Lasting' serves to bring both stone and linen together: 'Lasting' both being the property of stone, and having as a secondary meaning, 'a durable kind of cloth'. When I spoke to Di Stefano about this second sense he quipped "A durable kind of cloth': that could be the most basic definition of a painting.' The remark highlighted for me the strange paradox of painting —

how, due precisely to what is placed on the canvas, this fragile weave can indeed prove more durable than stone, and be more carefully preserved. *Aere perennius*? Or linen outlasting bronze? Poetry's ambition to outlive stone is heard in Shakespeare's

> Not marble, nor the gilded monuments
> Of princes, shall outlive this powerful rhyme;
> But you shall shine more bright in these contents
> Than unswept stone, besmear'd with sluttish time.
> When wasteful war shall statues overturn,
> And broils root out the work of masonry,
> Nor Mars his sword, nor war's quick fire shall burn
> The living record of your memory.

Di Stefano's paintings are so often a record of 'unswept stone' and in themselves make a bold claim to 'outlive'. The negative description of 'besmeared with sluttish time', however, is one that these paintings reverse — they celebrate the marks and erosions of time and, as it were, gather and reassemble them. In another sonnet, Shakespeare speaks of: 'Thy gift, thy tables, are within my brain | Full character'd with lasting memory.' Memory is Di Stefano's element and architecture embodies it. The frail stuff of linen preserves it. Lasting, the painting which gives the exhibition its title, celebrates the cloth itself. It is linen hung on linen. The top corners of the garment, as though pegged on a line, have a suggestion of shoulders and allude to the body that has vacated but left an impression on the form.

* * * * *

In this exhibition the explicit human form is rarely seen. Always implied by dwellings, and almost measured by doorways, the figure has, for the most part, been concealed. In earlier painting where the human figure appears, it's interesting how much privacy, almost *pudore*, Di Stefano's paintings exercise. They are at the furthest pole from the most conspicuous and lauded tendencies of Francis Bacon, or of Lucien Freud, where in the first there is a kind of dramatic reduction of the human to basic desire and need, and in the latter nakedness becomes both mass, force and animal vulnerability. Di Stefano's figures are most often demurely clad, even if in pyjamas, as in his delicate and haunting full-length *Portrait of Jan Di Stefano* (1991–92). They are either unaware of being observed or show a kind of reluctance to reveal themselves. Another contrast of this kind could be made between Chaim Soutine's almost always clothed and often intensely awkward figures and his friend Modigliani's reclining nudes, odalisques who are brazenly open to the painter's gaze. Of course these are tendencies, and only crudely distinguished here, but Di Stefano's work would very much fall on the side of Soutine. One of the few human figures that appear in the show is *Sibyl* — and interestingly she wears a headdress that is strongly reminiscent of the Muslim *hijab*: an image of modesty that relates the mythical Italic seer to the contemporary East End of London where the painter lives and works. She could equally be a girl from Turkey or a Southern Italian village.

Elsewhere the human is manifest in traces. In *St. Paul's* the whited interior is marked by gestural swirls of raw sienna, which pick up the gilded rail of the entablature that runs across the column heads and the wheaten — or oaken — field of chairs at the base of the pictures. These curves of colour seem not so much gratuitous as ghostly — the traces of what? — movements of air or organ music, draughts or drafts, *pentimenti* that paradoxically come after the composition rather than before. Similar swirls or gestures, abrasions, draggings or scuffings of paint figure in other of his paintings where they seem like ripples on the steady gaze, hints of movement that disrupt the stasis of architectural structures, or even seem to liquefy the stone.

In an essay contrasting cinema and the visual arts, John Berger, a discerning and early admirer of Di Stefano's paintings, writes of painting that

> It collects the world and brings it home. Infinity and the surface of the canvas play hide-and-seek in a room where a painting is hung. [...] And it can do this because its images are static and changeless.

Many of Di Stefano's paintings indeed 'collect the world and bring it home', but what is transported often remains mysterious, striated with history, even sibylline. Two other recent architectural paintings are on a grand scale and bring a glimpse of infinity. *Arcades, Bologna* (2009) depicts a stretch of via Fondazza where the painter Giorgio Morandi lived. Here again the arches are suffused or ghosted with an ancestral presence, and the vertical pink stucco far right may even allude to predominating colour of two 1956 Morandi paintings called *Cortile di via Fondazza.* There may be a temptation to discern Morandian bottle- and ampulla-shaped contours to the columns and arches, a meditative stillness to the composition, but there is no element of pastiche: the structures have a sturdy weight and actuality braced with tie rods that act like a perspectival grid drawing the eye towards a vanishing point. The mauve-pink tinge of the upper storey as well as the far right pink give promise of a radiant day beyond the shadowed walkway. The central column, for all its solidity, has paint dragged to the right and the ochre wall has a shadowy play of paint strokes, themselves arching, which effectively dematerialize the setting. The Renaissance arcades of Bologna, some thirty miles of them, have a history that stretches far further back in time, as the fretted and flaking walls witness. Morandi himself, in a radio interview, declared that 'there is nothing more surreal, nothing more abstract than reality' and this painting fuses dream and actuality in a remarkable manner. Another underlying connection with arcades and colonnades is the figure of Walter Benjamin whose *grisaille* portrait Di Stefano has painted in a sequence of writers. Benjamin's unfinished *Arcades Project,* a palimpsest of observations centred around Haussmann's Paris, at one point links the experience of the arcades with that of a collector's 'ensemble of items': 'all this shows him his affairs dissolved in a constant flux, like realities in a dream'.

The oneiric quality of architecture, the suggestion of infinity, is also notable in *Cloister: Ferrara,* the final picture completed for this exhibition, and one of his most extraordinary successes. The setting conjures up the presence of Giorgio de Chirico who painted some of his most important 'Metaphysical' cityscapes in Ferrara while he stayed there during the First World War. (And perhaps also that other Giorgio — Bassani — the poet and novelist whose major work is centred on the town.)

The complex geometry of *Arcades*, the off-centre, far from classical positioning of the viewer, suggestive of the *flâneur*'s circumnavigations of the city, is here only slightly simplified with the arches of one side of the cloister rhythmically intercutting those of the nearer side, but both suggesting an infinite spatial recession. The lozenge of bright green lawn framed and cut by the columns has a luminous vitality, evidence of the present moment held in the frame of the past.

Those leaves of grass, one of nature's simplest forms — and incidentally one of the hardest to do pictorial justice to — bring us back to the leaves scattered at the mouth of the Sibyl's cave. The contrast of the dark between the arches and this sunlit green is another re-evocation, another way in which Di Stefano has fused the most ancient elements of art with the absolutely contemporary, the mythical with the quotidian. His paintings are meditations on the actual that collect and reassemble the traces of time.

Introduction to Arturo Di Stefano, Lasting, *exhibition catalogue (London: Purdy Hicks Gallery, 2012)*

— 63 —

Tom Lubbock's *English Graphic*

The word 'Graphic' in the title — let's leave the 'English' for now — comes from the Greek *graphein*, meaning both to write and to draw. Although the word commonly refers to a range of media including sketches, printmaking and illustration, we are right to think of it as largely concerned with the linear rather than the plastic, with the tonal rather than the colouristic. In Tom Lubbock's hands the term becomes still broader and more flexible — earthwork, rose window, tube map — and even stretches to watercolours, but in each case the reason for the inclusion becomes immediately apparent. In his chosen examples, as well as in his treatment of them, this link between 'writing' and 'drawing' is reinforced. Frontispieces and illustrations declare their relationship with text ostensibly, and maps also conjoin word and representation, as do cartoons with their captions and speech-bubbles. All of these show a kind of hybridity in the art form, or even the instability of one thing becoming another, and in his concern with outlines and boundaries, Lubbock's enquiries again and again attend to the protean aspects of the image.

Blots, dots, lines, marks and so on all have a writerly aspect, a dual identity, and in this collection of his writings especially, Lubbock makes numerous sorties into literature and philosophy to 'illustrate' the chosen image or rather to think along parallel lines about it. Effortlessly and aptly, he draws on a vast store of poetry — Racine, Beddoes, Hopkins, Eliot, Les Murray and many others — as if to disrupt the frontiers established between the art forms, but also because he sees such disruptions as being inherent in the graphic art. To take just one instance, he equates what he calls a 'reaching out effect' in Keats's poem 'This living hand...' to *A Democrat*, Gillray's caricature of Fox with his blood-drenched hands. The mutual illumination is extraordinary, even shocking, given the opposed political sympathies of these two contemporaries. This 'reaching out effect', with the switch to plainer English which Lubbock observes in Keats's poem, is also a noticeable and frequent effect in his own writing about art: the sudden palpable presence of the speaker.

In the proposal for this book he describes the project:

> The connecting & overlapping ideas running through the book are: maps; islands; whales; clouds; enclosures; multitudes; swarms; wombs; contours; vignettes; creations; visions; miniatures; skins; containers; outlines; rows, lines; dots.

This list is plethoric and multitudinous but is also very intricately connected, and those connections emerge and re-emerge, like islands — an archipelago — or whales, or schools of isles. Clouds are sky islands, 'sometimes dragonish', sometimes 'very like a whale'. 'My island seemed to be | a sort of cloud-dump' as Elizabeth

Bishop writes in her poem 'Crusoe in England'. Even the shapes of Bewick's vignettes take on an islandish contour: 'the coastlines of these ovals can be very rough and fluctuating.' Here, as elsewhere, the prose assumes something of the delightful play of a Francis Ponge prose poem — with sudden candour the contours of the art work, and how we perceive it and the world beyond it, are imperceptibly shifted.

Swarms and crowds, crushes and clusters, hives and cells are other important strands in this work — a matrix of imagery. These concepts allow him to navigate between Hogarth's 'hugger-mugger' hundred *Characters and Caricaturas*, the frontispiece of Hobbes's *Leviathan*, its colossus crammed with a populace, the flying figures in Carwitham's astonishing drawing, Palmer's blossom-crowded trees and a host of other pictures that would include the dots in a Bridget Riley abstract. The slave ship *Brookes*, in one illustration, is the most infernal crowd scene devised by economic greed.

Lubbock is a great 'reader' of images — by this I don't mean to suggest his approach is an especially literary one but that his interpretations are acts of attention to what the marks on the page do as well as mean, and how that effects the way we respond to them. Always a significant part of what he looks for is what it tells us about the *ways* in which we look. Often enough he proposes a series of readings of a given shape, alert to its alternations and possibilities — just to give one example from his description of Lincoln cathedral's rose-window: 'like planets in orbit, spokes of a wheel, radiant beams, exfoliating petals'. 'The eye altering alters all' as Blake, one of the crucial figures in Lubbock's pantheon, writes in 'The Mental Traveller'.

Part of his concern with the protean is the question of how we perceive, but it is just as much a look at the artist's own potential for generating these perceptions. His essay on Romney, for example, is a masterly reassessment of a neglected artist but also a remarkable account of an explosive moment in which Romney alights on a black-and-white story-board technique that surpasses and outstrips everything he has elsewhere achieved. Here Lubbock is uncannily aware of what this, possibly a cul-de-sac for the individual painter, might lead to in the hands of future artists ('He inspired Blake but lacked Blake's inspiration').

Like *Great Works*, the first selection of Tom Lubbock's writings, but with a more tightly focused topic, this book has largely been compiled from the Great Works column Tom wrote on a weekly basis for the *Independent*. The constraints of the form proved exceptionally viable and liberating for his procedures. Providing a 'wiry outline', the form itself allowed for wit, *aperçu*, mental callisthenics, provocation, aphorism, meditation and surprisingly sustained argument. It means leaving the starting line at some velocity — and Tom developed some really stunning openings: 'Images are mostly not for looking at. They are for being there and having around' and 'You can be in two minds about the moon' are two of my favourites. But the pieces are never content to be merely eye-catching: they have to examine both the picture and their own premises; they have to advance a line of thought; and — here he also excels — suggest how it might develop. This is another gift to the reader

— a spur to do it themselves, to see where the thought leads. The essays that are included are a special bonus, because there we can see how this compactness could unfold on a larger canvas. We see how able he is to extend and deepen the insights that abound in his shorter pieces.

Another strand skilfully worked throughout this book has to do with bodily sensation, with the skin which is both a 'container' and our largest sensory organ. We see its vulnerability in Gillray's cartoon *The Gout*, and in both Thomas Rowlandson's *Six Stages of Marring a Face* and the anonymous folk artist's *West Bromwich Sweep* with the black contusions on the boxer's battered face (and with its rebuke to Hazlitt's breathless and bloodthirsty paean to pugilism) . But, more extensively, the physical experience of space, or lack of it, is examined with wonderful clarity in John Tenniel's illustration of *Alice Overgrowing the Room* as well as in the cramped and curled figures in Fuseli and Blake, set against the latter's 'starfish' Albion, stretched (almost) to his human — and spiritual — limits. Lubbock's alertness to the devices of 'framing', exactly where the picture ends, is a key and recurring element in his analyses — how our experience of space can be tampered with and unbalanced by the fronded edge of a Bewick vignette or by the subtle cropping of the left-hand margin of John Russell's *The Face of the Moon.*

What of 'English', then? *English Graphic* has no nationalist agenda, and it doesn't seek to impose a set of national characteristics. Unlike, say, R. H. Wilenski in *An Outline of English Painting* (1946) where there is a somewhat anhedonic argument for English art's persistent moralism, or even the far more subtle and observant Nikolaus Pevsner who speaks of the 'flaming Gothic line' in *The Englishness of English Art* (1956), the idea of a set of family resemblances doesn't seem to hold much interest for Lubbock — although at one point he declares that 'the tradition of English illustration has typically been devoted to the fantastic and visionary', in another piece he amusingly takes a scunner to this second term. But still there are lines and lineages (or 'lineaments' as Blake might say) — strands that become skeins and, beyond this, recurring arguments. One such central argument is between the visual and the visionary, between reality and imagination. It is rehearsed in the wonderful piece on Hooke's Flea from *Micrographia* where Lubbock commends the actual over the chimerical: 'We often take imagination as the great achievement of art. But the refraining from imagination can be just as great and often harder. What we see in *The Flea* is the discipline of observation.' (If only we had his thoughts on Blake's 'Ghost of a Flea', a macabre twin.) Again, in the contrast he draws between Bewick and Blake: 'His images are more faithful than Blake's are to "minute particulars", both in their knowledge of nature's details, and in their mastery of engraving at a miniature level. Their wonder lies, not in vision, but in eyesight.' Though this may seem like an argument for a stolid English empiricism, it is only half the story. It is part of an unresolved and creative dialectic and needs to be set beside his passionate appreciation of Blake's visionary imagination: 'Blake's great artistic discovery was the potentialities of two-dimensional life. No artist before him understood so clearly the uses of the flat page to create a transcendental world, a world in which things are simultaneously material bodies and spiritual forces.'

His two pieces on Blake's illuminations are among the most brilliant and searching readings both of the images and of the artist who forged them.

There are few references to art critics and historians, and often then just to show them the door. 'Wrong' he says to Panofsky, Rosenblum and James Hall. On another occasion, he makes fun of 'all the I-Spy stuff commentators on Hogarth like to go on about'. (Baudelaire and Robert Hughes, however, receive a brief but warm welcome.) This absence may be due to the constraints of space, but I think it's also very much of a piece with his whole procedure. Lubbock approaches pictures without the armoury of the specialist — it's an open engagement, *mano a mano*. Iconographical and historicist studies are not likely to appeal to a writer who delights so much in provocative anachronism — but anachronism, as he argues persuasively, is unavoidable in how we look at art: 'since we never shed our contemporary selves, anachronism is the air we breathe'. Unavoidable, and also fertile. He plays with this notion by uncovering, say, the seed of abstraction nascent in a Townes watercolour, the invention of collage in the random reassembly of a medieval rose window or a foreshadowing of abstract municipal sculptures in *The New Word in Golf*, the cartoon by H. M. Bateman, but also more generally in the rapid way he can traverse, backwards and forwards, vast tracts of art history, finding precedent and prolepsis.

One fuller engagement that does occur is with the critic John Berger, and his description of Samuel Palmer's paintings as being like 'furnished wombs'. It's an expertly loaded phrase — straight off you can see the damage it intends: Palmer has made the natural artificial, made his nature cosy, bourgeois, acquisitive. Why is he painting these little idyllic retreats at the height of the Industrial Revolution? What the phrase excludes is the way that the womb-like curves and swelling forms of Palmer's work, down to the embossed surfaces heightened and glistening with gum Arabic, are a true and valid modality of perception. And while Lubbock doesn't explicitly quarrel with the phrase, his description of the effects of Palmer's paintings — how the flowering branches are 'not so much blossom as like a shaggy fleece, or bubbling foam, or proliferating fungus growths, or clusters of pearls' allows the pictures to reply in their own terms. These alternative readings are superbly responsive to Palmer's own description of his surfaces 'sprinkled and showered with a thousand pretty eyes, and buds [...] and blossoms, gemmed with dew', albeit in a less conventional poetic style. But the ultimate rebuttal to Berger's critique comes in the sure judgement which Lubbock arrives at: 'Palmer believes in individuality to the end. Every bit of creation has its iconic character, distinctly outlined'.

As Laura Cumming notes in her introduction to *Great Works*, John Berger is almost the only art critic with whom Lubbock can be compared. Both have a rare and robustly independent cast of mind and give short shrift to cant and specialist jargon, and both have, and communicate, a joy in arguing. But Lubbock has no political design on the reader. Paradoxically that may make him the more radical: he works on the body rather than the body politic.

The revelation of Lubbock's Great Works series, and one borne out by all his art criticism, is how much there is in every painting to think *about*, even to think *with*;

how much thought — not just instinct, luck or genius — went into the making of a picture and, in generous exchange, how much thought each picture prompted. It is a grievous loss that he is no longer here to add to these thoughts, but this book is a celebration of his indomitable gifts.

Introduction to Tom Lubbock, English Graphic,
ed. by Marion Coutts (London: Frances Lincoln, 2012)

— 64 —

Valerio Magrelli: He Digesteth Harde Yron

'Prosegue il catalogo della vegetazione' [the catalogue of vegetation continues] begins one early poem by Valerio Magrelli. Only some lines later do we realize that the Linnaean impulse behind the poem has thought itself, its own thinking, rather than botany as its subject, but we already sense how the scene of possibly thankless, methodical labour is a wry image for the book he is writing:

> Like a canvas
> much over-painted
> on which many different
> hands have worked...

Before its end, this characteristically brief, untitled poem has set in play a series of oppositions: scientific/artistic, solitary/collaborative, internal/external.

Magrelli's remarkable first book, published in 1980 when he was twenty-three, bears the somewhat forbidding title *Ora serrata retinae*, which would seem more in the way of an oculist's textbook than a collection of poems. The term signifies the jagged edge, specifically 'the irregular anterior margin of the *pars optica* of the retina'. Each poem in the book is an instrument of perception, with a clear circumference and a scrupulously observed area of concern. They highlight a particular small feature of an internal, often nocturnal, landscape and yet cumulatively they bring a haunting and abundant panorama into view. A demonstrative quality is to the fore — and it's significant that as many as thirteen poems in the book have a 'questo' or 'questa' [this] in the first line. The poems examine the 'I', as well as the eye, that examines. Rhetorically, they also re-configure this infolding movement: 'I think of the tailor | who uses himself for a roll of cloth'. They proceed painstakingly with their 'catalogue of vegetation', describing the moods and torsions of perceiving. Only when they, the poems, have acquired sufficient surety of their own visual and conceptual bias do they gradually and inexorably move outwards.

The book was greeted with quite unprecedented acclaim by many of Italy's most significant writers and received praise from poets as far afield as Octavio Paz and Joseph Brodsky. Not since Eugenio Montale's *Ossi di seppia* has there been such a consensus that here, at last, was a voice inhabited by the whole language and culture, shaping it to its own purposes. Reading them again, a quarter of a century after their publication, what's striking is the sheer nerve of the enterprise: poems scribbled down like diary jottings in a notebook with what looks like a radical economy of means, often a single galvanizing metaphor, that focus so resolutely on an aspect of consciousness. The tone is dry and scientific, almost forensic, seemingly hostile to any lyrical effects, and yet again and again, almost despite itself, a fierce concentration propels the poems out beyond the familiar. Elizabeth Bishop's often quoted letter on Darwin, which praises his outwardly directed 'self-forgetful, perfectly useless concentration', 'sees the lonely young man, his eyes fixed on facts and minute details, sinking or sliding giddily off into the unknown.' Something analogous occurs in these poems with a procedure which is precisely contrary.

The compressed, punning title *Nature e venature* [Natures and Veinatures, or Veinings] (1987) of Magrelli's second volume retains an element of the physiological but places it in a wider landscape. Nothing could seem further from traditional nature poetry than these curt meditations, and yet they share with a poet like Hopkins an extraordinary impulse not merely to describe but to encompass, almost themselves to perform, the underlying principles of growth and form. Hopkins would be at home within this precisely observed, recursive and inscaped world of veinings, cloud formations, Fibonacci numbers. Unlike Hopkins though, with his flaming palette of 'gold-vermillion' and 'skies of couple colour like a brinded cow', Magrelli's poems have the subdued tones of Analytical Cubism or verge on monochrome, like Morandi: it's more often as though the world is seen by X-ray or lamplight or moonlight. Even the moonlight has artificial traits as in his poem 'The moonlight is a work of art...' — his coolly irreverent reprisal of a long-fatigued topos.

His third collection is *Esercizi in Tiptologia* (1992) — 'Exercises in Typtology' — the word comes from the Greek *typtein*, to beat or batter, and refers to the table-rapping in spiritualist séances and, in Italian, to the language of tapping which prisoners use to communicate. The title marks a shift from the first volume's concern with the visual to acoustic phenomena and, by extension, to language itself. 'Exercises' has a musical provenance and is far from the kind of communication we might expect of wall-tapping. The head-on collision in the title between leisure and urgency, between contemplation and need, is a paradox which the poems themselves bear witness to.

All this would seem to make of Magrelli a scholarly, philosophical, cerebral poet. And yet the astonishing immediacy of the images and the precision of the language carry an emotional charge. A love poem like 'The Embrace' from his third book excavates beneath the domestic, and by way of the central heating is led to the prospect of millennial destruction on which the frail moment of affection is based. The two flames recall the eerie double flame of Ulysses and Diomedes in Canto XXV of Dante's *Inferno*. This is one example of the way Magrelli's poems quietly situate themselves at the centre of a tradition which they question and qualify. His poems describe the process of their composition and their language keeps measuring its own capacity to observe the world.

Another example can be found in his poem 'Rosebud' whose first line in Italian, 'Non pretendo di dire la parola' [I do not claim to speak the word] can't fail for an Italian reader to evoke the first line of Montale's famous poem 'Non chiederci la parola che squadra da ogni lato | l'anima nostra informe...' [Don't ask from us the word which squares off on every side | our formless soul...]. It has the typically Montalian, negative incipit and the feel of a manifesto poem, concerned with a possible, and possibly threatened, language. The title alludes to Orson Welles's *Citizen Kane*: 'Rosebud' is what he called his childhood sled but is also a sly reference to the name that the newspaper magnate William Randolph Hearst gave to the sex of his mistress. With its sense of the evasiveness of language and its own peculiar, witty self-referentiality the poem moves a fair distance beyond its forebear.

If the technology of the first book was utterly basic — a pencil and a note book, the present moment of introspection — the third book is populated by current media, the TV, phone and computer screen, for example, and the fourth, *Didascalie per leggere un giornale*, by the image and sections of a newspaper. *Instructions for Reading a Newspaper* is a long poem in which each of the shorter poems corresponds to a section of the newspaper, such as Games, Horoscopes, Obituaries and so on. The Letters Page is a canny device for allowing entrance to the more personal and lyrical, otherwise excluded. Even the book's title suggests a kind of anti-poetry. The decision for poetry to found itself on the throw-away, the quotidian, the mechanically reproduced, recalls Joyce setting part of his epic *Ulysses* in a newspaper office — with an added, disturbing, almost elegiac touch now that newspapers are no longer our dominant mode of purveying information and news. The poem anatomizes an institution, its economics, its way of reproducing reality, and subjects the familiar to an estranging scrutiny. Walter Benjamin's argument that the organization of newspapers has a way of fragmenting our knowledge of the world is very apt here:

> Man's inner concerns do not have their issueless private character by nature. They do so only when he is increasingly unable to assimilate the data of the world around him by way of experience. Newspapers constitute one of many evidences of such an inability. If it were the intention of the press to have the reader assimilate the information as part of his own experience, it would not achieve its purpose. But its intention is just the opposite, and it is achieved: to isolate what happens from the realm in which it could affect the reader. The principles of journalistic information (freshness of the news, brevity, comprehensibility, and, above all, lack of connection between the individual news items) contribute as much to this as does the make-up of the pages and the paper's style.[1]

For all their brevity and their fragmentary style, these poems, as so often in Magrelli, combat that 'lack of connection' which Benjamin intuits. In mimicking a newspaper format, they work in the opposite direction and bristle with connectivity.

The idea of fragments and of anatomy, paradoxically, unites much of Magrelli's poetry. Throughout his work there is an insistence on the corporeal. One poem from his second book describes the extraction of a wisdom tooth (in Italian *il dente del giudizio*). It is not a simple operation, the tooth has to be worked at, broken into three parts, before it comes free. The tri-partite fate of the tooth is mirrored in the three stanzaic divisions of the poem as though in homage to the kind of exact

1 Walter Benjamin, *Illuminations*, trans. by Harry Zohn (London: Fontana, 1973), p. 107.

correspondence between poem and thing we encounter in Francis Ponge's work. The relief of sleep at the price of bodily integrity or of wisdom is quietly hinted at, and this kind of unconsoling awareness is often painfully evident in the poems.

But there are other threads to this eleven-line poem which give an odd sacral quality to the object, as though it was both suffering the process of martyrdom and itself being turned into a holy relic. It is referred to as a sacred fish, it's *segnato* — marked out as a target but also, in the context, signed with stigmata or with the cross — as well as *segato* (*segnato* with an extracted 'n') — sawn, as though it were a particularly luckless saint. Further seams of geological imagery and of artisan vocabulary run through the poem and it's in this context that the slow and freighted movement, the elaboration and unravelling of his language are utterly essential to the whole design.

As Jonathan Galassi, Montale's translator, remarked of Magrelli, 'his poems are not simply self-referential, but always advance an argument with and about life'. One among many examples is 'The Vanishing Point', a poem which tries to imagine how it might be to write a picture, say, like Uccello's 'Hunt by Night', but to inscribe it in the medium of time as opposed to space. This poem is a far cry from the run-of-the-mill picture-poem and an intriguing exploration of how we perceive through language. Its vanishing point, having become a temporal rather than a spatial coordinate, lets us re-think both kinds of composition — the pictorial and poetic.

Magrelli's most recent book *Disturbi nel sistema binario* [Disruptions within the Binary System] (2006) follows and reinforces the tendency of *Instructions for Reading a Newspaper* in making a book of poems an exploration of a unitary (or, in this case, binary) theme. The concerns of the poems range from the domestic to the political, considering notions of doubleness, hybrids and antitheses — its finale is a brilliantly inventive sequence on that visual pun, the *anatra-lepre* (the duck-hare, usually known here as the duck-rabbit), in this case a kind of zoological Jekyll and Hyde. The poems alternate roman and italic print. The idea of doubleness — and duplicity — so thoroughly explored in this sequence has been a feature of Magrelli's world from the start, and can be seen in miniature, though already fully formed, in an early poem such as 'A groove | like the vertical join | in plastic figurines | cuts me in two, two sides, | two slopes...' or in the poem on cloning 'Health: Dolly's Eye' in his penultimate book.

For all the variety of subject and approach, for all the formidable development from volume to volume, Magrelli's poetry has always had immense cohesion. Whole books can be read as sequences, and frequently the lack of titles for individual poems emphasizes this continuity. Tadeusz Różewicz, a poet with whom Magrelli has more in common than he has with most of his Italian contemporaries, speaks of his own 'dogged revision, repetition, returning to the same material and so [...] to the end' as 'the most valuable element' in all his work. In neither poet does this imply a narrowness, but rather a necessary depth and force. I can think of few living poets who have evolved a style so equal to and so inclusive of the most resistant aspects of modernity. A Magrelli poem is equipped to address and carry something back from subjects as various as hijackings, radio-active contamination, dinosaur toys, sheep cloning, recycling, graffiti, skateboarding, and environmental destruction. As Marianne Moore said of her ostrich, 'He Digesteth Harde Yron'.

A Note on the Translation

The first poem of Magrelli's that I read, some ten years ago, was 'L'abbraccio' [The Embrace]. My immediate response was such a turbulent mixture of recognition, awe and envy that the only way I could still the chaos was to see if I could write it in English. Besides, I was intensely curious to see if what I admired so much in it might survive the passage. Before this, I'd translated a few Italian poems but with little appetite and mixed results. Turning 'L'abbraccio' into English, I was surprised to discover, actually felt like writing a poem, carrying with it the same excitement and pleasure. It seemed to me a fluke, a one-off event, but some years later, in a slightly freer style, I translated his untitled 'Amo i gesti imprecisi' which I called 'The Tic'. For the reader who doesn't have Italian or *the* Italian, it's only fair to note what kind of liberties are taken. Apart from the addition of a title, there are other deviations. The sentry is given an 'insubordinate eyelid', and forgets what was in the cup where the original is starker. In the last line 'Dentro qualcosa balla', the verb *ballare* whose usual meaning is 'to dance', but in the case of machinery, as here, suggests something clanking or ticking, something out of kilter. My solution, 'throbbed', may not add up perfectly but it picks up the 'cuore', the heart, which Magrelli places exactly mid-point in his poem, and contains a sense of longing as well as a hint of physical peril. Magrelli's poem is like a modern, wittily dysfunctional up-date on that Provençal tradition of the *plazer*, a poem in which writers compile a list of favourite things. For all the departures from the original I feel I haven't betrayed its essential direction.

Another example that might stand for a different kind of making free is my version of 'Parlano' [They Talk] which was one of the next that I attempted. Here I have put the unrhymed poem into rhyme — a labour-intensive, counter-intuitive manoeuvre, where more normally in translation it's the reverse that occurs. My excuse for this is that I wanted to intensify the acoustics. With so much at risk of being lost, there has to be the chance of listening out for where a translation might go in the new language, of looking out for what the new language might possibly *add*.

When I had done a dozen or so translations I began to think a whole book might be possible, but it was only about ten years after that first encounter that I set about completing it in a less sporadic fashion. The initial feeling of excitement and possibility revived. Where earlier I'd thought of the process as a lucky, random, unrepeatable exchange, I began to sense the same engagement was possible with more and more of his poems — not just petty theft but grand-scale larceny. In other words, what had drawn me in the first instance to a particular poem was latent or lying in wait with the same intensity of recognition in far more poems than I'd expected.

Much theorizing about translation is, and has long been, concerned with arguments over the relative claims of domesticating or estranging strategies. Often ignored, where poetry's concerned, are the different kinds of strangeness that poetry itself brings into the equation. Far more interesting than general questions of the differences between two languages is the poem's own divergence from normal use in the original language. The translator must then come to terms with (at least) two different kinds of strangeness. It's probably easier to arrive at some untroubled and consistent-sounding theoretical approach if you know little about the language you're translating from, but, sadly, even an extensive knowledge guarantees practically nothing, except (only perhaps) the absence of gaffes. Aside from the genuinely bilingual and some rarely gifted linguists, however well you know another language it will always remain exterior and opaque in some respects, and poetry, in which that language is paradoxically both most at home and most idiosyncratic, will remain an even more vertiginous challenge. These spots of opacity, though, may have the effect on the foreign translator of heightening attention so that the act of reading is, in more than one sense, an act of listening out. The translator is in the first place a kind of 'listener-out', and then must go on to listen in, must thoroughly absorb what's alien to make it his or her own.

Even here the same problems return. Translating could then become an act of appropriation or, worse, expropriation. Lowell's *Imitations*, which continues to exert an influence today, belongs to this *virtuoso* tradition — although their triumphs tend to be most admired by those with little knowledge of the languages and the original poems he was 'imitating'. Elizabeth Bishop, who voiced serious misgivings about *Imitations*, offers an alternative in her translations of the Brazilian poets Carlos Drummond de Andrade and Vinicius de Moraes: a severe adherence to the original which doesn't sacrifice vitality and formal invention. These are just two points along an infinite succession, and they don't represent wholly opposed tendencies anyway — there is no way of miraculously ridding a translation of the translator's voice and limitations. Translators serve the original best by extending the former and coping with the latter as best they can. My own approach has been catholic, pragmatic, even opportunistic rather than consistent with any theory. I have tried to sense the possibility each poem, with its own peculiar demands, opens up within the new language. I've ditched those (a fair number at that) where I'd failed to bring over anything new into the English, and any which, on checking later, seemed too close to Anthony Molino's earlier, authoritative translations.

Introduction to Valerio Magrelli, The Embrace,
trans. by Jamie McKendrick (London: Faber & Faber, 2009)

— 65 —

Valerio Magrelli: Seeing Darkly

For more than thirty years now, since I first read and translated his poem 'L'abbraccio', I have been listening out for and tuning in to Valerio Magrelli's poems. Along with the work of four or five contemporary poets they have become something of a haunting soundscape and backdrop for my inner world. To be able to hear his poems in a language not my own has cost more effort but it's been an effort amply rewarded.

It's rare that a first volume of poetry, however original, makes one think differently of the art, but I believe that's the case with Valerio Magrelli's *Ora serrata retinae*, published in 1980, when he was twenty-three years old. Equally rare perhaps were the accolades it garnered not just within Italy but internationally, including enthusiastic responses from Joseph Brodsky and Octavio Paz. To read it again almost four decades later is to re-experience that delighted surprise that issues in baffled questions — Where does this come from? How did it happen? Why *him*? The materials are utterly basic — a pen, a page, a body, a room, and the language, despite the forbidding and technical title — which refers to the serrated edge attached to the retina — is also for the most part approachable, even idiomatic. A seemingly self-sufficient, almost a solipsistic perspective; a voice communing with itself about the surrounding phenomena in a manner that takes nothing for granted. Every act, however usual, sparks off an enquiry, and each enquiry is conducted with an unusual boldness of imagery and of heightened attention.

The quotidian is a given feature of this work. Take the untitled early poem — all of the poems in the first book are untitled — 'Domani mattina mi farò una doccia...' [Tomorrow morning I will take a shower] — an opening statement that might easily provoke in the reader a sardonic 'Well, I'm glad to hear it.' This natural response, however, doesn't outlast the second line: 'nient'altro è certo che questo' [Nothing other than this is certain]. The reader is already disconcerted by this certainty. Why should the act of taking a shower be so certain if nothing else is? The boiler could break down, a water pipe burst, the speaker come down with flu. However small the matter, it puts will and intention on an irrefutable plane. At the same time we become aware of how frail and suppositious is any use of the future tense and the 'future intentional'. The critic George Steiner once wrote, 'We also lack a history of the future tense', adding that the 'eternal "tomorrow" of utopian political vision became, as it were, Monday morning.' The poem is content to scrutinize what Steiner disparagingly calls Monday morning and yet finds in it material enough for extensive contemplation.

What follows in the fluid course of this seventeen-line poem is an evocation of what will happen *during* the shower. On one level: nothing — 'un futuro [...] in cui non succederà nulla' [a future in which nothing will happen] — but as the poem progresses this nothing has become if not everything at least something significant, a succession of significances. The water turns into a river, into steam, into rain, into infinite rivulets, into the current of a river and finally into a delta of rivers, and the speaker into a hermit, a tree trunk, a dead horse. Though the steamed-up mirror shows no reflections, this rite of ablution has transformed the quotidian into something rich and strange. The whole poem supplies a history of the future tense, and it ends with a peculiar prophesy:

> e finirò incagliato nei pensieri
> lungo il delta dello spirito
> intricato come il sesso di una donna.

> [and I will end up tangled in thoughts | along the spirit's delta | intricate as a woman's sex.]

Here I'll only pause to notice 'incagliato' (derived from the Spanish 'encallar') carries the idea of a boat being stranded, stuck. To be stranded in one's thought suggests, like the earlier image of a motionless and silent hermit, a state of melancholia or accidie, and yet the final two lines that merge geography and female anatomy have an arresting beauty to them — perhaps the triangular formation of a delta, and of the Greek letter the word is derived from, has suggested the final image. And with the earlier image of the 'eremita' (hermit susceptible to 'né miraggi né tentazione' [neither mirages nor temptation]) suggests this state is not one of erotic reverie but of detached meditation. That a poem so embedded in the body, in physical sensation, should end with 'spirit', both a philosophical and a religious term, and then in a final dazzling turn to associate the spirit with an image of a woman's sex indicates the vast distance covered in this short poem with its almost banal opening. Any number of poems in the book would show a comparable trajectory and reach.

It's intriguing that a poem with the Spanish title 'El memorioso', from Magrelli's most recent book *Il sangue amaro* (2014), revisits this same topic, but this time the protagonist is the speaker's son, who is taking what seems to be an endless shower while he commits the Ugolino canto to memory. Although the title alluding to Borges's parable 'Funes el memorioso' and the Dante reference would seem to make the poem metapoetic, it wears these references lightly. Humorous, urbane and ironic at the poet's expense (the literal expense of the hot water) it deftly sets the quotidian against the backdrop of a poem written seven centuries ago. Like a faint hum in the background, behind the son murmuring the verses, is the thought of the desperate family relations of the starving Ugolino and his four sons in the tower of famine, but the absolute contrast in circumstances is neither complacent nor emphatic.

The first poem is without apparent irony: it describes the process of showering with fertile and patient attention. The second has a wry and appealing humour, as the speaker tots up his electricity bill, and at the same time we infer a kind of pleasure that the son is devoting himself to this act of memory, to the father's *métier*, and will emerge not only perfumed but brimful of hendecasyllables. The first has an engagement with the self and its perceptions, and overtly with language and the future tense, the second is more communal, more social, and makes fluent cultural connections. I dwell on these examples not to show either progress or retreat but to suggest the range even in treating the same theme that Magrelli's writing is capable of.

Another poem which shares this domestic and Dantesque connection, chronologically midway between these two, is the poem 'L'abbraccio' [The Embrace] from his 1992 collection *Esercizi di tiptologia*. Here the reference is far less explicit and acts as a subliminal source of unease. The two night lights on the central heating boiler recall the twin flames of Ulysses and Diomedes in Canto XXV of the *Inferno* but even if the allusion were missed, the threat of millennial destruction underpinning the intimate scene with a couple in bed has a compelling and unmistakeable chill.

Lest this repetition of a domestic motif gives the impression of a limited subject matter, it's worth stressing the omnivorousness and modernity of Magrelli's poems. Anything and everything is potentially to his purposes. As I wrote elsewhere: 'A Magrelli poem is equipped to bring something back from subjects as various as hijackings, radio-active contamination, dinosaur toys, sheep cloning, recycling, graffiti, skate-boarding and environmental destruction'. That list could be extended with ease.

But to dwell a little longer on the ritual of washing, in a ruefully witty poem, again from his first book, Magrelli himself worries about the nature, and the limits, of what he is writing:

Dieci poesie scritte in un mese
non è molto anche se questa
sarebbe l'undicesima.
Neanche i temi poi sono diversi
anzi c'è un solo tema
ed ha per tema il tema, come adesso.
Questo per dire quanto
resta di qua della pagina
e bussa e non può entrare,
e non deve. La scrittura
non è specchio, piuttosto
il vetro zigrinato delle docce,
dove il corpo si sgretola
e solo la sua ombra traspare...[1]

Wallace Stevens in a critique of an unnamed poet (probably T. S. Eliot) wrote that he 'lacks this venerable complication': his poems 'do not make the visible a little hard | To see'. In the case of Magrelli, perhaps as a result of myopia, a persistent

1 'Ten poems written in one month | isn't that much to show for it | even if this would make the eleventh, | and the themes are not exactly various — | rather, there's just the one theme, which has | for its theme, as here, the theme. | Which goes to show how much | remains beyond the page, | knocks but cannot — must not — | gain admittance. Writing's not | a mirror but rather | the shower screen's frosted glass | — behind which, real enough, | but darkly, a body | is discerned...'.

theme in the first book, the world is always a little hard to see, is always perceived with a fierce struggle which makes the achieved clarity all the more rewarding. Writing is not a mirror, but rather the shower screen's frosted glass... we see darkly, but then face to face.

In these lines we encounter a characteristic Magrellian trope — 'anzi c'è un solo tema | ed ha per tema il tema' — which we could call the recursive or *mise en abyme* though neither term quite accounts for the effect. It recurs on the level of imagery throughout his work. To give a couple of early examples, the lines

Penso ad un sarto
che sia la sua stessa stoffa
('Di sera quando è poco la luce')

[I think of a tailor | who uses himself as a roll of cloth.]

are another uncomfortable example of this infolded perspective which questions both the medium of language and the role of the poet. Or again in another poem :

È come se una nube
arrivasse ad avere
forma di nube
('Scivola la penna')

[It's as though a cloud | should have taken on | the shape of a cloud.]

we find a similarly vertiginous self-reflection. A later example can be found in his extraordinary and disquieting 'Xochimilco': 'palafitta del nulla | palo nel nulla fitto' [piles driven into nothing | a stake stuck in the void] where the language itself stares down into the abyss.

As Jonathan Galassi, the translator of Montale, remarked of Magrelli: 'his poems are not simply self-referential, but always advance an argument with and about life'. This is certainly true, but it's also worth noting that their self-referentiality is a crucial part of the way they advance this argument: they continuously interrogate their medium to assess the distortion imposed, or the degree of deviation:

come con un'arma difettosa
di cui conosco ormai
lo scarto

[as though handling a faulty weapon | of which by this stage | I know the exact degree | of deviation]

as he writes in 'Rosebud', and it's the precision and resourcefulness with which they do so that makes his work so trenchant, unforgettable and essential.

Introduction to Valerio Magrelli, 66 poemas: antologia, *translated into Spanish by David Huerta (Mexico City: anDante, 2018)*

— 66 —

Antonella Anedda
Island and Mainland

'One must have a mind of winter' begins Wallace Stevens's 'The Snow Man'. Antonella Anedda in her first book of poems would seem to have taken this perspective to heart, along with its final stanza:

> For the listener, who listens in the snow,
> And, nothing himself, beholds
> Nothing that is not there and the nothing that is.

Its title *Residenze invernali* [Winter Residences] (1992), could hardly strike a less Italian note — and in fact these dwellings appear to be sited mostly in some northern zone, a St Petersburg of the soul, as though Tsarskoye Selo has been crossed with an ancient, dilapidated hospital in Rome. They are dream interiors — dream bordering on nightmare — and at the same time they have the frosty clarity of Joseph Cornell's *Setting for a Fairy Tale*, a detail from which she would later use in her prose book *La vita dei dettagli*. The inmates or patients of these imagined hospital wards are ailing or dying, deprived almost of movement or communication though they may 'signal as from distant boats' to each other.

Not only is the weather inclement and un-Mediterranean, but the spiritual atmosphere is senescent, reduced and bitten back to the core. It's a curious debut for a poet not yet thirty years old. It has more affinities with Anna Akhmatova and Osip Mandelstam, perhaps even with Marina Tsvetaeva, than with the Italian lyrical tradition, even that lineage of poets like Franco Fortini and Amelia Rosselli who, following Montale, have sought to challenge it. The Russian Acmeists are not so much a direct influence as an example — and the same could be said of Philippe Jaccottet, whose collection *La Semaison* (mixing prose and poetry) she translated into Italian. The opening of one of his prose pieces — 'L'attachement à soi augmente l'opacité de la vie' — sounds a warning note that will recur in her own poems.

If the perspective of Anedda's first book of poems was Eastern European, the title of her second, *Notti di pace occidentale* (1999), signals an apparent move westward, though it retains the sense of an outsider's, even a foreigner's view. The poems were written in the wake of the first Gulf War and of the break-up of the former Yugoslavia — the latter a war very close to Italy's borders and involving territories such as Slovenia with an intimate connection to Italy, and so the 'Western peace' it speaks of carries a bitter irony and a distinct uneasiness. As she writes in an afterword: 'The idea that lingers in the title is that of the West surrounded by apparently concluded wars and of a Europe which is not living in peace but in a frightened truce.' 'La tregua' (the title of Primo Levi's sequel to *If This Is a Man*) is a recurrent word in Anedda's lexicon — sometimes literally a truce, sometimes meaning a space for repose, or more idiomatically a relief, and the eponymous section first appeared under the title 'Versi per una tregua'. Is this a peace only maintained by exporting war to other places? A delusion or a deception? All of these questions are in play throughout the book, which has a decisive, if exhausted, tone of civic and ethical engagement.

As I've begun by considering the titles of Anedda's first two books, it may be helpful to offer some notes of a similar kind on the succeeding three volumes to date. *Il catalogo della gioia* [Catalogue of Joy] (2003), Anedda's third collection, again presents an ambiguous title, but its references to the Zohar and its epigraph from the Hasidic Rabbi Nachman of Breslov ('To someone who asked him what difference there was between being sad and having a broken heart, Nachman replied that to have a broken heart was not an impediment to joy') strongly suggests a movement towards a poetics which might counter the bleaker landscapes that preceded it. The concluding sequence on La Maddalena, an island off Sardinia, puts this island perspective further into the foreground of her poetry; dream, memory and reality are all reconfigured in this archipelagic setting.

The title of her fourth volume, *Dal balcone del corpo* [From the Body's Balcony] (2007), may be recalling her own earlier poem from *Notti di pace occidentale*: 'I see from the darkness | as from the most radiant balcony', but the image in both cases recalls Baudelaire's famous sonnet 'Recueillement' with its self-estranged and paradoxical consideration of suffering: 'Sois sage, ô ma Douleur, et tiens-toi plus tranquille', and more particularly its architecture of the psyche: 'Vois se pencher les défuntes Années, | Sur les balcons du ciel, en robes surannée' — in Robert Lowell's translation: 'Look, the dead years dressed | in old clothes crowd the balconies of the sky' (though that misses the slightly sinister or perilous way the years lean out over the sky's balconies). The book's initial working title was *Cori* [Choruses] — there are a number of poems simply entitled 'Coro' — and perhaps here more than before in Anedda's work, as from a balcony, we hear the voices and the lives of others.

Although some critics saw the title as indicating a feminist slant to the work, Anedda in an interview has remarked that she hadn't considered this body as having a specific gender, but that, in reference to a statement by Husserl, all of us 'lean out from our own body as from a balcony, attached to an interior yet suspended above something, unable properly to turn around'.

Salva con nome (2012), her fifth volume, has yet another ambiguous title. The phrase corresponds, as a computer direction, to the English 'Save As', but may also be read as an imperative (second person singular) 'save with the name' as well as a third person indicative 'he/she saves by naming'. The book opens with the prose poem 'Il Componidori' (a figure in a Sardinian festival who sheds his actual name and gender) and ends with a visual collage composed of pieces of anonymous faces. The visual element of photographs and images which accompany the poems has been excluded from the translation for reasons of space and to give priority to the poems themselves, but it is undeniably a striking component of the original book.

★ ★ ★ ★ ★

Anedda's ambivalence, which I note above, towards the Italian lyric tradition — rich and various as it undoubtedly is — has become, if anything, more marked with each new collection. It is a kind of temperamental opposition — even to the language itself. Her own language, effortlessly musical, throws obstacles and calthrops in its course, and gives space to quotidian things such as pots, pans, cutlery, needles. Such imagery might be considered feminine or domestic, but her handling of it tends to emphasize the metallic, angular and obdurate qualities of these objects, their *Dinglichkeit* or thingish quiddity, and a kitchen rather than offering an image of domestic peace is as likely to be the site of a haunting — see her poem 'Cucina' [Kitchen].

One immediately notable feature of her writing from the outset is how her poems can stray into prose, and return, or start in prose and turn to poetry, breaking the line, breaking with the line, then reconstructing it. Many years later, she would also break with the language, and her last two collections both include poems written in Logudorese, a language of central Sardinia. The languages she was brought up hearing, apart from Italian, were Logudorese, Catalan from Alghero, and Corsican French mixed with the dialect of la Maddalena. Best here to have her own account of this linguistic sidestep or re-rooting:

> It began after an operation [...]. I can only say that at a certain time the sounds that rose in my memory were those harsh ones of a pre-school language, thick with consonants and shorn of adjectives. And I understood my own Italian in the light of those sounds. When I translated these poems from Sardinian into Italian I saw that one language steered or guided the other and that most likely I had always 'translated' into Italian from that language.

She adds that the experience involved a descent into 'una lingua non bassa, ma profonda' [a language that isn't low, or vernacular, but deep] such as the writer Luigi Meneghello speaks of. I think that for the reader too, these new poems in Logudorese shed light on her earlier poems in Italian. From her first book, with its insistently Russian atmosphere, a sense of otherness and estrangement has always been audible in her poetry, which has a slow, resistant compactness of phrasing. The new poems in Sardinian suggest that those qualities may also involve an encounter between two distinct languages and cultures.

The significance of Sardinia in the mental and actual landscape of this Roman-born poet is worth dwelling on. Sardinia and Rome are poles of her imagination, both geographical and historical. Had dialect per se attracted her, *romanesco* might have been the more obvious, the more local choice. It also has a rich literary history from Belli's satirical and brilliant sonnets to Pasolini's novels and stories from the Roman *borgate*. But Logudorese, with its harsh, consonantal acoustics, of all the languages of Italy (Albanian apart) stands perhaps at the greatest distance from Tuscan Italian — it is called 'limba' (*lingua*: language not dialect even if that distinction is dubious at best) — and also, arguably, at the greatest distance in terms of culture. The depth of that schism can be heard in her poem 'Contro Scauro' [Against Scaurus], which describes how the island's inhabitants were held in contempt by the Imperium, and their plea for justice was dismissed by the Roman orator Cicero: 'A truthless people [...] land where even the honey is gall.' Incidentally in the original Logudorese, as in Italian, the pun on 'Cicerone', identical for the orator's name and the term for a tourist guide, has been sacrificed in my version, although of course it could have been heard, somewhat mangled by English, if I'd kept Cicero/cicerone. Instead the orator has been transmogrified into a lizard among the ruins.

Even if Sardinia is remote from the mainland of Italy, the most visited site of her poems is a small island at a remove from the island itself. The archipelago of the title, and which many of her poems refer to, is La Maddalena, a chain of islands off the northeast coast of Sardinia, in the wind-scoured Straits of Bonifacio stretching out towards Corsica. Her most recent prose book *Isolatria* (2013) offers a revealing backdrop to the poems, with its acute and original mixture of travel writing and spiritual biography, of meteorology and meditation. The *continente*, as the mainland is called by Italian islanders, works as a kind of oppositional field of force to the weather, history and landscape of the island itself. 'September 2001, Maddalena Archipelago, Island of S. Stefano' begins:

> This small island riven underwater by U.S. submarines,
> where my great-grandfather planted citrus fruits and vines,
> built cowsheds and brought ten cows from the mainland...

The poem, set just over the threshold of the new millennium, but overshadowed by historic images of uprooting and undermining, is one example of the way her imagination seizes on this mainland–island polarity. However important such tensions are within her poems, to make Anedda a poet merely of conflicting local allegiances would be to oversimplify and trammel the force of her writing. In the same interview I mentioned, she gives the Greek etymology of the word 'ethos' as a space ('a habitual gathering place' as I've elsewhere seen it defined) preceding its later sense of mores and disposition. What's most unusual in her work is a severe distance of perspective and an abrupt, often searing intimacy of tone. Her poems, with their emphasis on space as much as place, are poems of solitude, though they occupy a site curiously equidistant from the self and from the world, the self and others. A place of solitude and gathering, an ethical space.

Introduction to Antonella Anedda, Archipelago,
trans. by Jamie McKendrick (Hexham: Bloodaxe Books, 2014)

Epilogue

Or envoi. One of the recurrent threads in this book has been the attempt to show how an image or a line is 'translated', carried onwards or transformed from age to age, from one art form to another; has been handed down and has found a regenerative function in its new setting. I've tried, in passing, to distinguish this phenomenon from Eliotic ideas of tradition or Bloomian ideas of influence, to which it certainly bears some resemblance. In the hope of clarifying this, I'd like to end by tracing a brief history of one final 'foreign connection', an image-thread that leads from Provençal poetry through the *dolce stil novo* to the final story of James Joyce's *Dubliners*. In thirteenth-century Provence's renaissance and tireless invention of poetic forms, one genre was known as the *plazer* which, as the name suggests, listed sources of joy. This is the premise also of one of Guido Cavalcanti's most celebrated sonnets, though the sestet introduces a radical turn by having his list of pleasures eclipsed by the beauty of 'la mia donna':

Biltà di donna e di saccente core
e cavalieri armati che sien genti;
cantar d'augelli e ragionar d'amore;
adorni legni 'n mar forte correnti;

aria serena quand' apar l'albore
e bianca neve scender senza venti;
rivera d'acqua e prato d'ogni fiore;
oro, argento, azzurro 'n ornamenti:

ciò passa la beltate e la valenza
de la mia donna e 'l su' gentil coraggio,
sì che rasembra vile a chi ciò guarda;

e tanto più d'ogn'altr'ha canoscenza,
quanto lo ciel de la terra è maggio.
A simil di natura ben non tarda.[1]

[Beauty of woman and of the knowing heart | and armed and noble horsemen | the singing of birds and speech about love | decorated galleys coursing over the sea; || the serenity of the air when dawn breaks | and white snow falling without wind; | water in the river and meadows full of every flower; | clothes adorned with gold, silver, and lapis lazuli: || all these are surpassed by the beauty and great value | of my lady and her noble bravery, | so that they seem base to whoever looks on them; || and she so far exceeds the wisdom of other women | as the sky is greater than the earth. | No virtue is lacking in such a creature.]

As if to acknowledge the poem's forebears, Cavalcanti uses two Provençal words ('genti' for 'gentile', 'albore' for 'alba') and two Gallicisms ('Biltà' and 'rivera').

1 Guido Cavalcanti, *Rime*, ed. by D. De Robertis (Turin: Einaudi, 1986).

The rough translation I've provided gives little sense of the linguistic depth of the original, the resonance for instance of 'saccente', 'genti' or 'canoscenza' — this last, like the Provençal *connoysense*, can mean wisdom, learning, knowledge, even experience. Dante would later give the word a different inflection in Ulysses's speech to his crew in *Inferno* Canto XXVI. Here, though, I just want to single out the line 'e bianca neve scender senza vento' which, perhaps of all the listed pleasures and things of beauty, is the most arresting. It's well known that his friend Dante uproots this very line and 'translates' or transplants it into a very different setting, that of *Inferno* Canto XIV, ll. 28–30:

> Sovra tutto 'l sabbion, d'un cader lento,
> piovean di foco dilatate falde,
> come di neve in alpe sanza vento.

> [Over everything the sand, falling slowly | rained swollen flakes of fire | like snow in the alps without wind.]

So Dante has taken Cavalcanti's great line and transformed it from an observation into a simile, from an image of beauty into an image of torture. Nevertheless the beauty of the line is by no means extinguished and seems to resist its translocation. The preceding descriptive phrase 'd'un cader lento' [of a slow falling] uses the infinitive as a verbal noun, where we would use the gerund, and thus retains a stylistic trait in Cavalcanti's poem ('cantar'; 'ragionar'; 'scender'). As Teodolinda Barolini notes,[2] line 8 of Cavalcanti's poem — the gold and silver and blue — gives rise to another Dantean passage, this time more consonant with the original: a description of the flowers in *Purgatory*, Canto VII, l. 73 and following: 'oro e argento fine, cocco e biacca...' [gold and fine silver, crimson and leaded white...]. It hardly matters whether this is rivalry or homage: what's undeniable in both cases is the generative force of Cavalcanti's poem.

Petrarch was to use this same image, as has been often noted, in his *Trionfo della Morte* (ll. 66–67): 'Pallida no, ma più che neve bianca, | che senza venti in un bel colle fiocchi...' [Not pale, but whiter than snow, which falls without wind on a lovely hill...]. But here, in his characteristic praise for feminine beauty, the image already seems a little tired and conventional and lacks the startling quality of Cavalcanti's invention or of Dante's repurposing and relocation.

Within the Petrarchan tradition snow becomes an attribute of praise as well as reproach, and Shakespeare's Sonnet 130 — 'If snow be white, why then her breasts are dim' — is a witty demolition of this convention of 'false compare'. However what interests me here is the more naturalistic observation of falling snow. An extension of this image-series, six centuries later, which as far as I know has passed unobserved, can be encountered in the ending of James Joyce's 'The Dead', where Cavalcanti's image of snow undergoes a further transformation:

2 Teodolinda Barolini, *Dante's Poets: Textuality and Truth in the 'Comedy'* (Princeton, NJ: Princeton University Press, 2014), p. 139. She also notes how Cavalcanti's sonnet is a variant of Guido Guinizelli's 'Io voglio del ver la mia donna laudare', with its list of flowers and minerals outshone by the beloved.

> Yes, the newspapers were right: snow was general all over Ireland. It was falling softly upon the Bog of Allen and, further westwards, softly falling into the dark mutinous Shannon waves. It was falling too upon every part of the lonely churchyard where Michael Furey lay buried. It lay thickly drifted on the crooked crosses and headstones, on the spears of the little gate, on the barren thorns. His soul swooned slowly as he heard the snow falling faintly through the universe and faintly falling, like the descent of their last end, upon all the living and the dead.[3]

From his student days in Trinity College, Cavalcanti was a favourite poet for Joyce, and he knew Dante well. Dante's 'd'un cader lento' has been transformed into the double chiasmic structure of Joyce's 'falling softly [...] softly falling' and 'falling faintly [...] and faintly falling', so the effect is slowed down even further. The suspended snow is sibilantly transferred to Gabriel Conroy's state: 'His soul swooned slowly...': in itself a Dantean effect, as his pilgrim on several occasions faints, most memorably at the end of *Inferno* Canto v. The transformation is all the more radical here in that Joyce has turned poem into prose, albeit prose that is cadenced in a way that makes the reader aware of how close prose can be to poetry. What begins with the flatness of a weather report ends in what Padraic Colum describes as 'the music of a requiem'. And while this conclusion evokes, like Dante's poem a 'last end', the emotional effect hovers between a benediction and a final erasure.

With the possible exception of Petrarch, in each of these cases, including Cavalcanti's handling of a Provençal convention, there is a dynamic change of consummate skill, where the grafted image takes root and bears original fruit, or where a stolen flame lights up a different world. A connection that is not a competition but an enabling, not a struggle but a rekindling.

3 James Joyce, *Dubliners* (New York: The Modern Library, 1926), pp. 287–88. The quote from Padraic Colum is from his introduction, p. xii.

INDEX

www.ingramcontent.com/pod-product-compliance
Lightning Source LLC
Chambersburg PA
CBHW081325020726
47506CB00006B/1188
* 9 7 8 1 7 8 1 8 8 5 0 4 8 *